T0357182

The Weaponization of Expertise

The Weaponization of Expertise

How Elites Fuel Populism

Jacob Hale Russell and Dennis Patterson

The MIT Press
Cambridge, Massachusetts
London, England

The MIT Press would like to thank the anonymous peer reviewers who provided comments on drafts of this book. The generous work of academic experts is essential for establishing the authority and quality of our publications. We acknowledge with gratitude the contributions of these otherwise uncredited readers.

This book was set in ITC Stone Serif Std and ITC Stone Sans Std by New Best-set Typesetters Ltd. Printed and bound in the United States of America.

Library of Congress Cataloging-in-Publication Data

Names: Russell, Jacob Hale, author. | Patterson, Dennis M. (Dennis Michael), 1955- author.
Title: The weaponization of expertise : how elites fuel populism / Jacob Hale Russell and Dennis Patterson.
Description: Cambridge, Massachusetts : MIT Press, [2025] | Includes bibliographical references and index.
Identifiers: LCCN 2024019083 (print) | LCCN 2024019084 (ebook) | ISBN 9780262049597 (hardcover) | ISBN 9780262382106 (epub) | ISBN 9780262382113 (pdf)
Subjects: LCSH: Expertise—Social aspects—United States. | Technocracy—Social aspects—United States. | Science—Social aspects—United States. | Elite (Social sciences)—United States. | Populism—United States. | United States—Social conditions—21st century. | United States—Politics and government—1989-
Classification: LCC HM651 .R88 2025 (print) | LCC HM651 (ebook) | DDC 306.20973—dc23/eng/20241009
LC record available at https://lccn.loc.gov/2024019083
LC ebook record available at https://lccn.loc.gov/2024019084

10 9 8 7 6 5 4 3 2 1

For Guy and Aija—J. H. R.
For Mac Joseph Patterson—D. P.

Learn from science that you must doubt the experts. As a matter of fact, I can also define science another way: Science is the belief in the ignorance of experts.
—Richard Feynman, "What Is Science?"

One can never know much about any subject. I would much prefer the following definition: an expert is someone who knows some of the worst mistakes that can be made in the subject, and how to avoid them.
—Werner Heisenberg, *Physics and Beyond*

Scientists! If we were as wrong as often as they are, they'd shoot us.
—Colby Young, Maine lobsterman, speaking to journalist Colin Woodard in *The Lobster Coast*

Contents

Preface: "Just Follow the Science"

In 2020, as the coronavirus pandemic swept across the globe, pundits and op-ed writers raced to heap praise on Governor Andrew Cuomo of New York. "Andrew Cuomo Gets It Right: Govern by Science," began a characteristically breathless headline in the *Washington Post*.[1]

Cuomo's fall from grace, of course, was equally rapid. Although the proximate cause of his resignation in November 2021 was a series of sexual harassment scandals, it was also widely understood by this point that Cuomo's pandemic victory lap was premature. In 2022, an audit by the New York comptroller confirmed what many had suspected: that Cuomo's administration had misled the public on the nursing home death count.[2] His autocratic, self-confident approach to pandemic management came under fire from many scientific quarters.[3] And after heaping lavish praise on his press conferences, pundits were largely silent as his speeches gave way to unscientific—not to mention cruel—claims. At one point, Cuomo claimed that deaths from COVID-19 were "all self-imposed," going on to make an analogy that simultaneously insulted anyone with uncontrollable obesity: "If you didn't eat the cheesecake, you wouldn't have a weight problem."[4]

As observers at the time, we were not surprised by the fact of Cuomo's missteps: many of them were transparent from the beginning of the pandemic.[5] Even without careful examination of the facts, basic norms of humility and common sense should have suggested that it would have been premature to crown anyone as infallible, much less victorious, over a novel, poorly understood, and rapidly spreading virus.

What surprised us instead was the degree to which academics, journalists, and other elites had been taken in by Cuomo. Few of them harbored any skepticism about Cuomo's pandemic behavior; they had, it seems, been genuinely swept up in the narrative of a heroic leader following the dictates of science. Perhaps we were simply naive, but we had always thought of academia and journalism as institutions forming the core bastion of healthy skepticism. Basic norms of these institutions require reservation of judgment, careful collection and evaluation of evidence, as well as a willingness to engage with opposing viewpoints and to actively acknowledge the possibility of being wrong. Few of those traits were on display in either academia or journalism. We fear that this has become the norm rather than the exception in contemporary discourse.

Anthony Fauci provides another and in some ways more interesting case in point. Whatever one thinks of his handling of the pandemic, doubt about his early views—over school closures, masking, lockdowns, and other topics—is now widespread and legitimately accepted as part of ongoing debate. But at the time Dr. Fauci made many of his recommendations, he was deemed by elites to be beyond criticism.[6] Again, we are not puzzled that Fauci might have been wrong about certain subjects. Rather, what is puzzling is how passionate elites became about lionizing Fauci's views as representing infallible scientific truth. Fauci himself got into the act when he infamously said, "Attacks on me, quite frankly, are attacks on science."[7]

Most troublingly, the idea that we had to defer to science extended even to claims that could not be adjudicated by science alone. Pandemic policies presented trade-offs that could not possibly be resolved without considering domains far beyond fields such as immunology. Few of the questions could legitimately be claimed as the sole dominion of experts of any sort. Experts could assist with predictions about particular aspects of an intervention, but most of the major policy choices implicated values and other political questions. By the time politicians acknowledged this, as Rishi Sunak later admitted of the British response to the pandemic, it was far too late.[8]

Treating science as a unitary religion with Fauci as its high priest had consequences. It turned people off. It degraded trust in public-health institutions, perhaps quite durably, as early overconfidence by public-health leaders turned into increasing doubt. It deprived the public of its rightful role in considering important questions: even if science could accurately and unanimously predict the health consequences of a lockdown, there were always going to be more ramifications for schools, civic institutions, social life, and community, which were often dismissed as mere "economy."

Scientific research itself was stifled in this atmosphere. Some basic questions were never answered. When we face our next pandemic, we won't know what interventions work best.

* * *

It has become fashionable of late to proclaim that the United States has become stupid, a nation rooted in a hapless public's stubborn and baseless disregard for experts. As one proponent of this view, Tom Nichols, puts it, the United States is "now a country obsessed with the worship of its own ignorance." Nichols asserts—while proffering little evidence—that we increasingly "lack basic knowledge, . . . reject fundamental rules of evidence and refuse to learn how to make a logical argument."[9] Elites knowingly nod their heads in agreement: the only reason anyone disagrees with them must be stupidity. President Barack Obama received cheers at a commencement address in 2016 for chiding that "ignorance is not a virtue" and that "facts and evidence matter," a rebuke to a nation where "actual experts are dismissed as elitists" due to a growing "strain of anti-intellectualism."[10] Other pundits are crasser, labeling America a "dumbass nation . . . of militantly ignorant people."[11]

Needless to say, there is more to this story. These commentators dismiss their critics without engaging them. They never grapple with the challenges to deploying expertise in a democratic society. Much of their account rests on false premises and gut suppositions about the current moment. Just to mention one example, which we discuss later, we are not living through a particularly unusual "age of misinformation." As an empirical claim, this is pure hyperbole.

But, perhaps more importantly, these commentators' claims are grounded in hubris: an implausible belief that elites and experts are infallible and that most of our societal problems are solvable by technical expertise if only the benighted would listen. These experts would arrogate to themselves the power to make all value judgments in society. It is hard to know what's worse: if this hubris is due to a hunger for power or instead to an obliviousness to the reality that most complex social questions in fact revolve around values, not the recitation of unambiguous facts.

The claims made by elites about the role of experts versus society in political judgment are disturbing. They are not only undemocratic but also deeply corrosive of expertise. Expertise should rest on humility, doubt, skepticism, and open dialogue, but the elite line of argument turns science into dogmatism. Elites, put simply, are doing exactly what they accuse their critics of doing. The consequences are tragic for expertise.

The philosopher Michael Sandel puts the matter bluntly in his recent takedown of meritocracy and the hubris it breeds in winners: elites "inhale too deeply of their success."[12] Blind to their own failings, they cannot seem to grasp the fact that their critics are rational and worth engaging with. This blindness has led them to disturbing policy conclusions that have stifled dissent and, in turn, fueled our current populist moment.

Our book proposes a corrective to this dangerous, blind faith in expertise. We do not denigrate expertise. We instead identify a cluster of pathologies that have enveloped many institutions meant to help referee expertise. Doubt, uncertainty, and counterarguments are now feared, but such habits are crucial to the accumulation of knowledge. Credentials are used as trump cards. Academia alternates between turf war and means to a political end.

To be sure, misinformation exists. But it always has, and the most challenging problems in public discourse do not revolve around denialism. Rather, our polarization and gridlock owe at least as much to technocratic elites who have taken their fears of misinformation too far toward the suppression of skepticism and healthy dissent. Experts are fallible, and expert consensus may be (and has been) wrong. Elites too often misuse the claim of "following the science" to mask complicated policy choices and trade-offs. This claim calls for more, not less, tolerance of healthy skepticism.

We live in an age of technocratic elitism. Government policymakers use the opinions of experts to justify all manner of laws, directives, and policies. Elites relentlessly employ credentials as a way of justifying their authority and foreclosing broad public debate. Disinformation—the province of denialists masquerading as skeptics—is indeed a feature of public discourse. But *disagreement* is not a reliable measure of disinformation. By conflating the two, elites spurn all critical voices—from populists to mainstream scientific skeptics—as "fringe" participants in public discourse. We think this is a serious mistake. It evinces little respect for public opinion or awareness of the difficulty of drawing a line around "wrongthink," and it only leads to more polarization.

Expertise—or at least the pretense of expertise—is everywhere. Experts grace headlines not only to tell us how we should think about domestic and foreign policy but also to remind us to watch more funny videos of cats for our mental health.[13] Experts dole out advice on everything from global-warming models to how to stay warm during power outages. (On the latter, experts have some creative solutions that ordinary folks might overlook: light your fireplace, or, if you don't have one, use a heater.[14]) We play an occasional game of going to the front page of the *New York Times* or the *Washington Post* and searching for how many times the word *expert* appears there. It seems to be there more often than not. These experts are deployed less to reason through difficult subjects with nuance and more to shore up the party line with the imprimatur of their credentials. The *New York Times* deploys its experts to great success: a reference to "experts" in a headline can insist on the paper's "just-the-facts" neutrality in a piece that is written primarily to disagree with Donald Trump ("Trump Tries to Improve His Environmental Record with a New Water Rule, but Experts Reject Its Efficacy"), provide an imprimatur of credibility because the journalist has talked to a professor or two ("What Can Be Deduced from the Length of Jury Deliberations in the Rittenhouse Case? Not Much, Experts Say"), or even serve as crass clickbait to steer readers to its more commerce-oriented offerings ("These Expert-Approved Gadgets Can Help Upgrade Your Kitchen for Less").[15] Every field needs its experts: not just "infectious-disease experts," "policing experts," and "experts on the weapons of 1791" (of which we have "a sudden need," the *Times* tells us), but also now "gift experts," "tailgating experts," and even "Wordle experts." Browsing the news, you can hear from a parenting expert, skincare expert, bathing-suit expert, living expert, lifestyle expert, *digital*-lifestyle expert, social inclusion expert, burnout-prevention expert, tidying expert, vacuum expert, downsizing and decluttering expert, and even a ritual expert.[16]

Many of these examples of alleged experts are amusing, to be sure, but they also mark a culture in thrall with expertise. From 1954 to 1999, the term *expert* or *experts* appeared in *New York Times* headlines in this usage—experts sharing their consensus—just 15 times; in 2021 alone, it decorated more headlines than over the entire previous 45-year period.[17] In the *Huffington Post*, never one for half-measures, it appears in the title or byline more than 2,000 times between 2012 and 2022 (expertise to the rescue: "etiquette experts share faux pas to avoid while staying at a hotel, especially during the pandemic" and "from eye masks to neck pillows, here's what health experts keep in their bags when they take a trip").[18] This is a degraded off-brand imitation of expertise. Tragically, it seems to be the kind

of expertise that elites celebrate. Where a few decades ago academic institutions might have profiled their researchers and scholars—or, better yet,
written about the research itself—university web pages now prominently
boast of their "faculty experts," who inevitably are at least "noted" or "leading," if not "world renowned." A scholar pursues knowledge; an expert, it
seems, tells you what to think.

*   *   *

After a series of surprising results—from the Brexit referendum to the election of Trump—many publicly vowed to try to understand why so many
voters had made choices that seemed unimaginable from the perspective
of the mainstream. The effort to widen the circle of understanding sadly
seems to have been short-lived, and a collective amnesia about the consequences of ignoring wide swaths of the electorate has set in. Many of our
colleagues, for instance, were surprised by how close Trump came to a second term in 2020 despite his apparent mishandling of the COVID-19 pandemic and notwithstanding the many other obstacles in his way, including
the change to a politically unfavorable mail-in voting system. Although we
shared in our colleagues' repudiation of Trump's term in office, we were
hardly surprised by the closeness of this victory.

Our theory of populist epistemology developed out of a course we taught
at our law school, "Populism and the Law." If you had to reduce our course
to a single question, it would be: What does it mean to apply the label
populist equally to both Bernie Sanders supporters and Trump supporters?
Framing the question this way meant we had to avoid most straw-man narratives about populism (e.g., that populists are just angry racists or even just
angry conservatives). It forced us to examine the claims and perspectives of
populist voters. Careful analysis and attention to empirics shook up many
firmly held priors about populism—our students' and our own.

We see it as lazy to dismiss populism without first seeking to understand
it and take its claims seriously. Although seductive, the disdain for populism is dangerous.[19] The willful ignorance that makes one write off populists has in recent years resulted in the election of authoritarians. Despite
a brief window after 2016 when many sought to understand voters better,
mainstream commentary seems to have moved back to its old register of
contempt—which in turn begets yet more polarization, fear, and anger. The
contempt is lazy. Populist voters are full of surprises, and they are not easily

pigeonholed. We argue here that what most unites populists—both left and right leaning—is neither their political agenda nor a set of attitudes such as racism but rather their skeptical perspective toward policy expertise.

*   *   *

Our book distills three dimensions of a flawed elite mindset that are as pervasive as they are corrosive. The first is *condescension*: because of a misguided faith in meritocracy, elites see an America plagued by the scourge of ignorance and the failure of common folk to trust their intellectual betters. Second, *technocratic paternalism*, a mindset that mischaracterizes our most important fights as being over facts. Elites wrongly believe that if we can agree on the facts, agreement on policy will follow. The third mindset is *intellectual tyranny*. Elites see doubt and dissent as the result of faulty processes, if not outright corruption. This view paves the way for an intellectual culture that brooks no dissent and assumes one's nonintellectual or nonelite opponents engage in bad faith. Each of these three views is interrelated, stemming from the same valorization of credentials and merit, and each is equally corrosive.

There have been some excellent books written about the pandemic. Naturally, the question that keeps coming up is "What can we do to be ready for the next pandemic?" Our answer is not one grounded in epidemiology, public health, or any other scientific endeavor, although we do discuss all of these approaches in this book. Our contribution is to do what we can to improve the quality of public discourse when the next pandemic arrives. To be frank, there is little hope of a successful response to the next pandemic if we are not honest about what went wrong with the debates over the most recent one. If the climate for debate does not improve, we are doomed to repeat the mistakes made this time around.

1 Expertise Corrupted

The past decade has handed a series of rebukes to the elite ruling classes and in particular to the experts they trot out. "People in this country have had enough of experts."[1] "People are not stupid; and you can rely on their wisdom in the long run, more than on the so-called experts."[2] Although these statements are strikingly similar, they come from opposite ends of the political spectrum. The first was uttered during the Brexit campaign by the right-leaning Michael Gove; the second came from the political left, President Ólafur Ragnar Grímsson of Iceland in defense of his decision to veto a parliamentary decision and send it to public referendum, a power never previously exercised by a president of Iceland.[3] Even when the line of attack is being levied by other elites, the critique resonates. The left-wing Greek politician Yanis Varoufakis explains that he became an economist "because I refused to leave it to the experts," having decided that "so-called experts in our great universities, on our TV screens, in the banks and finance industries did not have a clue."[4] Voters on both sides of the aisle are increasingly fed up with being told what to think.

Elites have responded by circling the wagons. Science and expertise, they say, are under attack. Question-begging platitudes—"we believe in science," "follow the science," and "defer to experts"—became the obligatory mantras of politicians, pundits, and yard signs during the COVID-19 pandemic. A paranoid obsession with misinformation developed. For these elites, disagreement, rather than representing a healthy sign of democracy, proved that shadowy forces were leading Americans astray. Commentators on populism offered impressionistic portraits, inevitably sneering and one dimensional, of the ignorance of antiestablishment voters.

Were these explanations correct in depicting a mass of angry, hopeless "deplorables," fomented by a cabal of authoritarian lunatics? At a minimum, this elite diagnosis did not seem to provide much of a cure. In 2020, just 43,000 more votes—Biden's combined margin of victory in Georgia, Arizona, and Wisconsin—would have handed Trump a second term. Yet in response to Trump receiving 74 million votes, the second-highest vote total in US history, elites doubled down on their dismissal of Trump voters.

The conventional wisdom on antiestablishment voters has other anomalies. If populism is nothing more than the dying rage of racist nationalists, how can we understand the rise of antiestablishment voters on the left, epitomized by Bernie Sanders in the United States and left populist parties across Europe and Latin America? The caricatured impression of populists as xenophobes cannot easily explain the nuances of recent populist uprisings, whether the *gilets jaunes* protests in France or the Canadian convoy protest of 2022. But elites seem increasingly disinterested in the messy complexity of the public sphere. Brexit, or "British exit," provides a case in point: elites continue to perceive the "Leave" (the European Union) vote as proof that voters were ignorant and easily duped. But given the robust debate that proceeded the vote and an election where a remarkable 72 percent of voters turned out, Brexit could just as easily be seen as an ideal manifestation of democracy in action—regardless of the outcome. That is, a country had a public, open, and vigorous debate about its core values and identity, unearthing profound grievances and fractures that lay beneath the surface of British political life. Dismissing the process because you didn't like the result betrays a contempt for democracy.[5]

Elites, as Jackson Lears puts it, have reduced "a complex populist ferment . . . to a creation of conniving politicians manipulating an illiberal population."[6] It rarely seems to occur to elites to ask why populists are angry. To be sure, a minority of thoughtful analysts have offered some explanations for the cultural disdain felt by working-class voters, the political ails of a polarized country, and the pernicious psychological impact of meritocracy on elites.[7] But far more commentators have simply written off populist voters.

The term *elite* is controversial. Scholars and pundits dispute its meaning and in many instances deny its plausibility. We detail our understanding of the term in chapter 2, but the hallmark of an elite is academic credentials. Elites are found in the halls of academe and government as well as in newspapers and the media generally. Although there are conservative elites, they are often politically left of center on social issues.[8] Their home is urban, and their demeanor is that of the confident and successful professional. Elites valorize smarts, diplomas, and expertise, all of which they have in overabundance. We have much more to say about elites as we develop our arguments.[9]

Our book focuses on a highly visible and pernicious source of antiestablishment fervor: the routine misuse of expertise in the public sphere. Expertise is the primary tool by which elites claim legitimacy and justify their authority. Thus, when expertise is routinely and demonstrably misused, legitimacy erodes. Elites are very good at diagnosing the failure of voters to heed expert warnings. They are less successful at diagnosing themselves. "Follow the science," to take an overworn axiom from recent years, represents a painful abuse of the idea of expertise. It begs the question and implies that complicated trade-offs over societal values are not matters of public judgment, which in turn stifles discussion and debate.

We are defenders of expertise. Expertise is indispensable. It is often used well and wisely to inform debate and decision. But as we document in this book, its hypocritical, selective, and exaggerated misuse has become routine in the public sphere. That abuse is corrosive of true expertise. It fuels antiestablishment sentiments. When elites take to the ramparts, allegedly in defense of science and expertise but in reality in service of their preferred policy agenda, they denigrate expertise further.

The current conventional wisdom of elites—that science and knowledge are under attack by a growing slice of the population—is simply not justified. Nor is it helpful: calling your opponents "deniers" seems unlikely to be persuasive. Elites have developed a lexicon for dismissing the claims made by others: *misinformation, denialism, whataboutism, bothsidesism*. Ideas one disagrees with are labeled *dangerous*, which marks them as out of bounds for civilized discussion. To be sure, misinformation exists and warrants our attention. And ideas might, in some sense, be "dangerous"—it could hardly be otherwise if you believe, as we do, that ideas matter. But when these terms are casually bandied about so widely, they cease to have any real meaning, and their main consequence is to make vigorous debate, even within the ivory tower, impossible.

We must return to some basic, commonsense habits: not silencing others, not attacking straw men, not resorting to ad hominem attacks. It strikes us as peculiar that we need to defend skepticism, a philosophical stance with a long pedigree. In the context of intellectual culture, with its practice of tenure, skepticism is precisely the type of practice that should be defended or encouraged. Skeptical inquiry is the essence of the academic temperament. Or so we thought. But skepticism has gotten decidedly bad press of late. It is sometimes associated with a "post-truth" environment where misinformation and denialism are rampant. Many academics now seem to believe that all skepticism is shoddy at best and dangerous at worst. This stance is both intellectually indefensible and pragmatically unworkable.

Populists and Experts

Expert overreach actuates populist skepticism. Elites would have us believe that skepticism is either misplaced or, worse, the source of misinformation and disinformation, but we argue that populist skepticism is firmly grounded and hardly a principal cause of mis- or disinformation.

Contrary to some of its modern critics, populism does not have a particular political valence—which explains why voters as disparate as Sanders and Trump supporters are often labeled *populists*. Populism is also commonly and wrongly conflated with other political phenomena, including authoritarianism, demagoguery, and nationalism. These political beliefs are distinct from populism. Populist movements may have elements of each of them, but so can other movements, including mainstream liberalism. The lens we use instead to understand populist voters is epistemological—a focus on their skepticism toward elite expertise, a skepticism that is often grounded in experience.

This populist skepticism is strikingly defensible and rational. It serves as a useful corrective to a growing elite pathology in overreaching when it comes to expertise, and it responds to a sense that technocracy has deprived the public sphere of its voice. A. O. Hirschman famously said there were two ways one could express disagreement with an institution: voice (speaking up) or exit (quitting).[10] The strictures of today's globalized liberal institutions make both avenues difficult. Populism's apparent destructiveness, then, is strategic: it creates options in the face of being told there are none. When Angela Merkel told Germans that her expert-driven monetary policy was *alternativlos*, "without alternative," she unwittingly provided the perfect name for a new, far-right populist party, Alternative für Deutschland (AfD).[11] Merkel, of course, was not the first or the last elite to tell voters that a chosen policy had "no alternative," nor the last to whom voters responded by creating an unexpected, unpredictable set of alternatives.

Many wondered why the COVID-19 pandemic didn't hand Biden a landslide victory. Honing in on Trump's mishandling of the outbreak, Biden's campaign focused on a pledge to "follow the science." The clichéd mantra, both illiberal and unscientific, fell flat with many. When Governor Gavin Newsom of California admitted in 2023 that "we would've done everything differently," he emphasized how "we, collectively"—"hardly I," he added to underscore his unwillingness to be held to account—knew little in 2020 and thus could hardly be held to account.[12] But the 2020 version of Newsom showed little humility or doubt as he admonished residents to mask "between bites" while dining outside. And elites worked hard throughout 2020 and beyond to suppress debate about how to respond to the pandemic, behavior that is hardly consistent with their new claim to humility. As we show throughout the book, elitism during the pandemic degraded public discourse, and populists, with their radar tuned to elite hypocrisy, took notice. Quick to blame gullible Trump voters and antivaxxers for predictable failings of policy design, elites created a climate where scientific values and the integrity of public debate were undermined.[13]

Our chief antagonist is those who have little interest in understanding populist voters, instead sneering at them as ignorant and naive at best, racist at worst. These elites litter the op-ed pages of newspapers and are common in the ranks of public intellectuals. This patronizing tone has unfortunately pervaded discourse more broadly. It is easy for people to roll their eyes at almost everything the "masses" do. When confronted by disagreement, we no longer attempt to understand the other side, much less to argue back—although both approaches are a necessity for a healthy democracy. Instead, it is tempting to yield to contempt and disregard. These attitudes, far more than populism, are responsible for the hollowed-out and polarized landscape we face today.

Consider this description of a group of 12 million Americans who voted in the 2016 presidential election: They are middle class and educated. They are strongly in favor of increasing taxes on the rich. They distrust elites and think our system is rigged: they overwhelmingly believe our economy is biased toward the rich, that money is distributed unfairly, and that they have no real voice in politics. Their social views are fairly moderate. Who are we describing? Sanders voters or Trump voters? This is an extrapolation from a study of Trump voters.[14] This group does not form the majority of Trump's base, though—in 2016, they constituted 19 percent of it, more than enough to swing an election. In fact, they had the most favorable views of both Sanders and Clinton of any subset of Trump voters. Most Trump voters are not populists, nor is Trump necessarily a populist. Rather, a subset of those voters is populist, and they are the group whom we seek to understand.

Although it is tempting to lump all Trump voters together, doing so is analytically sloppy. Populists are distinct in values and outlook from other constituencies, ranging from the alt-right to mainline conservatives, that might have voted for Trump in 2016 and might do so again. Voting coalitions are not a monolith. More Trump voters were traditional mainline Republican voters—for instance, those who favor lower taxes or those who are culturally conservative—than populists.

At its most basic level, populism is the rejection of the elites by the masses. In recent years, the concept of populism has been muddied and misused, largely by those who are strongly critical of certain forms of populism. We have more to say about this in chapter 2. In particular, though, we are most interested in populist voters, not whom they vote for. Both Sanders and Trump attracted populist voters. We are more interested in those voters—who, as the study referred to earlier suggests, share much in common—than we are in the imperfect politicians who attract their support. Populism is misunderstood in part because many analysts start with the conclusion that it is bad and needs to be stopped. They thus magnify its ugliest elements and ignore the rest. In our view, to talk about populists you need to be able to explain multiple phenomena at once: Bernie Sanders, Donald Trump, Hugo Chavez, the nineteenth-century populists. Excluding variation that is inconvenient to your worldview is not helpful.

Populists level a serious critique of elites. The elite use of expertise is often motivated not by facts but by values masquerading as judgments. The expert shores up the authority of the claim to knowledge, licensing a particular policy agenda. As we say repeatedly in this book, facts alone rarely if ever settle matters of public policy. But many elites, speaking in their technological argot, dismiss the concerns of ordinary citizens and shut them out of the policy discussion. Elites would rather not hear from ordinary folks because such people, as the elites see them, lack the competence even to enter the discussion. Taking populism's critique of experts seriously helps explain populism's enduring appeal. It does so without blaming the voters, redirecting the spotlight to ask whether our governing institutions might bear some responsibility for what some call a crisis in democracy. The populist critique is a response to a real elite pathology. Many elites are no doubt well intentioned, but that is not enough.

Overreach

Our book tells a story in three parts. In the first act, elites overreach. In the second, populists call them out. In the third, rather than taking this critique seriously, elites double down.

In part I, we detail the phenomenon of elite overreach. We show how in the deployment of expertise, elites have overplayed their hand. We start by explaining why we use the term *elite* despite pushback from some colleagues. Like any social category, elites are not a monolith. But certain tendencies and habits predominate among the elite, such as the claim that the masses are ignorant and, as such, should defer to their elite handlers, who are possessed of superior knowledge and skill. Many elites display a nostalgic view of rationality and knowledge, but one that does not withstand critical scrutiny. In chapter 3, we show how faulty claims to expertise are deployed in public policy. In chapter 4, we show why expertise is inherently problematic, discussing systematic issues in the generation and interpretation of expertise. This nuance is characteristically ignored by elites.

Part II takes a close look at the chief critics of elites, the populists. The conventional wisdom contains many inaccuracies about populism, which we clarify in chapter 5 by focusing on populist voters. We understand populism as a rational response to a public sphere that is the product of elite capture. Populism emerges out of being told "no" and dealing with a politics of exclusion. Populists bring a unique epistemology to the table (chapter 6). They are skeptical of the claims made by elites, believing instead that wisdom can come from common sense and experience. In chapter 7, we defend that epistemology, showing that it holds its own against the epistemology of expertise.

Rather than taking these critiques seriously, elites double down on their exclusivity, as we show in part III. One trope of elite commentary is that we live in an age of mis- and disinformation, a public sphere flooded with garbage. In chapter 8, we show this view is empirically and theoretically shallow. Things are now no different than they have ever been, and facts matter less to opinion than elites assume. Troublingly, elites have extended their obsession with misinformation to the scholarly sphere, the subject of chapter 9. Here we examine the claim that academia is awash in "merchants of doubt," a claim that has led to the mislabeling and stifling of ordinary debate. The epistemology advanced by proponents of this view turns out to be more a matter of favoring the members of one's own club than a matter of the facts of science. In chapter 10, we link these behaviors to a growing close-mindedness among elites. Many agree the United States faces a free-speech problem, with rising censorship and self-censorship. In response, many elites shrug. Their minds are so made up, so lacking in curiosity, that they see no reason to rise in defense of basic values of open inquiry.

Some may read this book and perhaps misunderstand its message. We are not here to criticize rationality, facts, and knowledge. We are academics. We believe deeply that the virtues of the academic temperament—openness to critique, entertainment of contrary opinion, and full-throated debate—are the best way to pursue knowledge. But we think the technocratic elite capture of the public sphere has damaged the enterprise we hold so dear. Our book is written in the hope that our fellow elites will consider our claims and give us a fair hearing. Many of our friends have read our work and replied, "Sure, elites overreach, but what is the alternative?" Even if one thinks there is no alternative to elite dominance of the sphere of public discourse, elites could be infinitely more effective if they were to develop a better sense of how their conduct undermines their own agendas.[15] Our primary goal in this book is to dissect what is wrong with discourse in the public sphere. We are critical of elite approaches to policy discourse, and we think there are several dimensions to the problem. In addition, we think that much of the nonelite population has been driven from the public sphere. We think this is a mistake both on its own and relative to the objectives of technocratic elites. Our highest aspiration is to reexamine what it means to be a member of a polity, for that is what joins us together.

I An Overplayed Hand: The Age of Mindless Expertise

2 Elites and Expert Culture

Elites—a group we explain in this chapter—see the world as little more than a series of technocratic challenges that only their "smarts" can address, especially since the world is "increasingly" complex. This is a natural extension of their meritocratic mindset. But their view of knowledge is shallow, and their expertise amounts to a cheap parlor trick.

Does democracy let too many people vote? That is the claim of a widely praised book by the philosopher Jason Brennan, who suggests our contemporary problems call for an "epistocracy." One cure might be to disenfranchise most Americans, as voters routinely prove themselves "ignorant, misinformed, irrational, biased, and sometimes immoral." Alternatively, an "epistocratic veto" could grant additional legislative power to "a cognitively elite body."[1] Brennan may go to extremes in his plan to eliminate the scourge of ignorance, but he is hardly alone in his diagnosis of what ails democracy. Yascha Mounk, a well-regarded pundit on the "crisis of democracy," believes that modern society is so complicated that most decisions inevitably turn on technical know-how. Not only do we need experts to sort out these issues, but for him it is "difficult to imagine that most citizens would take an active interest in them."[2] Tom Nichols, a regular writer for outlets such as *The Atlantic*, proclaims that we are living through the "death of expertise," arguing that "Americans have reached a point where ignorance, especially of anything related to public policy, is an actual virtue."[3]

These are representative accounts of an attitude that has taken hold in elite circles. We discuss the elite mindset in detail in this chapter, but first we must answer the question "Who is an 'elite'?"[4] The moniker *elites*, roughly speaking, refers to university-credentialed experts in high-paying, usually urban-centric jobs, alongside the politicians and members of the media who enable them.[5] Elites who subscribe to the views voiced by Brennan, Mounk, and Nichols valorize expertise, believing that only experts have the needed insight and intelligence to inform our most important public-policy decisions. They disdain laypeople as apathetic and naive at best and militantly ignorant at worst. Because policy is highly technical, laypeople, in the elites' view, have little right to an opinion. Elites assume that disagreement with their worldview cannot be the result of a rational or good-faith process. Dissent from the elite consensus must instead be the result of emotion, groupthink, or misinformation and deception. But elites fail to apply this lens to their own consensus, which they assume rests on neutral grounds.

Surely not all elites hold the most extreme versions of these views, but the essential premise is foundational for modern elites: expertise is idealized, and common sense and intuition are denigrated. This perspective is factually wrong, antidemocratic, and profoundly unhelpful. It also begets populism, which arises in defense of lay knowledge, and quite correctly so. To be very clear, expertise is important. Frankly, nobody would argue otherwise. When elites such as Tom Nichols shadowbox against populists who supposedly would replace all expertise with a fanatical and reflexive worship of ignorance, they argue against a straw man. The kind of "expertise" elites frequently turn to in practice—and that populists execrate—is instead more of a pose than anything else. It is not so much the use of expertise to inform public policy as a resort to credentialism to foreclose debate.

Populism emerges as a response to the three elite mindsets we described in chapter 1: *condescension*, a disdain for a citizenry seen as besotted by ignorance, coupled with a belief in the wisdom and benevolence of elites; *technocratic paternalism*, the misguided view that facts, not values, can settle all important debates; and *intellectual tyranny*, the assumption that dissent is grounded in bad faith and misinformation. These mindsets have gained the status of conventional wisdom but originate in the elites' rarefied bubble. In this chapter, we first explain what we mean by *elite* and why we use that term. We then explore the elite mindset, which stems from the founding myth of elite culture, an excessive faith in meritocracy. In principle, it is hard to argue with calls for more knowledge. But although elites are quite passionate in their contempt for the unenlightened masses, they provide only a narrow, flimsy account of what knowledge looks like. Besotted by credentials and word counts, they forget that these metrics measure neither wisdom nor knowledge, which are more subtle and diffuse.

Defending an Unpopular Term

Although the term *elites* has a long-standing academic pedigree and is both useful and essential for our account, we have gotten occasional pushback—always from elites—about it. They seem baffled by it. Many of them will use it only in phrases such as "so-called elites" or in queries such as "Who are these elites?" The distinction between "real Americans" and "coastal elites" is a "total crock," one pundit put it.[6] We're frequently asked—especially by fellow elites—why we use the term *elites*.

The befuddlement is somewhat peculiar. Since its inception, American politics has been concerned about the power struggle between "the masses" and the political elite. This struggle was, after all, a dominant concern of the framers and a central theme of the *Federalist Papers*. From the dawn of the American republic, there were always some who defended the elite, believing that a select group of refined and educated citizens could best protect democracy against its most dangerous instincts. This was the explicit tack of multiple presidents of the past century, from Franklin D. Roosevelt and his so-called Brains Trust to John F. Kennedy and his "best and the brightest" and Obama in his recurrent use of the word *smarts* in talking about policy.[7] Likewise, there is a long-standing tradition of a backlash against elites. Most notably, in the historical moment that gave us the term *populism*, the nineteenth century saw a growing divide and distrust between the moneyed financial class and populists. Composed initially of farmers but ultimately made up of a wider collective, the populists—and ultimately the short-lived Populist Party—endorsed a series of political reforms and ideas that remain alive and contested today.

A little genealogy might be in order. The term *elite* was put into widespread use by the sociologist C. Wright Mills, whose book *The Power Elite* (1956) explored three power structures—big business, government, and military—and noted the deep connections between the powerful few who ran their associated institutions. Research into the idea of a power elite spread within sociology and political science, and the term *elite* remains alive and well in academic research today. For example, it appears in nearly 3,000 articles in the *American Political Science Review*, the top-ranked political science journal.[8] In many of those articles, the word *elite* is so widely understood and seemingly neutral in its meaning that authors rarely pause to define or clarify it. As two political scientists put it in a discussion on the increased focus on surveying elite opinion in recent years, "Many of our theories of politics are either directly or indirectly about the beliefs or behavior of elites, whether at the local, national, or international level."[9] Echoing many others in his field who study labor economics, automation, globalization, and outsourcing, the economist Daron Acemoglu talks of "elites . . . making choices that are not good news for non-college workers," which will fuel inequality.[10]

Why, then, are elites so ruffled by the term despite its long pedigree? Most likely, they don't like its implications. Americans have long been uncomfortable with ideas of class and class distinctions. But social and cultural classes do exist, and they do matter. They are formed when people, through common circumstances, "interact with each other, develop in-group social organizations, and share a common lifestyle, while at the same time excluding people they do not see as similar to themselves." Of the elites (upper-middle-class professionals who make up about one-fifth of the population), a leading sociologist notes that they "tend to live together in high-status suburbs and to perceive each other as equals."[11]

In recent years, the term *elite* has been deployed pejoratively, but here we mean it neutrally. It is a description of a social group with a recognizable worldview. Its pejorative use is in part a symptom of the uptick in populism—both left leaning and right leaning—in our era. Distrust of elites is the defining feature of populism. Donald Trump and other political candidates and commentators have deployed it regularly as an epithet, but it is by no means predominantly used by the Right.

Many commentators increasingly link pathologies in the public sphere, including the populist backlash, to elites' disconnection from the real experience of others. A growing slate of liberal commentators—including academics such as Michael Sandel, Jackson Lears, Joan Williams, and Daniel Markovits as well as celebrity journalists such as Chris Hayes and Anand Giridharadas—express concern that our obsession with "meritocracy" has created a system that empowers elites at the expense of all others.[12] Some worry that our flawed meritocracy corrodes the democratic ideal. Others note that elite culture is harmful to elites themselves. But all agree that there is such a thing as the elite, that the elite wield tremendous influence and power, and that something is rotten in the balance between elites and the rest of society.

Complaints about the term *elite* seem to coalesce around three claims: the term is imprecise; the term is applied hypocritically by other elites or conspiratorially by the ignorant; and the term suggests elites have a degree of power that they in fact do not enjoy.

None of these objections survives scrutiny. Of course, elites aren't a monolith: all the people who belong to the elite don't share the same opinions or have identical social status. This is a truism of any sociological category (e.g., "working class"). However, an imprecise category can still be useful and have a commonly shared meaning. A similar and equally flawed objection is sometimes levied against the idea of "the people," a concept that is essential to populism, which asserts that the "people" rather than the "elite" are the authentic voice of society. Many elites consider the term *the people* to be meaningless because there is no singular "people."[13] Yet this view ignores the role of "the people" in a deep tradition in political theory extending at least back to the concept of the "populus" in ancient Rome, which carried "favorable connotations that 'democracy' lacked."[14] The inexactness of terms such as *the elite* and *the people* do not make them useless as a concept, any more than the terms *love* and *hope* are meaningless because they are inexact.

Others object that the term *elite* is fundamentally flawed because some politicians have played on resentment against elites despite the fact that they themselves are quite wealthy and powerful and thus fit within this category. As one writer for *Salon* put it, "If Donald Trump is not an 'elite,' then the term is entirely meaningless, as it signifies nothing."[15] This argument is nonsensical—that someone uses a term opportunistically does not make it "entirely meaningless." Others dislike the fact that elites are often the loudest critics of other elites, but even if these elites are "class traitors" or "self-loathing" elites, that has no bearing on the validity of their critique.

*   *   *

As originally described by Mills, elites were defined by their disproportionate power in decision-making. Put simply, elites were those who have more influence than nonelites. Elites, for Mills, "occupy positions in American society from which they can look down upon, so to speak, and by their decisions mightily affect, the everyday worlds of ordinary men and women." But Mills's point was not just that elites had power and prestige. He saw those characteristics not as inherent features of them as people but rather as a result of the concentration of authority in the institutions they led: business, the military, and government. As a keen observer of the people occupying those roles, Mills was more interested in the fact that elites also shared an identity, a culture. "The people of these higher circles are involved in a set of overlapping 'crowds' and intricately connected cliques," he noted, referring to the striking similarities in their origins and social networks.[16]

Perhaps the most defining trait of the elite are their educational credentials—carrying at least a college degree and often a postgraduate degree. The "diploma divide"—the gulf in political and cultural attitudes between those with and without college degrees—is central to today's divisions of modern American politics and life. Among Americans 25 and older, fewer than 40 percent have a four-year college degree.[17] Yet in Congress, fully 94 percent of the House and 99 percent of the Senate hold at least a bachelor's degree. The concentration is even more striking and nonrepresentative in other respects: for instance, about one in ten members of the House and one in eight members of the Senate hold a degree from a single institution, Harvard.[18]

The diploma divide explains the vertiginous flip in the Democratic Party since the era of Bill Clinton as the party transformed from its traditional focus on the working class to an emphasis on the economic and cultural elite. For most of the second half of the twentieth century, Americans without college degrees were more likely to be Democrats compared to more credentialed American voters. That did not change until 2004. As the party's educational composition changed, it also became richer. Since 2016, the wealthy now vote Democratic more than the middle class.[19]

The diploma divide has had many consequences. Among other things, it helps explain elites' disdain for the ignorant masses. Although some might assume that a "smarter" party produces better governance, credentials are hardly the same thing as good judgment.[20] Expertise, judgment, *and* the values held by citizens are supposed to inform decision-making in a democracy. The diploma divide unfortunately makes it more likely that we will forget the importance of this combination and that elites will assume all their political leanings are the inevitable result of their superior, educated understanding of the world. Some commentators, such as the philosopher

Michael Sandel, have noted credentialism's undemocratic effect: it excludes many voices from politics. It also has political consequences. For example, some have questioned whether the Democratic Party can sustain national power if it continues gaining wealthy, highly educated voters at the cost of losing working-class voters.[21] When elites exhibit relentless credentialism and embrace the argot of "smart versus dumb," they express their disinterest in the uninformed opinions of their fellow citizens. Elites increasingly believe that all problems have technocratic solutions and that they are uniquely qualified to identify those solutions and apply them.

The diploma divide insulates elites. The elite bubble tends to coalesce around similar ideological and psychological proclivities.[22] Moreover, elites tend to enjoy disproportionate power not just in the Democratic Party but also in other key institutions—including those where political issues are hashed out. Within the media, both financial and general-interest journalists tend to lean liberal.[23] Within academia, there are few self-identified conservatives or Republicans.[24] These biases do not, as some assume, mean the work produced by those institutions is inherently biased.[25] In fact, those institutions have safeguards—if increasingly imperfect—in the form of professional and ethical norms that are meant to check against ideological bias. For instance, journalists have long been trained to interview and quote dissenting perspectives. But the safeguards are eroding, perhaps in part because of the intense concentration of a particular ideological and social class.

Some elites have tried to deny the problem of ideological concentration—either that it exists or that this bias represents a problem. The work of the historian of science Naomi Oreskes plays a central role in later chapters of our book because many have relied on her work about trust in science to argue for greater censorship and less tolerance of dissenting views in academic research. In a recent essay, she has dismissed concerns about the low numbers of conservative faculty.[26] But even the numbers she cites—which suggest that the critique understates the number of centrist faculty members—still show that academia fails to draw widely, much less representatively, from across ideological perspectives. Indeed, given the diploma divide, it probably cannot do so—the pool to select professors from is limited by the pool of advanced degree holders, as Oreskes points out. But there is reason to think that more than the diploma divide is at work. There is also an overt prejudice, increasingly overt in some faculties, against hiring conservatives. Arguments that faculties should deliberately seek out conservative perspectives to increase the diversity of opinions on campus are under fire. This state of affairs should trouble Oreskes because in other work she argues that pluralism and viewpoint diversity are part of what enables the scientific community to arrive at trustworthy truths, but she apparently does not believe that the need for such diversity is necessary when it comes to political views.

At elite institutions, liberal ideological dominance is even more pronounced than at community colleges and professional schools. More than 80 percent of faculty at Harvard identify as liberal, including almost 40 percent as "very liberal," whereas less than 1.5 percent choose the moniker *conservative*.[27] And only 9 percent of incoming students at Harvard describe themselves as conservative.[28] The issue is not just that the faculty has sorted that way but also that many on the faculty want it sorted that way. Forty percent would bar anyone who worked in the Trump administration from holding a faculty appointment. Even when we take Trump out of the equation, the numbers do not suggest much more of an embrace of pluralism: "31 percent opposed hiring conservative professors to increase ideological diversity."[29]

Oreskes dismisses critics' focus on elite institutions as misguided because, she says, they center on institutions that are "by definition unusual."[30] But those few institutions disproportionately dominate public policy and national discourse—recall again that more than one in ten members of Congress went to Harvard, where Oreskes teaches. It makes little sense to dismiss a critique for its focus on the rarefied ether of elite institutions. Such a dismissal reflects precisely the bubble mindset that makes many Americans doubt the elite. And doubt they do: in 2015, 57 percent of Americans had "a great deal" or "quite a lot" of confidence in higher education. By 2023, that share had plummeted to 36 percent.[31]

The Worldview of Elites

Is it fair to paint elite attitudes with a broad brush? That is, how can we be so sure, beyond anecdotes, that elites generally share particular perspectives on decision-making in a democracy? Because we are talking about a group as a whole, our account is necessarily somewhat stylized, but it aligns with empirical research on elites. Some scholars have tried to directly measure elite attitudes through public-opinion research. One such study suggests that there is indeed an "elite mindset" that transcends narrow political preference. The authors wonder whether Silicon Valley elites, who are growing in economic influence, have distinct views from other elites. Indeed, they do: although they mostly identify as Democrats, they are more strongly opposed to regulation and more libertarian in their mindset than most other Democrats. As part of the study, the authors examined several distinct groups: the general public, self-identified Democrats and Republicans, Democratic and Republican donors (as a proxy for elites), and Silicon Valley elites. Their approach identified certain values and predispositions among elites. Most notably, elites scored highly in "cosmopolitanism." These cosmopolitans shared both beliefs—identifying as a "citizen of the world"—and behavioral traits, such as a propensity to travel more and to eat sushi. Both Republican and Democratic elites scored notably higher on this measure than the other groups in the research.[32]

More sociological research suggests that, in general, elites tend to be culturally liberal. They support "post-material" policies that further "big-picture" social goals rather than those that relate to immediate material and physical security—presumably their wealth and status make them less focused on material needs. They tend to see "structural and systemic problems" rather than "individualist" explanations. Psychologically, they tend to score high for "openness to experience."[33] Others have found that they tend to be more "rationalist" in outlook than less-credentialed individuals, who are more prone to "intuitionism."[34]

These perspectives aren't the problem, of course. The problem arises instead when elites mistakenly see their attitudes as universally shared or objectively correct. These attitudes, however, are values, which are not reducible to data and which will never tell us whether being "open to experiences" or identifying as a "citizen of the world" is a moral good.[35] Unfortunately, because elites go to school for longer and have more educational pedigree, it is easy for them to assume that their opinions are simply "smarter."[36] The fact that more educated people tend to hold those views is not evidence that these views are the result of that education. Many of these views are self-serving in that they are adapted for the kind of high-performing professional jobs that the college educated seek.[37] College graduates are also more likely, on the whole, to have material security, which could change their priorities and focus. Like-minded people also tend to cluster near each other—in turn reinforcing their bubble mentality.

In 2021, Nate Silver was widely mocked by fellow elites for a tweet where he contended that "a lot of elites would fail a pop quiz on how the median American thinks and behaves."[38] Research, however, suggests he may have had a point: elites do seem to make many mistakes when trying to interpret public opinion.[39] As one political scientist puts it, much elite research suggests that "elites are fundamentally misreading the room."[40] This misreading is based in part on elites' failure to understand that their values and tastes are not universal, a blind spot that can be subtly reinforced by the bubble in which they live. Consider a minor example: the mainstream media's treatment of the television show *Yellowstone*, which in 2022 was America's most-watched show. Steve Krakauer, a journalist and media watcher with a keen eye for hypocrisy in the mainstream press, noted that the show was barely reviewed or mentioned by major media outlets for its first several years, in stark contrast to media darlings such as *Succession*, which had a fraction of *Yellowstone*'s audience. Krakauer's explanation was that the show didn't check the right boxes for a "culturally 'acceptable' prestige show."[41] Another critic explained that it perhaps seemed like a "'red-state show,' loved more by Texas gun-toters than Brooklyn hipsters."[42] A reader of the *New York Times* could be forgiven for not even knowing about *Yellowstone* because its popularity stemmed in part from its success with audiences that could not be more different from the typical *Times* reader: Americans who still use cable television and don't use social media. Although television viewing choices are a trivial example, they illustrate the blind spots created by bubbles.

Why Elites Matter

How much do elites really matter? Some elites dislike the moniker *elite* in part because they reject the idea that they have real power. If anything, much of the time they feel as if they are screaming into the void. The contrary view, held by most Americans, finds it almost self-evident that elites have too much power. More than eight in ten Americans think that politicians, big business, and the rich have too much power and influence in today's economy.[43]

Tom Nichols thinks ordinary Americans should stop passing the buck. For Nichols, a staunch defender of the expert class, voters alone bear responsibility for whatever ails us: "citizens are the masters of their fate."

Blaming elites, says Nichols, is a "hell of a story," but "it is not new and it is not true." Ordinary Americans, instead, are to blame for the ravages of globalization—if, indeed, there are any ravages. They brought it on themselves because they love the material goods that modern capitalism produces—say, bigger and brighter televisions—and simultaneously love paying less for them. For Nichols, what we really have in populism is a crisis of accountability, where ordinary people fail to take responsibility for their own bad political decisions.[44]

Is he right? To be sure, deciding who has power—"elites" or "the people" —isn't a simple question of arithmetic. Elites could indeed be losing power and influence, given the apparent profound distrust in them, even while they simultaneously maintain a firm grip over important structures of power. Martin Gurri, whose book *The Revolt of the Public and the Crisis of Authority in the New Millennium* (2014) was seen by some as presaging the rise of Trump, expressed that ambivalence in an interview in 2021: "What we have is this collision between a public that is in repudiation mode and these elites who have lost control to the degree that they can't hoist these utopian promises upon us anymore because no one believes it, but they're still acting like zombie elites in zombie institutions. They still have power. They can still take us to war. They can still throw the police out there, and the police could shoot us, but they have no authority or legitimacy."[45]

Nichols's claim cuts against the grain of much political science research, which seems to more closely track the intuition of eight in ten Americans. Most political scientists see contemporary politics as an elite-driven phenomenon. Voters take their cues from elites rather than the reverse. Indeed, many elites evince precisely that attitude when they describe Trump voters as a credulous public in the thrall of a master manipulator. But they never turn the lens back on themselves, hardly recognizing the role that elite cues play in forming the counterreaction against Trump.

One clever test of the power of elites came from two political scientists. They identified nearly 2,000 instances between 1981 and 2002 where the public was surveyed about a proposed policy change. They then estimated how closely the ultimate outcome of each of those proposals matched the view of different groups of voters. They concluded: "Economic elites and organized groups representing business interests have substantial independent impacts on U.S. government policy, while average citizens and mass-based interest groups have little or no independent influence."[46]

We certainly do not mean to suggest that one journal article proves that elites have outsized power. Nor do the study's authors, who, showing the kind of humility we wish was more on display in contemporary academia, label their own efforts a "tentative and preliminary" attempt to bring data to bear on a long-standing question in political science. But their finding is consistent with others and with commonsense intuition about the influence of elite attitudes. In foreign policy, for example, elites seem to have disproportionate sway over public opinion and are seen as credible voices even by those who differ politically.[47] A leading scholar of international relations describes the result as "the hell of good intentions," highlighting the folly of a foreign-policy "blob" that makes repeated mistakes and is never held accountable.[48] In the world of law, two authors put the elite bias succinctly: "Supreme Court Justices care more about the views of academics, journalists, and other elites than they do about public opinion." This, they say, is especially true of swing justices, whose opinions are most important in close decisions. Why do the justices care so much about elites? Drawing on social psychology, the authors propose that it is as simple as the "human need for approval from individuals and groups that are important to them."[49] And what groups might those be? Eight of the nine current justices were produced by the same two law schools, Yale and Harvard.

The Technocratic Mindset

Elites valorize expertise. Their mindset is technocratic. Public-policy questions are, to them, ultimately technical puzzles to be solved by experts. This epistemic stance is what interests us about the elite because we think it is this attitude—more than any particular political vision—that ignites the ire of populists. Otherwise, both left-leaning and right-leaning populists could not be so united in their dislike of the elite.

The technocratic view of policy is a consequence of seeing the world as a meritocracy. Elites have always been told that smarts matter most for success, so their successes confirm their superior gifts of intelligence. They naturally assume that their credentials mean they will enact wise policy. Two versions of the technocratic mindset sometimes get elided. As we show, one of them is significantly more problematic than the other. First, elites believe—more so than the general public—that we should "follow the science" or "listen to experts": that is, decision-making should be primarily evidence based. Second, likely owing to their tendency to be quite educated, elites believe that what they do is listen to experts. In fact, however, this flips the cart and the horse. More often, elites choose a preferred public-policy outcome and then find an expert—whether a real expert or not—to shore up their claim.

Although the success of our arguments does not depend on knowing why elites hold their views, we can mention two compelling possibilities. The first is a bureaucratic explanation in the tradition of Max Weber: elites have constructed a philosophy of governance that makes them indispensable and that leads to the need for more and more elite-led institutions. Throughout the first half of the twentieth century, a "policy-planning" network—large think tanks and other foundations—developed to help big business understand increasingly complex issues of a national economy and to advocate for big business on a national level.[50]

The second explanation is more philosophical in nature and roots elite behavior in meritocracy and perfectionism. From an early age, education has taught elites that problems are solvable with the right knowledge and skills. It is assumed that anything—even a global pandemic—is something that is entirely preventable or solvable, which yields unrealistic policy prescriptions followed by recriminations when they are not heeded. Joe Biden famously said that if Trump hadn't failed in his management of the pandemic, "all the people would still be alive"—that is, there would have been zero deaths. This, of course, is malarkey even for those who agree that others might have managed our response to coronavirus better than Trump did. But the structure of Biden's claim nicely captures the elite perfectionist mindset. The technology critic Evgeny Morozov invented a useful term to describe big-tech elites who hold a similar attitude: *solutionism*, the conviction that with the right algorithms and data we can eliminate all the problems of modern life. But solutionism only works by fundamentally misunderstanding and narrowing those problems.[51]

A Shallow View of Knowledge

Many elites sneer at the supposed ignorance of the public. This stance exposes not only elite paternalism—which is part of what inflames populists—but also a superficial conception of knowledge and citizenship. When it comes to real knowledge, elites themselves make many mistakes, too—relying too heavily on credentialism and misunderstanding the application of that knowledge, which we focus on in chapter 3. But there is an even more fundamental problem. Elites talk a big game about "knowledge" (and against ignorance), but their idea of knowledge, on further probing, sounds more like trivia and memorization, not wisdom or insight.

Recall Jason Brennan, the philosopher who proposes restricting the right to vote. Brennan is regularly praised by elites and pundits, in some cases for his plan but in other cases for how he is raising awareness of the very important problem of voters who, according to the elites, are just too darn stupid.

Brennan's account is mistaken for several reasons. For one, ignorance isn't the same thing as stupidity, as the legal scholar Ilya Somin has argued. That is, voters sometimes choose not to be informed because their vote so rarely matters.[52] Those who consider themselves well informed, meanwhile, may not be as smart as they think they are. The political scientist Eitan Hersh has written about the rising problem of "political hobbyists," where people feel politically active because they engage in "obsessive news-following and online slacktivism, by feeling the need to offer a hot take for each daily political flare-up, by emoting and arguing and debating, almost all of this from behind screens." This, argues Hersh, is not real engagement in politics because it is not committed to solving problems or to using the political process. Instead, it's more of a form of entertainment, politics as a feel-good spectator sport.[53]

In addition, even if Brennan's concern is legitimate, his idea of political knowledge seems hollow. In that regard, it echoes many other elites diagnosing our epidemic of national stupidity. To decide who can vote, Brennan suggests a test consisting of questions such as "Which item is the largest part of the federal budget?"[54] His questions are borrowed from a political science tool that was developed for other reasons—not for disenfranchising voters. But in this case, pass the test, and you're licensed to vote.

But democracy, one hopes, hardly reduces to a series of mundane facts. There is a millennia-long history of advocacy for more involved, knowledgeable citizens, but engaged citizenship is not, in most philosophical traditions, about memorizing facts of dubious importance. That is not to say that it's good when half of Americans can't name any Supreme Court justices.[55] Interrogating why they can't might even be useful as a matter of civics: Is it because of education, disillusionment with the Court, or something else? But it seems a stretch to say that being unable to name the justices on the Supreme Court makes your voice on all political issues unimportant or unworthy. Nor is the flip side true: we know plenty of people who can reel off all nine names but do not have depth or breadth of knowledge on any number of other subjects. By the Brennan standard, the person who gets the perfect score on the widely criticized citizenship test—correctly naming the president during World War I, identifying the two longest rivers in the United States, and describing the "rule of law" in four words (an essentially contested concept on which countless books have been written)—might as well be appointed benevolent dictator. ChatGPT could do even better.

This test makes little sense to those who see political judgment as a human endeavor that is more than the sum of trivia. The fact that many Americans (almost 40 percent, according to a *Newsweek* poll in 2011) would fail the US citizenship test may say less about our uninformed electorate and more about the poor design of the citizenship test.[56]

Perhaps because elites tend to live in large cities where local and national politics converge, tests like the one Brennan advocates ignore local political knowledge and engagement. Elite law schools and legal academics are sometimes criticized for focusing too much on federal law and federal courts at the expense of state and local governments—a skew that seems to have to do primarily with a perception that federal courts are more "prestigious" than state courts. But for many citizens, the politics that matter most on a day-to-day level are local, even hyperlocal, with issues around school boards, zoning commissions, and even sanitation commissions that have huge impacts on citizens' daily life. In one of our hometowns, which is governed in part by town meetings, key recent issues have included debates over local infrastructure repair, the best way to grant the public access to conservation land, and housing developments. Nearly all of these issues, despite being quite technical and complicated, are ultimately hashed out and decided by citizens exercising lay knowledge and judgment. It is hard to see how being able to recite the current number of representatives in the House or the number of amendments to the Constitution would indicate much about someone's ability to contribute on these or many other issues.

The conservative journalist David Harsanyi has proffered ideas similar to Brennan's, suggesting that "by weeding out millions of irresponsible voters who can't be bothered to learn the rudimentary workings of the

Constitution, or their preferred candidate's proposals or even their history, we may be able to mitigate the recklessness of the electorate." His proposed questions include the banal—"If both the President and the Vice President can no longer serve, who becomes President?"—and the tendentious— "What is freedom of religion?" (a question that has provoked centuries of debate among scholars of freedom of religion and is hardly answerable as trivia).[57] Like other elites, Harsanyi reduces the idea of civic engagement to rote memorization.

*   *   *

Like many elites, Jonathan Rauch diagnoses America as suffering from an epistemic crisis—a collective inability to agree on truth—in his book *The Constitution of Knowledge* (2021). Rauch is likely wrong about the empirics: like most elites, he overdiagnoses the prevalence of misinformation, as we discuss in chapter 8. But our focus now is Rauch's defense of "knowledge," which ultimately reveals a hollowness similar to Brennan's and others' defenses.

Rauch's book draws attention to the institutions that supposedly help us converge on truth—the institutions that make up the "reality-based community," which he calls the "constitution of knowledge," a phrase he considers more descriptive than the usual "marketplace of ideas" metaphor. Rauch offers thoughtful critiques of how these institutions are under attack from both the left (cancel culture) and the right (troll culture), a rare balance in contemporary elite critiques. He is less compelling, though, when explaining what he thinks has happened, which tends to rest on cherry-picked behavioral science. He jumps between opposing behavioral biases when it suits his narrative. "Modern neurology" shows that we have sympathy for others and thus can cooperate regardless of tribal boundaries. But a few pages earlier he says that neurology instead shows that our minds "divide us against other teams and blind us to the truth." Scientific communities find truth because scientists have different biases and spot each other's, which seems to contradict his reasoning from a previous chapter about how groups are also subject to herd mentality that cause them to double down on the same biases.[58]

Rauch makes a key move early on that is typical of the elite attitude toward "smarts." He asserts that liberalism rests on three systems, economic, political, and epistemic. For our epistemic system, liberalism relies on a series of "social rules for turning disagreement into knowledge" through norms and institutions.[59] At first, this assertion seems innocuous enough—after all, each system sounds quite important—but separating them out allows him to make a clever move. By isolating these systems, Rauch essentially removes most arguments from politics. Instead, arguments happen at some neutral epistemic layer, where facts are sorted out without the messiness of politics. Thus, if only we could fix the epistemic system—which essentially amounts to returning it to elites who lead the institutions that Rauch thinks we should trust—our political system would work smoothly because we all would agree on everything.

But our epistemic system—at least to the extent we mean the kind of facts that are brought to bear on political decisions on a daily basis—has always been entangled with politics. The kinds of facts that are of interest to Rauch must be fundamentally political because he is trying to understand our polarized politics; we are not talking about which molecule a pharmaceutical startup should try next for curing cancer, a topic that does not typically polarize voters and where he would be unable to find a real breakdown in our epistemic system. When it comes to political facts, disagreement is inevitably part of our civic fabric because which facts we fight over and how we fight over them are inevitably value laden and interpretive.

Meaningful knowledge is inextricably embedded in society. Saying that facts are constructed through social processes is not the same as saying facts are unimportant or made up. Nor does it mean that facts don't matter: they do. But we have never had a system that can always start out with complete and correct facts, even for nonpolitical questions. That's why so many of us learn the metaphor of the marketplace of ideas. Rauch's idea of knowledge as a kind of elite-controlled Wikipedia does not get us very far on any question that matters.

Rauch himself illustrates our assessment with a story that he sees as helpful but is in fact quite problematic for his point: the arrival at a contemporary theory of geological change in the nineteenth century after decades of conflict when a "cumulating, community-building strategy" generated a "mass of evidence" that solved an "intractable clash of dogmas."[60] The story suggests that evidence solved the "creed wars" of centuries, but it ignores the fact that evidence was accumulated only because there was a creed war. In other words, because scientists harbored sharply different prior views about what divided them, they were motivated to collect and bring evidence to the fight. In other words, science occurred only *because* we had a creed war. This is troubling for Rauch's theory but not surprising in light of how knowledge works. Theory comes first. We don't simply look out at a sea of accurate facts and divine the truth. Rather, we theorize about what might be true, and then test it, generating facts based on our desire to test those theories. What he dismisses as "creedal war" is really epistemic institutions at work—a mechanism that produces the very kind of knowledge he valorizes.

At times, Rauch slips into an even shallower view of knowledge, most acutely on view when he tries to show off the successes of the elite-led, "reality-based" institutions. He proffers "mountains of . . . data on the growing breadth and depth of the reality-based community—and on its growing capacity and efficacy." These data are mostly trivia about the quantity of research in the world, measured in units that have no bearing on their meaning, accuracy, or utility. He "marvel[s]" at the fact that there are 24,000 academic journals (as of 2010), as if the number is a meaningful indicator of quality.[61]

And in a stunning example of trivializing "knowledge," he gushes that more than 100,000 academic papers were published in the first year of the pandemic, more than doubling each month from March to August 2020.[62] But he seems to assume that all these papers were worthwhile and that each additional paper added an additional "increment" of knowledge—as opposed to noise, mistake, or sheer opportunism. To the contrary, many scientists have noted that journals' obsession with COVID-19 drove out other crucial research and induced scientists who had little useful to say about the virus—not because they weren't good scientists but because their area of science was not especially relevant—to contort their research agenda to match the hot topic of the day. As one medical journal editor noted, "Alarms were raised early on about the mix of sheer volume and unprecedented speed. Commentators decried a flood of junk in the literature: observational studies, opinion articles, and duplicated efforts as researchers rushed to capitalise on covid [*sic*] related funding calls. . . . Concerns are being raised that the domination of covid related papers in medical journals came at the cost of other health issues such as non-communicable conditions, violence, and mental health."[63]

Indeed, quantity is rarely a measure of quality. Instead, it can indicate a "gold rush" caused by a "publish or perish" system within academia.[64]

Researchers are rewarded for quantity, speed, and opportunism. According to one research paper published in 2022, there were far more articles on COVID-19 than on influenza in 2020, alongside an extreme rush to publish them—with papers accepted within an average of 8 days after submission rather than the usual 92 days, suggesting less careful review and editorial vetting. That was not a harmless error as the rate of retractions and withdrawals of COVID-19 papers far exceeded those for influenza papers, "a warning sign about the possible lack of a quality control process in scientific publishing and the peer review process."[65]

Another by-product of the "covidization" of scientific research was the creation of superstar hype around those who could publish the most and the most quickly. Some scientists received many times more citations to their COVID-19 work than to the entirety of their work in the rest of their career, which researchers worry "may have major repercussions for research priorities and the evolution of research on COVID-19 and beyond." Universities increasingly reward academics for citation counts and media attention, which has created what these scholars call a "citation elite." That creates a siren song for young scientists and "the incentives of scientists motivated by the lure of such scientific rewards." In other words, choosing a trendy field would reward them with higher rankings in citation counts, an overvalued and sticky measure of academic success. Conversely, new academics might avoid more gradual, subtle areas of research, where research moves incrementally, garnering fewer citations, but with the possibility of more value for society in the long run.[66]

If the measures of quantity that Rauch cites are what matter most, we should cheer the possibility that modern-day chatbots such as ChatGPT can get us to an even faster rate—tripling each month! quadrupling each day!—of the production of text, which presumably fewer and fewer people will read or use. Indeed, many academic papers are never cited.[67] This doesn't mean that they shouldn't be written or that they won't have value later on. And citations, as we have already said, are imperfect measures that can reward quality but also hype. The primary point is that quantitative measures should give us pause: we can do better than celebrate the "reality-based community" for giving us 24,000 separate journals.

In a more troubling example, Rauch forgives the "reality-based community" for the fact that wrong answers "can linger too long because scientists are too biased or too lazy to challenge them."[68] He is willing to forgive the mental health community's refusal to give up its long-standing claim that homosexuality is a mental illness—because, he says, we can't expect that every error be caught immediately. But most are caught eventually, he proffers. How would we know that? And at what cost were the wrong answers defended? Rather, examples like this should give us pause if one purpose of a reality-based community is to converge on a truth and then take dissent off the table by labeling it "misinformation."

The results of Rauch's readiness to find misinformation can be quite comical. Rauch complains of Republicans believing "bizarre" claims about Bill Gates and microchips in the vaccines but then in the next sentence moves to mocking Republicans for being "twice as likely as Democrats to believe that the COVID-19 virus was intentionally created in a lab," suggesting it is part of the same type of herd-driven delusion.[69] To be sure, he cannot be faulted for not having the benefit of hindsight, as we do, that this "conspiracy" about a lab leak is now widely accepted as credible.[70] But he can be faulted for dismissing it so readily because, unlike the Gates conspiracy, a lab leak was always plausible. In fact, there was relatively little evidence *against* the lab leak other than a loud insistence by certain voices that it was absurd or dangerous to consider. One hopes that is not the kind of reality-based consensus Rauch would have us defer to—one based on groupthink and the shouting down of questions to prevent further research. Elite mistakes, it seems from Rauch's discussion, are always forgivable one-off accidents, never plausibly part of anything more systematic—a perspective shared in many elite accounts.

*   *   *

Tom Nichols, five-time *Jeopardy!* winner, teacher at the Naval War College, and perhaps the nation's most ardent fan of experts, believes most of our ills stem from our self-imposed crisis of ignorance. In his two books, *The Death of Expertise* (2017) and its follow-up, *Our Own Worst Enemy* (2021), he provides a heavily anecdotal, armchair psychologist's account of the many "disturbing ways in which people reject established knowledge and argue with experts as if they know what they're talking about."[71] He displays palpable frustration at the sense that he and other experts are ignored. Judging from the books' sales and reviews, this feeling resonated with other credential-wielding experts, but Nichols never really makes the case for this supposed phenomenon. He rests far too much of his case on breezy anecdotes, such as doctors who feel they are asked too many annoying questions by their patients. It is hard to feel much sorrow for professionals whose clients push back: answering such questions is their job, not to mention that the resulting conversation might yield a better outcome.

Nichols is most indicative of elites in his vexation at the whining of the masses. A favored theme is that people are wrong to express frustration with many aspects of modern life. Nichols sees little room for complaints, given the present era of peace and prosperity. This is where Nichols embodies the flawed mindset of elites: it is a bad-faith reading of the American public to so readily dismiss widespread feelings as factually mistaken. Not only are these matters *not* subject to factual resolution, but Nichols's grip on the relevant facts is also much looser than he claims.

Nichols's central fear is that an antiexpert turn has led us to "dismiss the progress of the past fifty years achieved by free societies—and the experts that serve them" and in turn has produced an antidemocratic backlash.[72] Nichols exudes disdain for the American electorate. We apparently cannot sustain our country because it is populated by "people who contribute almost nothing and yet complain endlessly and talk about how shafted they are by their own system of government."[73] He denounces what he calls the "burn it all down" attitude, a "jaundiced view of life in the early twenty-first century" that is in fact "nonsense" because we are "living in a time of peace and plenty that was unimaginable a half century ago." How he evaluates this standard of life—how one measures, for instance, the benefits of cheap clothing against environmental degradation and income inequality—is never detailed. To see anything but progress, for Nichols, is just factually incorrect. That same attitude pervades modern liberal politics. Nichols quotes Obama saying, "We are fortunate to be living in the most peaceful, most prosperous, most progressive era in human history." Nichols never considers that the young people surprised by this claim might have a point, because "the facts allow no other conclusion."[74]

In other words, laypeople are wrong even when it comes to an *opinion* about how their lives *feel*. What does it mean in a democracy to call someone's grievance "wrong"? If people perceive themselves as aggrieved, shouldn't that mean something even before we get to an accounting of the facts? Nichols directly rejects this possibility—"feelings are an unreliable

way to know if our institutions are making life better or worse"—a typical sentiment of the technocratic elite, who see only facts where others
might see a range of possible emotions and value-laden judgments.[75] But
how—other than feelings—can we compare apples and oranges? How do
we decide if consumerism is worth its emotional cost without considering
how people feel about it?

It should be noted that the dissenting voices are hardly limited to populists. To his credit, Nichols at least takes on the populists' worldview—a
belief that elites have put us on a negative trajectory that is motivated by
a sense of economic, cultural, and political grievance—rather than simply
dismissing them as gullible racists. Nichols acknowledges, correctly, that
populism responds to a sense that liberal democracy has failed. But he
does not seem to take this critique seriously, even though the perception
of social failure is deep and widespread. In a National Opinion Research
Center survey in 2023, which has asked many of the same questions since
1972, four out of five respondents said the economy was "not so good"
or "poor." Fewer than three in ten thought people like them were likely
to improve their standard of living. Seventy-eight percent said they didn't
think their children's generation would have a better life, the most pessimistic result since the question was first asked three decades ago. Roughly
one in ten said they were "very happy," and three in ten said they were "not
too happy."[76] One wonders what it means to label this level of pervasive
dissatisfaction as "wrong." To do so requires a profound indifference to the
beliefs of voters.

*   *   *

Nichols is a prime example of elite punditry that falls short of its claims. He
asserts that the world is better because it is more peaceful, a point he says is
not open to argument because "there is no point in arguing over things we
can look up."[77] But it is not so easy to accept this assertion. The case Nichols
builds was made, at greater length and with more empirics, by the Harvard
psychologist and linguist Steven Pinker in a best-selling book *The Better
Angels of Our Nature* (2011), which purported to document both short-term
and long-term declines in violence. The book was a favorite among elites.
Bill Gates once announced to graduating college students that "if I could
give each of you a graduation present, it would be this—the most inspiring
book I've ever read."[78]

Subsequent research has not been kind to Pinker's claim. Many who reanalyzed Pinker's data think the basic premise of the book is false and rests on a misunderstanding of how to interpret random noise in data.[79] As one special issue of *Historical Reflections*, a journal of historians, put it, Pinker's book isn't just "problematic" but "patently tendentious"; "the overall verdict is that Pinker's thesis . . . is seriously, if not fatally, flawed" because of methodological problems, "the unquestioning use of dubious sources," and "the tendency to exaggerate the violence of the past in order to contrast it with the supposed peacefulness of the modern era."[80]

Nichols does not acknowledge, much less grapple with, any of this. Even if he did, he wouldn't accomplish what he has mainly set out to do: to prove that those who complain are factually misguided. Even if violence has declined, would that mean we have reached a state where we should be happy with the results? Would people be obligated to credit government with the decline in violence? Even the idea that we should blindly reduce violence is not so clear cut: if we could lower violence by trading off other things we cared about—for instance, by trammeling on civil liberties— would it be worth it? These questions do not lend themselves to simplistic answers. Within a democracy, we must be willing to look at feelings to have any sense of measurement. Political life is always interpreted. Sentiment is based on argument, rhetoric, persuasion—and thank goodness it is, or nothing could ever change as we would be locked into whatever the data tell us.

Consider one more of many examples: Nichols's irritation with those who complain about the economy (income inequality) and thus fail to recognize the West's collective affluence. Although income inequality is real, he seems to suggest our real problem is a "fixation" on it because inequality seems to matter most "when citizens are highly aware of it"—a tautology masquerading as an insight. Painting his rosy picture, Nichols cites the Estonian leader Toomas Ilves for the proposition that the Gini coefficient— one (highly imperfect) measure of income inequality—has been stable or declining in the European Union (EU). In the original statement, however, Ilves noted that this coefficient is high and rising in the United States, which Nichols mysteriously ignores. We say all this not to pick on Nichols but rather to make an observation: it is this kind of loosey-goosey relationship to the facts that makes Nichols's account so characteristic of elites like him. A nugget of data can always be found—who cares if it's true or contextualized?—to dismiss what "people" think. He rolls his eyes, without apparently needing to say more, at an Ohio steelworker who told the *New York Times* in 1994 that "if inflation is so low, how come cereal is $4.75 a box?"[81] Nichols's argument is just sloppy. Income and wealth inequality are serious problems, as modern economics makes clear.[82]

Nichols wants the deference accorded an expert but does not want to grapple with the complexity of modern evidence. He cites an argument between two economists, Donald Boudreaux (who argues that material standards of living have increased so much that the middle class cannot be said to stagnating) and Branko Milanovic (who considers smartphones and streaming music to be a "peculiar metric" for understanding income stagnation). Nichols comes down on Boudreaux's side but never says why, insisting he doesn't want to get "caught in a brawl between two economists."[83] This superficial, half-baked engagement is typical enough of Nichols. And even if he did, it hardly seems that expertise could really referee the ultimate question Nichols is seeking to answer: How should the good life be measured, and should people be happy with the standard of living they have? These are not questions over which economists, experts, or Nichols have any particular jurisdiction.

Nichols would aver, however, that facts show that populist rage against economic inequality is misplaced. To justify his dismissal of populist claims about inequality, he frequently references cognitive biases that supposedly cause us to underestimate how good we have it. The problem is that it's not clear that these biases are all that relevant, and that for many of them there are offsetting biases, and he fails to engage with this complicated literature in any useful way. But, more importantly, even if biases are a biologically and evolutionarily deeply determined part of how humans think, is it fair, appropriate, or useful to dismiss them? Or might they actually be part of what makes us human and therefore worthy of at least some deference? Nichols's hollowed-out view of how we measure life—some glibly cited statistics cherry-picked and decontextualized to prove whatever point he wants—is hardly going to convince many angry voters to come around to see things his way.

His most interesting critique of populism is that populism deflects blame by harboring an "unfocused rage at the culture, at the elites, or at some other culprit," in turn producing opportunities for "savvy operators" to "exploit."[84] But here he gives short shrift to the very real causes of that rage and seems to misunderstand how politics and civic life work in a democracy. Ironically, he denigrates right-wing populism for its "nostalgia," but nostalgia is also a central feature of the elite worldview. Nostalgia, in fact, animates Nichols as much as it does Rauch: they yearn for a supposed golden era in which expertise was followed, by which they mean an era in which their authority as elites was unchallenged. Nevertheless, Nichols also makes much out of the problem of nostalgia, calling it an "insidious challenge for almost any form of government" that will eventually put a government "on a treadmill that will produce exhaustion and eventual collapse."[85]

Nichols's account is riddled with grand assertions buttressed by half-baked anecdotes. On the COVID-19 pandemic, he mocks the "spate of 'the pandemic means the end of globalization' pieces in early 2020," considering that "the globalized economy proved to be a great advantage in fighting the pandemic."[86] He wrote this in 2021. By 2022, pundits had switched their narrative in the other direction. This is not to pick on Nichols for not having a prescient crystal ball; instead, it's to pick on him for pretending to have such a crystal ball rather than recognizing that grandiose predictions are about as likely to be flawed as confident proclamations made by many public intellectuals in the years leading up to World War I that globalization had rendered war obsolete.

In another telling section of *Our Own Worst Enemy*, he mocks voters who liked Sanders or Trump (without speaking directly to any of their views or identifying their prevalence) for being deluded into thinking they are "true to a set of political ideas but are really acting out of contradictory emotions and conflicting rationalizations."[87] It is this hollowing out of voting— the idea that there is a "correct" answer, which happens to coincide with his choice—that makes Nichols (and others who express similar views) so unappealing as a spokesperson for liberal democracy. It also makes him incapable of understanding the phenomenon that he describes.

For all his valorization of facts and expertise, Nichols employs little of either in sustaining his claims about the state of the economy and about people's complaints that things are unequal. Again, our point is not that Nichols is wrong and populists are right. Rather, we are arguing that elite commentary and criticism fail to live up to the elites' own standards of discourse. Nichols decries populists with the very terms he ascribes to them. Were he to make an argument, we would see that things are rather more complicated than he lets on and, perhaps, not quite as clear as he would like us to believe. '

Fanatical Certitude

A seductive explanation for the world's ailments has taken grip among elites: the ignorance of the common voter and their failure to listen to their intellectual betters. This diagnosis is obviously attractive for elites because it suggests that elites have the solution and are not part of the problem. It is further shored up by elites' faith in meritocracy and technocracy. But it rests on hollow premises, including the reduction of wisdom into a kind of currency that can be accumulated through credentials.

Unfortunately, this reduction creates a close-mindedness to other perspectives—even though many elites themselves (especially Rauch) proffer that openness to perspectives, the "marketplace of ideas," is what leads us to greater wisdom as a society. Unfortunately, they do not heed that advice when it comes to ideas different from their own.

We can see this contradiction manifest in elites' attempt to define "truth" or "knowledge." Their best explanation for truth amounts to little more than Supreme Court justice Potter Stewart's line about pornography: they know it when they see it. But knowledge is more complicated than that, more tentative, more uncertain, and ever changing. The unreliableness of this definition in application—our inability to distinguish some "knowledge" from "misinformation" for reasons other than personal taste—should make us particularly worried when elites call for censorship or suppression of dissent, a problem we return to in the third part of this book.

Taylor Dotson has diagnosed America as suffering from "fanatical certitude," an overconfidence that afflicts both sides and prevents us from engaging in real debate.[88] His is a most insightful observation on the quality of discourse in the public sphere today. In this book *The Divide: How Fanatical Certitude Is Destroying Democracy* (2021), we focus on one side of that "fanatical certitude," those of elites. We certainly don't mean to suggest that they are the only ones who seem overly confident in their answers, but they do have a unique megaphone and ability to influence social outcomes. If at times it feels as if we are overly harsh toward these elites, it is precisely because their platforms give them a kind of power and security that means they can take a sharp critique.

In our next chapter, we demonstrate how the elite mentality plays out in decision-making: overreach, the misuse of expertise, and a resort to "credentialism" rather than true expertise. These approaches to knowledge are quite corrosive to knowledge itself. By turning expertise into a game, elites prove precisely what their critics claim: that "expertise" and "science" are really just politics in disguise.

3 The Misuse of Expertise

Expertise has been degraded in public discourse, where it is routinely deployed as a trope that adds a patina of legitimacy and authority to elite assertions. These assertions of legitimacy and authority, however, come not from "following facts" but from elite priors. The way expertise is used routinely exaggerates, minimizes uncertainty, and rests primarily on credentialism.

The theoretical physicist Richard Feynman once defined science as "the belief in the ignorance of experts." Feynman loved science, understanding it to be a practice defined by doubt and an instinct to ask questions. He feared "intellectual tyranny in the name of science."[1] His definition is a far cry from today's elite-held portrayal of expertise: that we should "follow the science" and "defer to experts." These mantras, which were deployed unironically and ubiquitously throughout the COVID-19 pandemic, encapsulate how expertise has come to be misused in public policy. The catchphrases mislead in two important respects. First, they imply that science—or other claims about the world, some of which are more socially contingent—is always readily settled. Second, they suggest that facts alone can determine complex public policy without the need to face up to real trade-offs. Both implications are falsehoods. Genuine science rarely offers immediate, binary, and certain answers to novel, complex questions. That is even more true in the social sciences and other areas that cross multiple disciplines, which matter for the vast majority of public-policy issues. Public policy in a democracy nearly always involves uncertainty and painful trade-offs that can be informed but never decided by science. Real experts know this. Pseudo-experts, who regularly hog the spotlight, are full of hubris and overconfidence.

This stultified view of the relationship between knowledge and action is destructive. When we drive out uncertainty and debate and falsely or prematurely declare consensus or that a question is "settled," we make it more likely that a mistaken policy will be widely adopted in its most extreme form. Policy is sticky, and bad policy can be hard to undo. We also make it far less likely that research will be done to evaluate whether a given policy decision was correct. And the public is misled about the true basis for policy decisions, which ultimately rest not just on neutral facts but on the political preferences of those who anoint themselves the keepers of the facts. Elites who disdain the public find it plausible that a handful of experts can provide all necessary solutions, that the public cannot be trusted with complicated information, and that dissent is dangerous because skepticism leads inexorably to radical denialism. This contempt for public deliberation has become normalized and reflects a sorry relationship between elite culture and society at large. On this front, elites are blinder to reality than their populist critics, who are acutely attuned to elites' disregard and hypocrisy.[2]

In this chapter, we use expert overreach in the COVID-19 pandemic as a case study. The misuse of expertise politicized the pandemic, especially in the United States. It engendered cynicism and predictable misbehavior and created a toxic environment for discussion of policy. And yet the debate was always framed by elites as a battle of "science" (which they represented, even when it turned out science was not on their side) versus ignorance (represented by anyone who asked questions).

We focus on the extended closure of schools and then on mask policies, two major policy issues where decision-making suffered from warped debates. Both provide examples of more general pathologies of expertise. To be very clear, our criticism is not of expertise in itself, which has necessary and valuable insight to offer. Rather, we are critical of its misuse to add a patina of legitimacy and authority to elite assertions. Expert overreach deploys a veneer of expertise to marginalize or censor dissenting views. This distortion of expertise claims certainty rather than facing up to complicated unknowns, and it blames all failures on those who ignore the supposed expert consensus. It removes tough questions and difficult, even tragic trade-offs from their proper sphere of political judgment and public debate.

Such overreach cannot be said to be the genuine exercise of expertise because to truly use knowledge requires perspective, integrity, and humility. In contrast, what we see when expertise is misused is the exaggeration of findings and the misunderstanding of what a particular study can or cannot offer. Empirical results are conflated with models, op-eds, and even tweets. The trump card is credentials—often exaggerated or irrelevant ones. Petty academic turf wars predominate. Doubt, uncertainty, and counterarguments are cast aside, notwithstanding that they are in fact central to the accumulation of wisdom.

Examples of overreach in the pandemic are legion, but the pandemic is not an isolated example. In recent years, many academics have worried about growing attacks on science and expertise, typically associated with industry groups or with the Republican Right. These attacks are problematic, but their mirror image is less discussed and just as problematic: the degradation of science and expertise by the very elites who claim to practice and protect it. In constructing what they claim is a defense of science, they have instead created a false idol that bears little resemblance to the open-minded mode of inquiry described by Feynman.

We conclude this chapter by linking expert overreach to global populism. Populists see that elites are bluffing. Populist skepticism represents, in many instances, a rational backlash against the misuse of expertise. Elites are quite deliberately blind to this charge of misuse because their authority rests largely on their claim to be "following" expertise.

Even if populists' critique of "expert-led" policy were more misguided than it is, that would still not make their claim one to ignore or dismiss out of hand. Yet that is exactly what elites do, at their own peril. After the 2020 election, many seemed surprised that Biden's margin of victory was narrower than they anticipated and thus that it did not deliver the decisive repudiation of Trump's pandemic strategy that they expected. A characteristic response, unfortunately, was that of *Science* editor-in-chief Holden Thorp, who declared beyond hope the 74 million Americans who voted for Trump: "Science was on the ballot and this means that a significant portion of America doesn't want science. . . . Science is now something for a subset of America."[3] We are alarmed that this cynical view, which is nonsensical, has become so mainstream.[4] If anything, it mostly confirms populists' perception of elites as out of touch and condescending. As Martin Gurri puts it, "Elites today have no idea how to speak to the public or what to say to it."[5] To judge from Thorp's statement—and those of many other elites who similarly spurn much of the country—they also have little interest in introspection or understanding others' views.

Keeping Schools Closed

Kids who were locked out of schools during their extended closures across the United States represent one of the primary victims of the toxic climate for discourse created by elites. Even after public-health experts started urging schools to reopen—a cause they took up later than they should have—it took many months before schools returned to some semblance of normal. Many schools in blue states remained closed for even longer. More than a year after the pandemic began, the majority of students in Democratic states still weren't back full time in the classroom in what one commentator called the "most significant failure of public policy in a generation."[6]

The results were as predictable as they were tragic. As one World Bank research paper put it concisely in the title of a report, "The longer students were out of school, the less they learned." On average, the report found, students globally lost roughly half a year of schooling.[7] Other studies have come to similar findings, and the effects have been worst on children in the poorest school districts. Many elite children attended private schools that reopened safely and quickly. Even those who were initially architects of school closures came to see them as problematic. Few today argue that the degree and extent of closures were justified by their purported benefits— something that was known from early on. Even the head of the American Federation of Teachers, Randi Weingarten, whose view was a major reason why schools were closed, now claims that she "spent every day [of the pandemic] . . . trying to get schools open" because "remote education was not a substitute for opening schools."[8] The costs to kids were incredible, or as Anthony Fauci later described it in language only a bureaucrat could love, the closures had "deleterious collateral consequences."[9]

Why did this happen? First and foremost because the application of "expertise" was misleadingly framed by pundits, politicians, and the public-health elite, which crippled the national debate through fear and censorship. Risks were exaggerated, creating a climate of hysteria where those who questioned school closures were accused of playing "Russian roulette" with respect to children or teachers. Policy blinders made it impossible to discuss the collateral consequences of decisions. It was a mistake to describe any decision—such as school closures—as solely about the transmission of infectious disease. (Of course, even seen through that narrow lens, closing schools proved a likely mistake.) The decision to do something as drastic as closing schools would necessarily depend on a more complicated set of social trade-offs, but because the structure of the debate was so toxic, few reasonable voices could be heard.

By June 2020, the evidence was fairly clear on one fortunate, if unusual, aspect of COVID-19 when compared to many other respiratory diseases: it was orders of magnitude less dangerous to children. Americans 65 or older made up 76 percent of the share of total deaths involving COVID-19, while those 18 and younger constituted less than two-tenths of a percent of total deaths.[10] That's why even the American Academy of Pediatrics, usually known for its caution, came out in favor of a return to in-person learning in June 2020, although it later flipped under apparent political pressure from teachers' unions.[11] Given the low risk to children if schools were open, there were only two medical risks left to consider on the downsides of reopening schools: the health effect on teachers and the effect on community spread. On that front, evidence was already mounting that schools were not especially risky and certainly not in comparison to other parts of society that reopened more quickly. On the flip side, there were downsides to prolonged closures that got hardly any airing or were dismissed until it was too late, including the effects on the education and mental health of students.

Consider the very typical framing offered by Chancellor Richard A. Carranza of New York City Schools in July 2020: "We can make up learning for students. We cannot bring a student back who is infected and passed away."[12] This implied that the deadliness of COVID-19 for children represented a serious reason to keep schools closed. In January 2021, a school board president earnestly posed the following choice to parents seeking to reopen schools: "Do you want your child to be alive, or educated?"[13] Even as evidence mounted about the relative safety of teaching during the pandemic, many teachers' unions and talking heads continued to proclaim that reopening schools was a death sentence for teachers. The more Trump tweeted about schools reopening, the more Democrats appeared to reflexively endorse the opposite conclusion.[14]

This exaggeration was systematic, not isolated. When researchers from Dartmouth analyzed mainstream media's coverage of school reopenings through November 2020, they found that it was 90 percent negative in the United States, compared to just 56 percent in other countries.[15] As a result, many Americans held an overexaggerated view of certain aspects of the pandemic. At the end of 2020, with schools preparing to stay closed into 2021, polling showed that Americans massively overestimated the risk of the disease to children. All deaths are a tragedy, but COVID-19's toll on youth was low compared to other threats that they routinely face.

The same polling confirmed that Americans were given an imbalanced diet of facts that amplified their fears. Americans massively overestimated the likelihood that a COVID-19 infection would lead to hospitalization. At the end of 2020, 41 percent of Democrats held the completely implausible view that *most* COVID infections resulted in hospitalization. Ironically, despite the widespread assumption that Republicans underplayed the disease, Republicans were more than twice as likely to identify the correct rate of hospitalization than Democrats, according to the same study.[16]

As part of the toxic structure of the debate, opponents of reopening schools questioned the motives of those advocating it rather than their actual arguments. Supporters of reopening were labeled "conservative" or even "Trumpian." This was, of course, a poor way of arguing: not only false but ad hominem and irrelevant to the substance of the issues. Such extreme opinions also made it difficult to adjust as the consensus swung increasingly in favor of opening schools. Many blamed teachers' unions for delaying reopening—even progressives who normally defend them—but the inflexible positions of teachers' unions were just as much a symptom of elite overconfidence and a year of doom and gloom with little counter-balance. Even if union leadership believed the science had changed, how could it admit to its members that it had been wrong all along?

The public was led to believe that scientific discourse had narrowed to a small consensus, when in fact consensus eluded experts on *many* issues concerning COVID-19. Consensus was strongest on issues that were not implicated in public debate, but any appearance of consensus had more to do with cherry-picking by a limited pool of talking heads on cable news.[17] Experts hadn't converged on a singular consensus about most questions at that point. Intolerance to dissent was regularly justified because of fears of misinformation, but the elite mentality toward misinformation during the pandemic was far too simplistic. It can be hard to draw a clear line between misinformation and disagreement. Some views were so far-fetched that they deserved little audience—those that denied the very existence of COVID-19 or that believed the pandemic was caused by 5G technology—but these views were scarcely influential. To focus on them was to distract from the real debates or to create false guilt by association (i.e., that questioning the merits of a lockdown must mean one also denied the existence of a pandemic).

In one delightful example of the complexity of distinguishing "misinformation," the World Health Organization opposed mask wearing for children between the ages of two and five because of developmental concerns, while the US Centers for Disease Control (CDC) recommended masks starting at age two. If one asserts that not obeying public-health authorities is being prey to "misinformation," how does one decide which of these incompatible positions constitutes "misinformation"? Elites who lambasted opponents for spreading misinformation ignored this question—precisely because it would have been hard to answer coherently and impossible to answer in a way consistent with their political priors.

The result of the warped discourse was a patchwork of closures that appeared to reflect politics, not public health. This became evident in the fact that the pattern of closing had nothing to do with local factors, such as how prevalent COVID-19 cases were in a particular school district. Studies repeatedly concluded that there was no relationship between reopening decisions and COVID-19 case counts. Closures instead appeared to be based on whether the locals were pro- or anti-Trump. Schools in Democratic-leaning locations were more likely to close, even during periods of low disease prevalence. Partly as a result, school closures also demonstrated a strong racial gap, with white students more likely to have had the option of in-person schooling than were Black or brown students. Meanwhile, nearly all private schools—95 percent by one count—stayed open for in-person learning, compared with 40 percent for public schools in the fall.[18] As others have noted, many of the most vocal advocates for school closures in fact had their own children in private school all along, just one of the many ways elites bought their way out of pandemic restrictions.

Lost in nearly all the discussion were the downsides of closing schools, not simply because the downsides were unknown but because they were simply assumed not to exist, as in the quote from Carranza, or sidelined from the conversation. The few who considered the effects of school closures vis-à-vis the pandemic often did so in disturbing, almost dystopian ways that normalized the idea of permanent school closures and online education. In May 2020, Governor Andrew Cuomo of New York proudly launched a commission, with participation from former Google CEO Eric Schmidt and Bill Gates, that would use the pandemic as an opportunity to accelerate online learning. "We now have a moment in history where we can actually incorporate and advance those ideas," Cuomo said in one of many dystopian quotes.[19] Tyler Black, a psychiatrist and self-proclaimed "data geek," spent much of the pandemic building up a Twitter brand for his forceful insistence that school closures were *good* for the mental health of kids, the evidence notwithstanding.

By normalizing the abnormal and insisting that kids were "resilient" in response to any objection to the closures, it became easy to forget that we were running an unprecedented experiment by depriving children of school. Even talking about "learning loss" was deemed off-limits. The euphemism was apparently too negative and thus declared a myth. "There is no such thing as learning loss," said the head of the most powerful teachers' union in Los Angeles: "Our kids didn't lose anything. It's OK that our babies may not have learned all their times tables. They learned resilience. They learned survival. They learned critical-thinking skills. They know the difference between a riot and a protest. They know the words insurrection and coup."[20]

Piling on, others suggested that even talking about learning loss was racist. Others said that it wasn't "learning loss" because you couldn't lose what you didn't have. All of this was understandably interpreted by parents as an attempt to downplay what was happening to their children. The political consequences of this approach are now widely known, from Republican Glenn Youngkin's upset victory in the Virginia governor's race in part because of furor over school closures to the growth of parents' groups taking an interest in politics across the country.[21]

Of course, we now have better evidence of what many suggested was the most likely outcome: children *did* lose, and quite a bit. Not surprisingly, the worst effects were felt in schools in high-poverty neighborhoods. In those that stayed remote for the first full school year after the pandemic (fall 2021 and spring 2022), students in poorer schools lost out on the equivalent of roughly 60 percent of the math they would have learned in person (compared to closer to a third in low-poverty schools). According to one of the best efforts to quantify the gap, those losses were *directly* attributable to remote and online learning, not just to the stress of living through a pandemic. Math gaps between the highest-achieving and lowest-achieving districts, for instance, did not widen so long as schools stayed open. The gaps emerged instead when the lowest-achieving districts closed their classrooms.[22]

School closures had the social and psychological consequences one might expect, notwithstanding efforts by Twitter celebrities who pushed an opposing narrative. One meta-analysis of 36 studies found consistent documentation of adverse effects from lockdowns and school closures, including higher levels of distress, anxiety, and depression, probable under-reporting of child maltreatment, and less healthy behaviors, such as more screen time and less physical activity.[23] None of this was terribly surprising; in fact, it was quite predictable. Yet it was ignored or, worse, suppressed as outside the bounds of debate by those who policed the COVID-19 discourse in 2020 and beyond.

Masquerading as Evidence

If schools were the most tragic, masks were perhaps the most visible example of the misuse of expertise during the pandemic. Masking was subject to some of the strongest scientific overclaims and reversals. Fauci famously proclaimed confidently that they weren't necessary, only to reverse that position under political pressure. Later, as the pandemic subsided, he flip-flopped again toward a more modulated view that masks probably helped public health only "at the margins" and that he was not sure if they were worth it given the divisiveness. The new party line seems to be that masks that fit properly (N95s) work for individuals but that masking as a policy doesn't do much for public health. Ironically, this is precisely the view that mask advocates initially spent all their firepower opposing during the "my mask helps you" phase of messaging.

Debates about masking were corrupted from the start by the mask zealots who dominated elite discourse.[24] Masks were portrayed as a panacea—even better than a vaccine, in the profoundly unscientific words of the former CDC director testifying before Congress.[25] Yet at the same time, masks also weren't good enough to quickly reopen many closed schools, even given that an unvaccinated child faced lower risk than a vaccinated grandparent.[26] The incoherence also existed in the gap between the earnest, even hysterical messaging around masking and the behavior of elites pushing those messages. Perhaps nothing illustrated the absurdity of lockdown culture more than the performative spectacle of diners donning masks as they entered a restaurant, only to remove them at their table as they sat for several hours shoulder to shoulder with other patrons. And perhaps nothing inflamed populists, with their sensitively tuned antenna for hypocrisy, more than the scores of photographs of unmasked politicians—many of them posing with masked children.[27] The covering of toddlers' faces always made the United States an international outlier and constituted outright defiance of World Health Organization guidance.

Some elites seemed puzzled why anyone cared about these photos. The answer should be obvious, but for populists the hypocrisy confirmed their suspicions about elite corruption. It also underscored how unimportant elites actually thought the masking recommendations were other than as virtue signaling and an example of "do-something" politics. Governor Gavin Newsom of California, who tweeted the baffling recommendation that people should pull their mask up *in between bites* when eating, was discovered attending a lavish indoor party at the French Laundry. When caught, his bizarre defense was that he thought the indoor space was actually outdoors. Others posed for photos without masks during the height of elite masking fervor and then justified their mask removal with unbelievable claims—like that of Mayor Eric Garcetti of Los Angeles, who maintained that he "held his breath."[28] Such hypocrisy by politicians was legion throughout the pandemic. Boris Johnson's partying during the most intense days of the British lockdown led to his downfall. The British scientist whose work prompted the lockdown was also ousted after he repeatedly broke the social-distancing rules he advocated.[29]

Was masking ever worth the divisive fuss? Today, evidence continues to suggest what infectious-disease scientists already believed before the pandemic: that imposing society-wide mask mandates was probably not an effective measure to curb the spread of a respiratory disease.[30] The single-minded obsession with masking and masking mandates created deep divisiveness and prevented people, perhaps most especially toddlers, from seeing each other's faces—all with little benefit and all the while displacing energy that could have been put toward more useful policies.

Some of this divisiveness was the result of politicization in our partisan moment. When Donald Trump casually denigrated cloth masks, the stage was set for an immediate backlash by Democrats. The moment turned masks into a partisan emblem more than a public-health measure: a talismanic symbol of virtue signaling on one side and a rallying cry about freedom for the other.[31]

But polarization is only part of the story. More interesting for our purposes are the parallels to the discourse about schools. The debate quickly degenerated, with elite participants exuding a profound disregard for curiosity and a disdain for open debate and declaring that the science was settled. The result was overconfident, hyperbolic messaging that conditioned us to assume that all dissenting opinions were misinformation rather than reflections of good-faith disagreement or differing priorities. In doing so, elites drove out scientific research that might have separated valuable interventions from the less valuable and corroded much-needed public trust. The mask debate, perhaps even more than the school debate, offers examples of pseudo-expertise and the overselling of policies based on dubious evidence.

The earliest push for cloth face coverings came from a citizen-activist group calling itself #masks4all, spearheaded by the artificial-intelligence entrepreneur Jeremy Howard. The group published a narrative review claiming to vindicate the usefulness of cloth masks. It offered no original evidence but came to a different conclusion from existing reviews, which had generally suggested that masks, especially cloth masks, were not useful as a society-wide effort.[32] At a minimum, the scene should have been set for an active debate. Instead, Howard and others confidently proclaimed the science to be clear and settled—a claim that was picked up by Democratic pundits and was used to drown out any real discussion.[33]

Silencing doubt, even mild doubt, was a key part of the #masks4all playbook. Howard pushed back against anyone who questioned his results, going so far as to email demands to the boss of one virologist, Angela Rasmussen, who raised questions about the #masks4all analysis. Michael Osterholm, later a Biden adviser and very much a COVID-19 hawk on other issues, has described how Howard mischaracterized Osterholm's views with a seeming indifference to the rules of argumentation.[34] Because Howard's group gained the upper hand with the press during this hostile climate to dissent, most people reading coverage throughout 2020 and 2021 would have been surprised by the weakness of evidence behind the public-health recommendation that everyone wear cloth masks if they had been given a chance to hear or read it. It was not until 2022 that the CDC itself began admitting the inefficacy of cloth masks, which had been known all along. If Fauci and others were overconfident in recommending against masks, the #masks4all people went even further in the other direction, proclaiming instantly that the science was "settled": "The science is simple"; "the science says yes."[35]

Early mask proponents made no effort to distinguish situations in which masks would be helpful from ones where they would not. In 2020, a lawyer dressed up as the grim reaper and walked the beaches of Miami, garnering extensive media coverage and praise, even as there was no particular reason to think masks would be helpful on beaches—and lots of reasons to think that mask shaming would be ineffective.[36] No attempt was ever made to have nuanced masking policies that accounted for density, transmission, and community spread. This would have been particularly important given the inevitability of policy fatigue—that is, that people would naturally get tired of wearing masks.

A thin or contradictory evidence base does not always represent a scientific failing. In fact, uncertainty is generally how science works. Research works slowly—or quickly, if necessary—but always by testing, repeated testing, and returning to alternative hypotheses. Rather, the failure comes in exaggerating the strength of evidence and thus preventing necessary *further* research from being done. In our hypercharged, expert-obsessed culture, people aren't willing to devote the time for the truth to gradually emerge or to allow for the kind of nuanced answer in the gray zone, with concomitant uncertainty, that should accompany most findings. On top of that, the use of expertise is often quite circular: people who hold one position find experts who shore up that position. On more than one occasion, we have mentioned to others a study that casts a problematic light on a conventional view. Within moments, a colleague will pronounce that study "discredited" and provide a link to an *Atlantic* article that summarizes a tweet by someone who didn't like the study and probably never read it. This is not the academic research process at work. Instead, it is more like a game of telephone, where one's preferred speculations are elevated to findings, then to theories, and finally into indisputable, inarguable truths—all with no new research or analysis.

*   *   *

Can scientists provide a bulwark against this kind of exaggeration? The Science Media Centre is a website dedicated to what seems like a noble task: providing rapid responses to new studies so that journalists and others can get necessary context in interpreting them. Unfortunately, much of its content shows that the participating scientists are playing politics, not science. In one telling example, the Science Media Centre solicited expert quotes on a modeling study on the effects of mask wearing, which purported to buttress the recommendations for universal masking. The study was very weak—it later produced a letter of concern and a call for a retraction. Nonetheless, one prominent doctor and early mask proponent, Trisha Greenhalgh, told the center that the study was "well-conducted using appropriate methods." That conclusion, it appears, was reached without reading the paper: because it confirmed her strong prior views, she assumed its methods were solid. She later retracted her comment, changing her view entirely to "we cannot confidently conclude anything from this paper."[37] So much for her prior praise for the "well-conducted" study. One wonders about a system where papers are apparently endorsed based on their bottom-line outcome without regard to methodology, but such behavior is common.

Scholarly credentials rather than evidence were routinely deployed as trump cards in the mask debate. Greenhalgh, for example, later proclaimed that people should listen to her because she published "peer-reviewed" scholarship—one example of which was a personal-opinion essay. Scholars were eager to be quoted as an "expert" even on subjects they have not read about. We know this practice all too well from our own realm of legal academia, where many agree to be quoted as experts based only on their general knowledge of the topic and facts garnered in the morning newspaper. It is quite clear that many of the most quoted experts do not always read the research they talk about, but they happily amplify research that confirms their priors.

This culture of loose expertise and credentials was amplified by the media, which throughout the pandemic held low, inconsistent standards in its use of terms such as *expert* and *epidemiologist*. At times, any scientist, regardless of domain-specific knowledge, appeared to qualify as an expert. At other times, when their views were less popular, their credentials were subject to excessive qualification. Consider the case of Emily Oster, a prominent public-health economist who took an unpopular—if ultimately vindicated—position in favor of reopening schools. Media accounts falsely disparaged her as "the go-to academic . . . who doesn't have a background in public health" and elevated her critics to true "experts."[38] Oster's publications were, in fact, in public health and economics.

Doctors were routinely trotted out to inform us about what "science" says, but not all doctors are necessarily experts in how to respond to a pandemic. That someone is a hand surgeon makes them an expert at hand surgery, not at pandemic response. Even an infectious-diseases doctor, although far more relevant, may have more expertise in how to treat patients than in thinking about the optimal global policy responses. The public-health field has more claim to advising on the latter, but there are also many boundaries in that field, and many who were quoted widely were experts in areas of public health that lacked infectious-disease expertise but nevertheless tried to silence others who *did* have relevant expertise but had come to different conclusions. Moreover, public health as a field has adopted a particular ideology, which causes it to make value judgments. Although it is surely entitled to those judgments, it has no particular *authority* to impose those values on others. The *New York Times* featured routine surveys of epidemiologists' views on the pandemic. While it is impossible to know who responds to surveys, almost none of the participants quoted in the articles specialized in infectious diseases.

Throughout COVID-19 coverage, the term *study* was used as a trump card to buttress anything from a blog post to a tweet to a model to a gold-standard randomized-control trial (RCT), with little discussion of the differences between these forms or their underlying assumptions. One article purported to describe a university study demonstrating the number of lives saved in a local lockdown. It would take a very careful reader to realize that the professors had done no original modeling and had instead relied on a *New York Times* interactive visualization.[39]

In the fall of 2021, many believed a few mask holdouts were the primary source of the continued pandemic. As evidence, many continued to cite a model—widely reported on—that the mask holdouts would cause an additional 130,000 deaths.[40] That claim was later retracted and the study corrected because it rested on data the authors knew were inaccurate at the time.[41] The retraction, of course, garnered little coverage. This kind of a vicious cycle—a circular loop connecting Twitter, the media, and quotable experts—only amplifies ignorance. The cycle is not just a phenomenon in journalism; many scientists have reverted to using the claim of "peer review" as a talisman, routinely referring to their ideas as "peer reviewed" even when the articles under question are personal essays and opinions.

In 2020, Danish researchers released the results of an RCT to study the efficacy of masks in protecting mask wearers. The study was widely turned into a straw man by experts on both sides. The study found no evidence that masks worked, which some antimask advocates characterized to an extreme.[42] But they were better than mask proponents, who dismissed the study or its implications on spurious grounds—or simply lied about what the study found. It is nearly impossible to understand the contortions that would allow the *Los Angeles Times* to write a headline stating that the study "shows why more mask-wearing is needed."[43] Elites' apparent readiness to use any study—regardless of its outcome or strength—to confirm their prior beliefs engenders valid cynicism about expertise in public policy.

Nearly all experts now concede the inadequacy of the cloth face coverings they promoted for much of the pandemic. Few, of course, are willing to admit or discuss the implications of the fact that they spent months recommending something that did not work. In 2023, Cochrane, the most respected arbiter of scientific studies for medical practitioners, reviewed all the evidence and concluded that it did not suggest community masking slowed the spread of COVID-19. This conclusion gave rise to predictably tendentious headlines, such as ABC's "Masks Are Effective but Here's How a Study from a Respected Group Was Misinterpreted to Say They Weren't."[44] Zeynep Tufecki, one of the original authors of the #masks4all paper, used her new pulpit as a *Times* columnist to strike back.[45] But her column never responded to the key point of the Cochrane study, which was not about the individual effectiveness of masks to protect a wearer but about the use of masking as a public policy. She mostly tried to imply—falsely—that Cochrane itself had backed off from its own finding. And nowhere in her column did she disclose that she had perhaps the biggest bias of all: she had staked her credibility on her early claim that masks, including *cloth masks*, were highly effective.

*　　*　　*

Why does this flip-flopping matter, especially if one remains convinced, even without more evidence, that masks were at least helpful at the margins? This is perhaps the most interesting part because the pro-mask contingent proclaimed that evidence wasn't necessary because masking was "costless." They also saw little reason or ability to study the benefits of masking because the benefits were self-evident. Some analogized masks to the need for parachutes when jumping out of airplanes but ignored the obvious dissimilarities—such as certain death without the intervention in the latter case.

It rapidly became conventional wisdom in liberal circles that masks needed no further consideration in part because they had "no downsides whatsoever." If anyone questioned that conventional wisdom, their critique was interpreted quite literally and then dismissed—as if the only potential downside to mask wearing could be literal suffocation. This no-downsides framing made it nearly impossible for masks to ever go away: if they had no downsides whatsoever, why not wear them permanently to protect against other respiratory viruses?

But this claim of masks' costlessness was always untrue. For one, the drama over masking—including hysteria over mask noncompliance—led to collateral social consequences. It decreased trust as recommendations changed, fueling polarization as masking became a partisan issue and amping up the costs of that polarization as masking turned into enforcement of mask mandates. As anyone who thinks about public policy can tell you, such collateral consequences must be considered as *part of a policy*. The masking contingent always denied this. Yet even Fauci recently admitted that putting so much energy into masking may not have been worth the polarization.[46]

Mandates fueled polarization, and the flip-flopping undermined public trust. That flip-flopping included the reversal from no masks to masks; the view that protesters, as long as they had the right cause, did not need masks while others outdoors did; the belated recognition that outdoor masking was not logical; the CDC's famous shift after widespread vaccination from dropping mask recommendations to reinstating them; and now the about-face on the (lack of) effectiveness of cloth masks. It took almost a year after the media began to accept the absurdity of outdoor masking for outdoor mandates to begin fading away, albeit in fits and starts.[47]

The loss of public trust isn't the only cost. There were also always direct costs to masking, which elites marked off as socially unacceptable to discuss. If masks were truly costless and helpful in preventing diseases, we would wear masks all the time. Of course, we do not. Society has always valued seeing faces. To claim masks had "no costs" was effectively to deny this. For many, seeing faces was important, and the normalization of a forever-masking regime was, in fact, a real cost. For others, seeing faces was essential, and insisting otherwise was magical thinking.[48] But insist they did—the *New York Times* ran many pieces about the benefits of *not* seeing faces, as if masking were a normal, desirable feature of human society that we had somehow failed to notice until now. This reasoning was either delusional or the product of the same kind of technocratic mindset that conceives of children as "mosquitos" who should "circulate less or will become vectors," in one telling and disturbing analogy adopted by a top Biden pandemic adviser.[49]

Some mask opponents were no better than mask zealots when it came to nuanced treatment of evidence. A few scientists suggested increased carbon dioxide intake as a potential downside to masking, which was quickly dismissed by mask proponents. In 2023, researchers published a "scoping review" on the topic that pointed to a "possible negative impact" and "circumstantial evidence" about the harms from increased carbon dioxide intake while wearing a mask.[50] *Scoping review* is a term of art for a preliminary examination of the existing literature: that is, the authors do not conduct new experiments but canvas existing studies to see what evidence is out there, in part to suggest avenues for further research. (It is less comprehensive than other types of reviews, such as a meta-analysis, which seeks to combine data from previously published studies to produce potentially more robust results.) Showing that neither side has much dignity when it comes to asserting that a single literature review is a "study" that "proves" their point, some leaped on this study as vindication. One article headlined "The Harm Caused by Masks" characterized the paper with undue certainty, calling it a "new study" that demonstrated masks "have major health consequences."[51] By the time the story reached Twitter, conclusions were even more exaggerated. It is understandable that patience wears thin when science cannot give a definitive answer, but the race to draw conclusions hardly promotes an even-handed evaluation of evidence or fosters nuanced policy.

What would a more appropriate policy have been from those who genuinely believed masking was our best line of defense? Simple humility about the evidence would have helped. Say something like, "We don't know for sure, but here's why we think it's worth the temporary cost, and here's what we're going to do to collect evidence to evaluate the efficacy of masks in the meantime." But that was hardly the message shared. Meanwhile, no evidence was collected. Instead, running rigorous trials of masks was immediately declared unethical. This approach does not represent the best use of expertise in public policy. The largest single impetus for universal masking appeared to be the feel-good politics of masking, which produced a visible way to show that we were "doing something" and to separate the virtuous from the ignorant. Worse still was the claim that this policy was simply a neutral "proclamation" from science and the belief that anyone who had doubts about universal masking was a card-carrying member of the flat-earth society.

Lessons Not Learned

Some say it is unfair to criticize public-health offices for messaging flip-flops—whether about cloth masks, herd immunity, natural immunity, or the vaccines' effects on transmissibility—because they were just "following the science" as it changed.[52] But in these cases and many others, what evolved was politics, not science. In one of many priceless examples, Eric Topol, a widely quoted physician, expressed pride in his efforts to delay the vaccine to avoid Trump getting credit for it.[53] Most critics of public-health messaging do not begrudge scientific progress—indeed, most of them want more research. Rather, people are upset by unjustified dogmatic certainty in one direction, followed by an immediate swoop to utter confidence in the opposite course of action. The pandemic produced a headfirst leap into a series of unprecedented interventions, from masks to lockdowns to school closures. In the first weeks of the pandemic, speed was necessary, and mistakes were inevitable. What was not necessary or inevitable was the suppression of healthy skepticism and discussion.

Masks are just one of many examples where the hypercharged discourse prevented us from doing good science. In the early days of the pandemic, the Stanford scientist John Ioannidis issued a warning, later much misrepresented, that our response to the pandemic might prove a fiasco because of insufficient data. His warning may hold up as one of the only accurate predictions from the early days of the pandemic. Because positions were set in stone, there was no appetite to do RCTs of masking, the gold standard for evidence, which were badly needed to evaluate when and how masks should be used. Unfortunately, proponents of masking proclaimed almost immediately that masks were so obviously useful that it would be unethical to study masking. Ethics aside, who in their right mind would study something that was known to be a panacea—and who would want to come to a "pro-Trump" finding? Even today, mask zealots misrepresent this issue, falsely claiming that masking can't be studied through RCTs. It's hard to know if that claim represents a lack of understanding of science or an attempt to fortify a preferred policy. The consequence of it, however, is that we have learned very little about when, how, or which masking policies are beneficial to help us respond to a future respiratory-disease outbreak. And masks were just one example during the pandemic of many missed opportunities to do RCTs, the result of stubborn polarization.

Warning signs of the toxic climate for scientific discourse emerged as early as March 2020. Jeff Flier, the former dean of Harvard Medical School, and Vinay Prasad, a well-known commentator on evidence-based medicine, published a piece expressing alarm that scientists with dissenting views were being "demonized" and subjected to ad hominem attacks.[54] Almost proving their point, many readers loudly rushed to criticize the op-ed and its authors. By June, a different duo of authors wrote to bemoan "medical tribalism in the era of Covid-19," again to no avail. Six months later, the same authors returned to write a further account of "the COVID science wars," which was again met with surprising criticism.[55] In what suggests an unprecedented moment within scientific discourse, concerns about incivility have been repeated again and again in editorials in top medical journals, where scientists express concern about silencing caused by a climate of fear and personal attacks.

These attacks distorted scientific communication. Some chose to cast their public statements to fit partisan narratives, while other scientists stayed silent so as not to be accused of having "Trumpian" motives. In our current moment, labels such as *right wing*, *Trumper*, and *antiscience* are sticky and often terminal in elite institutions, regardless of their veracity. By contrast, you can rarely if ever go wrong parroting the partisan consensus, even when it causes widespread damage to the actual human beings in whose name the consensus claims to speak.

When Exaggeration Backfires

What is especially ironic about elites' exaggeration is that it fails at its *own* goal: persuasion. That is, it isn't even a case where the ends justify the means. Contemporary science communications research has repeatedly found what should be obvious to any thinking person. Trust depends crucially on honesty. Honesty requires that we acknowledge uncertainty, complexity, and counterarguments. David Spiegelhalter, one of the best thinkers on how to communicate data and science, and his colleagues suggest that given inherent uncertainty, public-health communications "had better be certain, and right—or we should more humbly state our uncertainties."[56] His research and that of many others who have studied issues around the calibration of trust suggest that acknowledging conflicting issues enhances rather than undermines trust. Yet, as he documents, many public-health agencies in both the United States and the United Kingdom have declined to do so in the dubious belief that it would confuse people.

Of exaggerations during the pandemic, Spiegelhalter writes, "Scientists can feel as if they're in a communications arms race," which leads to their "denying uncertainty." However much good they think they are doing, their denial only backfires. Much simpler is to be thoughtful about presenting evidence in a way that people can "understand it, trust it and then decide for themselves."[57] This attitude represents the antidote to the condescension mindset that pervades contemporary elite culture.

The politicization of public health, in some cases quite overtly and proudly, had a quite predictable outcome. To the extent it shifted any minds, it shifted those who disagreed to have less trust in science. That is, at best it was utterly ineffective, and at worst it was counterproductive. In October 2020, *Nature*, by any account one of the most impactful and respected peer-reviewed scientific journals, published an editorial endorsing Joe Biden's presidential bid.[58] A week earlier the journal had published an explanation of the unusual nature of the coming editorial, titled "Why *Nature* Needs to Cover Politics Now More Than Ever."[59] (The explanation noted correctly that science and politics are intertwined in the public sphere; this account, however, never really answered or dealt with the question of whether it made sense for a scientific journal to endorse a presidential candidate.)

What was the effect of the editorial? Most likely it had little effect: it's hard to imagine that voters were going to peruse *Nature* to figure out which candidate to support. But to the extent it could have had an effect, the only likely consequence was *contrary* to what *Nature* should have wanted. In an experiment published by *Nature* in 2023, a researcher shared information on the endorsement with a range of voters across the political spectrum.

The primary effect? Trump supporters reduced their trust in *Nature* and reduced their interest in information on *other* topics on which *Nature* had more purview—vaccine efficacy or other COVID-19-related topics. The editorial also reduced their (already low) trust in scientists. The effect on Biden supporters was largely insignificant, and the effect on outcomes was also insignificant. In other words, according to this study of *Nature*'s endorsement, all the editorial did was confirm and exacerbate Trump voters' view that scientists are ideologues rather than scientists.[60]

Although *Nature* even-handedly published that study and its response, it nevertheless doubled down on its decision. Its reason? "Inaction has costs, too. Considering the record of Trump's four years in office, this journal judged that silence was not an option."[61] This empty rhetoric utterly fails to grapple with the point. What is the "cost" of a scientific journal's editorial page *not* printing such an editorial? The editors seem to equate the cost of inaction with the cost of a Trump presidency, but this implies that they think their editorial in fact had an effect on political outcomes—the lack of evidence notwithstanding. The author of the study in 2023 did not challenge the editors' contentions about Trump; he challenged only the efficacy of their methods. "We had to do something" is not a response to "what you did affirmatively hurt your cause." The only way to make the editorial cohere is to understand it as an exercise in virtue signaling: the *Nature* editors had to do something to make themselves look and feel good rather than to do something that made a difference.

The best argument the *Nature* editors could have made might have been to state that all science is political and that they had decided to play in the realm of politics, not just science. But they could not do this because at the same time they want to preserve their ability to fall back on the naive realism that they ask of their listeners: that there is a "science" out there to "defer to." The problem is that these people want to have their cake and eat it, too: they simultaneously believe (correctly) that science is embedded in social practice and want everyone to "follow" them as purveyors of objective, neutral truths. Any reader of this bifurcation is left seeing little more than hypocrisy.

In a further undermining of public trust, repeated oversimplifications leave a residue of dishonesty. Many have questioned Fauci's admission in the *New York Times* in December 2020 that he modified his public views on the necessary percentage of the population to achieve herd immunity, which he based less on the evolution of science and more on his views about what the public was likely to accept.[62] But expert overreach consistently evinces its lack of faith in the public. Fauci repeatedly said the biggest problem facing a vaccine rollout was that many Americans believed COVID-19 was a hoax. That claim appears to be more about pointing fingers because it is not supported by data: the segment of the population that truly believed this was vanishingly small. Some may have believed our response to the pandemic was misguided, which is absolutely not the same as thinking COVID-19 was a hoax or that it was not to be taken seriously. *Denial* has become a catchall term misused to label a range of views, many of which do not fit it.

Elites seem unwilling to recognize the difference between skepticism and denial. Studies repeatedly found that many Americans believed the media exaggerated the pandemic, even as they overwhelmingly deemed the pandemic to be a serious public-health threat. Unfortunately, statistics like that were routinely misrepresented as evidence that Americans believed the pandemic to be a "hoax" rather than as evidence that Americans distrusted the framing of many issues in exaggerated headlines. Such mislabeling is routine. One publication used the phrase "COVID-19 deniers" to describe voters who in exit polls ranked the economy as the most important issue in November 2020—an important dispute over values that represents a critical fault line in American politics, which mainstream coverage instead chalked up as conspiratorial thinking.[63]

Aside from being unjustified, overconfidence and censorship are not useful palliatives for what misinformation is out there. As the singer Seal told the *New York Times* in reference to the conspiracy-theory-laden video *Plandemic: The Hidden Agenda behind Covid-19*, which was widely watched in the early days of the pandemic, "They keep pulling it down, which in and of itself tells you everything."[64] Although the quote was no doubt intended to produce chuckles and eyerolls among *Times* readers, his point is actually worth reflecting on. Censorship and suppression lead to less, not more, trust. It may be reassuring to note that "most" people did not think the pandemic was intentionally planned by powerful people, but it is perhaps more important to reflect on why 25 percent of Americans found the conspiracy "probably or definitely" true.[65] Writing off a third of Americans is the sort of strategy that leads, for instance, to surprise electoral failures. But this is increasingly the elite mentality: either to ignore dissenting views or to suggest we protect the people who hold these views from their own stupidity by exaggerating or oversimplifying science.

Never Having to Say You're Sorry

What perhaps is ultimately most inflammatory about the misuse of expertise is the lengths to which experts will go to take credit and then later to avoid blame. Expert overreach backfires. When expertise is abused and misused, populist skepticism is not only a rational response but also often the correct response. Elites conflate any skepticism with the most extreme versions of it, such that someone who asks a simple question about masks or lockdowns is deemed to be identical with the most vehement antievolution, antivaccine advocate. But genuine dissent is different from crackpot conspiracy theory. Skepticism is a defensible, rational, and useful epistemology. And when genuine dissent is mocked, ignored, or suppressed, it creates anger, resentment, and a sense of being ignored. Throughout history, populism's role has nearly always been to create an alternative in response to being told that there is "no alternative."

Meanwhile, wishful amnesia has set in among elites. We have already mentioned Randi Weingarten, the head of the national teachers' union who now denies her role in promoting school closures. Although few take her revisionist history seriously, even pundits who are willing to admit mistakes do seem to have forgotten the scale of our policy blunders. For instance, Jonathan Chait contends that Democrats got school closures wrong, but, unlike Republicans, they fixed their mistakes.[66] But he understates how long the Democrats' mistake lasted and how hard it was to change; he implies that schools were open by the beginning of 2021, when most students in blue states still had remote learning. Others have gone to great lengths to suggest that all disagreement was in bad faith and evil in intention. Jonathan Howard, a neurologist who grew his Twitter following during the pandemic, wrote a book with the tendentious title *We Want Them Infected* (2023). Blurbs written about the book come from many of the people who refused, and still do, to engage in good faith with alternative perspectives about the best public-health control mechanisms for a pandemic. In other words, we have learned little from our pandemic debacle.

As we write in late 2023, the conversation over elite management of the pandemic has now come full circle. Those who were most adamant in their demands for harsher government measures to eradicate the virus now admit they were wrong. A prominent example is Scott Galloway, a New York University professor of marketing and pundit. Appearing with former governor Andrew Cuomo on *Real Time with Bill Maher*, Galloway admitted that during the pandemic he wanted stricter shutdown measures for his children's school, but, he says, he got this and other things wrong. In the video, Galloway claimed, "We were doing our best." We beg to differ. In the same video, Cuomo took no responsibility for his decision to send thousands of elderly people to nursing homes without COVID-19 testing (he even blames Fauci for "misinformation"). In addition, he equivocated on how deaths from COVID-19 were counted.[67]

To repeat what we hope is self-evident: the problem is not with expertise but with its misuse. The most common form of misuse is overconfidence: exaggerating the certainty behind the evidence or treating a prediction as infallible. When we create a culture that is open to mistakes, we create a more honest, trustworthy system that describes the real grounds on which decisions are made and that is capable of evolving.

The venomous debate over our responses to the pandemic represent just a recent case study in a dangerous trajectory. Overclaiming for the role of expertise in decisions corrodes both expertise and democracy. In most decisions—about both policy and even day-to-day life—expertise has an important but rarely decisive role because decisions are usually based on values in addition to data. In a democratic society, rendering judgment on these values is traditionally seen as the purview of the governed, not experts.

We are left with two obvious questions. First, how widespread is expert overreach? And second, why does it happen? In the next chapter, we turn to those problems, suggesting that there really is a systematic problem that has developed both because of problematic incentives and because of a growing intellectual case among elites that has sidelined open inquiry and debate in favor of exaggeration and deception.

4   Explaining the Abuse of Expertise

Expertise is under threat from within. There are systemic problems in its creation, description, and deployment. From the mischaracterization or exaggeration of research findings to the "replication crisis" within academic research itself, much expertise is less trustworthy than elites claim. These problems are exacerbated by structural incentives for scholars and journalists that do not reward the most rigorous, nuanced work. Elites ignore or minimize these issues to keep the conversation free of doubt and to maintain control of the discourse.

One weird trick has been recommended for you to try the next time you have to speak in public. Before you go into the room, spend a minute standing in a superhero pose, hands to your hips. Now go in and experience the magical power of "your body language shap[ing] who you are." Your brain will start to believe you're a superhero, and your anxieties will dissipate. You'll be following the science because the idea—sometimes called "power posing"—comes out of research popularized in a TED Talk by the social psychologist and motivational speaker Amy Cuddy in 2012. It remains the second most popular TED Talk, with nearly 70 million views.[1] Its advice has been amplified repeatedly since then. The *New York Times* lauded Cuddy in a profile in 2014, lavishing adjectives on her research: "Numerous well-documented follow-up studies by other prominent scholars showed significant effects on behavior outcomes."[2] Power posing worked its way into pop culture, featuring in an episode of *Grey's Anatomy* in 2018, and internet message boards are full of firsthand accounts of true believers in the technique.[3]

There's just one problem: power poses don't really work. The original research finding was wrong. Cuddy's first paper on the subject was published in 2010 with two collaborators who now disavow the research. Dana

Carney, a leading researcher in nonverbal communication, was the study's primary author but now puts her current perspective on power posing simply and eloquently: "Reasonable people, whom I respect, may disagree. However since early 2015 the evidence has been mounting suggesting there is unlikely any embodied effect of . . . 'power poses' . . . on internal or psychological outcomes. As evidence has come in over these past 2+ years, my views have updated to reflect the evidence. As such, I do not believe that 'power pose' effects are real."[4] Carney now thinks the evidence against "power posing" is so strong that the topic isn't worthy of additional research. She no longer teaches about the work or talks about it to the press. Rather than blindly defending work she wrote, she instead displays integrity and an admirable commitment to open-mindedness and truth in scholarly inquiry. The same cannot be said of Cuddy.

To be clear, the reversal of the finding doesn't mean the original research was in any sense unethical or bad. Preliminary findings will often be revised: revision is at the heart of the scientific method and its emphasis on repeated experiment and falsification. Because reversals *are* likely, the real culprits in the overreach of expertise are those who, like the *Times* and Cuddy, blindly elevate research to "numerous well-documented" status. As a result, the efficacy of power poses continues to circulate today as a robust psychological fact despite its falsity. This is typical of the "ideas economy": TED Talks, media pundits, and self-help book authors who invoke the authority of "science" to promote their favorite life hacks. Empirics and science are a marketing ploy rather than a method of inquiry in search of truth. The same behavior is seen when elites cherry-pick studies to "objectively" justify a preferred policy. Their rhetoric masks opinion as indisputable factual truth.

Power posing is just one of many examples of pseudoscientific advice that claims to draw on robust evidence. Perhaps you have heard the widespread claim that to develop mastery you have to put in 10,000 hours of practice. This idea was popularized by one of the most prolific and successful opportunists of the idea economy, the journalist Malcolm Gladwell, who dresses up vacuous clichés as scientifically based empirical insights. In his book *Outliers: The Story of Success* (2008), Gladwell claimed to base this "rule" on research by Anders Ericsson, who studied the intense practice habits of professional violinists. Unlike in the case of the power-pose research, the mistake in the science here wasn't revealed through research over time but was already admitted: Ericsson has long maintained that Gladwell mischaracterized his research to invent the rule.[5] Yet the "rule" is still widely repeated. Another example is the idea of "ego depletion," which suggests each of us has a "supply" of willpower that can get exhausted over time. This idea formed the kernel of the best-selling book *Willpower: Rediscovering the Greatest Human Strength* (2011) by Roy Baumeister and John Tierney. But as scientists have tried to replicate the original findings, they have increasingly been unable to reproduce the effect.[6]

These examples are perhaps trivial, but they illustrate a vicious circle in the dissemination of expertise. In what resembles the children's game of "telephone," a message gets distorted as it's repeated. Preliminary, tentative, and nuanced claims are exaggerated and then amplified. As the idea gets repeated, it seems to gain further credibility because it is restated by those with credentials—journalists or academics. (Consider the practice of authors and scholars writing enthusiastic jacket blurbs of each other's books, which they may not even have read. Gladwell admits to having lost count of how many adulatory blurbs he's written for his friends.[7]) But many of them are just repeating hearsay, and few put in the work to understand the limitations of the original finding. Academics are fallible, and nobody can read or check everything. We all rely on others' say-so, and it is easy to see why this practice persists. Everyone wants to be part of the latest findings, and each repetition individually may seem harmless. In aggregate, however, such sight-unseen repeated credentialing weakens the credibility of assertions made by credentialed sources.

In this chapter, we suggest that problems in expertise are systematic, not random or isolated. This indictment does not mean that all research is rotten or that the scholarly endeavor itself is unworthy. If we felt that way, we would not write this book or teach at a university. But we think academic integrity requires that we face up to systemic weaknesses in the way expertise is produced and disseminated.

The best credentials are no guarantee of true expertise. In July 2023, the president of Stanford, Marc Tessier-Lavigne, a distinguished neuroscientist, resigned after major flaws were uncovered in his research. They would have likely stayed uncovered had a student journalist not doggedly pursued the story. Some of the misconduct, including "obvious" data manipulation, the reporter says, was hiding in plain sight for years.[8] Following serious allegations of discrepancies and potentially doctored images, top scientists at

Harvard's Dana-Farber Cancer Institute retracted six studies and corrected a further 31 at the start of 2024.[9] The incident echoed another one involving top Harvard researcher in evolutionary biology Marc Hauser, renowned for his studies of monkey behavior and cognition. That research came to a halt with his abrupt resignation in 2010 after the discovery of fabricated data throughout his career.[10]

Since 1975, the number of articles retracted in scientific journals for fraud or misconduct—the most common reason for retraction—has increased tenfold.[11] In surveys, 2 percent of scientists say they have fabricated data at least once, and 14 percent say they personally know of other colleagues who have done so. Fully a third admit to other questionable practices.[12] Practices that are designed as an independent check on published research, such as peer review, have also been manipulated, as in a peer-review cheating ring that supplied fake reviewers to get articles published quickly.[13] These examples are a good reminder of why elites should not have blind faith in credentialism and simply rest on the pedigree of an institution rather than on the quality of evidence and argument.

As bad as it is, fraud pales in comparison to *intrinsic* limitations in research. As we explain in this chapter, it is plausible, even likely, that *most* published research in medicine is false—even when scientific fraud is set aside. Conventional wisdom is regularly reversed. Experts are terrible at predictions. There is a "replication crisis" in the social sciences, where findings—including many of the most celebrated claims—don't seem to hold up on subsequent experimentation. Scholarship may be biased toward clever but irrelevant results. All these problems are exacerbated once scholarship enters the public sphere and nuance is driven out.

This news is not surprising given problematic incentives within academia to "publish or perish" and the pressure to produce findings that will be widely cited and covered. It's easier to come to a robust-sounding and surprising conclusion—the kind that will attract top publishers and generate media interest—with a bad research design than with a good one.[14] "The persistence of poor methods results partly from incentives that favour them, leading to the natural selection of bad science," noted two scientists in 2016. "This dynamic requires no conscious strategizing—no deliberate cheating nor loafing—by scientists, only that publication is a principal factor for career advancement."[15] On top of these incentives, academics, like anyone, are biased. Although the scholarly enterprise is supposed to be based on methods that help reduce that bias, all scholars inevitably come to their research with prior views, which may overwhelm those safeguards.

These problems are well known and are not in and of themselves fatal to the academic enterprise—that is, if they are dealt with honestly. What is more troubling to us is many elites' desire to sweep these problems under the rug. Pointing out problems is seen as a "betrayal" of the elite claim of superior knowledge grounded in facts. Questions about the robustness of scholarly claims, elites fear, are dangerous because they only serve to undermine elites' ability to make wise policy. If people see that academics are only human, this reasoning goes, they will have no more reason to trust academics. We have a higher regard of voters, whom we think are capable of understanding the usefulness of expertise while being aware of its limitations and uncertainty, and we do not think voters are so easily fooled by overconfidence, at least not in the long run.

Technocratic paternalism, coupled with enlightened condescension, leads to the third mindset of elites: intellectual tyranny. An epistemic edifice is being built—and widely adopted—in favor of expert overreach. Many elites appear to have convinced themselves that limiting public debate is for the best. Although this conclusion is disturbing, it is quite likely reached in good faith. There appears to be a growing fear, the natural descendent of elites' meritocratic worldview, that the populace is simply too ignorant to deal with complexity. Although misinformation does exist, its role in public policy has been blown out of proportion (see chapter 8). And when elites circle the wagons in defense of expertise, they turn "evidence" into a tribal, partisan force that shuts down inquiry and discovery.

Cracks in the Expert Regime

In chapter 3, we showed the failure of public discourse to create a climate suited to evaluating expertise and bringing it to bear on public policy. But the problems start sooner, within the system that generates the expertise— made up of institutions such as universities, think tanks, and the media. Owning up to these problems is not nihilistic but rather a prerequisite to open inquiry. Real expertise means acknowledging with honesty the limits of our knowledge. In fact, it is precisely those limits and the enthusiastic questioning of "established" knowledge that drive discovery.

In 2005, the medical researcher John Ioannidis published an article with an eye-catching title: "Why Most Published Research Findings Are False." The article is well known, cited more than 12,000 times, and Ioannidis has become one of the most known and quoted researchers in academic medicine today. His interest is "metascience," or the study of how to improve research quality in medical sciences, in part by identifying its flaws. Few contest Ioannidis's central claim: "Simulations show that for most study designs and settings, it is more likely for a research claim to be false than true." To the extent there is disagreement with this claim, it is more about the implications of his finding.

How can what Ioannidis argues be true? He identifies several issues. Some sources of error are familiar and all too human, including bias and financial conflict. But one source is simply the nature of the type of research that goes on today, which is often focused on analyzing increasingly small effects. When you study something that may have only a very minor effect, the likelihood that the finding is overwhelmed by noise is much higher. In other words, the apparent effect of a particular vitamin on longevity—because the effect is likely small, if it exists at all—may be due to random chance, not to the vitamin. But medical science naturally must focus on increasingly small effect sizes because many of the biggest fish have already been caught.

Ioannidis argues that "claimed research findings may often be simply accurate measures of the prevailing bias." This means that scientists naturally *want* to find results—careers are made on results, not on negative findings or the absence of results. But in some areas of research, it is quite possible that there are no or few findings to be had! Consider nutrition research, which Ioannidis has been extremely critical of and which many scientists consider to be one of the more problematic fields in medicine. We all are familiar with the comic parade of newspaper headlines generated by nutrition research, where wine can flip-flop from a miracle cure for eternal life today to the deadliest sin tomorrow. Why does this happen? It might be that actually relatively few dietary patterns lead to consistent, large negative health outcomes. This makes sense because most food that society has regularly consumed over centuries is unlikely to be especially lethal. But nutrition researchers will still go in search of such novel findings because, as Ioannidis notes, "investigators working in any field are likely to resist accepting that the entire field in which they have spent their careers is a 'null field.'"[16] The result is that the rapid succession of breathless novel findings that make it into print are mainly a measure of the "net bias" in that field—not actual, meaningful findings.

Is it plausible that many fields are really "null" or close to null? It's not only probable but also extremely likely because we have eliminated much of the low-hanging fruit of research—say, the link between smoking and lung cancer, the ability of antibiotics to cure bacterial infection—and increasingly are studying phenomena with small effects. These small effects matter, of course, and are worthy of study, but they are also that much harder to study and to distinguish from random noise.

In later studies, Ioannidis has made further findings that buttress the possibility that much or most research—regardless of where it is published—is unreliable. Not all of his work bears as catchy a headline as "Why Most Published Research Findings Are False." Consider the unlovely title of his article "Assessment of Vibration of Effects due to Model Specification Can Demonstrate the Instability of Observational Associations" (2015). But bear with us for a moment because the point is crucial to understanding the inherent difficulty in trusting many published studies.

Imagine you are interested in understanding wine's effect on health, specifically longevity: Are two glasses of rosé each evening the secret elixir of diets in "blue zones" where people apparently live longer than average, or is wine unhealthy in any amount? The best way to answer the question would be a randomized-control trial, or RCT. In such a study, you would divide your participants into random groups, assigning each group a "treatment"—say, two glasses of wine a day for one group and complete abstinence for the other. The RCT is often called the "gold standard" for research because if the study is correctly designed, we can be quite confident that any difference in outcomes is the result of the "treatment." That is, if the rosé drinkers consistently outlive the nondrinkers, and the groups were truly randomly selected, we can be confident the wine is the *cause* of the effect we observe. But as you might imagine, this study would be expensive and difficult to conduct, not to mention that you would be waiting a long time for results if life expectancy is your interest. (The National Institutes of Health was funding a major trial of moderate alcohol consumption, but it was scuttled in 2018 following concerns about conflicts of interest from industry funding.[17])

So how would you go about answering the question? An alternative would be observational research: instead of conducting a controlled experiment, you would use data on what has happened in the real world, drawn from patient medical records, surveys, and other sources. But this methodology presents a major obstacle. Let's say these data show that wine drinkers live longer. Unfortunately, we can't jump to the conclusion that the wine *caused* their better health. Another conclusion could instead be that wealthier people drink more wine, and wealthier people have a leg up on health (better health care and more opportunities to engage unhealthier behaviors). These confounding factors exist in both directions. Binge drinkers may show up as "wine drinkers," but binge drinking is unhealthy, and alcohol abuse may be linked to other illnesses. As the saying goes, correlation is not causation. The result is we need to tease out more the role that wine plays.

This problem plagues all observational research. Unfortunately, observational data are often the only evidence we have. Certainly, observational data are more convenient for a researcher looking to get a publishable result quickly and cheaply. Researchers are well aware of the problem of confounding variables. One way to control for the problem is to add additional variables into the model. For our wine example, we might include data on our participants' income to *control* for the possibility that being rich, not drinking wine, is the real elixir. But a researcher cannot and should not include all variables. Which variables to include is a choice. There are methods to help guide that choice, but ultimately it is a judgment call for the study designer. And that is the key problem: the results may completely change because of very slight changes in which variables are included or excluded.

These slight changes are what Ioannidis and his coauthors call "vibration of effects"—how much the study result changes, or "vibrates," depending on what variables are or aren't included. Their concern is that many findings are robust only if we use the exact "model specification"—the exact interrelationship of input data—the experimenter happened to choose. The experimenter might even have chosen that model deliberately to obtain a publishable result, a practice called "p-hacking" that is considered unethical but hard to police. Or the experimenter's priors might have led them to make particular choices innocuously. Either way, the net result is that we cannot have high confidence in the results.

This problem is more fundamental than improving ethics and incentives because the "vibration" is a consequence of the reality of observational data.

Observational data are *always* limited in our ability to draw causal effects. We can improve on naively looking for correlations, but our confidence can never rise to the level of an RCT. The advantage of observational studies is availability, not accuracy. Moreover, many of the effects we are looking at these days are quite small. There are probably relatively few "huge" effects to find in, say, nutrition but rather lots and lots of really small effects. The same is probably true in the social sciences: most interventions probably have a small effect. The smaller the likely effect, the harder it is to measure because the harder it is to separate the effect from random noise.

These problems don't represent the failure of the academic enterprise. We *should* be looking at smaller effects because many of the best-known effects are quite obvious and well known. We don't need to continue studying whether the sun rises each day or whether binge drinking is unhealthy: we know the answers, and the effect size is large. The failures in studying small effects are our unwillingness to own up to inherent limitations in our methodology and to report and explain findings with the appropriate level of certainty.

How much does excessive certainty—exaggeration—matter? If the problem were simply a matter of mistakes in obscure journals, there might be hope that the "truth" would emerge over time through the natural working of academic processes. (There are reasons to be concerned that doesn't happen, though.) But when expertise enters the public sphere, the problem takes on a new dimension. Policies are often adopted long before research has run its course and settled on a consensus. Worse still, the wrong choices are often quite sticky. Vinay Prasad and Adam Cifu have studied "medical reversals," their term for practices or drugs adopted by medicine that later turn out to be ineffective or even harmful.[18] Some of these examples were quite widespread: routine stenting in stable coronary disease; the overuse of Atenolol for blood pressure compared to other, more effective drugs in the same class; or, perhaps best known, Vioxx, Merck's wonder drug for acute pain that made the company $2.5 billion in the year before it was permanently withdrawn from the market because it was causing tens if not hundreds of thousands of cases of heart disease.[19]

Prasad and Cifu document many such cases since the 1990s. What explains them? In some cases, they indicate the normal "run" of science, but these authors also point to a reluctance to run RCTs and to "financial incentives [that] are strongly aligned to promote new technologies." They call for a higher bar. Many have resisted this solution in part because of expense. Others seem resistant to the idea that evidence rather than common sense needs primacy.[20] The result is that more reversals are inevitable—and will inevitably diminish patient trust in medicine.

*   *   *

What about outside of medicine? At least in theory, medicine enjoys some of the most rigorous evidentiary standards, at least compared to social sciences. Federal agencies exist to evaluate evidence for drugs and procedures, and insurers cast a watchful eye to see if they can deny coverage for treatments deemed ineffective. The threat of malpractice litigation looms over harmful medical practices conducted without sufficient evidence. (Perhaps only physics has a higher standard of evidence—particle physics is known for its excruciating standards—but much of that work is not relevant for the kind of policy we're mostly concerned with in this book.) Medicine also benefits as a field from a robust infrastructure that allows RCTs to run, which are the gold standard in identifying whether a treatment is actually the *cause* of a particular outcome. This is all far less true in the social sciences, where it is challenging—and in many cases outright impossible—to run RCTs to determine the causes of war or violence, how to improve schools, and how best to run society.

So it should not be surprising to see the situation is likely even worse in the "soft" sciences of economics and political science. Philip Tetlock evaluated expert predictions and judgment in his book *Expert Political Judgment: How Good Is It? How Can We Know?* (2006). The book grew out of a well-known crisis in expertise at the time: the Iraq War, during which many experts and elites had rushed to judgments, but those judgments later proved to be incorrect. Although Tetlock concedes that it's difficult to measure and quantify how often experts get things right, he devoted decades to studying precisely that. His conclusions are damning. Over 20 years of surveying experts by asking them to forecast various scenarios within their areas of expertise, he collected more than 80,000 forecasts. The dismal findings: their predictions weren't great, often no better than random chance and no better than predictions made by nonexperts. Worse, many of the experts who were wrong wouldn't concede they were wrong, and many experts' predictions seemed motivated primarily by the experts' ideological priors.

This was not a novel result. In 1980, Professor J. Scott Armstrong of the Wharton School offered the "seer-sucker theory," which he put concisely: "No matter how much evidence exists that seers do not exist, suckers will pay for the existence of seers." Forecasting in particular was an area in which experts struggled yet was consistently valued and desired by others, notwithstanding its inaccuracy.[21]

Not just predictions but also existing findings suffer from widespread inaccuracy, however. *Replication crisis* is the term for an increasingly well-known problem in many fields of research, especially in the field of psychology. In general, the scientific method relies on replication. We develop a theory and test it, and through repeated testing that fails to "falsify" the theory, we gain more confidence in the truth of the theory. Replication is important because it can help separate out noise and random chance from a true finding. The finding of a particular effect in a single study could be the result of random chance, but once that study has been repeated enough times, and the same effect is reached, it's more likely that the effect does exist.

In recent years, scholars have sounded alarm bells about the fact that in many prominent cases, published research *can't* be replicated.[22] That is, when replication studies are performed, they don't come to the same result. The problem appears to be pervasive and does not concern just obscure findings. A variety of explanations have been advanced. They run the gamut from publication bias (we tend to publish "surprising" findings but not failed findings, so we are most likely to publish research that is the result of random chance) to "p-hacking," an unethical practice where researchers play with data to obtain a publishable result, and to outright fraud. Whatever the cause, the inability to replicate studies is another problem to contend with when elites insist that public policy must simply follow the evidence.

Asking the Wrong Questions

As we say often in this book, elites claim that if only the rest of us paid attention to the facts, all our problems would be solved. The hallmark of factual knowledge is data. When it comes to data, the mantra today is the more data we have, the better our conclusions. At first blush, this correlation looks promising: Who could contest that the more we know, the better our knowledge base? Alas, things are not quite as easy as this suggests. For one thing, empirical research can be seductive in that it can create conclusions that look irrefutable but are, like any other research, contingent and incomplete. Good empiricists know this, but many who seek to deploy empirical studies in support of their preferences—and who, in many cases, simply head to Google and quickly locate studies that support their priors—seem not to.

One of the most salient features of the embrace of more data is the way the data are deployed and disseminated. At the most extreme end, we have elevated a lightweight version of the empirical mindset into a kind of parlor trick. TED Talks and other elite favorites treat data as a game, carrying on a tradition from Freakonomics, a popular series of economic books that focused on counterintuitive empirical results. The authors and many of their students are part of a "credibility revolution" in economics that has made some important methodological advances in the field—many of which are really quite a bit more credible than some of the flawed methods that preceded them. But the popular reception of Freakonomics and the way it was taken up by others became little more than an academic version of the "one neat trick" meme. Cleverness has replaced careful and measured insight as the touchstone of quality research. This research culture sometimes borders on the superficial and the performative. For young academics who need a quick "aha!" result to establish themselves, it no longer makes sense to look at the big questions: the causes of war, the fundamentals of education or democracy, and so on.[23] These areas are less likely to have singular rigorous findings through large-scale data.

*   *   *

Are these issues serious, or are we making too much of too little? The most optimistic way of looking at these problems—one we in part endorse—is that most of them concern how expertise gets deployed and advanced within public discourse. That is, experts themselves aren't so bad. So what can we do about such issues? The rosiest view we have seen comes from the popular author Michael Lewis, who is quite fond of experts—and thinks our main problem is just that we listen to the wrong experts.[24] This is both the premise and the fatal flaw of *The Big Short: Inside the Doomsday Machine* (2010), his terrific book about the financial crisis of 2008. Although the book and the movie made from it explained many aspects of the crisis cleverly and concisely, they ultimately endorsed the patently false view that if only we had listened to those calling out that the "emperor has no clothes," we would have averted disaster. But, of course, Lewis wrote the book with the benefit of hindsight. One can always find retrospectively someone who was crying wolf; the problem is identifying them in advance. Many of the heroes of *The Big Short* should be just as famous for losing money before and after the financial crisis: they may, in other words, have just been lucky to have been right. Selecting heroes with the benefit of hindsight bias makes for great films but doesn't help much for setting policy, especially in the thick of a crisis.

In recent work, including a podcast series devoted to the topic of expertise, Lewis has suggested that the more pervasive problem is that we systematically valorize the wrong experts. He names talking heads who seem like experts and heads of agencies who have risen through bureaucracies but don't actually know that much as prime examples. Instead, Lewis suggests, the real experts toil away in obscurity in the basements of government buildings, corporations, and universities. He tells a terrific story about Arthur A. Allen, an employee of the US Coast Guard, whom Lewis reached while calling "nonessential" workers furloughed during a government shutdown.[25] Allen, far from "nonessential," had revolutionized the way we rescue people, saving countless lives. Yet he was furloughed, and few have heard of him, other than those who (like Lewis) read the citations given by the Partnership for Public Service to recognize unsung heroes in the US government.

It's a compelling story, but the lesson is entirely unclear. First of all, the Allen story actually seems like a story of expertise at work: Allen may not be world famous (except through Lewis's reporting), but his methods are in fact used by the Coast Guard. Isn't that what we want? Does Lewis want him to be more famous? As far as can be discerned from his interviews with Allen, Allen isn't bothered by his obscurity; rather, Lewis's holding Allen up as an exemplar of true expertise seems like Lewis wanting for others what he wants in his own professional career as a writer. It's not clear that society would better deploy expertise if it made the obscure but good experts famous—nor does Lewis suggest any particular way we can identify those people in a systematically useful way.

In the same podcast, Lewis gushes about his optimism about a new trend: the ability to directly engage with these backroom experts when they build a brand on Twitter. In particular, he cites his obsession with a certain military buff—someone who posts lots of colorful details about the nature and use of tanks in Ukraine. And thanks to Twitter, rather than hearing from a former general turned talking head on CNN who may know little about on-the-ground tactics in this particular conflict, Lewis and others can get it straight from the source.

But what problem is this kind of expertise solving? Was the problem really that random people—those of us who have no influence in military decision-making—didn't know enough specific details of tanks in Ukraine? Why should we celebrate the fact that Lewis can now read a nuanced analysis of tanks on social media? This is typical of the elite attitude toward expertise: it's an obsession with expertise *itself* rather than a more sophisticated understanding of the role of expertise *in context*. Yes, there should be a tank expert somewhere in the military hierarchy advising those making battlefield decisions, but there probably is one (or more), and if there isn't, a Twitter account isn't really the solution.

Lewis, like Nichols, rests much of his case on anecdotal evidence of people not trusting doctors or asking too many questions. But he's thin on evidence that asking questions from WebMD—even if it might annoy doctors—is a problem. Lewis notes that doctors know more and more, yet we trust them less and less. But even if this is true—and he has no evidence that it is—doesn't that actually evince a rational response to an era of lower-knowledge doctors? Trust will naturally take a while to calibrate, and it's quite plausible that transparency and access to information builds trust and makes people want to be more trustworthy. Again, there's no real evidence here that we have a problem that hurts outcomes: the best we can say is that some physicians don't like answering questions. If that's what elites mean by the "death of expertise," it's hard to be too upset.

Lewis proffers another policy, universal statistics literacy, because he believes we put too much stock in anecdotes. But there are a host of problems with this idea—not least of all the likely inefficacy of a statistical literacy class, given the well-documented failure of financial literacy efforts, in really changing how people reason.[26] Moreover, listening to stories and anecdotes *is* part of human experience—and a rational way of gathering information in many instances. It may not be how we want domain experts making decisions in their area of expertise, but for the rest of us anecdotes can be useful. (Of all people, Lewis should know this because the reason his books are successful is that they're heavily anecdotal—sometimes at the expense of nuance but with the consequence that they are engaging to a wide audience.) It's not clear that statistical literacy is relevant to most personal decisions: personal decisions about areas of individual autonomy are typically going to rest on more than some statistical fact.

Lewis contends, like many elites, that ordinary people have no right to an opinion on certain topics, such as global-warming models.[27] Fair enough: the models themselves are probably beyond our ken (and a statistical literacy class wouldn't help much with that!). But again, this assertion misses the bigger picture: How much of the real debate over global warming is really over the nuances of these statistical models? Admittedly, some people frame their arguments that way. But could it be that the real source of our polarized opinions on topics such as climate change stems from bigger and more fundamental fissures? We return to this point in chapter 6, but very few public-policy questions rest solely on facts, and the line between facts and values is much blurrier than Lewis and other elites seem to recognize.

Moreover, the biggest problem with most empirical results *isn't* in the technical aspects of the statistical methods. When one of us designed a class to teach basic statistics to law students, we learned that many of our students defer too much to the appearance of sophisticated data. They labor under the false assumption that they can't critique or engage with empirical papers because to do so would require detailed knowledge of complex methodology. But, in fact, the biggest problems with many academic papers are intuitive in nature—precisely the kinds of questions an intelligent law student can ask. The flaws often lie in faulty or questionable assumptions made or, worse, unnoticed by the author; in basic problems with survey design or data collection that anyone can learn to recognize; in alternative explanations not considered; or in the applicability of the study question to the public policy at issue (what can fancily be called "external validity").

A favorite example from the first week of our course on statistics for lawyers will illustrate that what we need is basic critical-thinking skills rather than more widespread understanding of technical methods or what Lewis calls "statistics literacy." Students were presented with a peer-reviewed article making a novel medical claim, supported by a seemingly impenetrable set of tables. Given that it was published in a peer-reviewed journal and consisted of rigorous-looking evidence, students assumed it was both accurate and beyond their purview. But once students paused and looked at the tables, they all were able to see a major flaw: the demographic details were completely implausible. To see this required no technical knowledge of statistics or medicine. It was plainly visible to a careful reader. What our students needed was not training but confidence and skepticism. The flaws could easily be overlooked because the paper had the appearance of reputable science. After the paper was posted, statisticians authored a letter of concern noting "multiple irregularities about the underlying data."[28] Many believed the underlying survey data were most likely compromised by a botnet that entered fake submissions. Later studies on different population data suggested the original finding was incorrect. The journal editor, however, declined to retract the flawed piece—which the editor had coauthored.

Most academic research—including empirical academic research with fancy regressions and lots of data—is open to engagement by anyone who reads closely. The problem is not our lack of training but rather that we are trained to believe in the credentials—to assume that well-presented tables indicate truth. To be sure, there are more technical methodological issues, but that is not where we (or most people who study empirical work) should begin when figuring out how much weight to accord a particular empirical study. Elites seem sadly unaware of this and all too willing to keep questions about empirical work away from "regular" people.

What is to be gleaned from the Michael Lewis story? And how does that story relate to our points about data and the performative aspects of elite deployment of experts? Lewis valorizes expertise and facts yet engages in pure narrative to sustain his claims about the financial crisis. In addition, he contradicts himself throughout his account of the power of expertise grounded in facts. He consistently fails to show how facts of any sort support his narrative. He denies "ordinary people" the right to opine on matters such as global warming while at no point showing how climate-change models tell us anything about the best global policy responses. Again, the facts alone will not settle policy debates. No matter how hard they try, elites cannot stifle the voices of the alienated portions of the polity.

Simplify, Then Exaggerate

Once expertise enters the public sphere, the problem gets worse. At least within the confines of the ivory tower, there is a collective awareness that research is contingent and imperfect. There are incentives to check and qualify previous findings. But when elites bring expertise into the public sphere, it is more as performance than anything else. Nuance is lost. Here we are focused on elites and experts' *incentives* to exaggerate evidence and overclaim about the strength of their findings as well as the flawed incentives to produce good research in this context.

The problematic economics of today's news environment are well known. Newspapers want to sell ads. People respond to clickbait headlines, especially ones that promote fear or other strong emotions. Scientists are rewarded by journalists for being influencers on Twitter. The combined results for scientific communication are inherently problematic. Nobody needs to want to behave badly, but it is hard to opt out of such a system where expertise is casually deployed, with little rigor, in support of a preferred view. Journalists want stories that will be read, academics want to be quoted, and politicians want to avoid blame. No doubt some are complicit, but bad results from such a system are likely, even when good intentions are at play.

There's an old joke about how to do journalism: "simplify, then exaggerate." In fact, it's not entirely a joke in that the first known use of the maxim came from the editor of the illustrious weekly *The Economist* in advice to new journalists.[29] If we accept it as clever more than literal, we can see some merit to it: journalism is successful only if it's read, and the weeds are often *not* what's important. In fact, there is usefulness to the idea in any endeavor. Teaching generally requires simplification, if not exaggeration, because getting students to see the big picture will help them understand the smaller pieces and is more memorable. But taken to an extreme, this approach results in the kind of coverage we typically see of science today: dire warnings that your summer barbecue will kill you or that eating more broccoli will bestow eternal life upon you. The outcomes would be almost comical if not so important.

Elite institutions amplify the most exaggerated views.[30] Mainstream media trip over themselves in search of hot takes. Consider the flurry of coverage in early 2023 about ChatGPT. The topic of generative artificial intelligence (AI) has produced countless pieces on long-term apocalyptic existential threats—ranging from those that enthusiastically endorse our robot overlords bringing in an extropian future to those that think the military should start bombing data centers to stop AI progress. Many who are in the former camp subscribe to a set of philosophical views given the unlovely label "Tescreal," which includes transhumanism and singularitarianism. One writer sums up these views as a "techno-utopian vision of the future in which we become radically 'enhanced,' immortal 'posthumans,' colonise the universe, re-engineer entire galaxies [and] create virtual-reality worlds in which trillions of 'digital people' exist."[31] These views are part of the rarefied world of the ultrawealthy, bubbled tech elites who have been enthusiastically planning their strategy for surviving doomsday since their teenage years.[32]

While entertaining, these views are taken seriously and drive out more nuanced conversations about immediate threats, which are not nearly as sexy or interesting as cosmism. Daron Acemoglu, an MIT labor economist, wrote a paper in 2021 on the "harms of AI," including potential economic harm (inequality, lost privacy, lost choices) and damage to our political system (by damaging democratic discourse). Acemoglu's summary is a model of academic thought in that he discusses these costs while also noting that there is "no conclusive evidence suggesting that these costs are imminent or substantial" and that the costs are "not inherent to the nature of AI technologies, but are related to how they are being used and developed at the moment—to empower corporations and governments against workers and citizens."[33]

This kind of nuanced approach—not only skeptical but also skeptical of its own skepticism—probably reflects something close to the mainstream view of those who have thought about AI in any serious way. But it is hard to get a headline about how AI may be both overhyped and problematic when others are willing to offer quotes about bombing data. In fact, some who share Acemoglu's view have suggested that our AI conversations would be immediately improved if we simply started calling AI something less science-fiction sounding and more descriptive of the actual technology. They're right, of course—but we have no way of getting there because hype sells, and, unfortunately, hype is now sold with a dose of "expertism": the hype is real this time, we are told, because experts say so. (Never mind that those experts are those who sell the technology and thus have the most to gain from hyping it or those who hope to profit off AI by styling themselves as AI ethicists.)

As an example of how even apparent balance can generate hype, look at a paragraph in a *New York Times* profile of Sam Altman, the chief executive of OpenAI. (The profile has other flaws, such as skipping over Altman's other eccentric projects, including Worldcoin, which proposes to create fake money, give it to everyone, and protect it with scans of their irises.) In the profile, this is how the *Times* summarizes the reaction to ChatGPT: "Some believe it will deliver a utopia where everyone has all the time and money ever needed. Others believe it could destroy humanity. Still others spend much of their time arguing that the technology is never as powerful as everyone says it is, insisting that neither nirvana nor doomsday is as close as it might seem."[34] Which of these three sentences is the wordiest and least compelling? It's not hard to see why the third sentence won't ever make for a good headline—even if it represents the "messy middle." And, unfortunately, that messy middle is probably where the truth almost always lies.

During the pandemic, the best way to get headlines was to make wild predictions—that COVID-19 would kill nearly everybody or nobody at all (as the law professor Richard Epstein famously did when he predicted fewer than 500 deaths, only to concede a math error and that he had meant to predict 5,000 deaths). Of course, these predictions, even the most scientifically dressed-up ones, were universally terrible. The most-referenced model throughout 2020, the Institute for Health Metrics and Evaluation at the University of Washington, was disliked by almost every epidemiologist asked about it.[35] Yet in part because of its readily available, exact-looking, and often extreme predictions and in part because it had extensive funding and marketing behind it (from the Gates Foundation, among other funders), it captivated press coverage and policymaking. That continued even when its forecasts repeatedly turned out to be badly wrong. A little bit of epistemic humility would have helped everyone.

*   *   *

The ivory tower increasingly plays along with and even encourages journalistic exaggeration rather than keeping it in check. For all sorts of reasons, academics want the prestige of popular press coverage—because they are human, because there is money in becoming established as an expert, and because universities increasingly value "public engagement" in making promotion and other decisions. There is nothing inherently wrong with engagement. Staying locked in the "ivory tower" and never speaking to the public isn't good, either. But when the rules of public engagement primarily reward exaggeration and rarely punish you for being wrong, the incentive structure becomes quite dangerous.

In 2014, several researchers examined nearly 500 press releases on scientific findings, alongside the original papers and the resulting news coverage. What they found makes clear that academia itself holds direct responsibility for exaggeration. News articles that exaggerated were "strongly associated with exaggeration in press releases." Those press releases frequently left out significant limitations and nuance that were necessary to interpret the result. The researchers blame the "increasing culture of university competition and promotion" as well as journalistic haste.[36] To be sure, the original authors of the underlying scholarship may well have had no hand in writing those press releases, having left that task to their universities' publicity offices. But that hardly absolves universities of blame because misleading, exaggerated, and misrepresented findings in the press ultimately stem from claims made by universities themselves.

Other researchers have documented the skyrocketing usage of words such as *robust, novel, innovative,* and *unprecedented* in abstracts of scientific findings.[37] The same happens outside science, too. In an article on "academic hype," cheekily titled "'Our Striking Results Demonstrate . . . ,'" two scholars found significant increases (roughly doubling per paper) in "hype" words over the past 50 years across a range of disciplines.[38] Young law professors are routinely told to assert that their paper is "the first ever" of its kind and appear to be rewarded for such novelty claims with better law review placements.

We are reminded of a meeting of law professors discussing "publicly engaged scholarship" and how to be a public intellectual. One faculty member raised a provocative claim: Is it possible that giving quotes to the *Times* or writing op-eds is inherently antithetical to the academic creed? To be successful, op-eds require making a strong argument and taking a strong stand. By contrast, most academic work requires carefully considering counterarguments and taking opposing ideas seriously—even at times *making* the best versions of those arguments—at a length and depth that would generally be impossible in a soundbite. So, he suggested, perhaps it is inherently impossible to be a "public intellectual." The most revealing part of the story is what happened next: not a single person took up his query, and the other participants eagerly returned to brainstorming how to get placements for op-eds in more famous newspapers.

Toward Epistemic Humility

The problems in the systems that produce academic knowledge are concerning. Still more concerning is the unwillingness to face up to these problems. Unfortunately, most elites seem now to equate legitimate questions about expertise and its misuse with illegitimate attacks on the entire enterprise of science and knowledge.[39] Especially if one is concerned about the latter, what elites do in circling the wagons is no better. This defensive posture reflects a narrow conception of the production of expertise and ultimately serves as little more than a kind of gatekeeping that tries to block outsider critiques. Rather than owning up to the limitations of expertise—which are inherent to the production of knowledge—elites ground their behavior in fear of misinformation. But this reasoning leads elites to some scary places, such as the belief that it's acceptable to communicate falsehoods to serve the greater good. By failing to grapple with the distrust of experts, elites only confirm their populist critics' sense that the system of expertise is antipluralist and antidemocratic.

Systematic issues in expertise do not undermine the enterprise. Those interested in metasciences, such as Ioannidis, study the problems that plague scholarship precisely in the hopes of improving scholarship. Nobody thinks researchers should throw in the towel. Rather, the shortcomings of the research method should suggest that a degree of epistemic humility or at least of carefulness is warranted when attempting to use knowledge to settle debate. But Ioannidis's central claim about problems in research is sometimes criticized in a very telling way. The critics don't think his claim is wrong. Rather, they think it will be misused by cranks who want to dismiss science they don't like. This is not a legitimate criticism of Ioannidis's work. It is borne out of fear and a desire for power rather than what should be the basic motivations behind research: curiosity and a love of knowledge.

A particular problem with the kind of "expertise" that Nichols and other elites celebrate is that it is blind to the quality of expertise. Because it has little substance other than credentialism, it cannot distinguish between research that is efficacious and research that is just noise. And it is impossible to create a magic wand that selects for true research and eliminates false research.

The solution to this problem is to do what academia has always done: engage in debate, dissent, discussion, repeated testing, and eventually consensus—but always a tentative consensus that in turn gives way to more debate, dissent, and revision of theories. Alas, this is not the kind of expertise that elites seem to have in mind when they tell us to "defer to experts." Expertise is a process, but they want to define it as an outcome.

On top of that, data are rarely unambiguous. They require our interpretation. The data sciences are really a form of storytelling—one driven by rigor, we hope, but nonetheless subject to all kinds of interpretive bias. So "more data" does not inherently mean "more knowledge," any more than a personal library with more books necessarily makes its owner smarter or well read. The accumulation of facts is not the same as wisdom.

Are we exaggerating when we say there is a growing case among intellectuals that *favors* public exaggeration and even minor deception as long as it is in the service of what they consider a good cause? We think not. As we detail in chapters 8 and 9, many elites are openly making the case that uncertainty and doubt should be suppressed. This climate of intellectual tyranny even features calls for a move away from evidence-based medicine on the fear that it is too easily misused.[40] During the pandemic, academics frequently wrote in *opposition* to randomized-control trials. Their reasons made little sense, so the best explanation was that these authors feared that such trials, if run, would not support their desired outcome. One column, published after Cochrane's review of the evidence on masks came to the conclusion that masks probably weren't effective in slowing the pandemic, was headlined "Randomized Controlled Trials Are the Worst Way to Answer the Question."[41] This assertion quickly garnered praise from many mask zealots, both inside science and outside it. But it is nonsense: RCTs *are* a good way to capture data on a population-wide intervention. Cluster RCTs are a specific method designed precisely for the problem of studying the effects of a policy on a wider group. More alarmingly, the authors of this column wrote that "RCTs have value only when researchers can be sure that the treatment is administered as intended." This is simply false. Researchers commonly do measure "intention to treat," which takes into account the possibility that a patient may not comply with a particular regimen. What we needed to know more about in the pandemic was the effectiveness of a policy, a mandate, or a recommendation that people wear masks. That scientists are now trumpeting the virtues of *not* collecting good evidence is a disturbing manifestation of the growing intellectual case against open inquiry.

In our first chapter, we talked about the elite belief in technocracy and perfectionism. Once one has decided that there is a singular, oracular science that can dispassionately decide complex policy issues, it becomes easy to exclude others. Of course, this belief rests on faulty premises: problems usually rely on multiple domains, some of which are more about values and less about expertise. And, even less noticed, not all problems are solvable—especially not in a world of scarce resources and competing priorities. By leaving decisions to an elite few and by labeling even good-faith backlash as disinformation, this attitude also inhibits the development of much-needed public trust—a resource whose value elites discount.

Owning up to the ambiguity of research frightens elites. If your mindset revolves around a singular, oracular science that can dispassionately decide complex policy issues, it becomes easy to exclude those who have a contrary opinion on the basis that they are ignorant and unable to handle complexity. And it is easy to fear that any questions about science will undermine your basis for governing. An instrumental view of research—as a way of producing public policy—leads inevitably to a protectionist, defensive stance toward research. The foundational premises of this worldview are faulty. Problems usually rely on multiple domains, some of which are more about values and less about expertise. Moreover, not all problems are solvable—especially not in a world of scarce resources and competing priorities. Seen from a different perspective, the mistakes in expertise are, in fact, part of the system at work. Through testing, retesting, debating, engaging with novel and strange ideas, we have a better hope of arriving at answers. More elites would benefit from a mindset of open inquiry like that of Dana Carney, the academic we mention at the start of this chapter who revised her opinion on power posing.

Most policy conflict is not a game where your opponent is badly intentioned. When you assume your opponent argues in bad faith, you do not attempt to engage in what should be the most basic behavior of any academic: to understand the strengths of opposing arguments and identify the weaknesses in your own. That simple kind of epistemic humility is the foundation of knowledge. But it is now under attack—and this particular attack, unlike others, comes from the managerial elite. We have more to say about that in chapter 9. But first we turn our attention to a group that has a finely tuned radar for elites' hypocrisy and internecine warfare: populists.

II Calling Their Bluff: Populists against Experts

5   Misunderstanding Populism

Populism is best understood by looking at populist voters, not politicians who court their votes, as many commentators have. Populism is a reaction to elites running along cultural, economic, and political dimensions and caused by the absence of opportunities for exit and voice.

In the winter of 2018–2019, France witnessed protests by citizens adorned in yellow vests. The *gilets jaunes* protested in response to President Emmanuel Macron's government raising taxes on diesel-fueled cars and trucks. The effects of this perhaps noble aspiration fell disproportionately on working-class citizens, largely in the French countryside. The protests widened and were not clearly aligned with any one political ideology.[1] Most seemed to agree that the government had fallen utterly out of touch with the working person and had little regard for how its policies would affect ordinary voters. The protests forced Macron to abandon the tax after protracted demonstrations across France, although it did little to dampen his technocratic-centrist proclivities. In 2023, a new wave of protests and strikes arose in response to his government's decision to increase the retirement age. The lingering feeling of a government both out of touch with the electorate and aloof from its needs would not subside.

Populism has been called many things, most of them bad: an existential threat to democracy; the final desperate howl of a dwindling horde of angry white men; a divisive tactic exploited by corrupt politicians to dupe witless voters. Even writers more inclined to understand what drives populist voters draw attention to populism's apparent irrationality. We see it differently. Populism is better understood as a rational form of politics, a tactic that responds to elite overreach and to a powerful sense of voiceless-ness.[2] Although populism can certainly manifest in emotional and even destructive forms, its tactics are designed to create an alternative in the face of being told by elites that there are no alternatives.

Discussions of populism are muddied by myths. For instance, populism is regularly invoked to explain Donald Trump's surprise election in 2016. But what does that mean? Calling Trump's election a "populist victory" conflates a complex coalition, as happens in any election. Were some of Trump's supporters populists, and was this important in understanding his surprise upset, including in previously blue states? Yes, absolutely. But that analysis sometimes obscures the equally important fact that *most* Trump supporters were not populists but rather mainline conservative Republicans. A well-off suburban voter, who loyally votes Republican and casts their ballot for Trump in the hopes of a lower tax bill, is neither a populist nor a challenge to the narrative of populism playing a role in the election.[3] Further confusion arises when we ask if Trump himself is a populist. There are numerous inconsistencies in Trump's record, such as populist rhetoric and policies on trade yet plutocratic economic choices in many other areas.[4] Such inconsistencies are hardly a challenge to populism as a movement, only a reminder that any candidate represents a flawed vessel for the hopes of multiple constituents of voters.[5]

Populism has become muddied because most analysts who study it start with a strongly held conclusion—that it poses a threat to democracy—and then magnify its ugliest sides.[6] The predictable results are contorted explanations that overtly exclude or quietly ignore left-leaning populists such as Bernie Sanders and Elizabeth Warren in the United States, the Syriza and Podemos parties in Europe, and various forms of Latin American populism. Few of those analysts show sustained interest in understanding what motivates populist voters. Many focus on politicians, and their work represents theories of demagoguery more than theories of populism. These supply-side theories fail to explain populist politicians' appeal or do so only by dismissing wide swaths of the electorate as stupid or misinformed.

In an article now more than half a century old, the philosopher W. B. Gallie described certain concepts as "essentially contested."[7] Concepts such as "justice" and "beauty," for example, are essentially contested because there exists widespread disagreement about the criteria that would satisfy their proper use in any given instance. The perennially contestable nature of these concepts sets them apart from most of language, and it is their fate to be forever debated and to largely escape any hope of settled meaning.

Is "populism" an essentially contested concept?[8] We think not. However, we acknowledge that there is widespread debate about the meaning of the term.[9]

In this chapter, we evaluate a leading account of populism, that of the political theorist Jan-Werner Müller, which represents the challenges in understanding populism by looking at populist politicians.[10] We then turn to an account that is more sympathetic to the concerns of populist voters from the British academics Roger Eatwell and Matthew Goodwin. Finally, we argue that populism across history and across the globe is a single phenomenon. As with any complex concept, populism has family resemblances to and evident differences from other concepts (e.g., think of populism versus nationalism). Properly understood, populism has three dimensions: economic, cultural, and political. Different dimensions will be accentuated or minimized in different institutional and cultural contexts. Populism is a proclivity found in the general population. It is not the province of any particular group. In fact, the spirit of populism can be found in places many would not think to look for it.

Our book began by identifying the overreaching claims and accompanying failures of contemporary elites. Ultimately, nothing incites populist ire more than the record of elite foul-ups—that is, the disasters visited upon the citizenry by the experts deployed by the elite class. Populists have a keen radar for the hypocrisy of elites. The progressive commentator Thomas Frank provides a succinct populist-tinged take on this litany of failures: "We are living through a period of elite failure every bit as spectacular as that of the 1890s. I refer not merely to the opioid crisis, the bank bailouts, and the failure to prosecute any bankers after their last fraud-frenzy; but also to disastrous trade agreements, stupid wars, and deindustrialization . . . basically, to the whole grand policy vision of the last few decades, as it has been imagined by a tiny clique of norm-worshipping D.C. professionals and think tankers."[11]

The rejection of this establishment is the key to understanding populism. The economist Albert O. Hirschman famously described the ultimatum of "exit or voice": when faced with a deteriorating situation, one can leave (exit) or do something, such as vote or protest (voice).[12] Populism responds to contemporary forces of globalization and neoliberalism that have made the costs of either strategy higher than ever. Proponents of globalization and neoliberalism admit this, quite proudly, when they proclaim the inexorable march of neoliberal progress.[13] Margaret Thatcher and Angela Merkel famously declared that voters had "no alternative" or were "*alternativlos.*" Populism is how voters respond when elites tell them, "You have no choice."

Populists or Demagogues?

A leading explanation of contemporary populism, Jan-Werner Müller's *What Is Populism?* (2016), demonstrates the pitfalls that plague even sophisticated analysts of the phenomenon. Müller advances a clear account of populism, but he is focused largely on what we call the "supply side" of populism, or those politicians who seek to capitalize on populist foment. From the outset, Müller identifies populism with political actors. He is quite explicit in his focus: "to give an account of what kind of political actor qualifies as populist."[14]

The populist political actor embodies two traits. First, he is representative of "the real people." Populists are "antipluralist" in that "they, and only they, represent the people." As the people's representative, they are aligned "against elites who are deemed corrupt or in some other way morally inferior."[15] The core of Müller's account of populism is that it is a form of identity politics. It is all a matter of "us versus them." The populists are the real deal, the only true members of the polity.

Müller considers what populists do when they enjoy power. Strongly against the notion that populists lack the ability to govern, he suggests that populists employ three techniques to govern: the occupation of the state, mass clientism, and the repression of civil society. Populists turn the state to partisan advantage, principally by installing "their people" in civil service positions, thereby taking control of state institutions. This behavior, he maintains, is not "illiberal democracy" but rather a form of "defective democracy."[16]

Finally, there is the matter of how to respond to populists. Populism is, well, popular, and Müller acknowledges this, but he thinks it is possible to take populists' claims "seriously without taking them at face value." His recommended approach, which he paints broadly, is one of building majorities within polities by bringing in the excluded without marginalizing the currently powerful.[17]

Much of Müller's book, in particular his discussions of what populists do once elected, do not help us understand populism as a movement. These discussions are really more theories of demagoguery. They tell us little about why voters choose populists in the first place. The successes such politicians have once in office, moreover, are not necessarily best character-ized as "populist" policies because no politician is the perfect representa-tive of their voters and especially because most politicians are elected by coalitions with divergent agendas. Trump may have enjoyed the support of many populists, but his tax policies, to take one example, seem more use-fully chalked up to traditional mainline Republicans, not to the small cadre of populists who focused on his protectionist trade rhetoric.

In an article published in the *London Review of Books* in 2019, Müller reprised his account of populism, adding texture to the three-part view just described. Here, he seems more inclined to understand populism as a response, in part, to failures of elites. He offers a sharp warning to elites:

> Not everything right-wing populists have done in government is a reflection of what the people wanted. Liberals should stop moaning that democracy is dying because "the people" don't care for it any more; their critics on the left have to do more than argue that democracy was never really born in the first place because our existing political institutions were shaped by racism and sexism. Not everything that populists say about elites is necessarily wrong—the talk of rigged economies resonates for a reason. . . . There has to be more to [liberals] than being "anti-populist": they have to start to figure out what they actually stand for.[18]

We will have more to say about the motivations of populist voters. We turn now to another account of populism, one that pays closer attention to populist voters than populist politicians.

The "Four D's" of National Populism

Roger Eatwell and Matthew Goodwin engage more deeply with the senti-ments of populist voters in their account of the phenomenon, *National Pop-ulism: The Revolt against Liberal Democracy* (2018). As their title suggests, they focus less on populist politicians and more on wider cultural tendencies, the attitudes of ordinary citizens who identify with the populist credo. They posit that national populism, far from a movement of a dwindling number of "angry white men," is just getting started.[19] They see the phenomenon as an exercise in ideas. It is those ideas that make their account of interest.

For Eatwell and Goodwin, nationalism is the missing ingredient that adds coherence to the "thin ideology" of populism. By itself, populism is a set of ideas that pits the masses against distant and corrupt elites. National-ism is characteristic of its current manifestation in Europe. This national-ism is grounded not in ethnicity but in "the belief that you are part of a group of people who share a common sense of history and identity and who are linked by a sense of mission or project."[20] This nationalism is "ter-ritorially bounded," thereby differentiating it from a basis in ethnic or reli-gious groups, and it involves more than love of one's homeland, which is often referred to as "patriotism." The maintenance of national identity and the desire to preserve it from radical change complete the picture.

The authors categorize the causes of national populism into the "four D's": *distrust, destruction, deprivation,* and *dealignment.* Distrust is directed at "elites." Nonelites feel their values are rejected by their better-educated, elite fellow citizens. To take one example, identity politics—a hallmark of cosmopolitan elite culture—is deployed to remind the working classes of their inferior status. Eatwell and Goodwin note that Gallup "found that 73 percent of Americans felt that political correctness had become a seri-ous problem in their country." But no such sentiment could be found in the C suite, liberal media outlets, or universities, where it is heresy to sug-gest that political correctness is even a problem. They find that the "politi-cal correctness agenda" has increased support for populism, quoting the work of a team of psychologists who in 2016 conducted research on restric-tions on communication norms and "found that priming people to think about political correctness—about the fact that there are norms in society that discourage them from saying anything that is offensive to particular groups—led them to become more supportive of Trump."[21]

The second of their four categories is "destruction." What they have in mind is destruction of national identity. The most global terms in which to discuss national identity are cosmopolitanism versus the national state. Much has been written about both the disappearance of the nation-state and its ongoing vitality. Despite critiques of the idea of national identity or pride by cosmopolitan-minded elites, it should surprise no one that "many people still feel very committed to their nation state."[22] By the same token, many voters are disenchanted with the apparatus of globalization, such as the EU. The numbers suggest that one-third of Europeans have a "negative view" of the EU.[23]

Attitudes toward immigration represent a stark divide between elites and populists in both the United States and the United Kingdom. For instance, "elites were more than twice as likely as the public to reject the ideas that immigration makes crime worse and puts a strain on the welfare state." Many with a favorable view of their nation see immigration as a threat. The concerns are not just economic in nature but also cultural. How is this cultural anxiety tied to immigration? Across ten European countries, "55 percent of respondents agreed that all further immigration from Muslim states should be stopped." Eatwell and Goodwin argue that this view relates in part to voters' understanding of national values. A long-standing commitment to gender equality sits uneasily with what is perceived to be the Islamic view of gender roles. Others are anxious about the loss of traditional markers of citizenship, such as learning the language of the host country. Large majorities in countries as diverse as the Netherlands, the United Kingdom, France, Germany, Greece, and Poland "feel that speaking the language is very or somewhat important."[24]

Yet these attitudes are largely ignored by elites; "the values of many people in politics and the media mean that they accept or celebrate these ethnic differences." Elites assume that those who are skeptical of immigration or its consequences are simply racist. But Eatwell and Goodwin argue that this assumption misunderstands the source of the clash, which is actually over widely shared cultural values. Racism, they argue, has actually diminished as a force in social life. Consider this question: "Would you feel comfortable if one of your relatives married somebody from a different ethnic group?" This question, they argue, "is a classic marker of traditional racism, and yet across much of the West the number of people who would feel uncomfortable has plummeted." In 1958, "more than 90 percent of Americans disapproved of interracial marriage. Today, 90 percent approve." The same is true in Britain.[25]

Eatwell and Goodwin turn their lens on the lives of ordinary people in Western economies in their discussion of deprivation. They identify neoliberalism, which they characterize as "market fundamentalism," as the root cause of decreased economic opportunities. As stagflation (inflation coupled with slower growth) took hold in the West, the middle classes suffered. Citing Thomas Piketty, Eatwell and Goodwin argue that "inequalities have returned to levels that were last seen over 100 years ago."[26]

What matters most to people drawn to Trump and Brexit, expressing the populist sentiment, is their state of mind—that is, their "subjective perceptions about how their own position and that of their wider group is changing compared to others in society." The scope of this angst is wide-spread as it "extends to full-time workers, parts of the middle class and also young voters."[27]

Eatwell and Goodwin are relentless in their emphasis that more is involved in the rise of national populist sentiment than pure numerical measures of economic output. Citing a study by the Harvard scholars Noam Gidron and Peter Hall, they make the point that neoliberal economic policies "[have] impacted strongly on people's perceived levels of respect, recognition and status relative to others in society." Having borne the ill effects of globalization, the financial crisis of 2008, and the decline in manufacturing work, many have "succumbed to opioid drug addiction."[28] Given all this, it is no wonder that many in America react to Hillary Clinton's dismissal of Trump voters as a "basket of deplorables" because of their resounding embrace of anti-elite policies and politics.

The final category for Eatwell and Goodwin is "dealignment." This cause of national populism is all about political parties and the realignment from the traditional to the extreme. Donald Trump, Marine Le Pen, and Matteo Salvini provide evidence of deep discontent with traditional political parties. As is well known, loyalty to traditional parties was a feature of postwar politics in both Europe and the United States. This loyalty began to erode in the 1960s and 1970s. Today in Europe, the antileft sentiment fueled what Eatwell and Goodwin describe as the "sudden rise of national populists like Jean-Marie Le Pen in France and Jorg Haeder in Austria, who were likewise symptoms of this emerging divide in values between liberals and traditionalists, as well as a growing gap between people and older political parties."[29]

People have drifted away from traditional political parties. As Eatwell and Goodwin note, "By 2009 the percentage of people who did not feel close to any political party had increased to 45 percent." Brexit confirmed the depth and breadth of dissatisfaction with traditional parties. The percentage of Labour districts in the United Kingdom who voted for Brexit was nothing less than shocking to traditional politicians. Citing a representative example, Eatwell and Goodwin point to "the working-class northern Labour district of Doncaster, where more than seven in ten had voted for Brexit."[30]

There is no greater evidence of an electorate's unhappiness with traditional parties than the election of Donald Trump in 2016. It is not Trump's election per se that is important but the switch in voter preferences from previous elections. More than "8 million of Obama's voters went to Trump, allowing him to win four states that Obama had carried in both 2008 and 2012. The key switchers were whites without degrees."[31] The situation in Europe is much the same, with support for political figures such as Angela Merkel and Emmanuel Macron experiencing pronounced volatility. And, of course, there is Italy. The technocratic government of Mario Draghi collapsed as populist support for his government was withdrawn. A populist government, led by Giorgia Meloni, was elected in its place. None of this bodes well for the future of traditional parties in Europe.

Culture and Resentment

As we see it, there are three dimensions to populism: cultural, economic, and political. In the United States, populism's cultural dimension begins with the diploma divide, which we discussed in chapter 2. The consequences of the diploma divide are not just economic: just as notable is the growing schism between the one-third of adults who have a college diploma and the remaining two-thirds with respect to their values and belief systems. Although the white working class do not hold exclusive claim to the moniker *populist*, they are probably the best-known populist demographic in the United States in part because they carried special relevance in explaining Trump's surprise victory and equally in explaining how Biden managed to beat Trump by winning back (some) white working-class voters, especially in Pennsylvania, Wisconsin, and Michigan.[32]

In her work, Joan Williams goes a long way in identifying the salient characteristics of one of the prime repositories of populist sentiment. An interesting feature of the white working class is not their disdain for elites but their embrace of the rich, which might seem paradoxical. As Williams explains, drawing extensively on sociologists' research on voters who are often ignored by academics and the urban coastal-focused media, the divide is more a matter of class than money. The professional elites send their children to private schools, shop at Whole Foods, and get their coffee at an espresso bar. The white working class celebrates family and religion. Elites love their kids but don't speak to them nearly as much as working-class folk.[33] In short, for the white working class it is "family first"; for elites, career, networks, and setting up children for a life in the professional classes are priorities.

Nothing separates the white working class more from the elite, professional class than education. Williams captures this aspect brilliantly with the comment: "Educational levels do not just reflect social class, they are constitutive of it. Graduating from college is a class act that both enacts class status and reproduces it."[34] Elites see college as a "class escalator," which takes you to the top through education and investment. But to really make the investment in a college education worthwhile, an education at an elite college or university is preferred. Alas, the system is rigged against those who do not come from the ranks of the economically well heeled. According to the *New York Times*, 38 colleges—including five Ivy League institutions—have more students from the top 1 percent than from the entire bottom of the income distribution.[35]

What is the cost, if any, of the sneering attitude of successful, professional members of the elite managerial class? In his work on the corrosive effects of meritocracy, Michael Sandel gets it right: "The relentless credentialism of our day has driven working-class voters toward populist and nationalist parties and deepened the divide between those with and without a university degree."[36] As the United States continues to evolve (or descend) into two nations comprising red and blue states, elites have to be held accountable—at least in part—for the degradation in our politics. When the president of the United States gives a speech in front of Constitutional Hall where he openly derides those who voted for his predecessor, one has to wonder what it will take for the credentialed elite class to realize how much they contribute to the fractured state of politics in the United States.[37] It is simply not the case that those who are smarter, better educated, and drink espresso are more worthy of respect than those who work with their hands without the benefit of a four-year university education. And yet, as President Biden's speech made clear, we are a long way from recognition of the importance of including nonelite voices in the conversation about our collective political and social life.

The Death of the American Dream

We turn now to populism's economic dimension. Everyone is familiar with the growth statistic for middle-class wages: they have been stagnant for decades. A recent spike of inflation appears to have cooled (though some items remain stubborn), but shelter (housing) inflation continues to run high. The decline in the percentage of Americans who qualify as "middle class" has been a decades-long phenomenon.[38] There are many reasons for the decline of the middle class in America. Some blame outsourcing and offshoring, while others point to automation. Obviously, both factors have a role to play in explaining the decline in the middle-class standard of living. The anger over the loss of middle-class earning power and its attendant status is palpable. We have not seen any serious effort to stem this decline because, as we argue here, governments have not really grasped the underlying, fundamental problem, which has to do with the changing nature of work in the global economy.

Margaret Thatcher and Ronald Reagan are the political figures most associated with the rise of neoliberalism. Both politicians managed to change the perception of what the state owed citizens and how best to achieve its ends. Deregulation was a strong theme. Equally strong was the notion that when it came to economic opportunity, the job of the state was not to provide sustenance directly but to create to conditions for individual pursuit of economic opportunity.[39] These ideas were the province not only of right-wing thinkers but also of liberal politicians, as both Bill Clinton and Tony Blair championed free trade (Clinton and the North American Free Trade Agreement) and eschewed nationalization of industry (Blair). Clinton and others painted these ideas as an "inexorable force," and elite commentators rushed to praise their benefits for the economy both in the aggregate and individually.[40]

But scores of Americans registered their skepticism about the long-term benefits of globalization.[41] That skepticism became even more widespread after the global financial crisis of 2008, which many saw as another example of elites creating a crisis in which deregulation was the culprit. Characterized as "too big to fail," many banks in the United States and United Kingdom received government bailouts. Add on the Euro crisis on the Continent, and you have another source of fuel for the national populist backlash. Nothing has slowed the rise of anti-elite sentiment. Marine Le Pen in France and Trump's continuing hold on the Republican Party are evidence of this.

Globalization's proponents seriously underestimated its effects on the average working American. Coupled with automation, globalization accounted for the steady decline in domestic manufacturing jobs. When Thomas Friedman published *The World Is Flat* in 2005, elites thought they understood globalization and its impact on work. The explanation was easy. Manufacturing jobs that used to be found in the G7 countries had moved offshore (mainly the Far East, China), taking with them the prosperity that had been enjoyed by middle-class citizens with good manufacturing jobs. That, in a nutshell, was the story: offshoring was largely responsible for the loss of the middle-class level of economic prosperity.

It was against this background that Richard Baldwin published his first book on globalization, *The Great Convergence* (2016). In that book, Baldwin shows how developments in information and communications technology transformed the nature of globalization. His argument starts with the observation that three aspects of an economy require movement: things, ideas, and people. The Industrial Revolution was all about moving things (e.g., agricultural products) from one place to the other. The steam engine and then the internal-combustion engine solved that challenge. With the advent of telecommunications and then high-speed computers, the movement of ideas across the globe became an everyday occurrence. But something radical happened in the 1990s, something that took globalization to a place it had never been before.

The Information Technology Revolution made offshoring hyperprofitable. Not only could an American firm relocate manufacturing to a place with substantially lower labor costs, but it could also control that factory from afar. This development revolutionized global value chains and fundamentally changed the nature of globalization. Bringing first-world knowledge to third-world locales achieved far more than merely relocating manufacturing could provide. Baldwin dubs this configuration the "new globalization." What's new are the knowledge flows, something the first wave of globalization did not enjoy.

Populism arises in part as a response to the results of this kind of globalization. Populists rail against inequality and argue that the working class is being exploited by global manufacturers. In this claim, they are supported by the facts, at least some facts. Offshoring—at least in its initial phase—was driven by the comparative advantage of cheap labor and lax regulation. The people assembling iPhones at Foxconn plants were paid far less than any American worker might have earned, thereby driving down the base price of the phone and increasing Apple's profits. At the same time, China's role as a major contributor to both pollution (air and water) and global warming meant that the externalities created by the manufacturing boom in China would be visited not only upon Chinese workers but also upon the world at large.

There increasingly is and will likely continue to be a tug of war between large firms with manufacturing needs (e.g., Apple), the governments of the countries where they do their work (e.g., China), and the workers who give their labor to the firm in exchange for wages that are a pittance by Western standards. The COVID-19 pandemic and the conflict in Ukraine have cast a new light on the fragility of global supply chains, and the global elite now bandy about new buzzwords such as *reshoring* (bringing production back home) and *friendshoring* (ensuring that production happens in countries with allied political interests). This state of affairs raises the question whether the globalization model of the past 25 years can endure. Against the conventional narrative of globalization, some scholars argue that globalization was never as widespread as its proponents contended. Regionalization, not globalization, is the key to understanding global trade.[42]

The connection between work and populism is a function of the changing nature of work. Baldwin correctly notes that the discourse around populism—by both populists and their opponents—seems unwilling to face what has happened to work, especially manufacturing work. The nature of work has been forever altered by the growth and sophistication attendant to information technology. But things don't stop there. Globotics—the fusion of globalization and robotics—is the next destructive force to hit the middle class. As Nouriel Roubini notes in his recent book *Mega-Threats* (2022), in the fullness of time "robots or globots will replace service workers everywhere." He attributes to Baldwin the prediction of a "'globotics upheaval' ending in a violent confrontation between humans and the machines replacing them."[43] Can such a state of affairs be avoided? Baldwin thinks so but only if (at least in the United States) the government expands social welfare subvention, but this solution has its own problems.

The rise of big tech and the concentration of wealth that accompanies it (we could add the rise of AI) will prove disastrous for the middle classes, a point explored at length by Joel Kotkin.[44] The impending catastrophe is not just about the concentration of wealth, although that has reached unprecedented levels and engendered deleterious results. Rather, Kotkin argues that a new class of serfs is being created. Owning a home—especially in urban centers—is increasingly out of reach for many. Small business—once the bulwark of the US economy—is increasingly finding itself near extinction. Upward mobility is increasingly under threat, as is the ability to express oneself without fear of sanction. In all, a new feudal order is emerging.

Whether things get to the point where Kotkin's thesis is confirmed, there is little doubt that the economic prospects for the middle classes are dim, and no respite appears to be on the horizon. That lack of options, one could argue, is what leads to despair or worse. Once a country gives up on the notion that hard work and perseverance can better one's economic prospects, all manner of social ills is soon to follow. America's opioid crisis is but one example of such a tendency, but it may well be that continued political unrest will also follow as despair takes hold. Moreover, what voters want is not just a paycheck, and universal basic income is unpopular.[45] Esteem, respect, and dignity are as important as a paycheck.[46] To the degree we deny any one of these values to large swaths of the polity, we should not be surprised by their embrace of national populism and its attendant agenda of anti-elitism and equal respect.

An Alternative to No Alternatives

The final dimension of our three-part picture of populism is politics. Government is increasingly perceived as technocratic and elitist, and many elites defend its being so. Populism arises in direct response to this definition of what government should be: although its ideological tenor differs, populism in its American, European, and British manifestations is united by a sense that populist voters expect more from their political life than what they are now getting.

Of the many books authored by the economist and social scientist Albert O. Hirschman, his most well-known work is *Exit, Voice, and Loyalty*, published in 1970. The book is first and foremost an inquiry into human behavior. As mentioned previously, when faced with a deteriorating quality of life, be it political, economic, or cultural, citizens have two choices: they can either exercise their "voice" in criticism of their government, or they can "exit."[47] Exit is not an option for most people: they cannot just pick up and leave their country. But what about voice? Aren't people free to exercise voice by voting for different political parties, ones that at least hold out the prospect of responding to their concerns?

With the rise in social media, disgruntled citizens have found new ways to exercise their voice. And they are. The Tea Party, the UK Independence Party, Trump, and Brexit are examples of ordinary citizens amplifying their voice. But if they already have a voice—indeed, an amplified one—why is the movement toward populism so strong? Why is the demand for populist politicians and policies seeming to grow every day? And why are the demands made in the name of populism so strong and running counter to so much of traditional politics?

Our take is that the loudest voices in the populist camp no longer believe they have a voice in Hirschman's sense. The combination of elite, technocratic politics and the politics of resentment have perverted the normal course of exit and voice, at least as described by Hirschman. Deeply committed populists no longer believe that voice is enough because, we suspect, they feel that no one is listening to them. The populists do not appear to be wrong. After the United Kingdom voted to leave the EU in the Brexit referendum, many commentators suggested that the vote confirmed that important decisions were too important to be left to the people. With exit not viable and voice dwindling, the populist sentiment turns deeply negative and destructive.[48]

Unfortunately, rather than trying to understand, much less learn from, this anger, many elites have dismissed it. We see populism as a series of moves. It begins with a big bluff by elites, who overclaim about their expertise and arrogate public policy to themselves. The populists respond in anger. They are skeptical of the claims of elites and believe that common sense can and should guide policy. Rather than taking these challenges seriously, elites double down on their initial bluff, blaming populism on misinformation, wrongly interpreting disagreement as coming in bad faith, and censoring political discourse. That doubling down is the subject of part III of our book. But first we continue our exploration of populists, turning next to their approach to politics—one grounded in skepticism and a belief that "common sense" can matter in political decision-making.

6   Populist Habits of Mind

Populists believe in common sense and are skeptical of many elites' and experts' claims. Skepticism gets a bad rap these days. This is puzzling because skepticism has such a long and intellectually grounded pedigree. Populists are skeptics, but they aren't wild-eyed global skeptics. As we show in this chapter, their skepticism is grounded in experience and motivated by elite overclaiming. We also ask whether there is something akin to folk wisdom or the insight of the ordinary person. We think there is, and we flesh out this idea.

Mike Coughlin operates the Village Tavern and Grill in Carol Stream, Illinois, serving comfort food, including "world famous" chicken fingers and an enormous Nachorama platter. In March 2020, Governor J. B. Pritzker of Illinois, like many other governors across the country, ordered restaurant dining rooms across the state to shutter. As did other governors, he suggested the closure would last only two weeks, a timeframe that seemed implausible and naive—if not outright mendacious—to many onlookers. But Coughlin, like other restaurateurs, dutifully complied.

It was not until late May that restaurants were given the green light for limited outdoor dining, and still another month passed before Pritzker announced that, following the "overarching guardrails" of "science and data," restaurants could return to (limited) indoor seating.[1] Coughlin faithfully followed the state's guidance throughout. He shelled out tens of thousands of dollars for the Village Tavern to purchase safety equipment, such as air purifiers and booth dividers. Pritzker's administration hailed the midsummer reopening as a sign of progress in "overcoming the virus" and a boon to Illinois businesses.

But in the fall, Pritzker rapidly reversed course, banning indoor dining first in limited counties and then throughout the state in November.[2]

Although his initial spring shutdowns had received support, his surprise backsliding on reopening led to protests and lawsuits.[3] Like many officials during the pandemic, Pritzker seemed uninterested in engaging with commonsense objections levied by critics. Some pointed out that private, in-home gatherings, which were unrestricted, seemed to be bigger contributors to the spread of COVID-19 than limited, distanced indoor seating at restaurants with ventilation and masks. That sort of logical argumentation was of little interest to politicians at this point in the pandemic. It was enough to assert that the data had spoken, even when those data were not shared with the people, contradicted official proclamations, or at least raised important questions about trade-offs.[4]

With this second shutdown, Coughlin decided he wasn't playing anymore. He announced his restaurant would not close, come fines or other consequences. "You pay my bills, you pay my taxes, you pay my employees, and I'll close," he told the *Wall Street Journal*. "I'm not going to be the guy with a boarded-up building because I follow someone else's science."[5] In a later television interview, he added that he felt he had no choice: a second closure would be permanent. He articulately described the pain of having endured almost nine months since the first closure, adopting expensive new methods, pairing back capacity, and still being asked the impossible— with no apparent recognition of the harm it would impose or the hypocrisy in Pritzker's inconsistent orders.[6]

Is Coughlin an enemy of science? No: whatever one thinks of the merits of Pritzker's policy, the inconsistencies critics identified were real, and the shutdowns represented existential threats to Coughlin and many other small-business owners. By 2021, an additional 200,000 small businesses had shuttered in the nation than would normally be expected to close in an average, nonpandemic year. There were also plenty of reasons to be skeptical of the renewed ban, given mixed evidence about the role restaurants played in the spread of COVID-19 and given that restrictions not coupled with economic support are the kind of policies most likely to fail. But, most importantly, agree or disagree with him, Coughlin was not calling the pandemic a hoax. Instead, he was engaging in vigorous protest, even civil disobedience, in support of a good-faith view.

His is the kind of skepticism that interests us. We think skepticism and faith in common sense form the epistemic core of populism. We have no idea of Coughlin's politics, but his story exemplifies the populist spirit—and how easily it is misunderstood. Acutely so during the pandemic, the mainstream media reliably cast aspersions on anyone who doubted the party line. Doubt the oracular sayings of public-health officials, and you were labeled a denialist or fringe conspiracy theorist. This is part of a broader trend in recent years. Elites have cast new doubt on doubt. Thus, Coughlin's story is the rare case of nuanced skepticism—the kind we argue pervades populism—making its way through media coverage.

Americans, especially elites, think that skepticism's more extreme twins, radical skepticism and denialism, are widely pervasive and destructive. Ask Americans about climate change, and many of them assume far more Americans doubt global warming than actually do.[7] The same goes with other conspiracy theories and misperceptions. The result is we misconstrue most skepticism, which is neither radical nor primarily an emotional or tribal phenomenon. Dismissing it or attempting to extirpate it is antidemocratic and unhelpful. It fuels populism, which exists precisely as a response to being dismissed. Most alarming to us, the misdiagnosis of skepticism as misinformation and disinformation has led elites and experts to adopt increasingly troubling views about the importance of their own expertise that are inconsistent with science, public judgment, and common sense.

We see populists possessed of a quite traditional epistemic stance: skepticism. Populists are not the antirational, Luddite, know-nothings some of their detractors take them to be; they actually have an epistemology. It is fair to say that skepticism is out of fashion.[8] We think it's odd that such a venerable institution is under attack, so we begin with a survey of the history of skepticism.[9] We account for the importance of skepticism in the history of thought, and we canvas the views of eminent philosophers and critics. We then turn to some examples of populist skepticism, suggesting the appropriateness of populist critique of elite certitudes and discussing how elites commonly misconstrue or mischaracterize this skepticism.

Skepticism derives from another populist habit of mind: a belief in the value of common sense and lay wisdom.[10] In contrast, elite epistemology valorizes narrowly defined expertise, often reduced to credentialism, and technocracy. In chapter 7, we argue that populists have the upper hand on many of these points. But in this chapter, we explore what populists mean by "common sense." Populism has a certain mythology that is expressed in the idea that there is a certain wisdom—call it "folk wisdom"—associated with the common person. We explore how populists have taken the notion of the wisdom of the common person, an idea with a long philosophical pedigree, and politicized it.

We explore skepticism in some detail for three reasons. First, readers unfamiliar with the intellectual history of skepticism may come to appreciate its long lineage in the history of thought. Second, the intellectual history of skepticism enables us to locate the current populist skepticism along the spectrum of classic conceptions of skepticism. When this is done, it turns out that populist skepticism is relatively mild in form, particularly when assessed against the views of philosophers such as René Descartes and David Hume. Finally, we discuss how *skepticism* and *skeptic*, like so many terms in current discourse, are often employed as expressions of derision, which is patently absurd. Skepticism is part and parcel of any serious intellectual undertaking, and it is certainly part of the fabric of science. For all these reasons, a modest discussion of the intellectual history of skepticism is warranted.

The Tradition of Skepticism

It is important to be clear about the form of skepticism we attribute to the populist mindset. As a first approximation, skepticism comes in both moderate and radical forms. We all are moderate skeptics in many aspects of life: it serves us well to be so. Consider the teenaged child who has returned home late on a Friday night. As his parent walks to the edge of the driveway to collect the Saturday paper, she notices a fresh dent in the front fender of the family car, the very car used by her adolescent child the night before. When quizzed by his mother about the origin of the dent in the fender, her young son replies, "I have no idea how that got there. Maybe someone ran into the car overnight?" There can be any number of explanations for the presence of the dent. It is entirely possible that during the night some wayward person walked up the driveway and hit the fender with a hammer. But is that the most plausible explanation? Every parent knows the answer.

Another example. You are in the market for a used car, and you find the model you are looking for at a local used-car dealer. The dealer says to you, "This is a wonderful car: it's in perfect shape. I've had three people look at it this morning: if you want it, you need to act fast." Should you believe the car dealer's representations, or should you first have the car inspected by a reputable mechanic before making a purchase? Here again, it pays to be skeptical of the claims made by the car dealer.

This sort of doubt—let's call it "local skepticism"—is both healthy and entirely unobjectionable. Indeed, this type of skepticism is practiced by all prudent persons all the time. Some claims need to be doubted, and, where possible, reasonable measures need to be taken to verify the veracity of claims made. Contrast this form of skepticism with what me might call "globalized skepticism." With this form of skepticism, rather than some specific proposition (e.g., this car is in top form) being doubted, the possibility of ever knowing anything is posited as being in doubt.

The debates in and around the pandemic were centered on the degree and extent to which one could reasonably be skeptical of the claims of experts. As we have noted, as the pandemic narrative unfolded, many questioned whether it was proper to be skeptical of experts. This legitimate question morphed into the claim that we are now in a "post-truth" environment, one where critics of elites and their preferred policy choices are labeled "denialists," "trolls," or some other form of anti-intellectual Luddite. We discuss this environment in detail in chapter 8. Here we wish to do two things with our discussion of skepticism. First, we wish to remind readers that skepticism is nothing new and that it has a venerable history. Second, we wish to locate populist skepticism against this historical background. In the grand scheme of things, populist skepticism is well within the bounds of the historically available forms of skepticism. Many seem to have forgotten this tradition, so, in our view, a short reminder is in order.

Skepticism is part of a constellation of topics that concern belief, evidence, facts, reasoning, and judgment. Skepticism has a long and distinguished pedigree in the history of philosophy. It comes in ancient and modern forms. Pyrrhonist skepticism traces its origins to Pyrrho of Elis (c. 365–270 BCE). Pyrrho himself wrote nothing, but his pupil, the satirical poet Timon of Phlius, developed the master's rejection of speculative philosophy and the embrace of a thoroughgoing dismissal of all claims to knowledge. Although we can certainly say how things in the world appear to us, we are utterly unable to say how they are in fact. This is not to deny that the world exists outside our minds (this way of thinking is not idealism, after all), but rather to say that we have no way of telling which of our beliefs comports with reality.

Pyrrhonism is clearly an example of global skepticism. Populists are often tagged with the criticism that if they have a view of knowledge at all, it is a form of global skepticism. We consider this claim in chapter 8, but before we do, we need to say a bit more about the history of skepticism and suggest why global skepticism is not quite as fanciful as it might appear at first blush.

In a more modern form in the seventeenth century, the French philosopher René Descartes based his entire approach to knowledge on a methodological commitment to doubt. The "evil-genius hypothesis" gets Descartes's philosophy off the ground, as it were. There is the world, and there are my beliefs about the world. Suppose that all of my beliefs are given to me by an evil genius who plants them in my mind. The view has been given a contemporary expression with the idea of a "brain in a vat."[11] Of course, I experience the world around me through my senses, and I form beliefs on the basis of my perceptions. But it might just be that "I" am nothing more than a brain suspended in a vat. My "beliefs" are the product of input sent to my brain, which is connected to a computer. My brain states, my beliefs, are simply the product of external stimulation having no basis in reality. Whether the doing of an evil genius or a computer, there is no knowledge of anything because I have no impressions of the world outside my brain. I am, to be sure, deceived.

What, one might ask, is the point of this seemingly wild thought experiment? It is to engender uncertainty about our beliefs, specifically our beliefs about the world, which is accomplished by undermining our faith in the ground of those beliefs, our experience. If we cannot trust our experiences, then we really have no basis for any of our beliefs. In short, by undermining the ground of our beliefs, skepticism—indeed, wide-ranging skepticism—gains a foothold.

It is against such arguments that Descartes mounted his method of skeptical doubt. He rejected any beliefs that were the deliverances of the senses because our senses do sometimes deceive us. He rejected our beliefs about physical reality because those beliefs could just be the product of dreams or hallucination. Finally, he rejected the conclusions of logical reasoning because those conclusions might be the product of the work of an evil genius.[12] All told, Descartes looked as if he had joined the camp of global skeptics, which, it becomes evident, he clearly wanted to avoid.

Descartes began to dig his way out of this abyss by asking, "What is the one thing I cannot doubt?" His answer was his own existence: if he was sure of anything, it was that he existed. Hence, his famous dictum "I think, therefore I am" (the Cogito). This observation devolved to the methodological principle of clear and distinct ideas. Whatever we can conceive of—in a clear and distinct fashion—is true. Accepting this principle, Descartes concluded not only that God existed but that God is perfect and, as such, incapable of deceiving us. Descartes believed his method of doubt had grounded epistemology and would save the world from the global skepticism with which he began his investigation.

However, it wasn't long before Descartes's philosophical views came under rigorous scrutiny. The assault came principally from English and Scottish philosophers. The Scottish philosopher David Hume is widely regarded as having made the most trenchant criticisms of Cartesian epistemology. Rather than grounding his approach to knowledge in concepts such as "clear and distinct ideas," Hume concentrated on causal knowledge grounded in experience.

We take ourselves to know many things. Hume's work gives us pause, or should, regarding the degree to which we really know as much as we think we do. Our reasoning takes two forms: deductive and inductive. In deductive reasoning, when we reason from certain premises, we will reach an absolutely certain conclusion. If all A is B, and all B is C, then all A is C. Inductive reasoning is another matter altogether. In inductive reasoning, the premises are true, but the conclusions are only probable, not logically certain. If we see that the sun rises each morning, we can infer that it will do so tomorrow. Although the future is probable, it is not certain.

The gravamen of Hume's account of skepticism is induction. Roughly speaking, induction supposes that the future will be like the past and present. We infer from past events to future events with some degree of certainty. All our knowledge, then, is based on previous experience.[13] We observe the world, and we see what appear to be causal interactions. Just because the sun has risen every day in our lives is no guarantee it will do so tomorrow. Our "knowledge" that the sun will rise tomorrow is not a logical conclusion but rather a prediction based on our experience: it may or may not happen. Because we can imagine the opposite of our prediction obtaining, our knowledge is unlike that of deductive knowledge, or knowledge that is certain.

Owing to the fact that most of our knowledge is the product of inductive reasoning, none of it is certain. This is where Hume's skepticism gains a footing. Empirical facts are grounded in observation. Our knowledge is knowledge of cause and effect. If I throw an apple in the air, it will return to earth. I can do it again and again with the same result. Hume argued that our knowledge from cause and effect is just inductive prediction and not certain knowledge. If we can conceive of an outcome contrary to our experience, then we cannot truly know the future. Cause and effect are not a natural process at all but rather a psychological phenomenon. A favorite example is the game of pool. We can send the white ball into the black again and again. When the white ball strikes the black, energy is transferred from white to black, and the black ball moves. But we can very rightly conceive of the black ball not moving tomorrow when we send the white ball into the black. Thus, we have no knowledge that when we send the white ball into the black tomorrow, the past will repeat itself. In short, we can gain no knowledge through our experiences.

The Humean account of skepticism remains the most well-articulated account of doubt. Despite centuries of attempts to get past Hume's skepticism, no one has been able to make a definitive case. Hume showed that there are real limits to our claims for knowledge. This does not mean that Hume denied the importance of knowledge. His point—indeed, the point of much philosophical skepticism—is that we should be humble in our claims to knowledge, for knowledge is both valuable and easily capable of being defeated in the face of reasonable doubt. Elites would do well to reflect on the fact that their certitude about facts is not nearly as well grounded as they would like. In other words, a bit of humility and a healthy awareness of the limits of certainty on their part would go a long way toward ameliorating the perception that elites are know-it-alls in possession of all the facts. Fine, but what about populists? What does the history of skepticism tell us about populist skepticism? We now turn to this question.

Fear of Skepticism

Most elites assume that populist doubt is unfounded. Populists are blamed for engendering a "post-truth" environment where misinformation and denialism are rampant. We emphasize that this assumption rests on a faulty empirical understanding about the role misinformation plays in our society. In chapter 8, we show that misinformation explains far less about our contemporary politics than elites would like. But for now, we are interested in understanding how elites construe populist skepticism.

Populists express doubts about many of the claims politicians and their experts deploy. Of course, it is not enough to have doubts about the knowledge claims of experts: doubt, to be rational, has to be grounded. As Ludwig Wittgenstein argued, ungrounded doubt is an impossibility, not an epistemic stance.[14] Doubt, like belief, has to be grounded. Thus, the views held by Descartes and Hume—seemingly global skeptics—might need to be tempered. Further, in assessing populist doubt, we must consider whether it is in fact grounded in reasonable objections to claims of expertise and is not just another form of global skepticism.

It strikes us as a bit peculiar that we need to defend skepticism given its long intellectual pedigree, especially among academics. In the context of intellectual culture, with its practice of tenure, skepticism should precisely be the type of practice that would be defended or encouraged. Skeptical inquiry is of the essence of the academic temperament. Or so we thought.

Yet today the conventional wisdom seems to be that skepticism is shoddy at best and perhaps dangerous. The philosopher Duncan Pritchard believes that wholesale skeptical doubt has led to a general "lack of concern for accuracy and the truth" in society.[15] Such a claim disparages populist skepticism not with arguments but with fallacious dismissals of populist sensibilities. As mentioned throughout this book, our primary focus is on the quality of discourse and argument in the public sphere. We believe that the populist impulse to skepticism is a healthy part of public debate about matters of public policy and that elite discourse improperly punishes this skeptical impulse.

Some scholars believe that skepticism regarding science, or "science skepticism," has become a defining feature of our age.[16] Skeptics, it seems, will never believe anything no matter how much evidence they are given. A *Guardian* editor accused dissenting scientists—some of whom count among the most influential medical scientists of recent decades—of being "agents of disinformation" for questioning received opinion regarding evidence and policy.[17] Anthony Fauci frequently talked about how his greatest problem was the widespread belief across America that COVID-19 was a hoax or nonexistent. Although this claim allowed him to pass the buck, the data did not support his observation. In fact, the vast majority of Americans were well aware that COVID-19 posed a threat. Disagreement centered not around the existence of a pandemic, but around the appropriate policies to adopt in response. In claiming that Americans were in denial of COVID-19, Fauci implicitly pigeonholed plausible, mainstream beliefs—such as the 41 percent of Americans who believed that "the threat of the coronavirus is being exaggerated for political reasons"—into the category of fringe conspiracies.[18]

It is common, indeed all too common, for social scientists to see skepticism as a psychological state bordering on an affliction.[19] The common trope in these discussions is to disparage common sense because it is "mobilized as a political argument against elites." Some go so far as to suggest that the common folk "think differently" by privileging firsthand experience over scientific evidence. The privileging is motivated by the belief that common sense "is virtuous and legitimate because it rests on authentic and unmediated everyday experience."[20]

This fear of skepticism ignores two important points. First, common sense—like skepticism—has long played a role in public life, a point we return to later in this chapter. Second, it assumes that the flip side of populist skepticism is an even-headed evaluation of the evidence when in fact the most educated often become the mirror image of the radical skeptics they oppose: dug-in believers regardless of evidence. *Cultural cognition* is the term for one school of research that has shown how our identity shapes our perception of information.[21] (Its findings are similar to those arrived at by other fields of research.) For instance, we tend to overcredit evidence that reflects our commitment to a particular group or belief system. We believe that if we fail to do that, we may lose status within our group, so agreement becomes more important than accuracy. Counterintuitively, the result is that more knowledge can actually make you *more* susceptible to misinformation because it is easier to figure out how to accept information that confirms your priors and to reject information that weakens it.[22]

What about populists—don't they get dug in, too? Populist rhetoric is often characterized by certainty, dogmatism, Manicheanism, and/or authoritarianism.[23] Recall, however, that populism responds to elite overconfidence. Elite overconfidence—claims made with utter certainty even in the face of obvious logical holes—comes first. Populists are skeptical of that unwarranted elite certainty. Their skepticism—hardly of the "global" variety—results in vigorous protest and can occur in different directions depending on the choices that elites make.

Failing to see skepticism at the heart of populism can lead to problems, even for commentators who seek to take populism seriously. Some elites may sympathize with the dissent but simultaneously assume that the experts are right. That is, they want to understand where the populists are coming from, but they also believe that the experts and elites with whom the populists disagree are correct. One of the only ways for them to resolve this incompatibility is to posit that external forces, such as misinformation, are leading the populists astray. We now see this explanation at play in how many scholars approached the surprising results when England voted to leave the EU in 2016. Aside from failing to understand voter preferences, this view can lead to some dark places: if the optimal level of disagreement with expert advice is considered to be zero, any means that can get us there is worth it. This is what gives rise to the intellectual tyranny prevalent among elites.

What is our point? Elite critique of populist skepticism is hyperbolic. Skepticism is not the same as radical denialism, nor is it a psychological affliction. The history of skepticism alone puts the lie to elite claims about populist sentiments. Populists are not substituting a form of intuition for scientific knowledge, feelings for facts. Rather, they are raising questions about the factual claims made by elites when those claims are grounded more in policy preferences than in facts, scientific or otherwise. Instead of denigrating populist questioning of elite certitudes, perhaps a better response is to admit that many policy matters are a matter of both facts *and* values and that some values (i.e., those of ordinary folks) are as worthy of protection as other values (i.e., elite preferences).

Misdiagnosing Brexit

Let's focus the lens a bit and look at a real-life political event. Consider Brexit as a case study in willfully misunderstanding why voters are motivated to make a choice—chalking up a preference to misinformation and ignorance. As all will know, in 2020 Great Britain left the European Union following a vote in 2016 in which a little more than 51 percent of those voting voted to leave. In the days and weeks leading up to the vote, many disputed claims were aired in both legacy and social media. Perhaps the most hotly contested claim was that £350 million a week would be saved if Britain left the EU.[24]

But we are not here to debate the economics of Brexit. Our interest lies in explaining why the Brexit vote occurred as it did. The conventional narrative has always been that those who voted to leave the EU were "ignorant" or worse. A frequently made claim was that the lower one's educational level, the greater the likelihood that one voted to leave. In other words, the less-educated people in Britain are responsible for the decision to leave.

How did elites interpret the Brexit vote? After initial shock, the elite narrative converged on misinformation and our "post-truth" environment. Leavers were naive dupes. Some elites used the vote as evidence that complex decisions shouldn't be put to the people.[25] Owing to their distrust of elites, ordinary citizens embrace a post-truth politics, some scholars claimed. These scholars understood Brexit as the result of "a politics which seeks to emit messages into the public domain which will lead to emotionally charged reactions, with the goal of having them spread widely and without concern for the accuracy of the messages provided."[26] Once the public turns its back on experts, they become susceptible to the fake news they find on social media. Claims to objective truth have become devalued and replaced with appeals to emotion and personal belief. In short, "the UK's 'Brexit' referendum to exit the European Union [was] shaped by post-truth politics."[27]

One of the more shocking (at least for Remainers) facts to come out of Brexit was the depth of Labour support to leave. In many ways, Brexit confirmed the depth and breadth of dissatisfaction with traditional parties. The percentage of Labour districts in the United Kingdon that voted for Brexit was nothing less than shocking to traditional politicians. As mentioned previously, Eatwell and Goodwin point to "the working-class northern Labour district of Doncaster, where more than seven in ten had voted for Brexit."[28] Why would working-class Britons vote to leave, and what does their vote mean in the larger scheme of things?

First, let's deal with the empirical question: the alleged correlation between education and the vote to leave. Again, the conventional wisdom was and remains that those who voted to leave have fewer educational credentials than those who voted to remain. Thus, the urban centers such as London voted heavily to remain, while the farther north one went, the greater likelihood of finding leave voters. A second empirical claim is that Brexit was largely about income, with mostly lower-income Britons voting with their pocketbook to leave.

Both claims are dubious. After the referendum, three academics surveyed what they described as "ordinary Brits" or an "intermediate class," which they describe thus: "This intermediate class refers to 'ordinary' families with intermediate or upper-intermediate levels of education, stable jobs, and median levels of income, but which nonetheless face an increasing challenge in maintaining their life-style." Citing Joan Williams, whose work we refer to elsewhere in this book, these authors argue that when one sifts the data, one finds "the Leave vote was not more popular among the low skilled, but rather among individuals with intermediate levels of education (A-Levels and GSCE high grades), especially when their socio-economic position was perceived to be declining and/or to be stagnant. These findings point to an alternative narrative to that of the left behind." Middle-class squeeze is identified as the main culprit. The narrative that Brexit was brought on by uneducated, low-earning Brits is simply false. Brexit was as much the product of well-educated but middle-class Britons who see their fortunes declining. As the authors conclude, "Brexit was the voice of this intermediate class who are in a declining financial position."[29]

Brexit was as much about immigration in Britain as it was a matter of EU finances. Immigration was nowhere more contentious than in the United Kingdom. In one of the best accounts, Robert Tombs explains the role of immigration in the United Kingdom's decision to cut ties with Europe. After the fall of the Berlin Wall in 1989, the EU began its eastward expansion. The Irish waffled on expansion but ultimately went along. In a show of support for Europe, Prime Minister Tony Blair permitted the free movement of people from the new eastern European member states to Britain. He supported immigration from a business point of view. Britain, he thought, needed more workers. As Tombs explains, "Officials predicted 5,000–13,000 workers to come per year from Eastern Europe: over 600,000 came in five years, and by 2012 there were some 700,000 Poles alone resident in the UK."[30] One could only characterize this as another instance of "elite failure."

But immigration is more than just numbers. One study observed that "those who voted for Remain and those who voted to leave have very different views about immigration."[31] Yes, many Leave voters wanted to see immigrants to the United Kingdom wait longer to receive the benefits of residency, but this study surmises that concern over immigration reflects more a worry about national identity. As the study authors put it, "Some may feel that everybody in society should acknowledge and accept a common set of social mores and cultural practices, as this helps to maintain a more cohesive society."[32] Others have commented on this sentiment about national identity.[33] There is something to it, but whether it "explains" Brexit, as the study authors believe, we prescind.

As in the United States, immigration in the United Kingdom benefited some but not all members of the polity. Employers did better than workers, and the middle classes fared better than the working classes. Again, as in the United States, those displaced by immigration embraced political opposition parties and candidates. Nigel Farage founded the UK Independence Party in 1993 and made "uncontrolled immigration from the EU" the core of the party's platform. It was this party's showing in the European Parliament elections that ultimately led to a vote on Brexit.

Tombs, in addition to his succinct reprise of the role immigration played in Brexit, describes Leavers and Remainers in terms that will sound familiar to Americans' ears. Immigration, Tombs observes, "worried both sides: before the referendum, three-quarters of the population thought it had been too high and too rapid." Despite widespread anxiety, there were two distinctly different reactions to the rapid rise of immigration. Remainers, wishing to stay in the EU, emphasized economic issues and individual rights. Elites benefited from cheap eastern European labor. The presence of so many immigrants made daily life much easier and cheaper. But Leavers had a different agenda: family, community, and national cohesion. Invoking David Goodhart's distinction between "Anywhere" and "Somewhere" people, Tombs concludes that the Leavers "still believe there is such a thing as society."[34] As any observer of the American scene knows, the Leavers were not alone in this view.

A Dose of Common Sense

Populists value common sense. What does that mean, and what role do they want it to play? Some scholars think populists would displace scientific knowledge with lay wisdom. In fact, they claim that what motivates populist skepticism is, in fact, a belief that lay insight is superior to expert knowledge, representing "a fundamental epistemological cleavage between lay and expert forms of knowledge."[35] Others, like us, believe there need not be a zero-sum battle between expertise and common sense.

What is "common sense"? Before it became entangled in discussions of populism, common sense—or "commonsense knowledge"—enjoyed a storied intellectual pedigree. It is the central concept in Alfred Schutz's phenomenological sociology and is featured importantly in Peter Berger and Thomas Luckmann's famous book *The Social Construction of Reality* (1967) as well as in the work of Anthony Giddens and Michael Polanyi (tacit knowledge) and, perhaps most surprisingly, of the anthropologist Émile Durkheim.[36]

The grand tradition of phenomenological sociology puts great stock in common sense as a basis for understanding everyday experience. Durkheim was a central figure in this tradition. He distilled common sense into collective habits or social conventions that have permanent existence. As Dieter Misgeld explains, commonsense knowledge is a genuine phenomenon that proceeds "from a reality held in common [and] is a reality for which responsibility is common as well."[37]

Thomas Paine famously wrote a pamphlet on the subject of common sense. In arguing for the separation of the American colonies from England, Paine claimed to be articulating self-evident truths that gave a clear and objective answer to the political question at hand. Although one might say there is a certain sort of reasoning involved, common sense—at least as Paine articulates it—is more a matter of insight, albeit rational insight.

Paine certainly had precedent for the view that common understanding was a distinct faculty of persons that could ground judgments deemed universal. In the same era, Immanuel Kant described the matter this way:

> Common human understanding which, as mere sound (not yet cultivated) understanding, is looked upon as the least we can expect from anyone claiming the name of man, has therefore the doubtful honour of having name of common sense (*sensus communis*) bestowed upon it; and bestowed, too, in an acceptation of the word common . . . which makes it amount to what is vulgar. . . . However, by the name sensus communis is to be understood the idea of a public sense, i.e. a critical faculty which in its reflective act takes account (a priori) of the mode of representation of everyone else, in order, as it were, to weigh its judgment with the collective reason of mankind.[38]

Kant drew the distinction between "common" and "cultivated" understanding. In a later passage in *Critique of Judgment*, he described two groups in a polis as "the more cultured and ruder sections of the community." The goal of a politics is "to bridge the difference between the amplitude and refinement of the former and the natural simplicity and originality of the latter."[39] Kant's insight is about the nature of politics. He thought there is a place—a necessary place—for both expertise and common sense. We agree. But the question is how to balance them or, perhaps better, how to know when one must give way to the other. That's the trick, and it's never easy.

Much of the outrage from populists during the pandemic seemed to focus in particular on propositions that simply defied common sense. More than anything else, this disconnect between what public-health officials said and what seemed obvious led to decreased trust. Consider the inconsistencies around mask policies—unmasked politicians posing with masked children or early signs advising one not to smell the flowers in the park lest it transmit COVID-19 to others or the claims that masking was necessary outdoors unless one was protesting for the right cause. At our own university, the mask regime varied with seeming randomness. At the end, students were required to wear a mask only in the classroom: they were otherwise free to do as they pleased. When we questioned the logic of this, we were simply told that it was what the science dictated. We asked, "Can you tell us what science allows students to eat together and sleep together (let alone recreate) but requires students to wear a mask in the classroom?" Of course, there was no answer.

Common sense would dictate that (some) public officials had lost the plot on the virus. In 2021, Jon Stewart appeared on Stephen Colbert's show and endorsed the possibility that COVID-19 had emerged from a lab leak. Asked for evidence by Colbert, who, like many elites at the time considered the lab leak a right-wing, fringe conspiracy theory with a zero percent probability, Stewart offered instead a dose of common sense: "The disease is the same name as the lab!" He continued, to the audience's applause and Colbert's increasing discomfort, "You work at the Wuhan respiratory coronavirus lab and you ask, how did this happen, and they say, oh, a pangolin kissed a turtle?"[40] Stewart, of course, was roundly mocked by elites for "slowly los[ing] his mind onstage."[41] Later he would be vindicated as subsequent evidence showed that the lab-leak hypothesis was plausible. As emails between scientists later made clear, the theory had been dismissed by elites not for scientific reasons, only for political ones.[42] Common sense here was useful in identifying cracks in an expert assertion.

Of course, the case for common sense can be taken too far. Common sense is not always enough. The Wuhan naming coincidence, for example, by itself does not permanently dispose of the matter (and we think Jon Stewart would agree).[43] To reject expertise entirely "rests on the assumption that there is an almost 'natural' or objective kind of reasoning that exists independently of culture but nevertheless remains always at the risk of being corrupted by it," as Taylor Dotson has put it.[44] This notion—the idea of a "natural faculty"—is corrupted in the hands of some populists when they argue for the rejection of what Kant described as the more "cultured" part of the political community.

How do such populists misappropriate and corrupt the notion of common sense? Dotson sees the move as a corruption of Rousseau's notion of the "general will." His account aligns perfectly with Müller's account of populism. Some populists—especially populist politicians—"[frame] the general will as unique to a subset of citizens."[45] Looked at this way, insight becomes a function not of cognition but of political valence. However, all claims to knowledge have to be backed up with something more than mere assertion or claim to know, so the mistake is in thinking that if one is the right kind of person, one's judgments are unassailable. We agree that this notion makes no sense. Just because one has a certain trait—such as being a member of a group—does not guarantee that one's judgments will be correct. This is as true of experts favored by elites as of politicians favored by populists. In fact, the reduction of knowledge to one's identity leads to a sort of sophomoric relativism. What is important is not who is reasoning but what and how that person is reasoning about. The expert does not triumph over the common person by beating them with facts. Rather, the average person assesses their situation relative to their knowledge of the world and asks whether the expert's claims are indeed plausible. Dialogue is possible, but only if there is a shared mode of discourse.

In Dotson's view, the struggle to find an absolute truth—one that will end the polarized state of contemporary politics—is the root cause of our troubles. Expert dominance makes government "seem increasingly distant and unresponsive, sowing discord among ordinary citizens." But he also notes that experts may double down in response to populists' attempts to "idealiz[e] the beliefs of laypeople or mythologiz[e] 'the majority.'" He sees both sides as being plagued by overconfidence and an obsession with being both right and certain that is destined to fail. "Any hope for a democratic future lies in finding a way out of the regress produced by a preoccupation with a monolithic Truth," he writes.[46]

"The People"

Some elites object to the idea of "common sense" because of the impossibility of identifying what sense "the people" share. For these commentators, there is no such thing as "the people"; there are just individual citizens. Jan-Werner Müller spends considerable time complaining that populism hankers for "holism," "someone speaking in the name of the people as a whole." The result is an antidemocratic, antipluralist vision of politics where "they, *and only they,* represent the people."[47] Others take Müller's point further. The economist Pierre Lemieux argues, in a framing only an elite could deploy, that populism is "ontologically impossible." (Never mind the inconvenient fact that populism exists!) Drawing on social choice theory, he says that populism, "defined as a regime where the people rule," is "impossible." He explains: "'The people' is not a social organism and does not have a mind that can govern like an individual who has coherent preferences and takes actions to pursue them. There is no voting method capable of producing a rational and democratic choice. As William Riker says, '[W]hat the people want cannot be known. Hence the populist goal is unattainable.' Populism is impossible because it is not clear who 'the people' is and what it wants."[48]

Clever though this explanation is, it speaks past populism. It arbitrarily tries to turn populism into some kind of mechanism for voting as opposed to a more capacious epistemology—a mindset about politics. Nobody believes that populism solves "all" problems of social choice, any more than any other theory ever has or will. Instead, populism is a defense of laypeople's expertise.

The idea of "the people" has a long tradition. Although it is ambiguous—surely it is true that we cannot always divine a singular perspective of "the people"—it is nonetheless a meaningful concept. The political theorist Margaret Canovan devotes her book *The People* (2005) to explaining why this is so. Canovan sees the inherent ambiguity of the "sovereign people" not as a flaw but as an inevitability. Its openness mirrors politics, which is "characterised by openness and contingency" and by "the spasmodic rise and fall of movements, and unpredictable changes of mood between enthusiasm and apathy."[49] This inexactness may frustrate the economist who wants to pin down an input into a model, but it is a constitutive feature of the world we inhabit.

When, why, and how should the people be listened to? The most clarity seems to come in the occasional moments where political mobilization leads to a "large-scale movement in which individuals are consciously united as the people and act as a collective body."[50] These moments might include the Glorious Revolution in seventeenth-century England, the American Revolution, and, more recently, the Solidarity movement in Poland. They may include what Bruce Ackerman terms a "Constitutional moment," which occurs when coalitions take up the mantle of "We the People" and change—either in a literal way or in terms of interpretation—our most basic legal institutions and rights, such as during Reconstruction.[51]

"The people" may also be glimpsed, perhaps more imperfectly, during large-scale social protests—the *gilets jaunes*, Occupy Wall Street, the Seattle protests against the World Trade Organization, the George Floyd protests, the Canada convoy protest, the Dakota Access Pipeline protests—that capture our imagination. These protests do not speak in one voice, and often— especially as they grow in attention—they get co-opted by or morph into other agendas. Nor, to be clear, do they speak for everyone. But many of them share a feature that captures the imagination of a wide range of viewers and often attracts a hodge-podge of disparate groups—often of opposing partisan ideologies—that briefly coalesce around a sense that elites are not listening to the lived experience of "the people." It is that sentiment, that "spirit" (if you will), that provides a glimpse of populist motivations.

Canovan does not mean to suggest that large-scale mobilizations are inevitably correct or should be accorded some kind of deference. Indeed, from a legal standpoint she agrees that this idea of a people is "profoundly unsatisfactory" because it is "occasional and unpredictable," and its boundaries are malleable. As she says, "It is never comprehensive enough to include all potential members, and its status as the *real* people is always more or less contestable." There are other limitations as well. The people cannot actually directly "rule" or form an institution, and the possibility of a descent into mob violence is real.[52]

But those who dismiss "the people" hardly offer a replacement that fares better. The idea that "experts" or "elites" can legitimately govern is just a less democratic version of faith in some kind of superstructure that will make the problems of society disappear. As Canovan writes, "The most potent (and most misleading) myth of all is surely the belief that somewhere . . . there must be some ultimate source of authority that could save us from the responsibility of muddling through as best we can."[53] On that front, elite technocracy is surely less honest about the challenges of modern democracy. We confront one of the leading expositors of the technocratic mindset, Cass Sunstein, in our next chapter. Although the "sovereign people" may be mythical, it is the foundational myth that overshadows all democracy, which should be evident to anyone who has read the first three words of the US Constitution.

7 Expertise in Policy

Although we are certainly in favor of expertise, expertise alone cannot settle most important questions of public policy for both an internal reason and an external reason. The internal reason is that experts are often systematically wrong. The external reason is that almost every real public policy depends on more than single-dimensional expertise; public policy is not the same as brain surgery. In this sense, the populist valorization of common sense has an important leg up on the elite valorization of expertise.

The Chernobyl nuclear plant accident in 1986 produced a large radioactive cloud that passed over the United Kingdom. As a result, elevated levels of radiocaesium started to show up in sheep, which led to a ban on slaughtering the sheep for their meat. The expert scientists predicted that the contamination would not last long, and so the argument was made that no compensation was due the sheep farmers.

For their part, the sheep farmers maintained that the contamination would last quite a long while. The sheep farmers proved to be correct, and the scientists "spectacularly wrong."[1] The sheep showed elevated levels of contamination a full six years after the incident. Did the sheep farmers just get lucky in their prediction, or was their doubt about the scientists' claims grounded in something actual? As the story goes, the sheep farmers knew things the scientists didn't, and those things turned out to be significant. Chief among them was the type of soil in the areas where the sheep grazed, the behavior of caesium in the soil, the local vegetation, and the sheep's diet. The scientists eventually listened to the sheep farmers, but at that point it was too late to save the experts' credibility (or the farmers' livelihood).

What is the lesson of the sheep recounted by Gil Eyal in his meditation on the current crisis in expertise? The story illustrates both the limits of expertise and the importance of lay insight into what would normally be considered the province of experts. Being charitable, one could say that the scientists lacked sufficient breadth of knowledge to correctly assess the situation. That is true: they did. But the problem with that assessment is that it leaves out the factor that they had the information right in front of them and chose to ignore it. By dismissing the sheep farmers' claims, the scientists precluded themselves from access to the information they needed to correctly diagnose the situation. As Eyal puts it, "To arrive at a correct assessment of contamination risk, it was necessary to know what the scientists knew, what the sheep farmers knew, plus a great deal more that was not yet known."[2] So the experts' hubris was the root cause of their diagnostic failure.

Political epistemology—how we know how to make decisions—is the arena in which the political, social, and economic rifts between populists and elites come to bear. We have outlined two competing claims for how decisions should be made. Elites valorize rule by experts.[3] Populists respond to elites with skepticism, valorizing instead the lay wisdom of the common people.

The populist epistemology—at least in its less extreme forms—is quite defensible. Very few public-policy questions rest solely on expertise: many implicate questions of values, morality, and trade-offs between different domains. The sphere where expertise can supply absolute "answers" is really quite narrow. Most purported uses of expertise are, in fact, a bluff, where experts are trotted out to shore up the political priors of elites. Moreover, expertise often carries considerable uncertainty, not to mention unresolved debates within the expert community—even under a narrow, elite-held definition. Experts themselves are human and prone to motivated reasoning (in fact, possibly more so than laypeople). And, as in the sheep example, "lay" expertise and experience, which are often excluded in elite-led accounts of policymaking, do matter.

Many elites claim that complex technical decisions—about the environment, about public health, about public safety, and so on—need to be insulated from public pressure lest "irrational" decisions be reached. Cass Sunstein is one of the leading expositors of this opinion: in his view, shared by many elites, the gold standard for public policymaking is a "cost–benefit" analysis by a technocrat shielded from public view. Many of them share Yascha Mounk's and Michael Lewis's view that the modern world has gotten too complex, that there is too much to be learned from the "big data" that only a few can understand, for citizen participation in policymaking. In this chapter, we show the hollowness of Sunstein's account. He, like many elites, is simply unable to see the varied values at play in almost any issue.

Lay Knowledge

Elites sometimes make ridiculous claims in dismissing populists' antiexpertise bent—for instance, that those who question their expert betters might ask their bartender rather than a cardiac surgeon to perform their upcoming heart surgery. This claim is, of course, a straw man: literally no one doubts that a heart surgeon is better than a bartender at performing heart surgery.

But *even* in that extreme example—perhaps the most obvious domain where credentialed expertise matters—lay knowledge matters. Nichols dismisses this possibility, ridiculing skeptical patients who ask too many questions of their doctors based on their Google research.[4] It has become popular for elites to warn of the perils of "doing your own research."[5] Now, of course, many people *do* come across bad medical information online, just as they might have received bad advice from their grandparents about how to treat a common cold. Many of us have had the experience of entering symptoms into Google, only to be told that a likely cause is some rare, fatal illness rather than the common cold that is far more likely. Most people are not scientists, and they may analyze data incorrectly.

But such occasional mistaken analysis does not mean that all lay expertise should be pushed to the side. Indeed, in Nichols's examples, the key is that all these patients have chosen to go to an expert, a doctor. They have decided not to self-diagnose. They evidently *do* respect expertise, his mockery notwithstanding. Also, it is well documented that patients do have to advocate for themselves in medicine. Patient advocacy—that is, family members who push providers and ask questions of doctors—has demonstrated benefits in treatment outcomes, which is why major medical regulators stress its importance.[6] Asking questions raises the possibility that a patient will supply new and relevant information that makes mistakes by the doctor less likely. Although questions may be time-consuming, any professional—doctor, lawyer, mechanic—should expect and accept them.

Moreover, patient advocacy has led, even in the face of disbelief by the medical profession, to important results as doctors eventually realized patients' complaints were real and worthy of further scientific evaluation. It has also helped numerous patients with rare diseases that fall between the cracks of medical specialties.[7] The medical profession hasn't always gotten it right. But we must also admit that the principle of patient advocacy can go too far. The view that a patient's self-experience is the only thing that matters and that it can be divorced from expertise and measurement does little to advance research and can exacerbate anxiety about problems that are likely not physical in nature.[8] As we said in chapter 6, the point is to balance expertise and common sense, not to pit them against each other in a zero-sum game.

The problem with Nichols's "defer to experts" logic goes deeper. Even the most technical decisions, such as decisions about surgery, sometimes involve trade-offs that are not mechanical and scientific in nature. Experts themselves can be blind to the ways in which values affect their own decisions. Consider an example from recent research. There is no clear clinical basis for choosing between hip replacement and hip fusion in teenage patients experiencing hip failure. Loosely speaking, hip replacement has better short- to midterm outcomes (a better range of motion and less pain) but more long-term complications (higher likelihood of wheelchair reliance later in life), whereas hip fusion has worse short-term outcomes (a limp) but fewer long-term complications (more acceptable follow-on treatments and lower likelihood of wheelchair reliance later).

How do patients make this seemingly impossible choice? Remarkably, a single, plainly irrelevant fact is most influential in determining which one a surgeon will recommend to their patient: the *age of the surgeon*, which apparently colors how the doctor personally sees the trade-off between short- and long-term complications.[9] How can a factor that is plainly irrelevant to the medical situation matter so much? We all presumably agree that which treatment a patient gets should not be based on the doctor's personal preferences outside of their medical practice. Yet that is almost certainly precisely what happens, likely without the surgeon's even being aware of this bias. There is no "correct" answer in this trade-off, but few would dispute that it is fundamentally a values choice that properly belongs to the lay participant (the patient), not the expert (the doctor).

These complexities aside, we all agree that surgery should be performed by experts. We know of no "populist" who disputes this. Our point is that *even* surgery is complicated when it comes to the role of lay expertise and values. With this in mind, consider dealing with climate change, setting interest-rate policy, or interpreting the Second Amendment—areas that provoke strong disagreement precisely because they touch on multiple spheres and invoke competing values. Expertise matters in each of these settings, but no one expert will have all the answers, and values will matter, too.

This point can be applied in concrete ways. For instance, some have focused on how expert-driven processes can be redesigned to include the public. By including members of the public in public-policy decisions with direct effect on the lives of ordinary citizens, the legitimacy of expert opinion is bolstered. Lay expertise has been a constituent feature of medical practice in the United Kingdom for decades.[10] Gil Eyal has studied the interplay between lay expertise and public policy: he sees lay expertise as the response to a "legitimacy crisis and declining trust" toward academic expertise.[11] Inclusion strategies are not without risk. One risk is that the wider the net is cast to bring in voices, the greater the chance that consensus fails to be achieved. Despite these risks, inclusion strategies have been employed in contexts as varied as decisions made by the Environmental Protection Agency (EPA) in the United States and the French mechanism of the "citizen conference."[12]

Some scholars see calibrating this kind of participation as the key to resolving the problems we discuss in this book. They are more optimistic than we are that a tidy distinction can be drawn. The two most prominent authors in the field, Harry Collins and Robert Evans, focus on legitimacy in "technical decision-making"—policy decisions that involve scientific matters but where the issues are "of visible relevance to the public."[13] They are responding to a problem created by twentieth-century scientific theory, when what was called "truth" began to be perceived, at least in part, as socially constructed and inevitably so. But that theory poses a problem: if scientists don't have "special access" to the truth, and if truth is what matters, it makes no sense to accord them deference. Collins and Evans see a simple solution: focus not on "truth" but on "expertise." But if one focuses on expertise—on how to bring expertise, not truth, into public policy—then what we need is a theory of which scientists have the right kind of expertise. This theory would permit us to decide when experts have legitimacy versus when "public" or "lay" expertise matters and needs to be brought in.

The focus, then, is on processes that allow for some citizen input and thus avoid unbridled technocracy. But Collins and Evans are just as worried about too much citizen participation as too little. Previous generations of scholars, Collins and Evans submit, correctly challenged monolithic claims that scientists had unique access to truth, but that critique went too far and "made it hard to distinguish between scientific expertise and political rights." Their solution: bring back the distinction but be more careful and precise about different types of expertise. For instance, they develop a taxonomy of types of expertise, such as "contributory expertise" (the kind that makes you a participant who can contribute in a particular field) versus "interactional expertise" (to understand and interact interestingly but not to contribute).[14]

Collins and Evans provide a more sophisticated picture of the problem than the more widespread elite mindset has. That is, the latter's "follow the science" and "the death of expertise" catch-phrases do not show a deep awareness of the distinction between "truth" and "expertise" or between different types of experts. But even with Collins and Evans's more nuanced picture, it's not clear how far their approach can get us in the real world. It seems at best just to shift the same contests—over fundamental values and who controls decision-making—to new terminology, where more and more people will claim expertise. In other words, it just becomes a fight over the definition of expertise, which is hardly helpful. Gil Eyal, whose work we have already mentioned, is a thoughtful analyst of the relationship between expertise and society. In his meditation on expertise, he notes that the term *expertise* itself started to be defined and complexified only as part of the battle for control of expert-led process. It exploded in popularity in literature in the 1960s during fights over the role of experts in public policy that Eyal traces. Thus, it's unlikely the term itself can settle the debate—we can finally agree on what an expert is and move on—because the term is the *result* of the debate.

Many have critiqued Collins and Evans. Sheila Jasanoff finds their terms and taxonomy unhelpfully reductive, attempting to impose an arbitrary and ultimately unwieldy order on "the complex dynamics of expertise in modern societies." As Jasanoff notes, science and policy have *always* interacted in a complex dance, and expertise has always been fundamentally contested and dependent on the particular issue at hand.[15]

For our purposes, the major point is that when citizens feel excluded, they become skeptical and mistrustful toward experts. Because facts always require interpretation, and because all scientific claims have some amount of uncertainty, the citizens' critique has no ready answer.[16] The populist critique, moreover, is not an attack on science; this is a misreading, willful or not. Rather, it is the unquestioned application of science to policy that is questioned.

Nevertheless, it is important to note that lay participation has chalked up some wins, which suggests the plausibility of the populist claim: lay expertise exists, matters, and can be harnessed. "Citizen science" has been formally integrated into many regulatory regimes not just because it is democratically sound but also because it is successful. In many cases, self-stewarded resources do quite well. Examples abound.[17] Fisheries councils—which have turned over control to local groups that involve fishermen instead of leaving all decisions to remote federal bureaucrats—have reversed and stabilized overfishing trends since the 1970s.[18] Robert Ellickson describes in *Order without Law* (1994) how ranchers in Shasta County, California, provided a model for how people commonly self-govern through self-defined social norms that are "located and shaped beyond the reach of law."[19] Elinor Ostrom's Nobel Prize–winning work on the "tragedy of the commons" in 1990 revealed how organic local groups—essentially a populist form of governance—have managed to avoid collective-action problems and to steward resources.[20]

This use of citizen science is not just "common sense" coming in to inform values and then deferring to experts. Rather, "common sense" serves as a replacement form of expertise. People are not as ignorant as elites would claim: a small-business person is likely to have both a personal, subjective understanding of how interest-rate decisions affect them, which matters, and a fairly knowledge-informed understanding of interest rates, even if it is not the same kind of purely theoretical view that an ivory tower economist might have. That theoretical knowledge is useful and worth encouraging and may ultimately inform wider debates, but that does not mean the person generating it is entitled to deference in setting public policy.

The False Use of Expertise

The failure to understand or admit the role values play in decision-making is precisely what ignites populism. During the pandemic, the public-health community lost considerable credibility in its policies on outdoor protests.

In the summer of 2020, it was essential that cloth masks be worn in all outdoor settings and that all gatherings be prohibited. This policy led to a zero-tolerance attitude toward antilockdown protests, including calls by medical ethicists for such protestors to forgo medical care if they contracted COVID-19.[21] But at the outbreak of the Black Lives Matter protests, the public-health community suddenly reversed course, actively encouraging individuals to join crowded protests.[22] Thousands of public-health practitioners signed a letter agreeing not to call Black Lives Matter protests a public-health risk, instead defining them as vital for public health, and insisting that this support "not be confused with a permissive stance on all gatherings, particularly protests against stay-at-home orders."[23] "In this moment the public health risks of not protesting to demand an end to systemic racism greatly exceed the harms of the virus," wrote Jennifer Nuzzo of Johns Hopkins.[24]

This stance strained credulity. The question for Nuzzo and others was not whether the protests were warranted or whether they posed a public-health threat but rather whether an epidemiologist had any particular expertise that permitted them to so weigh the substantive merits of one protest against another. Governments cannot pick and choose winners when it comes to free speech and protests, but can doctors? In 2020, the public-health community said yes, this was precisely what their field did.[25] Their field was not ideologically neutral, they said, and it had a duty to enter the fray. The claim was even more contorted as it appeared to conflate the *goal* of the protest with the *means*. The protests were worth it because the inevitable result would be better health care for Black Americans. That is, public health was evaluating the competing protests on the assumption that the protest would work and actually bring about what it set out to do—an assumption that would be a question for political science, not epidemiology.

For most Americans, this contradiction was simply too much. The about-face elicited eye rolls from many who already thought the public-health community was predominantly an ideological, result-driven, unscientific institution. It undermined the credibility of public health, which was already strained by the extremeness of its prior messaging—that all outdoor gatherings, even distanced walks in nature, were unsafe. The issue was not the moral judgment itself but rather the insistence that the moral judgment belonged to those who had the right diploma (apparently, a master's in public health).

So-called experts in public health are hardly alone in taking such a position. Experts in general, perhaps because they are human and have a strong interest in the fields they study, like to claim special knowledge over questions that are ultimately political or ideological or at least not ultimately derived entirely from expertise. In our own field, legal academics regularly try to arrogate high-stakes legal decisions to the ivory tower. Sometimes their claims *look* quite plausible. Thousands of law professors signed petitions against both the confirmations of Jeff Sessions (for Attorney General) and Brett Kavanaugh (to the Supreme Court), for example. But there was nothing in the letters that required the expertise of a law professor. They expressed opinions—valid opinions, maybe even ones we share personally—but ones whose authority rested on the signers as citizens and moral agents, *not* on their authority as law professors.

Once one becomes aware of this phenomenon of declaring special knowledge and thus more worthy judgments, one can see that it is ubiquitous. Law professors are regularly quoted in simple one-line reductions of the law, with "legal experts say" inevitably in the headline: that Bush "can't" declare war (even though he did) or that Trump "must" be indicted. "Experts say" in headlines is a pretty reliable indicator of an opinion piece masquerading as news or authority. Legal scholars aren't so much making predictions based on their knowledge as making a positive claim that the Supreme Court inevitably "must" do what these authors want. But these kinds of proclamations are problematic because the law *can* and *does* change. It's not clear what it means to call the Supreme Court factually "wrong" when it overturns precedent, given that the Supreme Court's latest interpretation does, in fact, become the law. "Wrong" here really means an author *disagrees* with the Supreme Court, which is entirely acceptable and may be based on solid arguments. Indeed, an author's opinion may be founded on higher-quality arguments than those proffered by the justices, but the way such opinion is often presented suggests that it is an inarguable matter that can be refereed solely by expertise.

To be very clear, we don't mean to suggest that our colleagues shouldn't share their opinions. What we mean is that their credibility rests on the *quality of their arguments*—which we all can judge because they do not require technical legal knowledge—not on *the credentials of the speaker or writer*. A petition "signed by thousands of law professors" is the latter. It wrongly asserts that the amassing of credentials makes a political opinion authoritative and unquestionably true. Of course, our colleagues are experts in their fields, but their views on political appointees are precisely what they sound like—primarily matters of their political opinion having little to do with expertise in law.

We can take this point further. Friends who are not lawyers routinely ask us questions about the Constitution. They assume that we, as law professors, might have a unique take on, say, the Second Amendment and the contours of the right to bear arms or on whether the Constitution prohibits affirmative action or gives rise to abortion rights. But on questions like that, there is no reason to defer to a constitutional law professor's interpretation of the Constitution. A law professor has certain relevant expertise for sure: they have no doubt read more judicial opinions, and they may be familiar with the intricacies of historical debates over the Second Amendment. Some of those intricacies may be relevant and certainly are interesting. But the professor's ultimate conclusions—the bottom line—usually reflects little more than politics. Expertise cannot "answer" a question like this, which ultimately rests on highly contested interpretations and most fundamentally on subjective opinion. Popular constitutionalism (discussed later), a widespread idea of constitutional interpretation popular before elites professionalized constitutional interpretation to a small circle, held that we *all* interpret the Constitution.

Journalists—and laypeople—frequently assume that lawyers know many "facts" about the Constitution that make their interpretations of it more valid. Although there is some truth to this assumption, there are also significant limits to it. For better or worse, interpretations of the Constitution change. The Supreme Court does not always uphold its precedents or may confront novel issues. The law can change—that is the nature of our system. So what does it mean when a law professor announces that the Constitution "says" such-and-such so that some particular thing "cannot" or "must" be done? It may mean that the professor believes that current Supreme Court precedent is clear on a particular matter. Or it may mean that the professor *wants* the Constitution to be interpreted in a particular way. It's frequently a bit of both. In any case, though, what warrant does a constitutional law professor have for deference to their interpretation? If much of constitutional interpretation is ultimately political, this deference amounts to little more than giving a nod to that professor's personal politics.

It is not for us to get into the thicket of how the Constitution ought to be interpreted. We observe only that interpretations *do* change and that law professors *do* disagree about interpretation: some are originalists, others are vehemently anti-originalists, to take just one area of disagreement. Although these professors may have honed their arguments and may know particular things about the Constitution that are quite relevant to their argument, it is hard to imagine that we could defer to "originalism" or "not originalism" simply because of the credentials of those espousing either view.

There are some who defend "popular constitutionalism," which is the idea that "the people" interpret the Constitution. This idea has a long pedigree, and Larry Kramer has persuasively argued that it was probably what the framers of the Constitution held because it was the closest to the idea that had arrived from England. Judicial review hadn't been invented yet; in fact, the idea of judicial supremacy over the Constitution didn't become popular until quite a bit later, in the second half of the twentieth century.[26] One needn't subscribe to this idea to see that it is plausible: there is nothing inherently special about a law professor that gives them particular wisdom about the nature of the right to bear arms. But the idea is quite upsetting to the power of those who study constitutional law and who would like to reserve it—and the right to be quoted in the *New York Times* pontificating about it—to themselves.

The Hollowness of Pure Expertise

As mentioned earlier, Cass Sunstein has devoted considerable research to "cost–benefit analysis." He is fond of noting our collective foolishness. In one of his early books, *Risk and Reason* (2004), and in many other places since then, he generates countless tables showing our inconsistencies in spending money to protect ourselves from risks.[27] We spend $107 million on regulations to avert a premature death from arsenic in the workforce, while we get a far better deal out of our trihalomethane drinking-water standards (just $0.2 million to save a life). Why? Because officials listen to "general public pressures," but "ordinary people . . . do not assess risks through a well-informed cost-benefit lens." The public, for example, is very afraid of industrial pollution of waterways (ranking it number 3 out of 26 risks), while EPA experts say the real risk is low. But the imprudent public doesn't care enough about radon (ranking it number 25 out of 26) compared to the EPA.[28]

Sunstein finds these inconsistencies hard to understand and hardly worthy of deference. Why would any person not prioritize whatever precaution saves the most lives for the fewest dollars? Of course, that assumes his numbers are correct. But many mistrust government risk estimates—and indeed they can be wrong. Our apparently inconsistent evaluations of risk may not really be that irrational.[29] They may be based on other judgments about the types of risks and benefits we are willing to endure as a society. For instance, we don't force people to exercise, despite its health benefits. This puzzles Sunstein. As one reviewer writes, "Sunstein's comparisons thus fly in the face of several hundred years of philosophical distinctions between acts of omission and commission, proximate and non-proximate causes, negative and welfare rights, justified and unjustified paternalism, causal chains of responsibility, and so on."[30] Ultimately, such inconsistencies may be a feature, not a bug, of living in a democracy.

That does not mean expertise does not have an important role to play in helping society set priorities and design regulations. Indeed, one purpose of the administrative state was to insulate the nitty-gritty of regulation from political pressure. But that is a political choice, not a divine right of regulators. Elites cannot understand how anyone would reach a different decision or how someone might want a certain matter to be subject to political oversight. In light of the diploma divide and the fact that the preferences of elites may in fact be quite systematically different from most of society, this is particularly problematic.

Sunstein famously argued that "the issues that most divide us are fundamentally about facts rather than values."[31] From this assertion, it follows that government policy should not be based on public opinion but on numbers—meaning careful consideration of costs and benefits. Thus, once people know the facts, they are in a position to make correct choices. Progress in matters of public policy is possible only when we depoliticize debates and come to terms with facts and numbers.

In *Averting Catastrophe* (2021), Sunstein brings his technocratic playbook to bear on a variety of hot-button issues, including climate change and COVID-19 policy. Sunstein promises a "decision theory" for disasters such as the pandemic and climate change. The book opens with an account of its origins. In his tenure as Obama's administrator of the White House Office of Information and Regulatory Affairs, Sunstein was tasked with developing a "social cost of carbon"—that is, an assessment of the damage caused by a ton of carbon emissions. The number was important because it determined the stringency of regulations for the control of greenhouse gases. The task was difficult. Why? Sunstein explains: "It was difficult in part because of the known unknowns, and the unknown unknowns and the challenge of deciding how to handle them."[32]

Sunstein believes the best way to go about formulating policy to avert catastrophe is to marry regulatory policy and decision theory. The promise is that "if we bring the two together, we should be able to make some progress in handling some of the most difficult problems of the current era, including those raised by pandemics." Sunstein channels John Maynard Keynes on uncertainty with these words: "Keynes's central claim is that some of the time, we cannot assign probabilities to imaginable outcomes." But Sunstein is unbowed. Sure, there are lots of things about the future that are unknown, but that does not preclude us from crafting policy. There are approaches to doing so, and although "they are not exactly pretty . . . they can save humanity a lot of distress."[33]

The first candidate for a policy principle is the maximin principle, "which calls for choosing the approach that eliminates the worst of the worst-case scenarios." The maximin principle has some problems, as Sunstein sees it. He mentions two. First, the principle does not allow for the possibility of "miracles"—that is, unlikely events with a strong upside.[34] In addition, the maximin principle may lead to the generation of externalities (i.e., bad outcomes), such as increasing poverty and suppressing the development of interventions (e.g., technology) that will avert the threat.

Sunstein clearly articulates the policy dilemma facing regulators: "In extreme situations, public officials of diverse kinds must decide what kinds of restrictions to put in place against low-probability risks of catastrophe or risks that have terrible worst-case scenarios, but to which probabilities cannot (yet) be assigned." In such a situation, two regulatory principles are possible candidates: quantitative cost–benefit analysis and the precautionary principle. Keeping with his long-standing commitment to cost–benefit analysis, Sunstein endorses it, but he does not abandon the maximin principle in its entirety, offering three conditions when its application would be appropriate: when the cost–benefit analysis is only moderately costly to implement; when there is a strong expectation that catastrophe will result from lack of regulatory intervention; and when it is impossible to reduce the uncertainty of a given outcome. Sunstein has consistently endorsed cost–benefit analysis as the basis of his approach to public policy. But in this book, one that ostensibly deals with disaster contexts such as the pandemic, Sunstein admits that "there are no simple rules. Judgments, not calculations, are required, and ideally, they will come from a well-functioning democratic process. But even when judgments are required, they can be bounded by applicable principles, which can prevent a lot of trouble."[35]

With the argumentative architecture now on the table, how does Sunstein bring it all to bear on the pandemic? He begins *Averting Catastrophe* with this paragraph: "In the face of a pandemic threatening to produce numerous deaths, should aggressive preventive measures be undertaken, even if we cannot specify the benefits of those measures? Should cities, states, and nations be locked down? Exactly when and how? Should people be required to wear masks?"[36] Although these questions may not be all the ones raised by the pandemic, they are surely some of the central ones. What are the benefits of aggressive measures, and when should people be required to wear masks? How does Sunstein answer?

Surprisingly, Sunstein provides few answers to the questions he poses. On his preferred normative modality, cost–benefit analysis, he says: "Consider, for example, the fact that the most aggressive responses to Covid-19, imposing something like a shutdown, can create severe economic distress (which is not good for one's physical health) and also an increase in mental health problems. Health–health tradeoffs might be inescapable. By contrast, breakeven analysis might turn out to solve the problem: If we know the lower bound of the upper bound for benefits, we might know what costs it does and does not make sense to incur."[37] As we assess the merits of this paragraph, let us not forget Sunstein's central claim that facts, not values, are what separate us. But there is little in this paragraph—the only paragraph in the book that puts cost–benefit analysis and the pandemic together—that anyone would disagree with. Elites and populists agree that fighting the pandemic involved trade-offs, so Sunstein's assertion there merits a yawn. What is important is identifying those trade-offs and finding a metric for weighing them. Sunstein disappoints in these tasks in that although first carefully setting up a decision procedure with clear and visible parameters, he then fails to take his analysis to the point where cost–benefit analysis is shown to be superior.

Another point involves some hedging on Sunstein's part. Recall his comment that there are no simple rules, and judgment is required. What sort of judgment? The kind that comes from "a well functioning democratic process."[38] To be fair, it is not clear whether Sunstein intends his one remark about the democratic process to apply to all disaster contexts. But what he fails to accomplish in his treatment of the pandemic is to make the case for his most cherished proposition: it is facts and not values that separate us. As we argued earlier in this book, school closures were a huge topic of debate. Perhaps second to that were the closures of businesses that put working-class Americans indoors with no chance to earn a living. Everyone knows the white-collar laptop class suffered minor inconvenience at worst by staying home and working. Zoom made certain that these workers lost little to nothing. Not so for the working class. They got government handouts (although many wealthy people benefited from Payback Protection Program loans).

Sunstein is utterly unconvincing in his claim that disasters such as the COVID-19 pandemic are not a matter of values and, worse, politics. In addition, it is quite difficult to discern just what "the facts" were with COVID-19. Did we need masks? First it was no, then it was yes. Did the vaccines stop transmission? First it was yes, then it was no. Should we be like Sweden or New Zealand in fashioning policy? These questions are difficult, and as Sunstein (invoking Keynes) reminds us, decisions have to be made in conditions of uncertainty. Again: no one disagrees. What is disappointing in Sunstein's work, however, is the failure to show how cost–benefit analysis provides greater insight into appropriate policy choices than, say, the political process. He has been severely criticized for propagating the view that public policy can proceed free of the political process.[39] The pandemic was a perfect opportunity to prove that view, and Sunstein came up short.

Decisions about threats such as the COVID-19 pandemic are matters of public health, but they have deep and uneven consequences on the lives of citizens. Although Sunstein fails to expand on the point, he mentions the importance of the democratic process in fashioning an appropriate response to catastrophes such as the pandemic. One of the key concepts in decision-making of any kind is authority. Who has the authority to make a particular decision? During the pandemic, state, local, and federal authorities arrogated the power to make decisions with regard to matters of public health. Their authority was grounded in law, but it was bolstered by scientific experts. Every time a US president appeared at a new press conference, he was flanked by his expert advisers. On some occasions, the president would ask an adviser to answer a question about government policy. The experts had no authority, but they did have tremendous influence on those in authority.

*   *   *

The legitimacy of an elected official (think of the president) is grounded in law. The legitimacy of the expert is grounded in science (the ground is methodological objectivity). But for a decision that affects all citizens to be legitimate, there has to be participation in making it by those affected. Decisions made by others and imposed on the rest of us have the greatest chance of success (that is, being seen as legitimate) when we, the persons affected, have a stake in the process. This is Zeynep Pamuk's view in her book *Politics and Expertise* (2021). We think this is correct.

There is a great deal of anxiety these days about public policy being ceded to experts. One of the chief complaints about the regulatory state is that so many aspects of life are governed by an unelected cadre of "deep-state" bureaucrats who are relatively free from criticism. What is the proper mix of expert knowledge and democracy? Pamuk notes that "determining scientific truth democratically would be irrational and dangerous."[40] We agree.

The question of the relationship between expertise and laypeople has been the subject of academic attention since Max Weber first gave an account of the relationship between bureaucracy and political leadership.[41] Pamuk comments that Weber was "pessimistic about the ability of bureaucracies to be truly neutral[, but] he held this up as the ideal to strive for."[42] Finally, Isaiah Berlin gave voice to the same notion in his classic essay "Two Concepts of Liberty" (1958): "Where ends are agreed, the only questions left are those of means, and these are not political but technical, that is to say, capable of being settled by experts or machines, like arguments between engineers or doctors."[43]

Does any of this help in determining the proper relationship between scientific expertise and democratic decision-making? Such a determination would be easier if facts and values could be separated in a real-time discussion, but the pandemic illustrated that cannot always be done. As all know, modeling was a big factor in the United Kingdom and the United States. Pamuk treats this well in her discussion of the Imperial College and University of Washington Institute for Health Metrics and Evaluation models for the virus. She makes the point that in fashioning the models, the scientists involved made value choices that were hidden from view. Specifically, "they failed to take a holistic approach to health outcomes overall, and left out the mental and physical health toll of social isolation and severe economic downturn, increased domestic violence and substance abuse rates, delayed treatments for other diseases, and missed vaccination schedules for children." In addition to these factors, Pamuk relates that "some UK advisers initially dismissed the possibility of a strict lockdown on the grounds that it would be politically unthinkable." She leans heavily on the fact that the modelers advising governments made choices—that is, attempted to balance competing interests—without disclosing their process. She observes that in such cases many citizens would make choices rather different from those of the scientific modelers. This obviously leads to conflicts, which, she argues, "must be resolved politically." How is that to be done? Pamuk recommends "adopting public-facing approaches that would allow real scrutiny and accountability." She is against what she terms "the ideal of neutrality in scientific advice," asserting "that it is essential for different values to be represented in public advice."[44]

Although we find Pamuk convincing on the need for democratic participation in fashioning public policy, her recommendations for accomplishing it are muddled. Take school closures during the pandemic. We now know that the US Centers for Disease Control (CDC) and the American Federation of Teachers (AFT) fashioned closure policy. It appears that the CDC sent a draft of its policy recommendations to the teachers' union weeks before a public release.[45] There is little one can think of that damages the already compromised legitimacy of the CDC than the revelation that it sought the input of the teachers' union prior to formulating policy. So much for following the science. And so much for the claim—consistently made—that the matter had to be handled by experts. Like so many decisions during the pandemic, the decision to keep schools closed and mask children was largely political in nature.

Of course, all of this could have been avoided and the CDC's credibility bolstered if the agency had made any effort to bring in the primary stakeholder into the discussion: parents. We recognize that school closures are controlled by local school districts and not the federal government, but local school boards are composed of people who are well meaning and risk averse. It is simply too much to ask them to go against the advice of government experts. Thus, as Eyal points out, "including lay members of the public in the deliberations of expert advisory bodies, especially in matters directly relevant to them, thereby render[s] decision-making processes more accountable, transparent and responsive."[46]

So what do populists want? As we argued in chapter 5, they want a voice. Hirschman's exit-voice-loyalty paradigm is at home in this context as much as it is in the ballot box. On the issue of school closures, the public was never consulted. That was the mistake. In one of the more thoughtful articles about the role of the AFT and its president, Randi Weingarten, David Leonhardt quotes an email from a Cal Berkeley philosopher that distills the problem with great clarity:

> It is clear that extended school closures were a mistake—they harmed children while having no measurable effect on the pandemic. It is also clear that teachers' unions were a major factor behind the closures. But remember that the unions were just doing their job. Their remit is to advocate for their members and that is exactly what they did.
>
> Seen like this, the problem was not the teachers' union per se—I am personally in favor of public sector unions—but the absence of a comparable organization at the bargaining table to represent the interests of students and their caregivers. It was a failure of democratic decision-making.[47]

One of the most important things in solving a problem is figuring out what sort of problem one has. The problem of school closures is but a microcosm of the larger problem of participation and choice in making public policy. The executive branch, the CDC, and the AFT colluded to keep the public out of the discussion on school closures and favor the interests of the members of the AFT. The revelations surrounding this issue hurt the credibility of the CDC enormously. Quite apart from the question of democratic participation, the revelations surrounding the CDC's consultations with the AFT serve only to confirm populists' worst fears about elite hubris. This is what fuels populism. Why anyone is surprised about that outcome is a mystery to us.

Why Are Facts and Values Conflated?

Mark Kelman, a left-leaning legal scholar who is known for engaging conservative arguments more seriously on their own terms, once participated in a panel discussion at a Federalist Society conference. The audience comprised largely right-leaning libertarians, and Kelman sought to describe what he saw in their most recent theories.[48] The changes in argument he had observed appeared to be more factual in nature than anything else. That is, early libertarians rested their theories on a relatively stylized and ultimately historically inaccurate portrayal of the "state of nature." As libertarianism evolved, it became more focused on comparative institutional study—that is, it substituted a new factual story about the types of American regulatory institutions that promoted libertarian ideals for the "state of nature" story. The new story was proving no more accurate, but empirical challenges seemed not to shake libertarians of their faith. Several continued to teach debunked stories—for instance, a claim that seatbelts made drivers less safe, which numerous empirical studies had discredited—because they "fit" the narrative.

But this was not a problem unique to right-leaning libertarians. It reminded him, Kelman said, of "watching the kooky leftists I hung out with in the late 60s." Their theories went through similar tumult. But one thing never changed: their commitment to factual stories that supported their underlying value system. The most reliable barometer of left- and right-leaning students came when there were arguments over blame in police shootings. Members of Students for a Democratic Society "believed in every single case that the police shot first, and . . . the young Republicans . . . in every single case believe the Panthers shot first." As Kelman pointed out, that's a factual question that needn't be inflected by politics (except perhaps as a first estimate): making a determination should require evaluating evidence. But both sides were "utterly unshakable."[49]

Kelman drew a surprising and important conclusion from his armchair sociological observations of his left and right colleagues. Since the Enlightenment, most of us have assumed that theories are hard to ground, but facts can be settled. We don't expect a philosophical proof to crush Humean skepticism or to resolve libertarian versus communitarian conceptions of political goods. But we do think facts can be settled. Kelman came to the opposite conclusion. "People lose faith in their theories because they're incredibly intellectually incoherent. They fall back on beliefs about the empirical world that are fairly badly grounded, but they can't be shaken out of them regardless of the level of proof. I think this is a fairly general tendency of people with strong political beliefs."[50]

Kelman made these statements in 1987, but little seems to have changed. Among very liberal Americans, most believe that police kill more than 1,000 unarmed Black men each year and that the majority of people killed by police are Black. (The actual total number of police killings in 2019, when the question was asked, was less than 100, and roughly 25 percent of those killed were Black.)[51] Republicans massively overestimate the number of immigrants and their dependence on government welfare.[52] The one thing both "sides" agree on is their dislike of each other: more than 75 percent of voters think supporters of the other party represent "a clear and present danger to the American way of life."[53]

*   *   *

We do not pretend to offer a solution, but elites' intentional elision of values in the decision-making process does not help our politics. It is a fiction to pretend there is some kind of prepolitical, neutral playing ground consisting of bare-bones facts, nothing more. That perspective hardens disagreements because it makes it easy to see the other side as illegitimate in its promotion of what it says are facts. If the other side is truly fabricating facts, there is no point in engaging that side. Fighting over deep political values, while difficult, is at least honest.

For some reason, we seem to be more comfortable chalking up many disputes to facts, when they are really about values. This may be because disputes about values feel hard to resolve. Values may feel incommensurate, while factual fights feel tractable. If my opponent genuinely believes, contrary to all evidence, that $2 + 2 = 5$ or that the earth is flat, there is very little I can do. If one goal of disagreement is to understand the other side such that one can recognize them as a fellow subject, there is no room for understanding in disputes over facts. The best I can "understand" about my math-denying colleague is that they are hopeless or crazy; at my most empathetic, I might conclude that they are the victims of poor education or a math-denying demagogue. That empathy would hardly mean much to my interlocutor, however, if they hold their view in good faith and would instead smack of paternalism and condescension.

If I can see my opponent's claim as something different—a claim about values or a claim about an ideology, a structure of viewing the world—there may be room for disagreement and understanding. These disagreements may still prove intractable. I may be unwilling to budge and maybe even less willing to budge because my foundational moral views are sacrosanct. But at least I can recognize my opponent's claim as similar in structure to my own: their claim is a genuine expression of their values, however disagreeable or even repugnant I might find it. In other words, in focusing on values and ideology we are fighting on the actual ground of our debate rather than an imagined ground on which neither of us has based our opinion. I might even be prepared to compromise, not in the sense that I would give ground on my values but in the sense that I could realize the only valid democratic outcome is one that gives each side a little ground. It is much harder to imagine splitting the baby on facts, such that we agree in the name of political expediency that $2 + 2 = 4.5$.

Many fear we have become tribal, but belief in a value structure or ideology isn't necessarily "tribal." No doubt some voters are tribal partisans, but not all disagreements are the result of tribal partisanship. More voters than ever identify as independents (albeit with a lean), suggesting a distaste for party polarization. And our populist era has given rise to interesting swing voters—Obama-Trump voters, Sanders-Trump supporters—who can easily turn an election and are not voting primarily on party loyalty.

Many would assume rational discussion—say, in universities—should be about developing empirical clarity. There are certainly questions for which that is true, and nothing we say here should be taken as a denigration of more empirical research. But many politically salient questions are unlikely to be clarified by more empirical research. Indeed, disputes over certain highly charged issues—guns, policing—have not been improved when academics label them as disputes over facts.

*   *   *

It's commonly asserted that facts are facts—or, as the cliché goes, "facts are stubborn things." But is this even true? We will say more in a moment about the definition of the term *fact* but start here with a simple example. Imagine a doctor tells you that eating bacon leads to cancer. Isn't this a straightforward factual claim that we can adjudicate? In reality, it is a complex claim in several regards. For one, it involves an evidentiary issue—that is, it is hard to assess the truth of the claim. We cannot easily run an experiment where we force people to eat bacon and see what happens. We are instead reliant on observational data, which, as discussed earlier in this book, are fraught with peril. Interpreting observational data requires judgment calls by the study's author, to which the final result is likely quite sensitive.

But there is also an issue of narrative—of how the relationship between bacon and cancer is framed. How much bacon and how much risk are we talking about? Assuming the evidence suggests a link, there are always multiple ways to state a risk that are equally accurate but have very different meanings.[54] Let's put aside the evidentiary problems and say that the rate of cancer among nonbacon eaters is 6 percent, and among bacon eaters it is 7 percent. Both of the following statements would be fully accurate: "Eating bacon increases the risk of cancer by 1 percent." "Eating bacon makes you 17 percent more likely to get cancer than someone who doesn't." Both are true. One points to the increase in absolute risk, the other to the increase in relative risk. But one sounds far worse than the other. There are countless ways we could package the evidence. Perhaps we avoid percentages and ask people to imagine 100 hypothetical people who eat bacon and 100 who don't. Seven in the first group will get cancer, compared to six in the second. Still accurate, but any better? Each of these statements may be interpreted very differently by listeners.

The decision of how to describe this seemingly simple statistic is, like any exploration of data, inherently a judgment call about a *narrative*, and which narrative we choose makes a great deal of difference, but we cannot decide between them simply on the basis of facts. Sometimes there may be a clear choice to avoid confusion given the narrative's context, but the main basis for the choice is the author's preference. As the statistician Nate Silver says, "The numbers have no way of speaking for themselves. We speak for them. We imbue them with meaning. Like Caesar, we may construe them in self-serving ways that are detached from their objective reality."[55] It is unfortunate that elites rarely provide the context when they insist on mindlessly "following the data."

We can take our bacon example one step further. Even once we have communicated the fact, it doesn't answer any question on its own. It tells us nothing about how an individual perceives the relative value of the trade-off. How much is the ability to eat a particular food valued, relative to a particular form of health? What should we make of the possibility that people may later regret their choices? Does our evaluation change if we frame it as a population-wide question (the global impacts of one set of choices) or as an individual trade-off? Are these questions for society or for the individual to answer? These normative questions are in no way the particular purview of experts. A public-health professional may have thought deeply about the question and may form a strong view about the appropriate trade-off, but their expertise does not grant them moral superiority to decide the trade-off. This argument is not relativistic or postmodern. It's not antifact or antiknowledge. Rather, we are simply recognizing what any expert should admit: that facts are always and only *in context*.

Let's approach this issue from a more general level. How should we think about the concept of a "fact"? The National Academy of Sciences defines "fact" thus: "In science, an observation that has been repeatedly confirmed and for all practical purposes is accepted as 'true.' Truth in science, however, is never final, and what is accepted as a fact today may be modified or even discarded tomorrow."[56] "Truth in science" is an interesting phrase because it suggests a degree of relativism or at least context dependence.

What this means is that facts should be accorded a degree of weight in certain contexts. The degree to which truth is settled is context dependent. "In science, 'fact' can only mean 'confirmed to such a degree that it would be perverse to withhold provisional assent,'" says Stephen Jay Gould. "I suppose that apples might start to rise tomorrow, but the possibility does not merit equal time in physics classrooms."[57]

But an exploration of contrary facts might well warrant time elsewhere. In legal investigation, for example, the exploration of warring accounts is not only a central right but the basis on which judicial decisions are believed to be sound. In the realm of public opinion, contravening facts also play a critical role. Suffice it to say, facts play an important role in many aspects of life. In the realm of public discourse and the setting of policy, facts play an essential if not a pivotal role.

In giving a definition of "fact," we could have just said that a fact is a statement of what is the case. But once we investigate that locution—what is "the case"—we quickly come to see that things are not quite as simple as they might first appear. To gain some purchase on the matter of "fact," we discuss the concept and provide some illustrations to demonstrate that the idea of a "fact" is not as simple as some would suppose. We don't intend to provide a detailed philosophical account of "facts," although it is quite possible to do so.[58] Our interest is in giving enough detail to an account of facts that enables us to see what is at stake in ideas such as "appealing to the facts" and "making claims based in fact," for it is these sorts of locutions one finds regularly in public discourse.

Facts are the sort of thing about which we can be right or wrong. In the argot of philosophy, we do say that facts are what is the case. Facts and truth are related, of course. When we say something is true, it is usually because what we say accords with the facts. Philosophers traditionally understood truth as "correspondence with reality." The so-called correspondence theory of truth understood facts as expressed by sentences that were made true in virtue of the way the world is. The sentence corresponded with the facts and, as such, was made true by the facts.

Science is in the business of facts. In fact, one often hears that what makes science so useful is its devotion to "hard facts." The hardness of hard facts is often expressed by the idea of objectivity. That is, scientific facts are truths about the natural world. It is that world that science investigates, and it is the facts of nature that give scientific truth its place in the pantheon of truth. Inflation may be a "real" thing, but it cannot compete with, say, gravity in terms of the hardness of its "factness."

The correspondence theory of truth has its competitors—that is, different ways of understanding truth. On the pragmatist view of truth, the hardness of facts owes more to the ways in which the word *true* is deployed and less to the way the world is. Richard Rorty was a leading proponent of the pragmatist view of truth, and his conception of truth strikes us as a profitable way to think about truth and science in the current environment.

Rorty sets out to explain why certain facts seem to be "hard." The correspondence theorist would argue that what makes certain facts hard is that they correspond to the way the world is. Rorty is skeptical of this explanation. True statements, he concedes, do depend on facts—no disagreement there—but what makes something a fact, he argues, is not the way the world is: rather, it has to do with the reaction of members of a scientific community to a data point. If the litmus paper in an experiment turns blue, do we have objective proof or verification of a truth? In Rorty's view, "The hardness of fact . . . is simply the hardness of the previous agreements within a community about the consequences of a certain event." Rorty is not denying causation; something causal is definitely taking place, but that causality does not translate directly into truth. As he puts it, the pragmatist "sees no way of transferring this nonlinguistic brutality to facts, the truth of sentences." Facts, he concludes, are "hybrid entities; that is, the causes of the assertability of sentences include both physical stimuli and our antecedent choice of response to such stimuli."[59]

We leave the question of whether the pragmatist account of truth is the best to another day. What we can say is that this account of truth captures a great deal of discourse about the pandemic. Consider one example, that of deaths during the pandemic. A man contracts coronavirus, has trouble breathing, and dies. Did COVID-19 kill him? Was COVID-19 his "cause of death"? As countless articles and books suggested, "It's complicated."[60] Is there a fact of the matter about what kills someone who tests positive for COVID-19 at the time of death? If there are comorbidities, such as diabetes and coronary heart disease, the situation can be enormously complicated. We all want to say there is a truth of the matter about what killed someone; they died from something, but it's just not obvious that we can always say just what that something was. Facts are stubborn things, yes, but figuring out what is a fact is not always easy.

How does this discussion of facts impact our critique of the discourse of elites? First, the realism of elites—the notion that the world delivers truths that can never be doubted—is naive and implausible. One need not be a relativist about facticity to acknowledge that facts are both context dependent and subject to revision. Second, facts rarely do their work in isolation: they are embedded in cultural values about which there are genuine, good-faith disagreements. The elite trope of shutting down debate over values in the guise of science is the most pernicious rhetorical trope we know of. Much of the populist anger about being dismissed can be traced to this one rhetorical move.

In Defense of Expressive Voting

Told by the elites "no, there is no other way," populism seeks to find another way. This sometimes leads to voting in anger or protest, a kind of vote that is called "expressive" voting. It may be contrasted with "instrumental" voting, where one evaluates only the expected costs and benefits of the policies that may result from a particular candidate.[61] Most of us probably engage in a bit of both. It is common during elections to hear people talk about which candidate they would like to have a beer with—an eventuality that, in practical terms, seems both unlikely and irrelevant—or about candidates who will make history by breaking down barriers. Politics has both emotional and logical aspects to it. But the real mark against populists, for some, is too much "expressivism." Pundits look down on Bernie Sanders supporters for not being "realistic" enough or complain that the white working class voted against its own self-interest by choosing Trump over Hillary Clinton. Clinton may have called the working class "deplorables," the argument goes, but her economic policies might have been better than Trump's tax cuts.[62] Is this a fair criticism?

Cass Sunstein certainly thinks so. The aim of one of his books is "to combat expressive approaches to policy issues," which he sees as "a great obstacle to progress."[63] The scholars of Brexit who chalked up the Leave vote to a post-truth environment also seem to denigrate the possibility of expressive voting. As voters "los[e] their respect for traditional elites and gatekeepers," they write, "emotionally charged voting has become more prevalent."[64] They bemoan that our post-truth era has given rise to more "value-based voting" and voters who set intentions based on their "heart" rather than on evidence.

But what's the problem with this emotional approach? Why can't voters make choices based on something other than a cost–benefit analysis? The disdain hearkens back to the voices in our first chapter who felt that populists' economic complaints were simply wrong and unjustifiable. We do not see a reason to pass judgment on how people form their votes. We note some hypocrisy in critiques of expressive voting: many people seem fine with their friends forming an emotional connection with a particular candidate as long as the candidate is acceptable to them. There is a similar blurring of facts and values here: elites who disdain "expressive" votes are trying to fight someone else's values on the value-laden grounds that they are "factually" mistaken or irrational.

The idea that politics involves both intuition and rationality seems like a perfectly ordinary, inevitable, and desirable feature of democracy. Hirschman's exit/voice dichotomy also plays a role here. The expressive and instrumental accounts of voting may be closer together than they sound. Protest votes may, in fact, be the only choice available when one is told there are no choices. Certainly, the wave of surprise populist victories around the world has gotten the attention of elites.

Expressive voting is a phenomenon that must be understood if it is to be addressed properly. When a substantial portion of the population is told their opinions don't matter and their point of view is irrelevant, they tend to respond in a negative fashion. This is one way of understanding expressive voting, and, we surmise, this is how elites understand it. But the point is not that people are voting in some irrational manner. In fact, given their situation, expressive voting may be just as "rational" as voting along the lines of cost–benefit analysis. Voting is all about motivation and perspective.

We have shown the plausibility of the populist rejoinder to the political epistemology of elites. A central contention of our book is that in matters of public policy almost nothing can be settled by scientific expertise alone. Expert knowledge enters the public sphere with the promise of resolution of contested facts, but, as the pandemic has shown us, it is exceedingly difficult to disentangle facts from values. In fact, expertise rarely makes its appearance without the freight of the moral values held by the purveyor of facts.

We are now in a position to see how elites respond to the populist pushback. Unfortunately, as we explore in part III, they have not taken the critique to heart. Instead, they have doubled down on their initial bluff. Many of the moves that we discuss in the remaining chapters—the hysteria over misinformation or claims that dissent is largely the result of "merchants of doubt"—are just a form of circling the wagons. Professions, once defined, tend to seek means of excluding nonprofessionals. The technocratic regime has done this, gradually arrogating to elites more and more control over all aspects of life for everyone. Every subject, not just complex medical or physics or engineering questions, has become "expertised." Expertise is used as a cudgel in debates over hotly contested issues—racism, abortion rights, censorship—to claim there is really no space for disagreement. Perhaps most troubling, that trend has overtaken the institutions that generate expertise, where groupthink increasingly predominates and dissenting voices are marginalized.

III Doubling Down: Weaponizing the Charge of Misinformation

8 Much Ado about Misinformation

We live in an age of misinformation and disinformation. Knowledge has been undermined by lies perpetrated on social media. Ignorance abounds because we are living in a post-truth environment. Such is the elite narrative. There is only one problem with it: it isn't true.

A presidential candidate secretly plots with congressional leaders in his party. If that candidate is not elected, a coup d'état will save their country and restore him to the Oval Office. Little evidence supports this conspiracy theory, but it is widely believed by his opponents. A typical tale from contemporary America's post-truth crisis? Hardly: the story dates from 1828, and the leader in question was Andrew Jackson.[1]

We are said to be awash in misinformation and disinformation.[2] The belief is pervasive that we live in a unique, post-truth age dominated by fake news.[3] This is the foundational myth that sustains the third elite habit of mind at issue in this book, *intellectual tyranny*. For many elites, our dangerous epistemic environment justifies a wholesale campaign against doubt and dissent—even in science, where it is foundational to the entire endeavor—and a climate of censorship and cancellation in the institutions that are supposed to foster public discourse. Populists question elites' epistemic culture, which requires deference to experts. In response, elites double down, weaponizing the claim of misinformation to legitimate the stifling of debate. In this chapter, we explain why the fever pitch over misinformation is misguided before we turn to the consequences of squelching dissent in our remaining chapters.

Terms such as *misinformation, disinformation, alternative facts, truthiness,* and *fake news* capture the zeitgeist of angst about our collective failure to simply face up to "reality." Headlines could practically be generated by an

AI bot: "The Death of Truth: How We Gave Up on Facts and Ended Up with Trump" reads a characteristic headline in *The Guardian*.[4] Americans largely seem to have bought into this narrative: according to the Pew Research Center, 85 percent of Americans think that our failure to agree on the facts is a moderately or very big problem.[5] A CBS poll indicates that 60 percent of Americans say people are more likely to believe in conspiracy theories today compared to 25 years ago.[6] So conventional is the wisdom that it is apparently the rare point we all agree on: "Americans know by now that democracy depends on a baseline of shared reality—when facts become fungible, we're lost," writes George Packer, the chronicler of America's great unraveling, in an *Atlantic* essay.[7] Some critics charge that the central epistemic doctrine of a wide swath of citizens evinces little more than a "generalized defiance towards established knowledge."[8]

But here's the problem. All the best social science research converges on the same finding: there is no evidence that we live in an age uniquely defined by misinformation or conspiratorial belief.[9] This is not to say misinformation doesn't exist but that it does not carry the kind of exceptional explanatory weight it is given.

Nor does there seem to be some kind of one-sided problem, as commonly charged, where Republican voters have become a "political party unhinged from truth."[10] "The GOP Has Become the Stupid Party—and Proud of It," reads one typical headline.[11] Try this exercise: name a political party where a third of members believe a presidential election was stolen through voter fraud. You probably didn't say the Democrats, but 34 percent of Democrats agreed with the statement "Republicans stole the '04 presidential election through voter fraud in Ohio." Lest you think we're arguing that this means the Democrats are the party with a problem, we hasten to add that 39 percent of Republicans rejected the statement that "Barack Obama was born in the United States."[12] To the extent all of use exist in a "post-truth" age, it is a bipartisan problem, and the problem is not limited to the "ignorant" masses whom elites despise: in fact, highly educated Democrats are *more* likely to endorse mistruths about climate change than less educated ones.

The key problem with the misinformation story is that "facts" don't matter in the ways we think they do. This nuance rarely makes it into coverage of our post-truth environment but is fundamental. That is, *why* do Democrats say the 2004 election was stolen, and *what effects* does that apparent misperception have on them? The call to arms about misinformation generally assumes that misinformation is the *source* of partisan divides rather than a consequence of it. That's largely wrong. The cause-and-effect relationship matters because if facts are the result of preexisting divides, our energies really should be applied elsewhere. We should recognize that fundamental tensions over deeply held values are inevitably at the center of our politics. Although recognizing this does not get us closer to resolving our disputes, we should at least be honest about playing on the right field.

If misinformation is not our central problem, why have we come to think this? Some of it is familiarity: we encounter misinformation, and it is plausible and satisfying to blame it for our woes. But the story is also highly consistent with the mindset of elites and useful to them. Deploying the charge of "misinformation" debases one's opponents and eliminates the necessity of engaging with their arguments. It reifies the technocratic view held by elites. Elites arrogate to themselves and to their preferred experts all aspects of public judgment. They justify this claim in part with the view that other people are ignorant and buttress it with the alleged sea of misinformation in which we all swim.

Here, we want to put misinformation into context. Doing so surely does not mean that truth is irrelevant. We are entirely in favor of pursuing truth and of improving institutions—such as academia and journalism—that have conventionally been seen as referees of facts. But most commentators go further: they rarely pause to consider that *truth* is a complex term. What they tend to mean by "truth" really means "what elites hold to be self-evident at the moment." As a result, they either explicitly devalue pluralism or merely pay lip service to it. The conventional solution to misinformation instead seems to be less pluralism and more of our contemporary tendency toward groupthink and ideological conformity. Hysteria over misinformation is leading us to some dark places where calls are made for the kind of censorship and conformity that breed resentment and prevent open inquiry.

This chapter lays out the empirical case for why misinformation in our time is hardly novel or unprecedented in scope. Of course, misinformation exists, and we do not mean to give it a free pass, but it probably does not play as much of a role in forming views as feared because of how people process information. That is, they are receptive to information that *already agrees* with their priors. Those who wring their hands about our post-truth moment rarely grapple with that, nor do they grapple with the thorny difficulties of identifying or correcting misinformation, which may be next to impossible *and* come at a tremendous cost to free and open discourse.

An Age of Misinformation?

After Trump's election in 2016, it was hard to escape commentators telling us about our post-truth world of facts and alternative facts. Pundits bemoaned a world in which voters—or at least some of them—no longer cared about facts, which is said to be central to our contemporary democratic crises. "A republic will not work if we don't have shared facts," Senator Ben Sasse said. Suggesting bipartisan consensus, President Obama expressed a similar sentiment in a 2018 interview with David Letterman: "One of the biggest challenges we have to our democracy is the degree to which we don't share a common baseline of facts." David Brooks sees the lack of truth as a central social fact, especially of right-leaning voters, claiming that conspiracy theories are now "the most effective community bonding mechanism of the 21st century" and describing populists as "floating on oceans of misinformation and falsehood."[13]

One of the most rigorous and thoughtful students of misinformation is the political scientist Brendan Nyhan. His research is sensitively attuned to the difficulty of getting a handle on misinformation. It turns out to be very hard to measure its prevalence, relevance, and effect. For instance, we might survey people to see if they believe well-known falsehoods and assess how widespread misperceptions are. Although this is a common approach, it is problematic. It skews toward well-known, controversial misperceptions that may not represent the overall prevalence of accuracy. (It's hard to test on subtle misperceptions because researchers may themselves not agree on the "truth.")

Moreover, such surveys may not really tell us what people think. Surveys—and other supposed evidence of misinformation—may produce "partisan cheerleading," expressive responding, and trolling. To take our earlier example: Do many Republicans *genuinely* believe Obama was born elsewhere, or are they answering that way for other reasons tied to their dislike of him? The extent to which other factors affect survey results remains an open question, but we know that it happens. In one study, researchers asked people to evaluate the relative size of the crowds that attended Obama's and Trump's inaugurations. When the pictures were not labeled, people accurately identified the larger crowd as at Obama's inauguration. Once the pictures were labeled with the candidate's names, however, partisan cheerleading took over, and accuracy became less relevant.[14] Experimenters have techniques for trying to reduce expressive responding, such as paying people for getting the right answer. But none of these techniques is perfect. Moreover, there is always a possibility that participants' responses change because of the context: they may be trying to please the experimenter or to feel as if they're answering on behalf of their in-group. Plus, people don't always have access to their "truest" thoughts, and so the survey methodology is always going to have limitations.

But even beyond the measurement challenges, such surveys do not answer the question that really matters: What comes first, facts or preferences? That is, do the facts inform the preference or rationalize an existing one?[15] If opinions come first, the conventional wisdom regarding misinformation—its diagnosis and its cure—is wrong. The attempt to cure our misinformation environment, were it even possible, would do little to help our partisan divide and is a distraction from the battle at hand. Politics is ultimately about helping us discuss and resolve—however tentatively—our divided opinions. If our division is really about opinions, not facts, that's where we should focus our energy.

The belief that our politics is warped by falsehoods is hardly novel. Indeed, complaining about misinformation in politics may be a little like complaining about the weather. More than two centuries ago, John Adams complained of rampant fake news: "There has been more new error propagated by the press in the last ten years than in a hundred years before 1798," he once jotted down.[16] The infamous Alien and Sedition Acts deployed censorship as an antidote to fear of dissent and discord. And the presidential contest between Adams and Jefferson in 1800 is sometimes said to have been an even dirtier, more mudslinging affair than those we are used to today. In 1964, the historian Richard Hofstadter famously described the "paranoid style" of American politics. He was, of course, stimulated to write his analysis by the politics of the 1950s and 1960s, but he also attempted to trace this instinct back further as a long-standing American trait that occurs and recurs across time.[17]

Evidence for the misinformation epidemic we are said to be experiencing today is generally anecdotal, and it fails to distinguish between influential and uninfluential misinformation. Even if we could identify and count every "wrong" sentence, it would be useless without knowing how important those sentences are. Did the misinformation appear on the front page of a major newspaper or on a bot-generated webpage that nobody actually read except perhaps other bots? For today's disciples of the misinformation crisis, the distinction hardly seems to matter.

Media headlines would have us believe that QAnon, the right-wing conspiracy theory centered around fabricated claims made by "Q" on an internet message board, is a dominant force in politics. A series of *Washington Post* headlines described it as a conspiracy theory "creeping into U.S. Politics" and a "menace" that "spread around the world," while the *New York Times* went so far as to claim in a headline, "QAnon Now as Popular in U.S. as Some Major Religions."[18] But a more level-headed account can be found in a paper published in 2022 by Adam Enders, a leading political scientist who studies conspiracy theories, and his coauthors, who conducted extensive empirical research into views on Q. Their sobering conclusion was that support for Q was "meager and stable across time," contradicting both aspects of the conventional wisdom. Far fewer people believe in Q than believe in various conspiracy theories about JFK's assassination. Media accounts to the contrary have made the mistake of conflating the *existence* of a large presence with actual support. This finding, the researchers note, is consistent with multiple other studies that suggest that fake news is much less influential than media accounts assume.[19]

Again, our purpose here is not to give Q a free pass or to celebrate the fact that some political candidates openly endorse Q or to suggest the number of Q's supporters could never grow. Our point is that it is important to maintain perspective rather than to begin believing that our *central* political problems involve activity on the margins. Instead of grasping the polarization at the heart of political life, we are focused instead on the fringes. Stanching the growth of something like Q also requires a level-headed understanding of the origins of Q. Contrary to popular accounts, most researchers who study conspiracy theories conclude the same thing: such theories are motivated predominantly by individual psychological predispositions toward conspiratorial beliefs, *not* by misinformation or political mistrust.[20]

Another canard is the view that misinformation must be on the rise because of the unique social and technological conditions of our time: a pervasive ignorance combined with technologies such as social media that allow falsehoods to spread rapidly. Some point fingers at particular institutions, such as the Republican Party. Others suggest that the problem is only going to get worse as digital large-language models make misinformation easier to generate and even customize. What is wrong with these intuitive-sounding ideas? Nyhan points out that "false information, misperceptions, and conspiracy theories are general features of human society." In his comprehensive review of evidence, he found nothing other than anecdotal accounts suggesting the problem is any worse today than in the past.[21]

Even if social media do increase the sheer *volume* of misinformation, the consequence of that is unclear. It is not evident that more misinformation means more *belief* in that misinformation. Indeed, some of what we widely assume—that fake-news bots are having lots of impact, for instance—is demonstrably false. Nyhan and his coauthors have demonstrated that Americans actually didn't see much "fake news" in 2016, despite all the media accounts to the contrary.[22] Others who study the phenomenon of social media have had similar findings. But this message cannot easily compete with headlines about numerous fake accounts and tweets, all of which lack context about whether most of those tweets actually mattered or were even read. This is part of why large-language models, which have given rise to recent fears about an even greater flood of misinformation, may matter less than many assume. For a rogue actor, the biggest problem with spreading misinformation is not the bottlenecks in creating it but the inadequate demand for it and inadequate channels for supply, which large-language models do not change.[23]

Nyhan and his coauthors are not alone in their conclusions. Others, such as researchers who study conspiracy theories, have found little evidence of a rise in conspiratorial worldviews. It appears instead that conspiracy theories are a long-standing—and bipartisan—feature of American politics. One group of prominent researchers looked over time and were able to identify more decreases than increases in conspiracy beliefs (although they did not go so far as to conclude that conspiratorial thinking is declining, either). The internet has not played the role many seem to believe it has.[24] Again, the essential mistake is confusing the ability to access misleading or conspiratorial information with *belief* in that information. Many saw the COVID-19 pandemic as a misinformation free-for-all, but actually there was probably *less belief* in misinformation than at other times in the past when disease was spreading widely.[25] General conspiratorial views—like the view that corporations are plotting against us—have actually *declined* over time.

Another myth in the conventional wisdom is that conspiratorial thinking is a partisan—specifically right-wing—problem. It turns out that most of us believe at least one conspiracy. (Examples of widely held conspiratorial views—held by roughly half of us—include the belief that Jeffrey Epstein was murdered in a cover-up, that President Kennedy wasn't assassinated by a lone gunman, and views about the deep state.[26]) That said, only a relatively small proportion of people have a strong conspiratorial proclivity that causes widespread belief in conspiracies. Nevertheless, right-leaning and left-leaning conspiracy theories do exist, and the partisan lean of such theories can change from country to country.

For instance, belief in Q, although rare, exists among *both* left- and right-leaning individuals. Rather than a particular partisan lean, believers tend to have a predisposition to "conspiratorial worldviews, dark triad personality traits, and a predisposition toward other nonnormative behavior." In other words, belief in conspiracy theories is a psychological phenomenon more than a political one, and a relatively minor one at that.[27]

Empirical research on our epistemic environment contradicts other favored chestnuts of elites. Many are convinced we live in our own filter bubbles, where we consume only information that agrees with us. It is certainly true that people have proclivities to engage with and trust information that supports their priors. But most Americans actually do *not* consume a heavily biased news diet. The best research shows that most people don't actually pay much attention to or consume political news or consume it in a fairly balanced measure. Relatively few of us live in the much-feared filter bubble.[28] We don't mean to let social media companies off the hook, but it may be that their contribution to our warped discourse is not mainly in the sphere of misinformation but rather in wrecking our mental health and contributing to a maladjusted national psyche.[29]

Overall, Nyhan and others reach the same sobering conclusion: our moral panic about "post-truth" far eclipses the evidence of its existence. "Misperceptions present a serious problem, but claims that we live in a 'post-truth' society with widespread consumption of 'fake news' are not empirically supported and should not be used to support interventions that threaten democratic values."[30] This does not mean we shouldn't continue to study this phenomenon or be attuned to the possibility that it will get worse, but it does mean we should be cautious about throwing out our basic commitments to free expression in a misguided effort to quash misinformation. Unfortunately, this more nuanced view of misperceptions—which seems widely shared by the academic community that researches it—has not made a dent in pundits' breathless panic about our novel post-truth society. In fact, few of them ever seem to have even paused to ask whether their confident assumptions about misinformation are, well, misinformation. In a way, this is unsurprising, for as we begin to elucidate next, facts and misperceptions more often follow beliefs than cause them.

Getting the Causal Arrow Right

Much of the panic about misinformation assumes a naive model for how we form our opinions: that facts come first, then opinions. Someone reads an untrue fact, believes and internalizes it, and then adopts a political conclusion that is "wrong" based on it—"wrong" in the sense that they would not hold that opinion but for their misperception. But our mental models are more complicated than that and largely work in the reverse direction. This is precisely why we have harped on how difficult it is to identify "pure facts" and why we believe values play an inescapable role in political decision-making. But let us pause to consider in greater depth the evidence on how people reason. In particular, we are interested in "motivated reasoning," a near-ubiquitous behavior where we process information in light of prior beliefs, values, or identity.

The basic idea behind motivated reasoning is straightforward and intuitive. When people reason through a problem, they may be motivated by "accuracy." In other words, they may want to obtain the truth, whatever it is, as impartially as possible. (Think of solving a simple math problem, such as adding the tip to your restaurant check.) But they may also be motivated by *directional* goals—the conclusion may come first. (Think of how you evaluate the latest political event—parsing the latest Supreme Court decision, for example.) In political reasoning, people often want to reach a conclusion that shores up their identity as part of a member of a particular partisan tribe. As Dan Kahan, a leading scholar of motivated reasoning, puts it, "People endorse whichever position reinforces their connection to others with whom they share important commitments."[31]

An interesting experiment demonstrates how a political framing can overwhelm the desire for accuracy. Researchers presented people with a simple table and several questions; to get the right answer, they had to make a quick calculation from the numbers in the table. For one group of participants, the column labels portrayed the data as being about something mundane: the effects of skin-care products on skin. People did reasonably well at getting the right answer. To the extent they struggled, their accuracy depended mainly on their numeracy. The better at math someone was, the more likely they answered correctly. But the story changed for a second group, where the same table was provided, but the labels were switched out, suggesting the table was actually about gun control. The numbers and correct answers were identical in both groups, but participants did much worse. In other words, people were perfectly happy to "do the work" to find the right answer in the skin-care example but were far more *directionally* motivated in the more politically charged case of gun control. Strikingly, the *more numerate* people were the most prone to polarization and thus to getting the wrong answer in the gun-control case. The explanation is that numeracy made them more able to warp the data to meet their preconceived ideas. This was true for both right- and left-leaning participants.[32]

This research may seem unnerving. It suggests that facts "don't matter"—or at least don't matter in the ways we want them to. Moreover, nobody is off the hook when it comes to motivated reasoning. It is not a "Republican" problem or an "ignorant person" problem. In fact, if anything, more educated people are *more likely* to engage in motivated reasoning in many situations—in part because they get good at figuring out how to make any fact buttress their narrative. (This may help explain why elites so genuinely seem to believe the facts are on their side.) Ignorance is not the problem.[33]

Many things that are described as "misinformation" seem to be primarily the result of increasing partisanship. There was a period not long ago when educated liberals had less accurate views on climate-change science than their highly educated Republican counterparts. Today, both educated Republicans and Democrats have similar knowledge about science but arrive at starkly different views, again suggesting that "ignorance" is not the problem. Views started to shift after the 1990s as climate change began being portrayed as a partisan issue in the media. Prior to that shift, "politically attentive conservatives, in fact, were *more likely to believe scientists about global warming than liberals were.*"[34] Unfortunately, once the issue became politicized, accuracy mattered less than motivated reasoning. The same holds true for other hot-button issues. Vaccine support appears to waffle back and forth depending on the current president. That is, partisans of the current president—whether Republican or Democrat—appear to be more likely to believe in the safety of vaccines and more likely to vaccinate their children.[35]

It is not nihilistic or relativistic to understand that facts play a more limited role in our politics than assumed. It is realistic and democratic. Our hardest debates—our biggest social conflicts, the largest partisan divides—aren't centrally debates over facts. They're just framed that way. Facts may still matter, for plenty of reasons. Lest someone make a straw-man argument out of our claim, we *of course* favor good-quality evidence and of systems that reliably produce and disseminate it. As lawyers, we are deeply attuned to both the importance of and the difficulty of achieving that goal. The law is a complicated, flawed system that at its core is designed to produce and evaluate competing evidence. It may falter in that goal, but the goal is a central precept nonetheless. Facts are central in many domains of life. Health-care decisions should be informed by the best possible information. Pundits seem much less bothered by medical quackery, unfortunately, than by shadowy Russian sources of misinformation that explain political outcomes they dislike.

We do not mean to suggest that we are telling a happier story when compared to the standard misinformation narrative that elites peddle. It is just a more accurate story. The problem isn't "following" or "not following" the science. Rather, the challenge arises in our partisan political divides and use of political rhetoric that fuels a herd mentality over certain issues. Putting out "more information" or censoring "misinformation" does not seem likely to help in overcoming this challenge. Whatever measure you use, the worst offenders tend to be the elites themselves. The more educated and more politically motivated an individual is, the more likely that person is to engage in motivated reasoning because such individuals have the most at stake in preserving their identity. There's less reason for a populist to do that. Populists believe that people like them "have no say in government[,] and [they] are relatively more likely to feel elections cannot change things."[36] That gives them less incentive to engage in the kind of partisan motivated reasoning than elites.

The Perils of Fact-Checking

The standard story about the prevalence of misinformation makes a second unsubstantiated leap from a faulty diagnosis to an even more dubious cure. Many elites have jumped to the conclusion that drastic measures—censorship by government and by tech monopolies—are warranted. At a minimum, most think, more "fact-checking" is warranted. At a more serious extreme, they propose Orwellian initiatives such as the ill-fated Disinformation Governance Board.[37] But these views only show, once again, how flimsy and thoughtless the elite conception of truth really is. Rather than something arrived at through process over time and always possessing some ambiguity, "truth" is simply whatever elites and their institutions declare at any point in time.

Misinformation is actually strikingly hard to identify. One person's obvious misinformation may be another's strongly held opinion. We do not mean facts can never be identified. We do not hold that there is much value if someone wants to claim that the earth is flat. But such examples are rare and of little practical import. The examples that matter are almost always more complicated than that. As such, censoring misinformation carries the strong risk of censoring a good-faith idea. This risk is hardly worth it, considering the thin evidence for misinformation's role in our contemporary maladies. But even if such a case could be made, would-be censors would have to show that their solution is worth other significant costs to the free flow of ideas and the silencing of important, good-faith ideas.

Consider a recent example: the rush to label the mere possibility that COVID-19 emanated from a lab in China as a dangerous conspiracy theory. Of course, as we now know, many intelligence agencies now deem the lab leak the most likely possibility. At a minimum, the theory is plausible, hardly conspiratorial. The rush to close debate about it by elite institutions suggested a casual indifference to the facts. It also created mistrust—quite rational mistrust. But even today some researchers maintain a close-minded attitude to the idea. Researchers in 2023 attempted to describe what they saw as misinformation by physicians and went so far as to suggest that professional and legal sanctions were warranted against offenders. Among the offending claims was the lab-leak hypothesis. Perhaps because by 2023 the idea could no longer be clearly called misinformation, the researchers explained that the idea was not supported by science "at the time" the tweets were issued. (This is also untrue in that there had always been significant debate within the scientific community, even if the theory was labeled off-limits by the *New York Times*.) In other words, even though the claim ultimately proved plausible and perhaps correct, that was not enough to cleanse it of the charge of "misinformation."[38] This nonsensical charge appeared in a peer-reviewed academic article. Imagine how much worse the potential mislabeling of something as misinformation would be if it is made the burden of low-wage, outsourced workers employed by private social media companies and subject to political pressure.

We don't have to imagine, of course. During the COVID-19 pandemic, social media companies raced to fact-check and "deplatform" unwelcome ideas. They made nobody happy and later rushed to distance themselves from their efforts. (Outside of the pandemic, Twitter also distanced itself from its decision to censor the *New York Post* for publishing a story about Hunter Biden.[39]) Many elites felt the fact-checking efforts did not go far enough, while others noted their hypocrisy and inconsistency. Innocuous ideas and rigorous scientists were caught in the crossfire. Hoping to avoid blame, companies farmed the work out to third-party fact-checkers. These fact-checkers' credentials and methodology were generally opaque. One aspect was clear and hardly robust: they leaned heavily on a select group of doctors, distinguished mainly by large Twitter followings, to arbitrate decisions. As two researchers concluded, "Greater transparency in the process of determining misinformation is needed."[40]

But that was not the most disquieting part of the flawed, inconsistent censorship regime that private companies imposed on our COVID-19 debate. More troubling was the fact that the White House leaned on these sites to censor information.[41] The Biden administration was apparently successful in its efforts to get Twitter to remove tweets and kick off users after Biden claimed that social media companies were literally "killing people."[42] Others were "shadow banned," a practice that essentially means a participant is shouting into the abyss without knowing it.[43] Pharmaceutical companies also joined in on the action as part of their "global lobbying blitz to ensure corporate dominance" over the drugs and vaccines developed during the pandemic.[44]

These results are unsurprising. The headlong rush to "improve" our factual environment can only lead to Orwellian places. The resulting censorship may be direct, but its indirect form is just as insidious. Indirect censorship can distort the types of views that are most accessible, giving people a warped perspective of consensus, and it can have a chilling effect, scaring people away from exploring or sharing their views because of fear of being accused of misinformation.[45] The efforts of the misinformation police also produce silly views of what facts actually are, which contributes further to polarization as people start to develop an unhealthy sense that their opinions are actually "facts" rather than opinions. Others just develop cynicism about the entire enterprise.

Two political scientists who study misinformation looked at the dubious epistemology behind "fact-checking." According to their study, PolitiFact assessed 800 facts related to the 2012 presidential campaign, awarding them various "Pinocchios" based on how false they were. But, the authors note, "if facts were as self-evident as the fact checkers take them to be, they [the fact-checkers] would not have to engage in methodologically questionable practices."[46] Instead, fact-checkers are highly selective in which "facts" and politicians they check. They confound different aspects of a compound claim—that is, where one subsidiary point may be false, but the overall statement is correct. They are sloppy about basic issues of causation. Fact-checking sites regularly "fact-check" predictions about the future, which are of course not facts. The entire enterprise indeed seems quite dubious when PolitiFact checks statements such as Trump's claim that he was "right about everything."[47]

For those worried about our so-called post-truth environment, there is some good news that does not rely on tendentious efforts such as PolitiFact's. Social beliefs over the long term do seem to trend toward agreement about basic truths.[48] It is generally accepted now that smoking causes lung cancer. Belief in creationism has consistently declined over time, although many seem to think otherwise.[49] In general, mistaken beliefs do seem to be amenable to factual correction.[50] (For a while, some had worried that corrections could backfire, but this effect seems less likely than originally thought.[51]) The good news is tempered, however: just because people change their facts doesn't mean they change their opinions. As we have said, less depends on these facts than is widely believed. Corrections do seem to fix factual misperception, but they don't usually seem to change overall candidate or policy support.[52] But that is why politics exists.

Why Elites Mythologize Shared Facts

"Everyone is entitled to his own opinion, but not his own facts." This famous saying has become one of the most overused op-ed phrases of the post-Trump era.[53] Why are elites so seduced by this perspective? We think it is because of the mindset we diagnosed earlier—technocratic paternalism. Elites *genuinely* believe that facts settle debates.[54] They also have immense faith in their own command of those facts, the result of another of the three elite mindsets, condescension. Therefore, the best way for them to avoid cognitive dissonance when debates continue is to assume their opponents are factually misguided. To accept otherwise would be to admit that the real conflict is one of values or strongly held opinions, which cuts against the technocratic grain.

Consider the cognitive dissonance created by Trump's surprise victory in 2016. It required an explanation, but the most likely explanation—that enough voters had diverging opinions that led them to prefer Trump and that elites had been utterly blind to this—was not appealing. Instead, blaming shadowy forces, such as Russian misinformation, was more consistent with elite priors.

When shown the best research on misinformation, as we have presented it here, our students and colleagues are surprised and skeptical. But when pushed, our colleagues can rarely cite any evidence for their view that misinformation is rampant. All they have is a strongly held anecdotal feeling. Misinformation is the bugaboo of the hour only because it's a convenient narrative. The convenience of the narrative means not having to contend with fundamental disagreements over values. One can simply assert that the other side is factually wrong, and therefore one need not hear them out.

Jonathan Rauch's *The Constitution of Knowledge* (2021), which we discussed in chapter 2, is characteristic in this regard. Although Rauch is more sensitive than many commentators to the bipartisan nature of our problems—what he terms "cancel culture" on the left finds its mirror in "troll culture" on the right—he ultimately reveals a simplistic model of the relationship between facts and political opinions. If we could stop disagreeing over facts, he urges, everything would come together. In other words, polarization and gridlock are first and foremost the result of unresolved factual misunderstandings.

Rauch never establishes that people's lack of trust in elite political institutions has explanatory force, and his approach has an inevitable and unfortunate corollary lesson: in any fundamental disagreement, one political party is right on the facts, and the other is wrong. This lesson is self-serving but also reflects a game where pride of place is automatically given to the current conventional wisdom of elite institutions. Because we defer to expertise, those who control expertise and the process of expert judgment, by and large members of the elite, will always have the right take on the facts.

Rauch and others say a republic can't work without shared facts, but what we think they mean, without realizing it, is that a republic cannot work without shared opinions—in particular their opinions. This, needless to say, is a very different claim—and a deeply undemocratic, ultimately indefensible one. If we are right, hand-wringing over the disregard for facts is really a way of at best ignoring and at worst silencing your opponents' more fundamental disagreements with you.

Rauch does not grapple with the empirical challenges to his argument— the findings that misinformation does not appear to have a widespread explanatory causal role in contemporary politics. He also avoids grappling with the theoretical challenge. This failure hollows out the meaning of political judgment. As Michael Sandel notes in his take-down of meritocracy, "Attributing political disagreement to a simple refusal to face facts or accept science misunderstands the interplay of facts and opinion in political persuasion." Sandel continues: "The idea that we should all agree on the facts, as a pre-political baseline, and then proceed to debate our opinions and convictions, is a technocratic conceit. Political debate is often about how to identify and characterize the facts relevant to the controversy in question. Whoever succeeds in framing the facts is already a long way to winning the argument. . . . [O]ur opinions direct our perceptions; they do not arrive on the scene only after the facts are cut and dried."[55]

Facts as Creed

In recent years, a sign has started popping up on the front lawns of blue neighborhoods across America. The yard sign begins, "In this house, we believe . . . ," and continues with a list of beliefs—one of which is "Science Is Real." Some progressives described the sign as "the most enduring symbol of anti-Trump resistance." It became popular after Trump's victory in 2016, although its words (which vary between renditions) are a mash-up of common progressive axioms.[56]

In a priceless emblem of our times, this sign is quite literally formulated in the form of a creed—the kind of statement of belief that is recited in church services. The sign is deliberately divisive, designed to run together a set of beliefs that are apparently considered to inherently run together. It is also deeply ironic in that it substitutes faith and dogmatism for the kind of critical thought that is inherent in some of its beliefs (such as science). It resonates precisely because it appeals to our tribal nature. One pundit insists the sign is not just virtue signaling, claiming it has done "a great deal of good" and made a "genuine difference in people's lives." But its real value seems to be like cheering on a favored team at a sports match. "Science is real," after all, is "a phrase millions of us have shouted at Fox News–watching relatives for years," he says.[57]

Elites eulogize a golden era when citizens purportedly accepted truth and shared facts. In contrast, the story goes, herd mentality now trumps epistemology, and "creedal conflict and political conflict [have] become indistinguishable."[58] The elite are nostalgic for the good old days, what Rauch calls the "reality-based community" or what Anne Applebaum rhapsodizes as "a world where we can say what we think with confidence, where rational debate is possible, where knowledge and expertise are respected, where borders can be crossed with ease."[59]

But the elite narrative founders when confronted by empirics. There is no novel misinformation epidemic, and facts have less role in shaping our views than elites assume. The false claim of misinformation not only erodes clarity over where our conflicts really lie but also has an even more insidious effect: it is weaponized to stifle dissent. Calling people misinformation or disinformation artists is an easy way to assert that their differing opinions have no value. That is the subject of our next chapter.

9   Merchants of Overconfidence

Can we trust research that is funded by an entity we deem undesirable or questionable? Should we question the motives of researchers who take money from corporations or other sources to fund their research? And what does it mean to practice science in the current context? These are some of the questions we take up in this chapter.

A school of economic theory known as "public-choice economics" deploys the tool kit of economics to explain political decisions. Many scholars working as public-choice theorists have a conservative or libertarian political bent. They treat political actors—politicians and policymakers—like any economic actor: as self-interested actors motivated by their own personal goals. The result of that approach can be quite critical to modern political institutions. Far from serving the public good, government agencies may be more interested in growing and gaining more power. Politicians may yield to the loudest or wealthiest voices rather than to the will of the people. Public-choice theory is a "politics without romance," which leads its proponents to be distrustful of politics and more trusting of markets, especially unregulated ones.[1]

It's not hard to imagine ways to argue against public-choice economics. You could unpack its assumptions, check its empirical work, or accept its description but disagree with its conclusions about markets. (Why should markets not be subject to the same problems as self-interested actors?) Many have done this and so have taken part in a debate that probably goes back millennia to long-standing fault lines over what makes a great society.

But here's another way you could disagree with public-choice scholars: you could impugn their motives. You could suggest that they have arrived at their conclusion only out of bias or malice. The historian Nancy MacLean does roughly this in her book *Democracy in Chains* (2018). The book is the latest entrant in a line of books that attempt to excavate the origins of conservative ideas that have gained power in recent years.[2] In principle, there is tremendous virtue in understanding how an idea was forged and the networks and institutions that were used to spread and popularize them, but today these accounts seem to be deployed simply to dismiss the arguments wholesale. Rather than taking such competing ideas seriously, these books treat them as little more than a conspiracy. MacLean describes her book as an "explosive exposé" of an "operation" by academics designed to "alter every branch of government to disempower the majority." An NPR review said the book revealed a "clear and present danger" to the country from these academics and fretted about "unsettling" tactics such as "a desire, at heart, to change the Constitution itself."[3] (Of course, the Constitution allows precisely that.)

Two historians of the public-choice movement sharply criticized MacLean's work as a conspiracy theory for liberal elites. They ask: "Why have so many left-wing readers embraced such a transparently flawed book? The most persuasive explanation is that MacLean confirms and extends their deep preexisting suspicions."[4] The book's approach amounts to a fallacy: an ad hominem attack on the scholars who first explored public-choice theory. It is therefore quite unsatisfying, and its basic claim about public-choice theorists unlikely. Unlikely because the public-choice theorists probably *did* believe what they were saying. They arrived at their conclusions in good faith, not because they wanted to "undermine" democracy or were "operat[ing]" together in a conspiracy. Unsatisfying because it fails to grapple with the ideas themselves and does not really explain why they found resonance. We are not here to praise public choice, but it's unfortunate that many Americans will never understand a major school of thought as anything more than a conspiracy to destroy democracy simply because they have read MacLean's book or a positive review of it.

This mode of critique avoids any serious engagement with ideas.[5] Understanding Trump's election as the consequence of Russian misinformation is easier than grappling with a complex populist foment. Explaining the ascendance of neoliberalism as the result of conservative funding is easier than trying to understand why the ideas resonated with society—above all even among liberals, such as Bill Clinton, who perhaps did more than anyone to popularize neoliberal concepts.[6] Such arguments *presume* that others come to the playing field in bad faith. MacLean continued this presumption in her response to her critiques, whom she falsely accused of being little more than paid shills for libertarian think tanks.[7]

In part II, we showed that elites misunderstand populists, writing them off as the ignorant myrmidons of demagogues. Here we show that elites also misunderstand each other, misreading intellectual opposition as bad faith. In doing so, elites are just as much responsible for the low quality of civic discourse as the populists they castigate. The rhetorical moves made in their critiques undermine democratic discourse and the search for truth. By rejecting the possibility that populists disagree with elites in good faith, these critiques instead rest on assumptions about the nefarious motives behind dissent. To those on the receiving end of these tactics, they appear as little more than attempts to avoid engaging in substantive argument. In this chapter, we focus in particular on the scientific trust offered by a leading public intellectual and historian of science, Naomi Oreskes, which we think encapsulates how elites misconstrue debate, doubt, and dissent.

Merchants of Doubt

During the pandemic, one observed widespread fretting about skepticism, dissent, and "denialism" during the pandemic. Two scholars went so far as to call it "the first post-truth pandemic."[8] Many turned for enlightenment and support to *Merchants of Doubt* (2010), a book by the historians of science Naomi Oreskes and Erik Conway that makes the case that scientists and corporations were complicit in falsely sowing doubt about nearly universally accepted research on climate change and tobacco. For many reasons we discuss, this research seems inapt when applied to a novel pandemic, yet its applicability was often assumed: the disparaging label *merchants of doubt* was applied aggressively to scientists who raised questions about the origin of COVID-19, the efficacy of particular treatments, and such interventions as school closures and lockdowns. Of the 6,000 works citing *Merchants*, almost 800 discuss COVID-19, according to Google Scholar.

This is not a harmless instance of name-calling. The conventional wisdom on a variety of issues flip-flopped over the course of the pandemic, as might well be expected, and some of the ideas that were once suppressed are now seen not only as valid but also highly plausible or even correct. Was the application of disparaging labels such as *merchants of doubt* to those who disagreed with the prevailing view simply the result of the fog of war during a novel infectious-disease outbreak? We think not. To illustrate this, we turn to another work by Naomi Oreskes, which develops an account of scientific trust grounded in the role played by consensus and community. This account values pluralism in debate over scientific claims. Yet Oreskes herself, like many scholars who share similar perspectives about scientific truth, vigorously censured dissenting scientists for their views about the pandemic.

Oreskes's work shares much in common with other elite-centric theories of epistemology, which hold that truth is best produced by communities of credentialed experts.[9] These accounts label particular views as out of bounds, but further examination of these accounts shows that their judgments as to the validity of experts and expert claims rest less on facts than on a preference for the authors' preexisting beliefs. We do not deny that Oreskes, Rauch, and others actually believe their opinions are grounded in facts. What we are suggesting is that their selection of *which* facts to deploy are driven by their priors. Just as many facts run contrary to their claims, but these authors choose not to engage with them.

We focus on Oreskes's work because it is both influential and emblematic of a widespread attitude toward scientific and populist dissent. We first describe her account of the nature of scientific practice. We then ask whether her theory, taken on its own terms, can be successfully deployed to delegitimize dissenting scientists (and nonscientists), as she and others do. We conclude that it cannot. First, her theory rests on gatekeeping institutions such as credentials and peer review, but many of the scientists she proposes to exclude are properly credentialed and have published peer-reviewed scholarship. Second, according to her theory, truth is established by the scientific community. Yet by this same token the theory cannot invalidate the work of ordinary citizens who claim to engage in science: that is, those who take the same data as scientific experts, employ the same or similar techniques of analysis with a high degree of data literacy, but come to vastly different conclusions about the data's significance. What really seems to demarcate science in Oreskes's account and others like it, instead, are the underlying priors of those seeking to draw lines of legitimacy in the sand. If one's conception of "science" is a function of one's priors, then "follow the science" may amount to a dogmatic insistence "to follow the science I think is right."

Trust and Consensus in Science

The COVID-19 pandemic brought the notion of "scientific consensus" into laser focus. Many policymakers as well as some scientists claimed throughout the pandemic that they were simply "following the science" or speaking "on behalf" of science and demanded that others "defer to experts." Some prominent scientists noted correctly that there was widespread disagreement within the scientific community both about particular scientific dimensions of the virus and about the appropriate response. But others, many of whom had primacy in media reporting on COVID-19, insisted that acknowledging any rift represented a false and opportunistic narrative propagated by a small number of deniers who stood well apart from the mainstream.[10]

Many of these commentators implicitly or explicitly drew upon the work of the historian of science Naomi Oreskes. A representative example, an opinion essay in the *British Medical Journal*'s online opinion blog was entitled "Covid-19 and the New Merchants of Doubt." Its authors, Gavin Yamey and David Gorski, argued that scientists with dissenting opinions on pandemic responses are like global-warming denialists, "using strategies straight out of the climate denial playbook." Much of their piece is given over to proposed links between prominent scientists and conservative causes. Ironically, some of their key factual allegations were ultimately retracted in a correction because they were not accurate. But, more importantly, Yamey and Gorski did not consider the possibility that these scientists came to their views in good faith, represented a wide swath of credentialed infectious-disease scientists, and might have had a point. They instead asserted but never demonstrated that these scientists' views were a product of a "well-funded sophisticated science denialist campaign based on ideological and corporate interests."[11] The rhetoric of "merchants of doubt" was deployed to powerful effect here, as elsewhere, to stifle scientific discussion.

Merchants of Doubt was largely a qualitative case study focused on telling the story of big tobacco and big oil's attempts to influence scientific debate. Its relevance to COVID-19 is doubtful. During the pandemic, there was no coherent industry or lobbying group that would consistently benefit from the (heterogeneous) views of dissenting scientists. There is no evidence that dissenting scientists were influenced by economic incentives. And, unlike tobacco and global warming, COVID-19 represented a novel threat that was poorly understood, where consensus could not plausibly have yet been reached. Indeed, that was the basic claim of one well-regarded scientist, John Ioannidis, who dissented from some of the conventional wisdom around the pandemic. In an op-ed authored in the first weeks of COVID-19's global spread, he argued that data, good data, would need to be collected and evaluated deliberately and continually if we were to develop a reasoned response. Although his op-ed was widely mischaracterized and pilloried, what he argued is an uncontroversial tenet within the field of evidence-based medicine.[12]

The philosophical core of Oreskes's work is made clearer in her later book *Why Trust Science?* (2019). Central to her work is the notion of consensus. To be able to identify merchants of doubt, one must first establish that there is consensus that they are attempting to undermine. Oreskes herself is well known for her empirical study of the high degree of consensus within the field of global warming in 2004. She analyzed all 928 peer-reviewed papers published between 1993 and 2003 that contain the word *climate change*, finding, strikingly, that none of the papers disagreed with the consensus position.[13] An analysis of peer-reviewed literature on how to respond to COVID-19 would have looked rather different in 2020, when the disease was novel. (It is also impossible to imagine that a similar consensus on global warming might be found today.) Consider, for instance, the continued debates, with knowledgeable scientists and intelligence agencies lining up on both sides, about whether the virus was more likely to have leaked from a lab or to have natural origins.[14] Or consider another contentious subject: masking. As discussed earlier in chapter 3, in 2023 a meta-analysis by Cochrane, one of the most respected arbiters of the state of medical consensus, concluded (based on "moderate-certainty evidence") that "wearing masks in the community probably makes little or no difference to the outcome of [flu or COVID-like] illness compared to not wearing masks." Yet many of those who had spent much of the pandemic promoting masking were entirely unconvinced by the Cochrane analysis.[15] The COVID-19-related issues with the most consensus appear to be ones that never generated much argument to begin with.

*   *   *

In *Why Trust Science?*, Oreskes argues that science is a community of inquirers. From the eighteenth century through today, the history of science has evolved from focusing on the method of the individual scientist to focusing on a community of scientific inquirers, whose trustworthiness is said to come primarily from social consensus. The details of this history reflect a changing consensus about both the nature of knowledge and the role of the individual scientist in generating knowledge of the natural world.

Evolution in the ways scientific knowledge is produced has the direct effect of undermining appeals to "reality" and "the way the world is." These forms of naive realism are a frequent component of elite discussion of the state of scientific knowledge and its production. But, as we will see, naive realism is no longer a plausible account of the nature of scientific knowledge. Once the notion of scientific truth as the product of "consensus" takes hold, the door is opened for competing knowledge communities to spring up and challenge the prevailing narrative. This is precisely what happened with so-called populist accounts of scientific facts in the context of the COVID-19 pandemic.

As Oreskes describes, scientific authority in the eighteenth and early nineteenth centuries sprang from "the man of science." Of course, the "man of science" required legitimation, usually from scientific societies. The nineteenth century witnessed a shift in the localization of authority for scientific knowledge. Interestingly, this shift was driven not by a scientist but by a sociologist, August Comte (1798–1857). Science, Comte believed, was uniquely positioned to provide "positive knowledge." By this, he meant knowledge that was reliable. The path to positive knowledge ran through method, which, he maintained, was far more reliable than religion or metaphysics.[16] It was by means of scientific method that the superstitions of religion and the dogma of metaphysics could be thrown off. Like Hume and many other empiricist philosophers, Comte believed that the basis of scientific reasoning was observation (experience). Comte shared with Francis Bacon (1561–1626) the idea that "there can be no real knowledge except that which rests upon observed facts."[17] For Comte, knowledge was in no way permanent: everything was on the table by way of claims about the natural world. Revision in belief was a normal part of the process of science. In fact, in his views about observation, Comte believed that the practice of science itself must be brought within the scope of observation.

Comte's view gave way to debates about competing approaches to science—experience versus ideas, confirmation versus falsification. These approaches became central to debates in the twentieth century on the nature of the scientific method and the role of experiment in the production of scientific knowledge. The hallmark of twentieth-century empiricist methodology is the idea that experience is the basis of knowledge.

Karl Popper (1902–1994) sowed the seeds of a radical change in the perception of the scientific enterprise. Popper denied the empiricist claim that induction was coextensive with scientific method. Knowledge, he maintained, was not grounded in experience because all observation is "theory laden."[18] He drew attention to the importance of individual attitude in the conduct of science, arguing that experience is always understood from the point of view of a theory. But his focus remained the individual scientist. Perhaps owing to his aversion to Marxism, Popper paid no attention to the collective nature of the scientific enterprise.

A focus on that collective nature would mark the next big turn in the story of the development of scientific method and practice. The work of Thomas Kuhn (1922–1996) stands out here: attracting consensus is the means by which scientists achieve stability when their practice moves from normal science to what Kuhn identified as "revolutionary science." In any scientific practice, anomalies appear. The moment when a paradigm breaks down is particularly fraught as competing theories attempt resolution of these anomalies. Those theories are often incapable of intertheoretical comparison—a problem commentators termed "methodological incommensurability."[19]

Kuhn's theory attracted the label *relativist*. Kuhn consistently denied the charge, but there is no denying its plausibility. When you aver that scientists "practice in different worlds," it is a short path to the conclusion that truth is a function of one's framework. The idea that theories are validated or not relative to a mind-independent reality is simply nowhere to be found. Kuhn finished off empiricism with the notion of a paradigm, thereby reconfiguring the entire notion of a "scientific fact." The most fundamental aspect of the change was the shift from the perceiving subject (the generator of hypotheses and validator of truths) to the "community of inquirers." Further developments in this line of argument, not surprisingly, increasingly drew on the field of sociology.

The end result, to which Oreskes subscribes, is the contemporary view that truth is the product of a scientific community. The community has norms that govern the assessment of truth claims. The community decides what is true and false. This account of scientific practice bears almost no relation to the empiricism it displaced. Moreover, this is the dominant view of scientific practice in the field of the philosophy of science.

*   *   *

On the specific topic of scientific trust, Oreskes asks: If scientists are "just people doing work, like plumbers or nurses or electricians . . . then what is the basis for trust in science?" Her answer is twofold: trust in science is based on "1) its sustained engagement with the world and 2) its social character." The reason we trust plumbers, electricians, and nurses is that they are "trained and licensed." Tradespeople are trained and licensed, and, as such, they are "experts." In a few telling sentences, Oreskes draws the connection between expertise and trust. She writes: "It is in the nature of expertise that we trust experts to do the jobs for which they are trained and we are not. Without this trust in experts, society would come to a standstill. Scientists are our designated experts for studying the world. Therefore, to the extent that we should trust anyone to tell us about the world, we should trust scientists."[20]

It is true that we trust scientists and that they are credentialed. Those credentials are a proxy for expertise. But Oreskes seems to be running together social and normative epistemology: the question of why and how we do trust scientists at any given point and the question of whether that trust is valid or misplaced. Consider: whence comes validation of scientific claims? Oreskes locates the process of validation in the "social practices and procedures of adjudication designed to ensure . . . that the process of review and correction are sufficiently robust as to lead to empirically verifiable results." Specifically, she focuses on two academic processes: peer review and tenure. Tenure, she states, "is effectively the academic version of licensing." Thus, the (social epistemological and, to her, normative epistemological) ground of intersubjective evaluation in science is social. In her view, because "the crucial element of these practices is their social and institutional character," this element "ensure[s] that the judgments and opinions of no one person dominate and therefore that the value preferences and biases of no one person are controlling."[21] This may indeed be the case, but whether it is sufficient grounds for trust is another matter.

In responses published alongside *Why Trust Science?*, several critics noted the many failures of these academic processes—such as the replication crisis in science. Depending on how systematic one views these problems to be, they may represent serious challenges to Oreskes's account of trustworthiness.[22] A second problem (which we elaborate on soon) is that the same argument for trusting scientific orthodoxy also justifies trusting critics of that orthodoxy—so long as we allow that they, too, constitute a community of inquirers.

We are now in a position to examine Oreskes's response to dissenting scientists in the pandemic. *Why Trust Science?* was originally published in 2019, with the pandemic a year away. In 2021, Oreskes wrote a preface for the paperback version, which begins with this paragraph: "COVID-19. Rarely does the world offer proof of an academic argument, and even more rarely in a single word or term. But there it is. COVID-19 has shown us in the starkest terms—life and death—what happens when we don't trust science and defy the advice of experts." She proceeded to identify a set of countries, including Vietnam, South Korea, and New Zealand, that had so far done well in contrast to the "disaster" manifest in the response in the United States. Attempting to identify why they were the "winners" in the COVID-response race, she claimed the answer was simple: "they did so by trusting science." The "science" in question consisted of recommendations by "public health experts [who] immediately made recommendations about how to minimize disease spread," especially hand washing, social distancing, testing and tracing, and lockdowns.[23]

After Oreskes wrote her preface, many of the measures she lauded were abandoned because they were ineffective, and debate continues about what measures were and were not helpful. To be sure, Oreskes did not have the benefit of hindsight. But that is our point. She claimed to have found "proof of an academic argument," but the evidence for that argument was incomplete at this early stage of the pandemic. This incompleteness may be, in part, because of the nature of the pandemic, but it may also be a product of the very nature of the scientific process—evidence may, in principle, *always* turn out to be incomplete at almost any point in the process. Even scientific consensus can be (and has been) overturned. Even if we *do* trust the scientific orthodoxy at any given point, that does not mean we *should*: trust may turn out to be misplaced, and thus we may find out that we were *over*trusting. This is not to say that the trust might not, in fact, be well placed, but it may be impossible or at least very difficult to know whether our trust is well founded.

Claims to "follow the science" may thus be a bit too quick, especially in the context of a complex society-wide response to a novel pandemic, where far more than scientific facts are at issue. Oreskes's claims in the preface were characteristic of the many scientists who suggested that doubt represented a problem, not a virtue, in the context of the pandemic. That conventional wisdom was summed up nicely in an article in the *Washington Post*: "Doubt is a cardinal virtue in the sciences, which advance through skeptics' willingness to question the experts. But it can be disastrous in public health, where lives depend on people's willingness to trust those same experts."[24]

The denigration of doubt was commonplace in the pandemic, as the hundreds of citations to Oreskes's work in essays about COVID-19 attest. One scientist who was quoted widely as a pandemic expert—despite repeated questions about his credentials and accuracy—described alarmism as a moral obligation. Another prominent scientist spoke in the first scientist's defense, describing the pandemic as an "all hands on deck" situation and thus not the time to complain about a fellow academic's "style or their tone."[25] Major newspaper reporters publicly urged that we avoid "insistence on [unnecessary] quantification and detail" because science is "not about evidence and detail per se."[26] It was argued that entire subjects should be marked off from discussion—even when done in a nuanced way—because they are "supremely unhelpful given the monumental Covid denialism we are all facing."[27] Others were less delicate, resorting to name-calling and ad hominem insults when scientists did not share their views. In many instances, these ad hominem attacks did not engage with the substance of the arguments proffered by dissenting scientists but instead impugned motives, labeled the criticisms "Trumpian" (even when they emanated from the left), and raised dubious questions about shadowy financial motives.[28]

Who Speaks in the Name of Science

Critiques of lockdowns and other nonpharmaceutical interventions during the pandemic fell largely into two categories. The first rightly interrogated the proper domain of science and the types of questions that science alone can answer. That is, even were the science established, almost any significant policy involved extensive nonscientific dimensions: social and economic trade-offs and costs that could not properly be deemed the domain of any one field of expertise. Consider the extended school closures in the United States, which had evident nonepidemiological implications. Put simply, "scientific" claims to necessity in many areas of policy were value judgments, yet because they were presented as objective factual claims, their evaluative and valuative aspects went unrecognized.

The second category of critique focused on the science itself. A purely scientific question, for example, might involve identifying the likely differences in effect between natural immunity and immunity produced by a vaccine. Pure science is what Oreskes claims to focus on in her preface to *Why Trust Science?*, so that will be the focus of our analysis here.[29] Our goal is not to evaluate the substantive truth of the competing claims of the scientific orthodoxy and its dissenters. Rather, the issue is the basis for demarcating dissent as inside or outside of the social boundaries of science. Oreskes provides no criteria for making such judgments. This is, in part, what makes her preface feel dated a mere two years after its publication: it did not anticipate the likelihood that certain claims written six months into a novel pandemic might be premature.

Oreskes's account of science is inherently ambiguous. On the one hand, it treats science as a community of inquirers, which presumes a degree of plurality and dissensus. On the other hand, it treats consensus as what determines scientific authority and, thus, appears to exclude the possibility of dissensus—or at least of *radical* dissensus. This ambiguity creates inherent instability and in some cases the inability to see consensus until long after it is reached. Indeed, this is a central implication of Kuhn's notion of a paradigm. As we discuss soon, this ambiguity is particularly peculiar given that the pandemic poses a particularly easy case for observing that scientific consensus had not (and has not) yet congealed about many aspects of interventions. There was clear dissent within mainstream science during the pandemic about the optimal pandemic response (dissent that still remains), including by those who were selected under the academic licensing procedures Oreskes describes and who were operating well within their "license" (field of expertise) in arguing over core facts about COVID-19.

Later, we turn to another indicative flaw in Oreskes's preface: her disdain for what might pejoratively be called "armchair" scientists—those who in her view were not the right "kind" of scientists or were not scientists at all. But, as we noted earlier, the philosophy of science itself—in particular the version of scientific trust she develops—actually sets the stage for these dissenters to make their cases against the claims of orthodox science. Once one is of the view that the "community" of inquirers is the basis for knowledge claims, the appeal to "reality" is thrown over. Those armchair interlopers might well be "wrong" in many important senses, but the community-based theory of science that Oreskes expounds cannot provide grounds for dismissing them altogether.

Our first critique of Oreskes, then, suggests that many in science apply her framework only selectively based on their priors about the data and facts rather than on the data and facts themselves and that the criteria of credentials and competence lack rigor. Our second critique suggests that Oreskes's framework is problematic because it does not provide a usable means to distinguish trustworthy and untrustworthy scientific communities.

*   *   *

As we detail in this section, Oreskes's preface dismisses some scientists out of hand based on who disseminated their ideas. In other words, their ideas are deemed guilty by association, which makes it easy to avoid engaging with their substantive claims. In the face of what might strike some as legitimate disagreement, she implies that the disagreement is illegitimate, for it stems, she claims, from certain scientists being "anti-experts."[30] But it is not at all clear what criteria yield this inference. The scientists whom she describes as hostile to expertise are experts by her own criteria of legitimate expertise. They hold the highest social "indicia" in their field—that is, they are tenured at top institutions in the fields of virology or epidemiology, have extensively published in peer-reviewed journals, and are widely cited. There is, then, something missing in Oreskes work: either something else must mark these specific claims about the pandemic as outside the bounds of expertise or other unspecified criteria are operating when Oreskes decides who is an expert. Her central claim—that science is formed by socially constructed consensus, tested in the context of academic institutions that serve as conduits for that consensus—would appear insufficient to sustain the substantive claims she makes in her preface about who is an expert and who is an "anti-expert."

Before we get to the details of Oreskes's charge, let us first recap the underlying debate. We oversimplify by dividing the complex patchwork of scientific opinion into two camps. To be clear, many scientists subscribed to neither camp, believing that both sides made excessive claims about the strength of their evidence given overwhelming uncertainty, and would have called for more nuanced policy options. Some were appalled at the very notion of "science by petition"—the idea that scientists should sign on to public letters in support of a particular claim.[31] Yet many scientists *did* sign on to two explicitly dueling statements that circulated in 2020.[32] The first, the Great Barrington Declaration, written by scientists at Oxford, Stanford, and Harvard, questioned lockdowns and called for "focused protection" of the elderly and for fewer restrictions on those who were likely to be less susceptible to COVID-19, allowing natural immunity to build in that group.[33] The second, the John Snow Memorandum, published in the *Lancet*, argued in favor of lockdowns, past and present, and insisted that pandemic management must not "rely upon immunity from natural infections." It described the Great Barrington proposal as "a dangerous fallacy unsupported by scientific evidence" and claimed that any disagreement was a "distraction."[34] The title of the memorandum is telling: "Scientific Consensus on the Covid-19 Pandemic: We Need to Act Now." This is the logical denouement of Oreskes's theory: if there is a scientific consensus, we must "follow the science" and act, closing the door for further discussion.

The very presence of a competing declaration favoring the theory of herd immunity indicates, however, a lack of scientific consensus on this issue. Peer-reviewed literature exhibited a range of views about the appropriateness of lockdowns and other nonpharmaceutical interventions. One *British Medical Journal* headline, published in late 2020, summarized that debate: "Experts Divide into Two Camps of Action—Shielding versus Blanket Policies."[35] None of the letters submitted to the journal in response challenged that claim—except for a letter that argued there were, in fact, not two but three warring camps.

The Great Barrington Declaration was authored by three scientists, all with expertise in epidemiology and infectious diseases. Their declaration was open to public sign-on, yielding signatures from 16,000 scientists and nearly 50,000 medical practitioners, but it also rested on the authority of an initial 47 key signatories. According to Oreskes's theory of science, these authors and signers should legitimately be considered part of the community of credentialed inquirers—and thus classified as experts. Yet Oreskes describes them as "anti-experts" who "muddy the intellectual waters around Covid-19."[36] Her argument, however, neglects their substantive claims and is based instead on an ad hominem argument that treats their theory as illegitimate through guilt by association.

Her primary evidence is that the declaration was written and disseminated following a meeting hosted by the American Institute for Economic Research (AIER), which "is, as its name suggests, an economic institute with no recognizable claim to biological or medical expertise." The AIER claims to have had little role in the statement other than hosting a meeting. But even if it had greater involvement, it made no claim to biological or medical expertise; rather, it rested any authority on the credentials of the scientists who wrote and signed the declaration and on the argument itself. Oreskes disdains the AIER because of what she calls its "political agenda" in favor of free markets, which, she says, "may or may not be good things, but they are not matters of science."[37]

Assuming arguendo that only science was implicated in this particular debate over lockdowns, the criticism that the declaration was written at or disseminated by the AIER is a purely ad hominem response. To be sure, information about authorship can warrant higher levels of skepticism and scrutiny, as in the case when a corporate drug manufacturer has paid a scientist to author a study of an expensive new pharmaceutical product. But even in that extreme case—which is not implicated here regardless—we do not get to dismiss the data out of hand. Rather, engagement with research results is the coin of the realm.

Most problematic for Oreskes's line of attack, the three lead authors of the statement had separately disseminated these and related views long before the meeting and apparently before they had even met or had any contact with the AIER.[38] In fact, their view on lockdowns stemmed clearly from their own priors—their past research and their particular scientific perspectives. There is no evidence that they came to it based on financial incentive, which is what Oreskes seems to imply. It is likely they accepted AIER's offer in an attempt to get more traction for their views (quite possibly a naive attempt because it allowed people to write them off based on the association). In addition, the Great Barrington Declaration was simply one statement, hardly the only or even primary critique of lockdowns, so discrediting the source of the declaration did not discredit more general criticisms of lockdowns or other aspects of our pandemic response. Many others who did not join or support the declaration were critical of much of the orthodox policy response, including lockdowns, school closures, and other restrictions.[39] And even today, questions remain unanswered about aspects of the most central tension underlying the dueling petitions—the relationship between vaccination and natural immunity.[40]

Focused as Oreskes is on spurious accusations about motivation, she engages substance only in passing, asserting that the Great Barrington approach was a "euphemism for allowing people to sicken and die" and that "if the United States had undertaken that approach, more than 200 million people would likely have become ill, with the potential for 2 million more deaths."[41] Neither point is backed up with citations, though the latter may refer to widely disseminated and later widely critiqued modeling by British researchers at Imperial College London in April 2020. Setting aside critiques of the model's methodology, its numbers were based on the crude data available in April 2020, months before the Great Barrington Declaration was written, and fashioned only a hypothetical scenario where there was *no mitigation whatsoever*—including no voluntary changes in individual behavior—which the researchers described as deeply unlikely.[42] If this is what Oreskes is referencing, it is irrelevant to the substantive dispute at hand.

*   *   *

Public, signed declarations of dueling opinions hardly seem an apt way to conduct an important scientific debate. Although science is built on vigorous disagreement, the publication of competing petitions feels more like an adulterated, performative version of science that values a public-relations strategy over scientific nuance. This kind of performance is a likely, if unfortunate, consequence of how many journalists and scientists have come to interpret the view of science, community, and consensus that Oreskes supports. If winning a policy debate can be accomplished by proving consensus, the most vocal factions—who may not reflect the majority and who may not preserve nuance—seek to prove that they represent a consensus. Scientific legitimacy then becomes a quantitative matter: tallying up the number of adherents on one side compared to the number on the other side or looking at the sheer volume of vocal public statements. This is hardly a model for scientific inquiry. Petitions are inherently anti-intellectual. The mathematician Wes Pegden eloquently described the emergence of dueling petitions as "the perfect phase for this moment, which involves remarkably little scientific curiosity or engagement."[43]

In the case of COVID-19, paradoxically, the position that Oreskes finds illegitimate should be, by her criteria of credentialism, more trustworthy than its competitor. While the John Snow Memorandum was certainly *popular* on social media, the Great Barrington Declaration counted slightly more established scientists among its signatories, based on a statistical analysis of citation counts in relevant fields carried out by John Ioannidis. Ioannidis concludes that the John Snow Memorandum's social media popularity led many journalists to falsely conclude that it reflected the consensus narrative, although the citation data about the authors (however imperfect and problematic) would suggest the reverse. As he points out, the "vast majority of the most influential scientists have not signed either document," perhaps because of the "adversarial" climate or perhaps because "neither document contains the perfect truth."[44]

We might further use the criteria Oreskes provides for *legitimately* distrusting science to see whether they are applicable to the pandemic debate. She identifies two reasons why one might legitimately be skeptical of science. The first is if the process is inadequate in some way: "If there is evidence that a community is not open or is dominated by a small clique or even a few aggressive individuals—or if we have evidence (and not just allegations) that some voices are being suppressed—this may be grounds for warranted skepticism." The second is if there is a conflict of interest. This is why, she argues, we should not trust the tobacco industry on smoking, energy companies on global warming, or soda companies on diabetes. The reason is the same for all: "the goals of profit-making can collide with the goals of critical scrutiny of knowledge claims."[45]

We agree that it is a cardinal virtue of science that it is skeptical of anyone with an agenda. Applying these criteria for doubting the legitimacy of science to the case of the pandemic yields some surprising conclusions, however. First, the orthodoxy that became "science" during the pandemic can be said to have formed by an exclusive clique.[46] There were open attempts to suppress dissent within the scientific community. Those most vocal in this suppression were scientists who belonged to the group that Oreskes endorses as the sole claimants to expertise. That suppression was fostered at the highest levels of the scientific community and science funders.[47] The tamping down of debate began as early as April 2020, just weeks into the US response to a novel pandemic and thus very early in the production of relevant research.[48] The timing here would suggest that, by Oreskes's standard, the first criterion for trusting in the science that Oreskes favored—that its process is inclusive and not cliquish—was not satisfied.

Second, there was little reason to think that the profit motive—or an "industry bias"—explains the fault lines between proponents of the John Snow Memorandum and those of the Great Barrington Declaration. It was often simply assumed that any divergence from the orthodoxy could be explained *only* by some kind of financial motivation. Yamey and Gorski noted that one of the declaration's authors, Sunetra Gupta, had received a research grant from a foundation named after Georg von Opel, a Conservative Party donor. They simply assumed that being affiliated with a conservative foundation turns scientists into mouthpieces for "billionaires aligned with industry." This is a controversial assumption, which they do not interrogate.[49] In any case, Gupta had made the same arguments before receiving the grant, which suggests that she received the grant *because* the donor approved of her opinions rather than that her opinions were motivated by a desire to receive the grant.

The kind of assumption at work here is prevalent. In this regard, we have previously mentioned Holden Thorp, the editor in chief of *Science*. In September 2022, Thorp declared that a doctor who dissented from a particular piece of scientific consensus and who offered to discuss his disagreement represented a "move . . . from page 1 of the anti-science playbook" that "undermines trust in science," just as in the tobacco and global-warming cases.[50] The issue here is not whether that particular disagreement was well founded but whether it is legitimate to describe as "anti-science" the act of a scientist attempting to provoke debate. Oreskes and others seemingly neglect the difficulty of drawing a line between those who are legitimately sparking such debate and those who are not.[51] This is not to say that such a line cannot be drawn but rather that this issue is often "resolved" simply by appealing to one's personal priors. There is little attempt to articulate criteria for making such a distinction. The implicit criterion for legitimacy instead becomes "it agrees with what I think is true." This standard, however, makes disagreement illegitimate by fiat, and it insulates "what I think is true" from objections by treating it as an inviolable truth rather than recognizing it as a fallible opinion.

This implicit criterion of legitimacy not only obviates the possibility of genuine disagreement but, in doing so, also leads to increasingly dismissive attitudes toward the other. This dismissiveness helps explain the rise in hostility as the pandemic unfolded. Recall the editor of *Science*, who proclaimed in early November 2020 that anyone who did not vote for Biden "doesn't want science."[52] It is telling that a hostility to science was the only possible reason he could deduce for the votes against Biden. He appears to rule out from the start the possibility that there could be legitimate skepticism about whether certain policies were scientifically mandated by facts about COVID-19 and that there could be other voting priorities. Instead of interrogating the epistemology of the other side, it is assumed that the other side, by virtue of being the other side, *cannot* have an epistemology.

This orientation puts the cart before the horse. Because it neglects the possibility that substantive *epistemic* issues may underlie the disagreement, it turns the epistemology of disagreement into a search to uncover the "real" motivational cause for such disagreement—that is, some hidden conflict of interest. This dynamic is manifest in the responses to the criticism made by John Ioannidis, one of the most cited medical researchers working today, who drew flak for his early views on the pandemic. His views were generally misrepresented by such critics of disagreement, but they were the result of a long publishing trajectory devoted to prioritizing the use of data in medicine and to skepticism of interventions that lack evidence. Ioannidis has long expressed concern about premature adoption of interventions, which might end up causing harm before evidence ultimately reverses their practice.[53] This approach to evidence and the conclusions Ioannidis associates with it are not necessarily correct and have thus been subject to disagreement, but they do appear to be consistent across his career and thus provide some evidence that his views in the pandemic debate were offered in good faith.[54] Yet when the founder of JetBlue airways granted Stanford (Ioannidis's home institution) a $5,000 grant (which Ioannidis did not personally receive), this was seen as explaining—and thus illegitimating—Ioannidis's opinions about responding to the pandemic.[55] This claim is implausible but more importantly drew attention away from the intellectual underpinnings of the disagreement.

Perhaps the biggest casualty of guilt by association is that it obscures the real origins of debates, which often involve conflicting interpretations and conflicting values that lie beneath those interpretations. Those conflicts are worthy of public discussion. Indeed, they are why we need science in the first place. "The facts" are not obvious but must be interpreted, and they are interpreted through theories and ideologies. Most of the fault lines in the

COVID-19 pandemic wars were not fundamentally about facts but about their interpretation and the values that underline medical responses. These methodological and theoretical fissures preexisted the pandemic.[56] On the scientific side, there is substantial—and we think genuine—disagreement about the proper role of evidence and the ease as well as ethics of generating more evidence through randomized-control trials. On the policy side, there are real disagreements about how to weigh different types of costs and benefits and how to reason under situations of uncertainty. A thoughtful and reasonable scientific discussion requires exploring these issues rather than tabling them, as occurs when skeptics of the orthodoxy are treated as "denying" science.

The Exclusion of Armchair Scientists

Let us shift from discussing the fault lines within the central corridors of the expert community and turn to some "armchair" scientists—members of the public who inhabited social media, did not necessarily have traditional scientific credentials, but attempted to engage with data in a quantitatively sophisticated manner and who were decidedly skeptical of governmental policy. Some of this skepticism may have been a product of conspiracy theorizing with respect to the virus, although that theorizing may have been less prevalent than widely believed.[57] We focus on the significant and sophisticated skepticism and suggest that, according to Oreskes's and other influential accounts of science, it should be categorized as science, despite its contestable results.

Five professors at MIT and Wellesley College investigated how COVID-19 skeptics employed social media to create an alternate account of pandemic data visualizations and first presented their findings in May 2021. The "counter-visualizations" manifest many of the tropes found in traditional scientific discourse. According to the researchers (who did not endorse the skeptics' conclusion), the skeptics "use rhetorics of scientific rigor to oppose public health measures." The researchers further conclude that the antimask communities they investigated are "more sophisticated in their understanding of how scientific knowledge is socially constructed than their ideological adversaries."[58] This study suggests that disagreement *among* sophisticated users of science cannot be resolved by simply appealing to "facts" and calling for one's adversary to "follow the science." The categories of "denier" and "antimasker" thus vastly simplify the way skeptics handled the publicly available data on the pandemic.

We can examine the dissent from conventional expert orthodoxy by examining the disagreement in greater detail. Using qualitative and quantitative methods, Crystal Lee and her colleagues reach some surprising conclusions. The first component of the study, the quantitative, consists in an analysis of more than half a million tweets and more than 41,000 images processed through a computer vision model. The investigators find that "anti-mask groups on Twitter often create polished counter-visualizations that would not be out of place in scientific papers, health department reports, and publications like the *Financial Times*."[59]

The qualitative dimension of the project consists of a six-month observational study of antimask groups on Facebook in 2020. The result of the embedding produced "an interactional view of how these groups leverage the language of scientific rigor—being critical about data sources, explicitly stating analytical limitations of specific models, and more—in order to support ending public health restrictions despite the consensus of the scientific establishment."[60] Following the lead of the renowned anthropologist Clifford Geertz, the researchers engaged in "deep hanging out" in the Facebook communities where participants discussed, debated, and mapped the data they took from public sources. What is of interest to us in this study are the conclusions the researchers reach with respect to the participants in the Facebook groups.

In the "discourse analysis" of the Facebook antimaskers, the researchers conclude that "anti-maskers are prolific producers and consumers of data visualizations, and that the graphs that they employ are similar to those found in orthodox narratives about the pandemic."[61] But, as with so much in the pandemic, the antimaskers' discussions are not driven by the data but rather by their interpretations of the data. For example, there is the question of which criterion matters most in setting policy: reducing cases or reducing deaths. Not surprisingly, the antimaskers believe deaths mattered more—not just death *with* COVID-19 but death *by* COVID-19, where, they claim, municipalities skewed the data to show that any death where the patient had COVID-19 at death was due to COVID-19.

How well do the antimaskers make their case? The researchers—no friends of this group—conclude that the group exhibits "expertise." For example, "data literacy is a quintessential criterion for membership within the community they have created." Data literacy, antibias, and "intellectual self reliance" are the hallmarks of this group's communications. When their work is compared to that of mainstream scientists, the researchers argue, the antimaskers "skillfully manipulate data to undermine mainstream science."[62]

The researchers also argue that these antimaskers are skilled in the *rhetoric* of scientific practices. For example, the skeptics "point to Thomas Kuhn's *The Structure of Scientific Revolutions* to show how their anomalous evidence—once dismissed by the scientific establishment—will pave the way to a new paradigm." The antimaskers have shown their deft skill at employing the language of recent philosophy of science. Science is a process with scientific knowledge produced by a "community." For antimaskers, "*increased* doubt, not consensus, is the marker of scientific certitude." Of course, purveyors of the conventional wisdom tend to dismiss the work of antimaskers as lacking scientific literacy. This disregard, the study authors maintain, is simply wrongheaded, for, "if anything, anti-mask science has extended the traditional tools of data analysis by taking up the theoretical mantle of recent critical studies of visualization."[63]

Antimaskers have proven themselves to be skilled at data analysis and visualization. Rather than denying science, they produce sophisticated skeptical counternarratives that bear the hallmarks of accepted scientific practice. But something deeper better explains the antimaskers' wholesale willingness to reject many claims made by "orthodox" and credentialed experts. The antimaskers "espouse a vision of science that is radically egalitarian and individualist," described by the researchers as an "epistemological rift."[64] Preaching naive scientific realism to antimaskers simply won't cut it. They have read their Kuhn, and they have mastered the mechanics of data visualization to such an extent that they think of themselves as their own scientific community with their own paradigm. In short, they play the game of scientific rhetoric as well as conventional scientists.

Nevertheless, while recognizing the sophisticated use of scientific methods, Lee and her colleagues do not, ultimately, think the antimaskers are on a par with conventional scientists because the epistemological rift between them is too great—that is, their worldviews are too divergent. The antimaskers are skeptical of the claims of public officials and are unintimidated when credentialed experts reject claims the antimaskers have come to through their own examination of the data. In this vein, however, we cannot dismiss the antimaskers' claims as antiscience because they are following the science—their science but a science that conforms to standard definitions of science. They have mastered the very same techniques as government experts and have built their own edifice. Perhaps the *substantive* gulf between antimaskers and their critics is too wide to be bridged—that is, they may have such divergent ways of interpreting the same data that they may never ultimately agree on what the data mean. But this suggests that a theory (such as Oreskes's) that treats this disagreement as stemming from a rejection of science misrepresents the nature of the disagreement.

Bringing Doubt Back In

In a recent column, the previously mentioned editor of *Science*, Holden Thorp, proclaimed that "teaching the controversy" is "page 1 in the antiscience playbook."[65] This assertion came as a surprise to us as teachers because "teaching the controversy" is, in our view, better known as "education." Perhaps because we come from a law school, where the entire adversarial system is premised on lawyers' ability to make convincing arguments and spot flaws in others', we would never shy away from teaching a controversy, even a manufactured one. To do so would suggest that we do not trust our students, that we do not think they are capable of seeing nuance or of understanding complexity. Thorp's disdain is, of course, precisely how he feels about his coparticipants in democracy—and is why populists are so rightly fed up with elites.

The case for doubt is not just theoretical but also quite practical: elites' judgment is fallible. The list of reversals during the pandemic is long, from masks to school closings to plasma treatments to estimates of vaccine availability. Hindsight is not the correct judge of a decision, which may have rested on stable grounds when first made, but reversals *made in hindsight* shed an uncomfortable spotlight on why silencing dissent is so problematic. The problem is not just the reversals themselves but the original overconfidence expressed by their proponents, who should have better calibrated their level of certainty. Indeed, humility and a willingness to admit uncertainty when it exists would go a long way to improving elite credibility.

We of course do not claim that no one denies basic scientific claims. There are surely bad-faith actors who misuse doubt or misconstrue evidence. But the claim of "post-truth" should be investigated domain by domain, and generalizing from one domain to another has little justification. Climate-change denial may rest on rather different processes than dissent about lockdowns. Concerned by the role "merchants of doubt" have played in one arena, elites have turned unjustifiably into merchants of overconfidence across all dimensions.

Used properly, doubt neither undermines expertise nor diminishes trust in science. In fact, without doubt the public will not trust the pronouncements of their political leaders even as those politicians invoke the authority of science. By "doubt," we mean an environment that permits—rather than fears—skepticism, uncertainty, and dissent. The heart of doubt is raising questions: no beliefs are above reasonable interrogation. Scrutinizing not only facts but, more importantly, also claims about what the facts entail is the hallmark of free and open inquiry. These values have been central to human rationality for centuries.

10 The Closing of the Elite Mind

The situation is fraught, if not perilous, in the wider cultural context within which ideas are discussed and debated. We consider challenges to free speech in American institutions from college campuses to the press. We critique the arguments of those who would label more ideas as off-bounds. Difficult, even bad, ideas play an important role.

Shortly after Russia invaded Ukraine, the diplomat and hawk Michael McFaul tweeted, apparently to nobody in particular, that "they" should get off his lawn. "Keep your BS whataboutism off my [Twitter] feed tonight."[1] His yawp was presumably directed at the many students of foreign policy who believed major US missteps had contributed to this tragic outbreak of war.[2] "Whataboutism," a favored assertion of elites in shutting down discussion, is an ungainly neologism for the tu quoque fallacy. The claim is that raising a related issue deflects from the actual issue at hand. McFaul has invoked it frequently, once tweeting that "whataboutism is always a sign of weakness." Anne Applebaum, another hawk, also adores the accusation.[3]

Charging whataboutism is a way to police discourse, shutting down any and all questions. Many would recognize that dissent and debate are needed perhaps more than ever on the brink of a major war. Yet for some elites there is no room for them. Their minds are already made up. Another favored epithet is *bothsidesism*, which refers to false balance—the idea that you claim to be presenting "both sides" but believe there's really only one side worth listening to. Elites apparently find it easy to know which side that is.

These terms contort ordinary features of rhetoric and reason. We *often* argue from comparisons, examples, and analogies. Like any form of rhetoric, they can be used in misleading ways, but for the most part they compose an entirely normal feature of human discourse and rationality. The accusation of whataboutism performs its own sleight of hand, deflecting focus on an issue by claiming that issue itself is the deflection. As Jackson Lears notes in a critical review of Applebaum where he takes on her obsession with "whataboutism," asking about US misbehavior is not misdirection. Rather, he says, "to recognize the bloody history of US foreign policy is not to equate this nation with amoral oligarchies but to call it to account for violating its own professed ideals and aspirations."[4] Applebaum, like many elites, would do well to listen more to those outside her own narrow circle.

The fear of bothsidesism has begun to undermine journalism, an institution that traditionally prided itself on doing precisely that—giving a voice to "both" sides. Eliciting contrary viewpoints from sources doesn't require that journalists repeat unchecked falsehoods or falsely imply that all sides share equal popularity. But that is not enough to satisfy younger journalists, especially in left-leaning publications. In surveys, they openly aver that equal coverage of divergent political views isn't warranted.[5] The main effect of this stance is, more than anything else, to confirm populists' sense that elites don't want to hear from them.

The darkest side of the elite mindset is perhaps its descent into intellectual tyranny. Skepticism is mislabeled denialism; dissent is censored as misinformation or derided as conspiracy thinking; open discussion is marked off bounds as bothsidesism. Expertise is replaced with a pale simulacrum that consists more of name-calling, tone policing, and censoring than of engaging in dialogue. In other words, elites are building even higher ramparts around their epistemic edifice to protect the very overreach that caused the public to distrust them in the first place.

In universities, newsrooms, and US corporations, discussion and debate over social issues has become fraught, if not perilous. In this chapter, we explore how, outside the realm of professional public-policy discourse, the same argumentative tropes are regularly deployed. The populist sentiment is not limited to the public sphere, for good reason. Its animating spirit is nourished by the treatment of populist opinion in a wide variety of settings. It is our purpose in this chapter to shine a light on these settings and to show the degree to which elite modes of discourse have made their way into the sphere of the ordinary.

Much ink is spilled denying the existence of "cancel culture." A characteristic example: "The phrase 'cancel culture' has been used as a false flag by anyone who feels threatened by the idea of accountability."[6] But the evidence is overwhelming that America has a problem with free speech. According to a poll conducted in 2022, whose findings are consistent with other surveys, only a third of Americans believed we all enjoyed complete freedom of speech in the United States, and some 84 percent said there was a "serious" problem of people being afraid to speak out in their everyday lives. Roughly half feel "less free" to express their viewpoints than they did 10 years ago.[7]

In July 2020, a distinguished and ideologically diverse group of writers penned an open letter in *Harper's Magazine* expressing concern about new "moral attitudes and political commitments that tend to weaken our norms of open debate and toleration of differences in favor of ideological conformity."[8] Reflecting our new normal, the letter—which was so short and whittled down as to be hard to argue with—garnered intense backlash.[9] Old-fashioned liberal ideals about freedom of speech increasingly require defense and explanation; being a free-speech absolutist is seen as archaic, perhaps even exotic. Nadine Strossen, the longtime president of the American Civil Liberties Union, increasingly seems like a relic. "The trope you hear over and over and over again is that free speech is a tool of the powerful," she told the *Wall Street Journal* recently, "that it's only benefiting white supremacists like the people in Charlottesville, or Donald Trump on Jan. 6, or antilabor crusaders, big, bad corporations . . . or fat cats."[10]

As with so many of our stories, the growing problem of intolerance toward expression in the United States is bipartisan in nature. Many left-leaning students seem today to assume that free speech is a conservative value. This is, of course, a historical falsehood, but it seems to have had a corrosive effect on getting liberal faculty to speak out in favor of open expression.[11] The classical-liberal defense of free speech speaks to values that do not belong solely to the Left or to the Right. On the flip side, the growing attacks on free speech come from both sides of the aisle. The Foundation for Individual Rights and Expression (FIRE) maintains a database of incidents against faculty members attacked for protected speech. The majority come from the left. But, strikingly, liberal newspapers cover those incidents far more than they cover attacks on campus free speech from the right. As Strossen says, there is plenty of illiberalism on both sides to go around: "Conservatives denounce cancel culture without admitting that they too engage in it, whereas liberals deny that cancel culture exists without acknowledging that they too are victims of it."[12]

What is the role of elites in stifling the conversation? To be sure, some, such as the deans we discuss later in this chapter, have risen in full-throated defense of free speech, though far fewer have done so than one might like. But many other elites, from editors to academics, have largely shrugged in response to the alarm bells of cancellation and self-censorship. The concern regarding their response is not so much that these elites defend an alternative conception of free speech, such as the idea that much speech is "harmful" and that listeners have a right to be protected against hearing it but that their response has been far too passive: they wring their hands over whether there really *is* a meaningful problem, or they believe it pales in comparison to other substantive ideological commitments. Close-mindedness, a casual indifference to free speech, and a lack of curiosity and rigor are what ultimately suborn cancel culture. That is the attitude we take on in this chapter. It is not hard to see how this stance emerged out of a combination of overconfidence and an anemic conception of "facts." If the facts are considered simple (i.e., noncontroversial) and dissent is assumed to come largely from bad-faith quarters, it is hard to get animated about the importance of robust debate.

Groupthink in the Ivory Tower

Perhaps no place illustrates rising groupthink and intolerance better than the atmosphere on college campuses. Universities might be expected to have some built-in immunities, including implicit and explicit guarantees of freedom of inquiry, such as tenure. Yet faculty are more likely to censor themselves today than they were during McCarthyism and the height of the Red Scare. As of 2023, a FIRE study found that more than 70 percent of conservative faculty members, 56 percent of moderate professors, and 40 percent of liberal faculty members report that they fear losing their jobs or reputations if they speak out. The numbers are better, but not by much, within the ranks of faculty who already have tenure—an institution designed to protect them from professional consequences for voicing their opinion. Yet roughly one-third of tenured faculty report self-censorship.[13] (The idea of tenure itself is on the decline as more teaching is assigned to non-tenure-track adjuncts and as schools increasingly openly contemplate the idea of revoking tenure based on a faculty member's ideas.)[14] The context of self-censorship is not just the classroom but also research. A quarter of faculty are "likely" or "very likely" to self-censor in academic publications. Less than one in ten don't self-censor anywhere.[15]

What are they so afraid of? The administration, their students, and each other, according to FIRE. As FIRE points out, they may have good reason to be afraid of each other: in the same surveys, many of them express support for what FIRE calls "soft authoritarianism." For instance, 36 percent of faculty would "endorse their college's administration launching an investigation into other faculty members for their controversial expression."[16]

Part of college is teaching students to engage with difficult ideas, to understand a range of perspectives, and to express themselves clearly and thoughtfully. Yet students also feel as if they cannot speak freely in classes: 83 percent of students sometimes self-censor in classes, and one in five students reports doing so "often." Students also contribute to that environment, with two-thirds of them saying it is "acceptable to shout down a speaker" and one in four suggesting violence is acceptable to prevent speech.[17] That confusion begins earlier. The psychologist Jonathan Haidt has recounted a surreal experience of giving a speech at a private high school. Students finger snapped during his talk—a common way to express disagreement with a speaker—and then aggressively interrogated him, yet in a smaller talk they identified intolerance toward viewpoints as a problem on their campus. He concludes that the "defensive self-censorship and vindictive protectiveness" they learn in high schools lead them to enter college looking for "new ways to gain status by expressing collective anger at those who disagree." The "only hope," Haidt concludes, "is to disrupt their repressively uniform moral matrices to make room for dissenting views."[18]

With Greg Lukianoff, the president of FIRE, Haidt wrote the best seller *The Coddling of the American Mind* (2018), a book blaming our campuses for intolerance on a complex set of social and psychological ideas. They identify and challenge our obsession with "safety," which has seduced many into believing that some difficult ideas are dangerous and thus should be avoided. They also point out that this is bad medicine: safetyism actually makes you feel less safe, and it fuels a vicious circle where students become less and less able to grapple with difference.

*   *   *

The story of campus intolerance is borne out not just in the statistics but also in countless recent incidents. We consider just a few, which show that speech can be targeted for both its content and for its speaker's other views.

Dorian Abbot is a respected geophysicist, a professor at the University of Chicago and described by the *New York Times* as a "scientific star" in the field of climate change.[19] In the fall of 2021, MIT invited him to give a distinguished lecture: the topic was climate and the potential for life on other planets. A "Twitter mob" protested, though, and ultimately got MIT to renege on the invitation. Their reason? Abbot had coauthored an article in *Newsweek* entitled "The Diversity Problem on Campus," raising questions about the role of diversity, equity, and inclusion (DEI) policies on campus. For instance, he suggested that requiring diversity statements from faculty applicants might "compromise . . . the core business of the university . . . the search for truth."[20] He is hardly unique in that assertion: many others have raised similar concerns, and, according to recent polls, faculty are split fifty–fifty on whether diversity statements are justified or a violation of academic freedom.[21] But, more importantly, Abbot had no intention of talking at MIT about his *Newsweek* piece or about faculty hiring. His talk was solely to be about his scientific research. After MIT bowed to pressure in canceling the talk, the administration faced considerable blowback from its own faculty, and Princeton invited him to give his lecture on its campus.[22]

In spring 2023, a group of Stanford law students protested and interrupted a talk by a conservative federal judge, heckling him until the talk was cut short. The students' behavior was further exacerbated by the school's dean of diversity, Tirien Steinbach, joining in the heckling of the jurist.[23] Lest it go without saying, the judge did not distinguish himself with his comments both during and subsequent to the event. After the incident, the dean of Stanford Law School, Jenny Martinez, issued an apology to the judge. Then, not to be outdone, a third of the school's students staged a protest against Dean Martinez. Clad in black and wearing masks, students disrupted her class and covered her classroom with signs. According to one report, "Hundreds more then formed a human corridor from Martinez's classroom to the building's exit—with those not joining in complaining that they were shunned."[24]

What happened next was a straightforward defense of free speech, a rarity in incidents like this today. In an usual and thoughtful memorandum, Dean Martinez patiently reexplained the basic ideas of free speech to students. She explained the "heckler's veto" and why protest and dissent, but not disruption, should be allowed. She prescribed a mandatory half-day session on free speech to the student body, noting that a law school of all places could not function if the community did not understand the value of legally protected speech. The dean of diversity was relieved of her duties before ultimately stepping down. Martinez insisted that the school's commitment to DEI, although real, was "not going to take the form of having the school administration announce institutional positions on a wide range of current social and political issues, make frequent institutional statements about current news events, or exclude or condemn speakers who hold views on social and political issues with whom some or even many in our community disagree."[25]

As contentious as the Stanford Law incident was, it was outdone by the appearance of the philosopher Kathleen Stock at Oxford University. Stock, who was awarded the title of officer of the Order of the British Empire in 2021, had been an object of intense student criticism at her university, Sussex, for her views on gender identification and transgender rights. Endless student protests, including posters and graffiti against her, ultimately led her to resign her position in 2021. Police even advised her that given the level of vitriol, she should beef up security at her home.[26]

In 2023, Stock was invited to speak at the Oxford Union, a debating society. Immediately, there were calls for the event to be canceled. The union did not budge, though, and Stock's invitation was honored. More than 40 dons signed a letter supporting Stock's right to speak at the Oxford Union and rejecting calls for cancellation of the event.[27] In response, students threatened the debating union that it would be cut off from funding and recruiting members if it did not cancel her talk.[28] She ultimately gave the speech under surreal and strange circumstances that largely overshadowed its substance.[29] In May 2023, the United Kingdom adopted the Higher Education Freedom of Speech Act, which makes interference in university speaking events an actionable offense.[30]

This kind of legislation leads some to claim a complicated and nuanced matter has been reduced to a simple formula by those worried about "cancel culture." The philosopher Amia Srinivasan worries in a recent essay that "right-wing culture warriors" have successfully "conflate[d] academic free-dom and free speech."[31] She makes a good case for the proposition that right-wing politicians such as Governor Ron DeSantis of Florida attack the very idea of academic freedom. Many of DeSantis's initiatives—from ban-ning TikTok to barring minors from drag shows, eliminating state fund-ing for DEI, and forbidding the teaching of critical race theory in state schools—exemplify the illiberal tendencies of our modern times. FIRE has convincingly argued that DeSantis's actions are unconstitutional.[32] Florida's Stop Woke Act is a deeply troubled piece of legislation. But, frankly, this is the easy part of the discussion. Lambasting DeSantis over his illiberalism toward college campuses is easy and deserved, but criticizing his conduct won't get us very far in figuring out how to handle free speech on campus.

In her discussion of the Kathleen Stock incident at Oxford, Srinivasan rehearses the back-and-forth between students, but she seems completely uninterested in the matter of principle that lies at the heart of incidents such as the Stock affair. She discusses "the long history of student protests" and asks self-reflective questions such as "Are today's students unpreceden-tially censorious?" She bemoans "the general fug of hysteria" around these issues. And she expresses concern about the new legislation: "The spectacle of the state coercively regulating student activism in this way should give any non-authoritarian pause."[33]

Yet Srinivasan never mentions the letter signed by more than 40 Oxford dons supporting Stock's right to speak. As the letter states, "Whether or not one agrees with Professor Stock's views, there is no plausible and attractive ideal of academic freedom, or of free speech more generally, which would condemn their expression as outside the bounds of permissible discourse."[34] And that is the point. What is the proper conception of academic freedom or free speech? Srinivasan purports to take up this question but never seems to engage it. This is the issue that requires debate and discussion.

On the one side, we have the liberal conception of free speech, which abjures censorship in all its forms. The free-speech mantra is that of John Stuart Mill: the best remedy for speech with which we disagree is more speech. Against this view are the purveyors of the "speech is violence" mantra. The core idea of those who opposed Stock's appearance at the Oxford Union is the claim that her speech is "harmful" to trans people. This claim—the notion that speech can "harm"—is central to the efforts of groups such as the Oxford LGBTQ+ Society and their efforts to prevent others from hearing speech they deem offensive. Similarly, the DEI dean at Stanford rebuked the invited judge for holding opinions that amounted to "an absolute disenfranchisement" of the rights of many in the Stanford community.

Perhaps no incident exposed the discursive problems in US higher education better than the congressional hearings in late 2023 on antisemitism on US campuses. When asked if calls for the genocide of Jews violated their college codes of conduct, three college presidents gave answers that seemed narrow and evasive, calling it "context dependent." The fallout ultimately led to the resignation of two college presidents, Liz Magill at the University of Pennsylvania and Claudine Gay at Harvard.[35] At a minimum, their answers—even if legally accurate—were tone deaf.[36] But the more telling concern was that the episode demonstrated the degree to which higher education in the United States has become deeply politicized. Many critics also noted the utter hypocrisy of elite academic administrators when it comes to speech. Even the most centrist of critics—those who would be expected to defend the elite establishment of which they are a part—appeared to agree with that assessment.[37]

Whether the outrage of late 2023 and early 2024 leads anywhere better is a different matter. The dethroned presidents may have been little more than convenient scapegoats, sacrificed to protect the university's brand above all else. It is not entirely promising that the revolt against the college presidents was led in part by billionaire donors with their own agenda. Their simplistic demand that universities simply return to "merit" rests on a mythical history of meritocracy.[38] The optics of universities bending to the will of their donors are troubling. So, too, are the optics of university professors defending their administrators purely on the basis that the critics are even worse. (As Charles Fried, a law professor at Harvard, said of the mounting plagiarism charges against Claudine Gay, "If it came from some other quarter, I might be granting [the charges] some credence. But not from these people."[39]) What we are sure of is that this incident confirms that elites in higher education are seriously out of touch.

The political scientist Greg Conti characterizes this issue as the rise of the "sectarian university." On one level, Harvard, with its nearly $50 billion endowment, is not meaningfully imperiled by criticism from Congress or the public. But the perception of these institutions as out of touch means "their authority will grow more brittle and their appeal more sectarian."[40]

The same phenomenon holds true at national papers such as the *New York Times*, which seem to have embraced their role as an elite "resistance" but at the cost of losing their national credibility.[41] What is most concerning is that these institutions' reaction to this phenomenon apparently is to double down on sectarianism rather than to reflect on whether sectarianism serves their institutional missions well.

The "Fug of Hysteria"?

Amia Srinivasan's concern that we may be in the "fug of hysteria," inflating the threats against free speech, is representative of a common reaction to the growth of groupthink. The problem is not so much that elites defend a narrower conception of free speech—not so much that they argue speech is "harmful"—but rather that they engage in hand-wringing about whether there is even a problem to begin with, all the evidence notwithstanding. This is borne out in the data: people overwhelmingly believe college campuses promote self-censorship and lack ideological diversity, but they are sharply split on whether this matters. Republicans and Democrats agree that colleges have a viewpoint bias (a view shared by roughly 60 percent of people, according to Pew). But within the group that agrees campuses are biased, only 26 percent of Democrats see this as a major problem, compared to 67 percent of Republicans. In other words, both sides agree that there's a liberal slant, but only one side is bothered by the existence of a slant. The consequences are a growing partisan split in attitudes toward universities. In 2015, the majority of Republican-leaning voters thought college had a "positive" effect on the country; by 2019, this portion had declined to 33 percent.[42]

Oreskes has sharply criticized those who contend academia has a liberal bias. In part, she disputes the fact that bias exists—a point we dismiss in chapter 2—but she also contends that the situation does not warrant attention. To do so, she says, would require "affirmative action for conservatives," given the disproportionate number of PhD holders who are liberal.[43] In other words, even if faculty were hired without regard to their politics, liberals would predominate because the available pool to supply such professors is already liberal.

She mocks conservatives for developing a claim that their views should be "epistemically privileged" because they are "marginalized," a claim that "adapts—and perverts—Marxist and feminist standpoint theory." But Oreskes's argument is a straw-man version of what most claim when they call for greater ideological diversity. Most of us want ideological diversity because we think it is how an academic community is formed. Inquiry requires the exchange of often contradictory ideas, arguments, and evidence. We all have had the experience of having our work improved by engaging with our deepest critics, and students learn from hearing competing ideas and understanding the diversity of viewpoints: not because they will adopt them but because this process will strengthen their ability to engage with, understand, and critique competing ideas. At a minimum, deciding that a third or half of Americans harbor a worldview *entirely unworthy of even trying to understand* is hardly a path to a productive politics, much less a healthy society or psychology.

A second way to dismiss the growing intellectual tyranny on campuses is to argue that there is no actual "censorship" because those censored can and do still speak—perhaps in different venues or outlets. This is sophistry. First of all, the question of *where* speech should be protected has long been a complicated one. It is not as simple as making a distinction between governments and private actors. In a famous case taught in first-year law school classes around the country, *Pruneyard Shopping Center v. Robins*, a privately owned mall was required to permit protestors because the state constitution's free-speech rights were broadly interpreted.[44] The private shopping center is in important ways one of our closest equivalents to a public square. Whether private actors should be constitutionally compelled to permit free speech or not—which varies between states—it's easy to see how permitting speech in a wider range of private venues might serve the foundational goals of free speech.

But, more importantly, the real concern here is the intellectual *climate* and its intolerance of dissent and viewpoint diversity. Whether it is literally "censorship" is a red herring. So, too, is the complaint that nobody should be forced to listen to an idea they disagree with. As a legal matter, that is of course correct. As a matter of creating good spaces for, say, education or public policy, that is nonsense. As legal educators, we could not possibly teach without helping students understand opposing viewpoints; our entire legal system is built on that enterprise, and effective advocacy requires it.

We have seen the narrowing of perspectives in our own professional lives. A few years ago, a group of faculty on our campuses started a reading group, engaging with texts that had become canonical or had a widespread influence on law, legal thought, and public policy. Texts came from a wide range of fields, including history, philosophy, and political science. The group was remarkably successful, but when it was suggested we read the philosopher Robert Nozick's *Anarchy, State, and Utopia* (1974), a classic defense of libertarianism, several colleagues said they disagreed with Nozick's policies and had no interest in engaging with the book. Had they read it? No, but they knew what it said. We have received similar pushback about inviting faculty with conservative perspectives, such as originalist constitutional thinkers, to our faculty workshops. Again, the excuse from several colleagues was that we already knew what they thought and knew we disagreed, so why bother? This response was perplexing to us because neither of us is an originalist—which is precisely why we would want to hear from one.

These anecdotes are illustrative in several regards. The "pushback" we are thinking of here does not resemble censorship or anything like it. Nobody threatened us or denied our right to invite such speakers, nor would they have—our colleagues are not like that. They were perfectly content to let us read Nozick. Rather, it was the utter indifference to competing viewpoints that surprised us. To be fair to our colleagues, many did show up when we had an originalist speaker come and engaged in substantive and thoughtful questioning, but their initial attitude was like that of a child refusing to eat their broccoli.

It is certainly the case that some will take advantage of the climate to make themselves out to be victims of censorship or to suppress others' speech. We are not here to defend those behaviors; they are just another example of what concerns us: an attitude that is not fundamentally curious or open to other ideas. But we do not think that attitude represents the mainstream critique of the current environment—the one espoused by groups such as FIRE, the Academic Freedom Alliance, and the Harvard Academic Freedom Council—which has more to do with the preconditions for a climate that encourages all the things we should value in academic inquiry: debate, discussion, understanding, complexity, and skepticism. And yet each of those groups, when formed, meets with skepticism and pushback about whether they are just contributing to a "fug of hysteria."

The clearest statement about free speech on campus is the Chicago Principles, adopted in 2014 following a series of incidents where students tried to block speakers. Authored by President Robert Zimmer and others, the statement reviewed the core values that underlie a university. Conflict is inevitable, it says, and the university's role is not "to shield individuals from ideas and opinions they find unwelcome, disagreeable, or even deeply offensive." The animating value is quite simple: "Debate or deliberation may not be suppressed because the ideas put forth are thought by some or even by most of members of the University community to be offensive, unwise, immoral, or wrong-headed." The Chicago Principles make it easy to decide a case like Dorian Abbot, the speaker disinvited from MIT. In response to a campaign to have Abbot sanctioned, Zimmer could simply point to the principles without further comment: "The University does not limit the comments of faculty members, mandate apologies or impose other disciplinary consequences for such comments, unless there has been a violation of University policy or the law."[45]

In a recent address at Chicago, his alma mater, the *New York Times* columnist Bret Stephens explained why the principles are important in today's toxic climate of cancel culture. Human nature, Stephens argued, is such that "most people just want to belong, and the most essential elements of belonging are agreeing and conforming." The result of wanting to belong, he argued, is "'preference falsification,' pretending to enjoy things they don't or subscribe to ideas they secretly reject." Intellectual independence is scary because it can lead to "loneliness and sometimes crippling self-doubt." Stephens noted that adopting the Chicago Principles is by itself not enough. What ultimately is needed is "academic leaders who are finally finding their nerve to stand up to the enemies of intellectual freedom."[46]

Neutrality and Facts

Holden Thorp has poo-pooed the Chicago Principles as "innocuous."[47] Thorp is no stranger to controversy (as we have noted previously). He has strong opinions. He tells us that he speaks his mind, and he thinks others—especially university presidents—should do the same. Thorp, the editor in chief of the *Science* family of journals, served as chancellor of the University of North Carolina at Chapel Hill from 2008 to 2013. The author of two books on higher education, he has strong views on how college presidents should conduct themselves when it comes to commenting on controversial policy issues. His views are of interest to us as his positions are a microcosm of elite opinion and of its befuddled relationship to "the facts."

In the essay "The Charade of Political Neutrality" (2022), Thorp argues that on some issues, university presidents need not—indeed, should not—maintain neutrality. Instead, on issues such as abortion, guns, and climate change, university presidents should speak their minds. Of course, he implies, on these issues there is only one point of view, one opinion that is correct, the opinion that university presidents should advance. Thorp argues against identifying these issues as "controversial" and, as such, against cautioning university presidents to eschew expressing personal opinions in the public sphere. In fact, he argues, neutrality on controversial issues plays into the hands of "[a] few rogue experts [who] come in and confuse the public just enough to forestall any policy actions based on established facts." He continues: "Tobacco, ozone, climate, Covid—it's always the same story. 'We doubt the science, it's not political,' they say. Whenever someone tells you something isn't political, it is. It's just that in such cases facts are in conflict with ideology." But facts, Thorp asserts, are "objective." That means many issues are beyond debate: there are simply facts of the matter. The notion that there could be more than one point of view on, say, climate change, is precisely the sort of obfuscation the purveyors of disinformation foment. Thorp derides the notion of "viewpoint diversity." We know, for example, that "climate mitigation is desperately needed." We know things like this "because we can measure them." We cannot be neutral about things "we can observe." After all, "we're not neutral about linear algebra or accounting."[48]

Thorp is remarkable in his insistence that some of the most controversial issues of the day are beyond debate because the facts are utterly clear. In this, one hears the echo of Sunstein's view that "the issues that most divide us are fundamentally about facts rather than value."[49] Thorp, in his insistence that certain matters are beyond debate, strikes the pose of the naive realist. Facts about the world are known to anyone who cares to look: all we need do is observe. Anyone who raises a question about the science of, say, climate change is just an obscurantist with a political ideology. But in response we want to ask, Are matters really all that simple?

Take climate change. Although Thorp doesn't tell us what "the facts" are, the conventional wisdom on climate change is that we are hurtling toward a climate apocalypse. Although Matthew Yglesias shows how such progressive hyperbole is—dare we say it—"misinformation" and routinely debunked, elite commentators continue to declare that the earth might "end" in a decade if emissions are not immediately reversed. Even Representative Alexandria Ocasio-Cortez (D–NY) has joined the chorus with her claim that "the world is gonna end in 12 years if we don't address climate change."[50] Many of these commentators claim to be "following the science," drawing on a line in an Intergovernmental Panel on Climate Change report, but their use of the report appears to be a willful or ignorant misreading. Yglesias points out that "the report is not measuring humanity's time to avert human extinction—it's measuring humanity's time to avert the 1.5 degrees of warming adopted as a global target in the 2015 Paris Climate Agreement." Most scientists believe we'll probably wind up with more warming than that, and it won't be good. "But it's not the actual end of the world . . . [a]nd even more importantly, there are no magic tipping points."[51]

The popular climate-change allegory "don't look up" was very much about an extinction-level event with no basis in fact. As a result of misinformation, many young people experience meaningful psychological distress. Contrary to this narrative, the facts are "that the world has been moving steadily away from this worst-case scenario outcome for some time," a view shared by some of the most thoughtful and urgent voices on climate change.[52]

It is hard to know, then, what Thorp means by "objective" facts about climate change that require no interpretation. He uses the word *objective* four times in his article "The Charade of Political Neutrality" to describe the facts that everyone seems to know. Not once does he explain what he means. The closest he comes to an explanation is his statement that facts are "measurable." But is it all really this simple? Even on basic questions about the causes of climate change, there are open questions among scientists who agree that the climate is changing. Some bad actors may blow these debates out of proportion, to be sure, but to deny the existence of the debates in response is equally unhelpful.

More importantly, even if we could convince everybody about the causes of climate change, that approach misses the real issue. Most people already agree that climate change is real. The real debate and widespread disagreement are over how to counter it and who should bear the costs.[53] Some point to the world's two major polluting regions, China and South America, as the primary sources for the production of greenhouse gases.

Others note the contributions of the meat industry to pollution: Should we all be vegans? And when some think everyone should be driving an electric vehicle, others point to the costs (human and environmental) of mining the minerals for electric-vehicle batteries. Even if the relative costs could neatly be sorted out by experts, most trade-offs do not lend themselves to a single objective frame. People, even those who admit the environmental consequences of their actions, are attached to the lifestyle choices that come with the ability to drive solo or to live the jet-set life despite the phenomenal carbon footprint of plane travel. Should we limit those rights? Although experts may be able to shed light on aspects relevant to those questions—perhaps helping us to approach consensus on how such restrictions would reduce emissions—they don't have any particular capacity to decide whether we as a society want to make those choices.

We raise these issues not to deny the reality of global warming—we are certainly convinced that it is occurring. But it will take a lot more than Thorp's glib pronouncement that "the facts are objective" to convince anyone, including us, that the policy choices with respect to global warming are anything but complicated. This is just another elite conceit that fuels skepticism about elite policy proposals. In failing to engage the details of the climate debate, Thorp not only hurts his own position but also undermines the very tenor of the debate because he thinks no debate is necessary. This way of thinking is fatuous.

Engaging Bad Ideas

Are some ideas so bad or repugnant that even discussing them is cause for consternation? Consider Aristotle. Not only did Aristotle endorse slavery, but he also thought slavery was good for the slave! By their nature, Aristotle argued, some people are at their best when controlled by others. The exercise of agency by a slave is counterproductive to the slave's own best interests. The slave, Aristotle averred, "is a part of the master, a living but separated part of his bodily frame."[54] Aristotle was not much better in his thoughts on women, whom he regarded as incapable of making decisions with any authority.

In her article "Should We Cancel Aristotle?," the philosopher Agnes Callard suggests that there are more than a few reasons for "canceling Aristotle"—that is, removing him from the basic philosophy curriculum.

Aristotle thought that the virtue—the worth—of a human being is something acquired as one grows up. Women, slaves, and manual laborers are, in his view, incapable of acquiring virtue and, as such, as Callard puts it, "have no grounds for demanding equal respect or recognition with those who do."[55] Aristotle was antiegalitarian, at least with respect to a significant portion of the population.

And yet Callard maintains that Aristotle deserves to stay in the curriculum. On what basis is such a decision justified? We are egalitarians. We believe in the rights of persons simply in virtue of their capacity to exercise their agency. Kant and other Enlightenment thinkers are the basis of our egalitarian mindset. Interestingly, Callard states that Aristotle "can help us identify the grounds of our own egalitarian commitments." By engaging with Aristotle, specifically his strong antiegalitarianism, we are forced to identify and justify our belief that everyone is deserving of equal concern and respect notwithstanding the fact that they may fall far short of the goal of excellence that Aristotle employs to root his inegalitarianism. In short, Aristotle motivates us to explain and justify our most basic political commitments.

Callard goes further, arguing that not only is engaging with Aristotle anything but a negative, but it is also, all things considered, a costless interaction. In short, as she puts it, "we have no reason to cancel Aristotle. Aristotle is simply not our enemy."

Callard emphasizes the virtues of the discipline of philosophy. "Philosophers," she maintains, "hold up as an ideal the aim of never treating our interlocutor as a hostile combatant." If our interlocutor articulates a view that directly contradicts our moral sensibilities, hostility is not the proper response. We should, she argues, take that person's words "purely as vehicles for the contents of his beliefs." This form of speech, which she calls "literal speech," contrasts with "messaging," which aims not at truth telling but at persuasion. Literal speech is a matter of evidence and argument, whereas messaging speech is a matter of struggle, specifically struggle for political power. Aristotle's views were grounded in his perceptions of the world around him. His claims were grounded in beliefs about the empirical world. We engage Aristotle when we engage the empirical claims that underwrite his strong inegalitarianism.

The Chicago Principles put the lie to Thorp's dubious certitude about hot-button political issues. Thorp fears the Chicago Principles set the stage for "neutrality," but their purpose is hardly that. Instead, it is to create a climate where, as Callard argues with respect to Aristotle, the possibility of reasoned disagreement is taken seriously. Nonconformity is the key to free and unfettered thinking. We need a public sphere that lives up to this ideal if we are to have any hope of progress through dialogue.

First Principles

The unfortunate tendency toward intellectual tyranny, which is on the rise inside the ivory tower, as elsewhere in elite culture, reflects a sharp break from the old conception of a university as a neutral setting for the free pursuit of ideas. Of course, an advocate for a less neutral university would not describe their goal as tyrannical. Rather, they would say that their goal is to serve justice, in particular "social justice."

Of course, nobody is against the idea of justice itself. Most who espouse the now old-fashioned mindset of neutral universities would agree that our commitment to a liberal education serves society's greatest ends. But what should a university do as a practical matter to further the good life or the cause of justice or freedom? There are many problems with the tyrannical mindset. Because it is inherently nonpluralist—it assumes one particular conception of "social justice" and excludes all others from debate—it is incapable of explaining why it is better than someone else's conception. Why should the university serve the vision of a particular version of DEI and not the vision of Ron DeSantis? By excluding the possibility of alternative visions, the tyrannical university cannot answer such a question. It simply asserts or assumes the vision it espouses—which means someone else can assert or assume a different view. The same is true of many who attack DEI—they simply substitute their own vision of morality and have no more commitment to free speech or inquiry than those they vilify.

By contrast, we think the old-fashioned conception—universities as neutral spaces for free inquiry—understands the institutional strengths and limitations of a university. Universities simply aren't that good at politics. If one wants to do direct political activism, perhaps being a labor organizer is a more useful career path than an academic. Universities *are* good at allowing many competing ideas to be hashed out. They are good at equipping students with the skills to question and debate tough ideas by providing an environment that encourages questions and debate. Despite our serious reservations about systematic problems in academic research (see chapter 4), we think many of those problems are less about the quality of the research itself and more about how that research is presented, characterized, and disseminated.

It is simply false to see justice and neutrality as being in tension. Those who are concerned about justice—whatever their conception of it—should celebrate the existence of neutral institutions that foster communities of scholars and students. Universities are not very good at taking positions on political issues. The past few months of universities scratching their heads at how to respond to the conflict in Israel and Gaza have demonstrated how their efforts to do so are likely to be clumsy and—no matter what they do—to win them few allies. This is not just because university presidents lack moral courage—although many presidents, like Supreme Court justices, increasingly seem to be selected for their ability to spend their entire careers avoiding staking out positions or commitments on any issues. It is also because most issues, if pursued with the academic and scholarly mindset, are complicated and fact intensive. They do not lend themselves to the kind of instantaneous statements that university presidents feel compelled to offer. As Jenny Martinez, the former dean of the Stanford Law School who is now the university's provost, and President Richard Saller wrote in October 2023:

> We believe it is important that the university, as an institution, generally refrain from taking institutional positions on complex political or global matters that extend beyond our immediate purview, which is the operations of the university itself. Maintaining university neutrality allows for our individual scholars to explore them freely. In recent years, many universities have gotten into the habit of issuing frequent statements about news events. This creates a number of difficulties. The decision to take a position about one event or issue yields implications for silence with regard to other issues; given that different subsets of a campus community may be more or less affected by particular issues, this inconsistency is felt acutely. It can enmesh universities in politics and create a sense of institutional orthodoxy that chills academic freedom. In addition, crafting each message is challenging, from gathering facts and context on complex issues at the speed of online media and the news cycle while also walking a line between platitudes and overly political positions.[56]

They conclude their statement against universities making political statements with a caution: "You should not expect frequent commentary from us in the future." This is sensible, as both a practical and a philosophical matter. The alternative is, as happened at our university, a president who issued three insipid statements on the conflict in Israel within two weeks. These platitude-laden documents bore little resemblance to the traditional fare of a university: they aspired to public relations rather than thoughtful scholarship. Of equal interest, they didn't work. As should have been no surprise, none of the statements satisfied anyone on any side. Instead, with each new statement, new demands grew that the president issue yet more statements.

Much the same can be said about the erosion of traditional principles in journalism. A commitment to social justice over traditional principles of neutrality has chipped away at the press's traditional role. It may have energized a new and loyal base of subscribers, but at the same time it has tanked the long-standing bipartisan credibility of many trusted sources. Was the trade-off worth it? Again, we should ask: What is a newspaper best at? Reassuring readers of their tribal allegiances? Or ferreting out and telling stories that would otherwise be overlooked and thus holding the powerful to account and equipping readers with the knowledge and tools to make their own decisions? The latter approach can still serve justice, while making far more powerful use of the unique institutional capacity of journalism.

Maintaining institutional neutrality is not "giving up." Nor does a commitment to free speech entail a spineless inability to make moral judgments. Rather, neutrality and free speech reflect first principles of institutional design. They yield communities that will produce useful knowledge and train informed citizens. The alternative yields third-rate political factions with little credibility.

Conclusion: Giving Political Judgment a Chance

In 2014, residents of Flint, Michigan, began noticing a funny smell and taste to their water. City officials dismissed the residents' complaints, maintaining the water was safe. Residents protested. The city brought in experts to tell Flint's residents that they were wrong. Representatives from the state and federal environmental agencies as well as a microbiologist doubled down on their reassurances.[1] Of course, as everyone now knows, the residents were right to trust their experience: the water in Flint was contaminated and unsafe.

We know this, however, only because residents refused to believe the experts. Instead, they organized their own effort to collect and test water. Their work demonstrated spiking levels of lead across the city, some to "very serious" levels. The water had other contaminants as well, including bacteria that very likely caused a serious outbreak of Legionnaires' disease (a form of pneumonia) and elevated total trihalomethanes, a chemical associated with cancer, a consequence of the city's efforts to eliminate the bacteria. The citizens petitioned the EPA for help, but none was forthcoming. Nothing improved until Flint residents got a federal judge to start ordering the city to step up and fix the water. In subsequent years, state officials, including experts, have been criminally charged for their role in the crisis. The reputation of expertise has not recovered.[2]

In 2007, police arrested a 15-year-old girl in a small town in Luzerne County, Pennsylvania. The crime was a MySpace page she created in which she parodied her vice principal. The judge, Mark Ciavarella, chastised her at a short hearing, with no lawyer present, before announcing the sentence: three months detention in a youth forestry camp. The student, Hillary Transue, remembered that the judge had once spoken at her school, warning them, "If you come before me, I'll send you away." He was not lying.

Ciavarella and another Luzerne judge, Michael Conahan, doled out unusually harsh sentences to juvenile shoplifters and trespassers, almost always after a cursory hearing with no defense counsel present and little discussion. Why did the judges administer such rough justice? Cash, as it turned out. They pocketed kickbacks to the tune of $2.8 million for supplying enough juvenile delinquents to fill a chain of for-profit detention centers.

The pair sentenced more than 2,300 kids in the "cash-for-kids" scandal.[3] During the years these judges "served" on the bench, experts and officials did nothing. Beginning in 2004, the FBI and the Pennsylvania Judicial Conduct Board began receiving complaints about improper sentencing and corruption in Luzerne's courtrooms. The Judicial Conduct Board later admitted it didn't take any steps to investigate, even in a cursory manner.[4] It took a concerted effort of concerned parents, joined by a legal-advocacy group, the Juvenile Law Center, ultimately to sue the judges and the county. After years of dogged legal work, all 2,300 kids' convictions were thrown out. The two judges were eventually criminally convicted and are now serving time in federal prison.

Luzerne County, historically a center of coal mining, voted for Obama in both 2008 and 2012. In 2016, it flipped for Trump, forming a crucial part of his critical victory in Pennsylvania.[5] The travesty of juvenile justice in Luzerne is hardly the only way in which its residents feel forgotten by America's elite, but it takes little imagination to see why you might lose trust in a system that literally sells your children to prisons for cash and then drags its heels in investigating the wrongdoing. "Trust the experts" is hardly a reassuring rejoinder.

*   *   *

Our gripe is not with expertise. After all, residents in both Flint and Luzerne needed and found experts—the right ones—to vindicate their suspicions. Rather, we have tried to make one basic point throughout this book: following expertise is not enough. Claiming otherwise, as many elites do, is disingenuous. Elites who think this way corrode, rather than fortify, expertise, turning it into a cheap shot that shuts down debate. They empty out politics, displacing the vital clash of values with an oracular elite.

Roughly a century ago, "legal realists" challenged traditional ideas of American legal thought. The classical perspective that preceded them was highly formalistic and asserted that cases could be "correctly" decided by the precise application of rules. The legal realists showed, in contrast, that law was always ultimately the expression of politics and judgment. How, after all, could it be otherwise? That conclusion remains sound—but also remains a source of deep discomfort to many lawyers and judges today.

We seem to be living through a revival of those discredited formalist ideas. Elites today claim that policy matters can be settled by deferring to experts. They maintain that many questions are not open for debate. This declaration, pronounced as a fact, produces cognitive dissonance when politics inevitably intrudes back in. Many Americans had been convinced wrongly that *Roe v. Wade* took politics out of abortion rights. The assumption was that abortion rights had been handed over to some magical constitutional sphere, led by the expert interpreters on the Supreme Court, which removed politics from the equation, rendering those rights durable and unassailable. It should have taken little imagination to see that the same process that created those rights could just as easily take them away. Many seemed utterly blindsided when this eventually came to pass. Even *Bush v. Gore*, which should have made it quite obvious that the Court as currently conceived could not avoid engaging in even the most partisan of politics, was unable to shake the mindset of many elites who saw the Supreme Court as structurally unique in its ability to protect certain rights from political influence. Politics, while obscured, was always there, as *Dobbs v. Jackson Women's Health Organization*, the decision reversing *Roe* in 2022, confirmed.[6]

Facts cannot simply displace politics. We have avoided expressing our own political views in this book in part because we do not think they should be of particular interest to our readers (nor do the two of us have a single political view). But we want to be clear that skeptical liberal-minded readers of this book—who may be most inclined to arrive with prior sympathies for the project of the technocratic elite—need not see our realism as inherently bleak. Technocrats have historically, after all, not been particularly effective in delivering on their promises, and their help may not be necessary. On many issues that our more liberal readers will worry about, most Americans share their concerns. For instance, polls consistently find that a majority of Americans tend to favor stricter gun laws, more climate-change regulation, and expanded abortion rights.[7] So why are we so afraid of using politics to engage one another on these issues? Why must they be settled by "facts," which cannot actually settle them?

We don't mean to minimize the messiness of politics. Hot-button issues are not simple. Even seemingly simple issues aren't simple. We do not live in a direct democracy, majorities do not rule, and the legislative process is flawed. (That said, many of our biggest accomplishments do actually originate with local, grassroots, bipartisan movements.) General agreement does not mean there is agreement as to the particulars. Our point is that it makes little sense to fear the inherent contingency and ambiguity of politics, while trusting supposed arbiters of fact to render extrapolitical judgment. The latter is simply fantasy. Punting political questions to allegedly neutral institutions, such as the Supreme Court, has failed in dramatic fashion. By restoring these issues to their proper sphere, politics, we again open up the door to a messier but more honest debate. "Following the experts" dissembles and shuts down that conversation.

There is rarely an entirely neutral or objective frame from which to pursue knowledge. Facts require interpretation. Honesty about this relationship can rebuild credibility. We need more nuance and less fanatical worship of "facts." Rather than fearing open-mindedness, scholars and journalists should return to their roots. Journalism does not exist to shore up the assertions of authorities but rather to probe the conventional wisdom. Academics and reporters are actually quite good at eliciting, understanding, and evaluating competing claims. Perhaps we should let them. "Bothsidesism" could be restored from epithet to compliment.

James Bennet edited the *New York Times* editorial pages until he was pushed out in 2020, following outrage by some employees at the paper's publication of an op-ed by Republican senator Tom Cotton. In a lengthy essay published in 2023, Bennet recounted what happened. Two things stand out. The first is his sense that the leaders of institutions such as the *Times* know—on some level—that they have lost their way. In other words, the editors and publishers have not missed out on the problem that the *Times* has "metastasised from liberal bias to illiberal bias, from an inclination to favour one side of the national debate to an impulse to shut debate down altogether."[8] Rather, Bennet charges, they lack the courage to unstick themselves. The second is Bennet's optimism, which derives from a habit of mind that is the opposite of the condescension we describe in this book. Bennet believes that journalists know how to ferret out good stories and believes that readers can be trusted with the truth rather than be sheltered from it. We believe the spirit of populism rests on a similar faith in people's ability to handle the nuance and ambiguity of our complex world.

*   *   *

America faces deep schisms, many of them about core values. But these schisms are not new: they are part of long-standing tensions that are the hallmark of all political societies from as early as people began thinking about how best to organize society. Our political tradition has never been on a straightforward trajectory toward a particular vision of democracy but rather has often changed course through "contention, argument, and power."[9]

Many of our deepest divides today are not "political" in the sense that is usually meant. That is, they are not necessarily about whether the Republicans or Democrats have the better policy for Social Security or welfare or education. In fact, Americans are increasingly disillusioned with both parties, as shown by the rise in unaffiliated voter registration. The real conflict is over what life in America *means* and how it *feels*. Does hard work matter most or luck? Are there structural impediments to equality? How fair is society? What does fairness even mean? How much should we celebrate the individual versus the community? These are tough questions. They implicate our deepest values and yearnings. We can't just look up the answers in a factbook.

Unfortunately, we are told otherwise by today's elites. Elites disdain the idea that we should listen to common sense and our national mood. Theirs is an attitude of *condescension*. It goes hand in hand with their mindset of *technocratic paternalism*, the idea that facts—specifically those held by elites—can inform social policies. Populists challenge this mindset, as we have seen. Told "no," they rebel. Elites double down with a third mindset, *intellectual tyranny*, which is perhaps the most troubling as it shuts down the avenues through which we debate and resolve our core problems.

These elite mindsets are deeply embedded. Once you assume that facts determine outcomes and that the facts are on your side, there is little reason to engage with others—and every reason to shut them down. We are also certain that the current elite strategy in dealing with populism primarily through more and more exclusion will fail. It only proves the core claim of populists, which is precisely that they feel excluded by a hypocritical elite. Elites can't evince much faith in the democracy they claim to protect when their tactics are based on fundamentally antidemocratic ideals of exclusion, censorship, and policing debates.

*   *   *

We have no easy solution. It would be incongruous to hold ourselves out as possessing the one quick trick to fix democracy. Many of the more promising ideas—more engagement at the local level, more grassroots movements, more participatory rulemaking—are neither easy to implement nor destined to succeed. Our main aim in this book is to reassert a basic, moral claim about democracy: political judgment belongs to all of us.

We have written this book primarily in the hope that we and our elite friends might engage in a bit of self-reflection about mistakes we make in assessing and judging our fellow citizens. What are populists trying to express? Their anger is seemingly easy to explain. It all comes down to exclusion and derision. Yet the more elites are called out for excluding and deriding, the more they double down. The plerophory of elites during the pandemic was as alienating as it was foolish. It failed to obscure their clear failures to evaluate evidence intelligently or to be honest about uncertainty. In the end, elites succeeded at only one thing: undermining trust.

The political theorist Ronald Beiner explains the idea that "political judgment" is a capability open to all of us. "Communication . . . in a community of rational dialogue," he writes, might yield "moral self-discovery that will lead us to a better insight into our own ends."[10] In recent years, we have been conditioned to recoil from disagreement. Disagreement might be dangerous, and our interlocutor may come in bad faith. This frame, however, makes rational and respectful dialogue impossible. It deprives us of insight not just into our opponent but into ourselves as well. To cure ourselves, we need mainly a little curiosity plus a dash of humility.

Acknowledgments

First and foremost, we thank our students across three years of teaching a course entitled "Populism and the Law," where we developed these ideas. Our students' discussions modeled the kind of open inquiry, curiosity, and willingness to change perspectives that we celebrate in this book. Several, including Tara Doherty, James Gregora, Chris Layton, and Stephanie Mignogna, commented at length on drafts or articles.

For brilliant research assistance, we are indebted to Jacob Davis, Ryan Duffy, Brian McCann, Henry Orlowski-Scherer, Samuel Shopp, and Ma'ayan Stein. We thank Johanna Bond, dean of Rutgers Law School, for her support of this project.

We thank colleagues, friends, and strangers who read and commented on drafts or who discussed ideas at length with us, sometimes vigorously disagreeing. The final product—and mistakes—are our own. We particularly thank Dave Allen, Julia Barnes, Laurie Bayless, Evelyn Burg, Julie Carlstrom, Alon Geva, Rebecca Hill, Sam Jacobs, Elizabeth Kaeser, Amelia Lester, Wade Malone, Rebecca O'Brien, Vinay Prasad, Sydney Pulver, Lauren Schuker, Mark Smith, Allan Stein, Barry Stern, David Wishnick, and David Withee.

We thank our editor at MIT Press, Phil Laughlin, for his sage advice throughout the journey to bring this book to publication. Anne Barva, Natalie Jones, and Ginny Crossman provided thoughtful and thorough edits. We thank the press's staff and the anonymous reviewers who provided thoughtful comments on our proposal and manuscript.

We were able to advance many of these ideas in *STAT*, *Tablet*, and *Critical Review*, and special acknowledgment is owed to the editors of those publications for their openness to perspectives that were seemingly controversial at the time. We acknowledge the late political theorist Jeffrey Friedman at *Critical Review* for inviting us to participate in a symposium on post-truth and for providing voluminous and thoughtful comments, and we thank Shterna Friedman for seeing the article through to publication.

Finally, we are grateful for our colleagues who make Rutgers a place where critical inquiry and debate are valued, especially Thea Johnson, Arthur Laby, Andy Shankman, Ray Solomon, Allan Stein, and Adnan Zulfiqar.

Notes

Preface

1. Rubin, "Andrew Cuomo Gets It Right."

2. Ferré-Sadurní, "Health Agency under Cuomo 'Misled the Public' on Nursing Home Deaths."

3. Thrasher, "Andrew Cuomo Should Resign."

4. "Governor Cuomo Announces Updated COVID-19 Micro-cluster Focus Zones." We use COVID-19 (coronavirus disease 2019) throughout rather than "the coronavirus" because there are, of course, other coronaviruses.

5. For an excellent summary of Cuomo's missteps, deceptions, and lies (especially with respect to nursing home deaths), see Nocera and McLean, *The Big Fail*, 204–209.

6. Even late-night comedy devolved into paeans: the actor Brad Pitt impersonated Fauci on *Saturday Night Live* before taking off his mask and praising Fauci. See *Saturday Night Live*, "Dr. Anthony Fauci Cold Open."

7. Sullivan, "Fauci."

8. Turner, "Rishi Sunak."

9. Nichols, *The Death of Expertise*, 3.

10. Obama, "Remarks by the President."

11. Karem, "Dumbass Nation."

12. Sandel, *The Tyranny of Merit*, 25.

13. See Bowen, "That Cat Lawyer Video Was Funny."

14. Diaz, "Trying to Stay Warm?"

15. L. Friedman, "Trump Tries to Improve His Environmental Record with a New Water Rule"; Hinkel, "What Can Be Deduced from the Length of Jury Deliberations

in the Rittenhouse Case?"; "These Expert-Approved Gadgets Can Help Upgrade Your Kitchen for Less."

16. All these examples are taken from real articles in major publications over the past few years.

17. Authors' calculations based on data collected from the *New York Times's* application programming interface in June 2022.

18. Authors' calculations using data from Misra, "News Category Dataset." For the examples given here, see Bologna, "The Rudest Things You Can Do at a Hotel"; Nayak, "The Essential Items Doctors Never Travel Without."

19. European politics has taken a decidedly right-wing turn. The rise of populism is part of this phenomenon but not reducible to it. Kundnani, "Europe May Be Headed for Something Unthinkable"; Goodwin, "Europe's Turning Right—Here's Why."

Chapter 1

1. Michael Gove said this in an interview on Sky News in June 2016. Gove's full statement is often truncated. The full quotation carries more nuance: "I think the people in this country have had enough of experts from organisations with acronyms saying that they know what is best and getting it consistently wrong." Steerpike, "What Did Michael Gove Actually Say about 'Experts'?"

2. President Ólafur Ragnar Grímsson of Iceland, quoted in Kestenbaum and Hedinsson, "A New Mom, Bjork's Dad and the President of Iceland."

3. Although the antiexpert turn is often associated with right-leaning movements, there are countless other examples from the political left, too. Alexis Tsipras, the left-populist former prime minister of Greece, routinely used such rhetoric in critiquing the economic establishment: "We don't believe the false promises of supposed experts." Quoted in "Greek Prime Minister Announced Minimum Wage Increase."

4. Varoufakis, *Talking to My Daughter about the Economy*, 193.

5. The academic and politician Michael Ignatieff—a liberal internationalist who is no friend of the "Leave" cause—has recognized this quite eloquently. In a recent podcast, he described Brexit as a "a liberal democratic society having the most fundamental debate about its future of any society I've seen since the Second World War. . . . Any person who loves democracy loved what happened . . . a rock 'em sock 'em debate. Democracy is about conflict. . . . People who say that because there's a lot of conflict and polarization that means democracy is in crisis, don't understand what a democracy is. Britain has just had one of the great democratic debates in any advanced liberal democracy that I've ever seen, and it's not over. This debate will go on. . . . It's a pretty inspiring example to the rest of the world. In other countries

these debates are suppressed, avoided, and pushed down. . . . The debate that then happened was fundamental. It surfaced discontents and hurts and anger that had been suppressed by the political system for 25 years. That's the sign of a healthy democracy." Fraser, "Michael Ignatieff's Confessions."

6. Lears, "Orthodoxy of the Elites."

7. On working-class voters, see, e.g., J. Williams, *White Working Class*, and Eatwell and Goodwin, *National Populism*; on polarization, see Lind, *The New Class War*; and on the psychology of a meritocracy, see Sandel, *The Tyranny of Merit*. See also Markovits, *The Meritocracy Trap*.

8. Nate Silver calls the "argumentative space" inhabited by many elites the "indigo blob"—"somewhere between left-wing (blue) and centrist (purple)." Silver, "Twitter, Elon and the Indigo Blob."

9. To be clear, as with any generalization, we do not suggest that every elite, in every situation, displays the traits we ascribe to elites. It would be pedantic to repeatedly hedge by saying "most elites" or "many elites." As we describe in chapter 2, when we deploy the concept of "elite," we are using a well-developed sociological category—and as with any such category, there are variations and even exceptions.

10. Hirschman, *Exit, Voice, and Loyalty*.

11. Lynch, "How the AfD Won Over Germany."

12. Quoted in Cadelago, "'We Would've Done Everything Differently.'"

13. Lears, "Orthodoxy of the Elites."

14. Ekins, "The Five Types of Trump Voters."

15. Some people point to the low uptake for the latest COVID vaccines as evidence of this. But more than one explanation might be valid. For discussion, see Scott, "Why Are so Few People Getting the Latest Covid-19 Vaccine?" The reckoning over the misuse of science during the pandemic is ongoing. Here is a recent example: Tuccille, "'The Science' Suffers from Self-Inflicted Political Wounds."

Chapter 2

1. Brennan, *Against Democracy*, 15, 217–219, 230.

2. Mounk, "The Undemocratic Dilemma," 110. Proponents of this view claim to be responding to the unique and novel complexity of twenty-first-century society but unwittingly repeat an idea that is quite old: that we live in complex times. In 1939, the sociologist Robert Lynd noted: "Many public issues today are of a highly technical character that should not be disposed of by a show of hands" (quoted in Lasch, *The True and Only Heaven*, 426). The problems of contemporary America "as Lynd

framed it," according to Christopher Lasch, "could have only one answer: all power to the experts. In order to make everyone happy and safe, America would have to institutionalize expertise" (426).

3. Nichols, *The Death of Expertise*, xx.

4. One could also speak of different elites, such as a "managerial elite," which is probably the closest to our focus here—although we think the qualifier *managerial* is cumbersome and largely unnecessary. *Managerial elite*, although not perfect as a term, either, has the benefit of defining elites by the role they play in society: a highly educated professional class that dominates government, business, and key institutions—from think tanks to journalists, academics, lawyers, doctors, and the like. We resist the term *liberal elite*, which risks putting too much focus on particular political goals that not all elites share. The similarities within elite culture that interest us are instead less political in nature and more about an approach or attitude toward how the world works.

5. Matthew Goodwin describes the current British elite thus: "Over the last fifty years . . . the new elite rebuilt society around people who look and sound like them, doubling down on [résumé] virtues. The only route to leading a valuable and virtuous life, worthy of respect from others, has come to be seen as having the right degree from one of the Oxbridge or Russell Group universities, and holding the right set of elite beliefs to accompany this education." Goodwin, *Values, Voice and Virtue*, 132.

6. Robinson, "'Real' Americans Are a Myth."

7. Michael Sandel counts over 9,000 instances of President Obama using the adjective "smart" to describe policy. Sandel, *The Tyranny of Merit*, 107.

8. Authors' search of JSTOR for the term *elite* in the *American Polical Science Review* from 1906 to 2017.

9. Kertzer and Renshon, "Experiments and Surveys on Political Elites," 530.

10. Acemoglu quoted in Edsall, "Elites Are Making Choices That Are Not Good News."

11. Domhoff, *Who Rules America?*, 4.

12. Sandel, *The Tyranny of Merit*; Lears, "Orthodoxy of the Elites"; J. Williams, "What so Many People Don't Get about the U.S. Working Class"; Markovits, *The Meritocracy Trap*; Hayes, *Twilight of the Elites*; Giridharadas, *Winners Take All.*

13. See the discussion of this topic in chapter 6.

14. Canovan, *The People*, 11.

15. Masciotra, "'Real Americans' vs. 'Coastal Elites.'"

16. Mills, *The Power Elite*, 3, 11.

17. US Census Bureau, "Census Bureau Releases New Educational Attainment Data."

18. Schaeffer, "Nearly All Members of the 118th Congress Have a Bachelor's Degree."

19. Levitz, "How the Diploma Divide Is Remaking American Politics."

20. For another elaboration of this point, see Sandel, *The Tyranny of Merit*, 99.

21. Levitz, "How the Diploma Divide Is Remaking American Politics."

22. Fredrik deBoer observes: "College does not merely marinate people in a particular political milieu but in social and cultural ones as well. . . . [C]ollege makes people more left-wing. There's even reason to believe that the relationship between college and ideology is now more certain than the one between ideology and race." DeBoer, *How Elites Ate the Social Justice Movement*, 146–147.

23. "The majority of [financial] journalists [in our study] (58%) describe their political views as very or somewhat liberal, while a small minority (4%) describe their political views as very or somewhat conservative. Thus, financial journalists lean more liberal than a recent sample of general-interest journalists (Willnat et al., 2017). Willnat et al. (2017) find that 39% (13%) of general-interest journalists have liberal (conservative) political views." Call et al., "Meet the Press."

24. Gross and Simmons, "The Social and Political Views of American Professors."

25. See Hassell, Hobbein, and Miles, "There Is No Liberal Media Bias" ("We find little evidence to comport with the idea that journalists across the United States are ideologically biased [in] choosing what political news to cover"). Other academics who have studied media coverage have come to sharply different conclusions; see, e.g., Groseclose, *Left Turn*.

26. Oreskes and Tyson, "Is Academe Awash in Liberal Bias?" Oreskes and Tyson also note the higher prevalence of conservative faculty in business and health science, which are popular majors for students.

27. Xu, "More Than 80 Percent of Surveyed Harvard Faculty Identify as Liberal."

28. "Class of 2025 by Numbers."

29. Xu, "More Than 80 Percent of Surveyed Harvard Faculty Identify as Liberal."

30. Oreskes and Tyson, "Is Academe Awash in Liberal Bias?"

31. Parker, "The Growing Partisan Divide in Views of Higher Education"; Brenan, "Americans' Confidence in Higher Education Down Sharply."

32. Broockman, Ferenstein, and Malhotra, "Predispositions and the Political Behavior of American Economic Elites."

33. Levitz, "How the Diploma Divide Is Remaking American Politics."

34. Oliver and Wood, *Enchanted America*, 4–5.

35. One can defend these views philosophically, of course. See, e.g., Appiah, *Cosmopolitanism*.

36. This problem is explored extensively in Sandel, *The Tyranny of Merit*.

37. Levitz, "How the Diploma Divide Is Remaking American Politics."

38. Nate Silver (@NateSilver538), Twitter, December 29, 2021, 6:20 p.m., https://twitter.com/NateSilver538/status/1476332200236929028.

39. Kertzer, "Re-assessing Elite–Public Gaps in Political Behavior."

40. Ward, "How Elites Misread Public Opinion."

41. Krakauer, "Rabbit Hole."

42. Murray, "Is *Yellowstone* a Red-State Show?"

43. Igielnik, "70% of Americans Say U.S. Economic System Unfairly Favors the Powerful."

44. Nichols, *Our Own Worst Enemy*, 8, 124, 137.

45. Illing, "The Elites Have Failed."

46. Gilens and Page, "Testing Theories of American Politics," 564. Because of data limitations, the study was conducted using an income-based standard for elites rather than an education-based standard. That is, they compared the voter of average income and the affluent voter (ninetieth-percentile income, which is probably well below the cutoff for what is considered "elite"). Nevertheless, given the strong correlation between income and education, there is little reason to think the overall results would change if we used the "diploma divide" as the metric for elites. Surveying elites can be difficult but is of increasing interest to political scientists. The difference between different definitions of elites—as defined by their roles or their economic class or their education, for instance—are sometimes elided in such surveys, but these definitions are "conceptually intertwined," and the focus on one may not produce terribly different results from a focus on another.

47. Lupton and Webb, "Wither Elites?"

48. Walt, *The Hell of Good Intentions*.

49. Baum and Devins, "Why the Supreme Court Cares about Elites."

50. Domhoff, *Who Rules America?*

51. Morozov, *To Save Everything, Click Here*. Outside of Morozov's focus on solutionism in Silicon Valley, the simplistic "solutionism" hawked by today's elite is routinely skewered in devastating fashion by Aaron Timms; see, e.g., Timms, "The Sameness of Cass Sunstein"; Timms, "Us vs. Him."

52. Somin, "Political Ignorance Is a Serious Problem."

53. Hersh, *Politics Is for Power*, 3.

54. Brennan, "The Right to Vote Should Be Restricted to Those with Knowledge." Brennan dismisses the problem that his test would result in overrepresentation of certain groups—such as rich white men. His remarkable defense is that this overrepresentation is fine in any case because they will vote for what they "perceive to be the common good rather than their self-interest."

55. Rosenblatt and Green, *Supreme Court Survey*.

56. "Take the Quiz: What We Don't Know."

57. Harsanyi, "We Must Weed out Ignorant Americans from the Electorate."

58. Rauch, *The Constitution of Knowledge*, 34–36, 73.

59. Rauch, 16.

60. Rauch, 65.

61. Rauch, 69.

62. Rauch, 70.

63. Clark, "How Covid-19 Bolstered an Already Perverse Publishing System."

64. Clark.

65. Schonhaut et al., "Scientific Publication Speed and Retractions of COVID-19 Pandemic Original Articles," 1, 4–5.

66. Ioannidis et al., "Massive Covidization of Research Citations."

67. S. Williams, "Are 90% of Academic Papers Really Never Cited?"

68. Rauch, *The Constitution of Knowledge*, 75.

69. Rauch, 178.

70. After various departments of the US government credited the lab-leak theory, those who originally dismissed it changed their tune and said the origin of the virus doesn't matter. However, if for no other reason than preparedness, it does matter. See Quammen, "Ongoing Mystery of Covid's Origin." Anne Applebaum never disavowed a tweet where she compared a Republican senator's suggestion that COVID-19 originated at a lab in Wuhan to "the Soviet propagandists who tried to convince the world that the CIA invented aids [*sic*]" (Anne Applebaum [@anneapplebaum], Twitter, February 16, 2020, 11:51 a.m., https://twitter.com/anneapplebaum/status /1229085936908034048).

71. Nichols, *Our Own Worst Enemy*, ix.

72. Nichols, 45. Of course, many who reject experts and "neoliberalism" would not agree with Nichols that they are rejecting democracy; rather, many would say their precise point is that technocratic neoliberalism is a perversion of democracy.

73. Nichols, "How to Confront the Growing Threat to American Democracy."

74. Nichols, *Our Own Worst Enemy*, 2, 27.

75. Nichols, 29.

76. Adamy, "Most Americans Doubt Their Children Will Be Better Off."

77. Nichols, *Our Own Worst Enemy*, 32. Granted, Nichols made this claim before Russia's invasion of Ukraine and the Israeli–Hamas war.

78. Bill Gates (@BillGates), Twitter, May 15, 2017, 8:56 a.m., https://x.com/BillGates/status/864102310250561537?lang=en.

79. See, for example, Cirillo and Taleb, "The Decline of Violent Conflicts," and Braumoeller, *Only the Dead*, 6–10.

80. Micale and Dwyer, "History, Violence, and Stephen Pinker," 4.

81. Nichols, *Our Own Worst Enemy*, 40–41.

82. On this point, see Piketty, *Capital in the Twenty-First Century*, and Milanovic, *Visions of Inequality*.

83. Nichols, *Our Own Worst Enemy*, 43.

84. Nichols, 112.

85. Nichols, 120.

86. Nichols, 53.

87. Nichols, 80.

88. Dotson, *The Divide*.

Chapter 3

1. Feynman made these comments in a lecture entitled "What Is Science?" delivered to a group of science teachers in 1966. In the same talk, he exhorted teachers to "have some hope and some self-confidence in common sense and natural intelligence." Feynman, *The Pleasure of Finding Things Out*, 186–188.

2. David Brooks articulates the sentiment thus: "Members of our class are always publicly speaking out for the marginalized, but somehow we always end up building systems that serve ourselves. The most important of those systems is the modern meritocracy. We built an entire social order that sorts and excludes people on the

basis of the quality that we possess most: academic achievement. Highly educated parents go to elite schools, marry each other, work at high-paying professional jobs and pour enormous resources into our children, who get into the same elite schools, marry each other and pass their exclusive class privileges down from generation to generation." Brooks, "What If We're the Bad Guys Here?"

3. Quoted in Florko, "'Science Was on the Ballot.'"

4. As three scholars who study the relationship between science and society put it in a later essay, "Was 'science' really on the ballot? Is it useful to imagine U.S. citizens as divided into pro-science and anti-science camps? Does the label antiscience serve the purposes of deliberative democracy? The answer to these questions is plainly no." Hilgartner, Hurlbut, and Jasanoff, "Was 'Science' on the Ballot?," 893.

5. Gurri, *The Revolt of the Public and the Crisis of Authority in the New Millenium*, 407.

6. Rouhanifard, "Blue States Are Failing Their Students by Not Reopening Schools."

7. Patrinos, "The Longer Students Were Out of School, the Less They Learned."

8. "Randi Weingarten's Incredible Covid Memory Loss."

9. Lantry, "As Dr. Fauci Prepares to Exit."

10. CDC, "Provisional COVID-19 Death Counts" (statistics as of 2022).

11. Kamenetz, "Nation's Pediatricians Walk Back Support for In-Person School."

12. Quoted in Shapiro, "N.Y.C. Schools."

13. Quoted in Cullum, "Alexandria School Board Member Lorber Apologizes."

14. The *New York Times* columnist Nicholas Kristof, a rare liberal voice in favor of school reopening, complained about this in the fall of 2020: "But after Trump, trying to project normalcy, blustered in July about schools needing to open, Republicans backed him and too many Democrats instinctively lined up on the other side. Joe Biden echoed their extreme caution, as did many Democratic mayors and governors." Kristof, "When Trump Was Right and Many Democrats Wrong."

15. Sacerdote, Sehgal, and Cook, "Why Is All COVID-19 News Bad News?," 4

16. Rothwell and Desai, "How Misinformation Is Distorting COVID Policies and Behaviors."

17. In 2022, a group of researchers put together a "Delphi study" where they attempted to obtain consensus across a large number of experts (386, in this instance). Because the process values high rates of agreement, it tends to result in extreme vagueness as statements are refined to garner greater consensus. For example, 99 percent agreed or strongly agreed with the claim "The COVID-19 pandemic

continues to reveal vulnerabilities in the global supply-chain framework for essential public health supplies." Lazarus et al., "A Multinational Delphi Consensus to End the COVID-19 Public Health Threat," 335. Although an important topic, supply-chain vulnerabilities were hardly an issue fraught with claims of denialism and misinformation in 2020.

18. Pandey, "Private Schools Pull Students Away from Public Schools."

19. Quoted in Schleifer, "Andrew Cuomo Is Leaning on Tech Billionaires to Help New York Rebuild."

20. Cecily Myart-Cruz quoted in McGahan, "Exclusive: Cecily Myart-Cruz's Hostile Takeover of L.A.'s Public Schools."

21. Barnum, "Did School Closures Help Youngkin Win in Virginia?"

22. Goldhaber et al., *The Consequences of Remote and Hybrid Instruction during the Pandemic.*

23. Viner et al., "School Closures during Social Lockdown and Mental Health."

24. As Nocera and McLean note, "The mask controversy was a microcosm of the pandemic itself." Nocera and McLean, *The Big Fail*, xi.

25. Brooks, Butler, and Redfield, "Universal Masking to Prevent SARS-CoV-2 Transmission"; Rummler, "CDC Director Suggests Face Masks Offer More COVID-19 Protection Than Vaccine Would."

26. Oster, "Your Unvaccinated Kid Is Like a Vaccinated Grandma."

27. Fortinsky, "Stacey Abrams Comes under Fire for Not Wearing a Mask."

28. Quoted in Li and Britton, "L.A. Mayor Eric Garcetti Defends Maskless Pictures."

29. Mikhailova et al., "Exclusive: Government Scientist Neil Ferguson Resigns."

30. This was the general prepandemic consensus. Jefferson et al., "Physical Interventions to Interrupt or Reduce the Spread of Respiratory Viruses."

31. Leonhardt, "Two Covid Americas."

32. Jefferson et al., "Physical Interventions to Interrupt or Reduce the Spread of Respiratory Viruses."

33. Greenhalgh and Howard, "Masks for All?"

34. Angela Rasmussen (@angie_rasmussen), Twitter, April 28, 2020, 12:30 a.m., https://twitter.com/angie_rasmussen/status/1254991422018605056; Osterholm, "My Views on Cloth Face Coverings."

35. Howard, "Masks Help Stop the Spread of Coronavirus."

36. Andrew, "A Lawyer Dressed as the Grim Reaper Is Haunting Florida Beaches"; Noor, "The Beach-Going Grim Reaper on His Florida Protest"; Marcus, "The Dudes Who Won't Wear Masks."

37. Science Media Centre, "Expert Reaction to a Study Looking at Mandatory Face Masks."

38. Cohen, "Why Reopening Schools Has Become the Most Fraught Debate of the Pandemic."

39. McCullough, "Drexel Researchers Estimate Philadelphia's Coronavirus Lockdown Saved 6,200 Lives."

40. Mandavilli, "The Price for Not Wearing Masks."

41. Reiner et al., "Modeling COVID-19 Scenarios for the United States."

42. Bundgaard et al., "Effectiveness of Adding a Mask Recommendation to Other Public Health Measures to Prevent SARS-CoV-2 Infection in Danish Mask Wearers"; Abbasi, "The Curious Case of the Danish Mask Study."

43. Kaplan, "Face Mask Trial Didn't Stop Coronavirus Spread, but It Shows Why More Mask-Wearing Is Needed."

44. Kekatos, "Masks Are Effective."

45. Tufekci, "Here's Why the Science Is Clear That Masks Work."

46. Wallace-Wells, "Dr. Fauci Looks Back." ("But I think anything that instigated or intensified the culture wars just made things worse," Fauci said in the interview. "And I have to be honest with you, David, when it comes to masking, I don't know.")

47. Bokat-Lindell, "Is It Time to End Outdoor Masking?"; Palus, "Do We Really Still Need to Wear Masks Outside?"; "Outdoor Mask Mandate Issued for Most Public Outdoor Settings."

48. National Deaf Children's Society, "Face Masks and Communication—Coronavirus Info for Families of Deaf Children."

49. Andy Slavitt (@ASlavitt), Twitter, January 3, 2021, 8:53 p.m., https://twitter.com /ASlavitt/status/1345911083211472896.

50. Kisielinski et al., "Possible Toxicity of Chronic Carbon Dioxide Exposure Associated with Face Mask Use."

51. Anderson, "The Harm Caused by Masks."

52. Tufekci, "The C.D.C. Needs to Stop Confusing the Public"; Guzman, "Fauci Says He Doesn't Regret Advising against Masks Early on in the Coronavirus Pandemic"; Mandavilli, "C.D.C. Says Cloth Masks Are Not as Effective as Others"; Aubrey, "CDC

Urges Vaccinated People to Mask Up Indoors in Places with High Virus Transmission"; McNeil, "How Much Herd Immunity Is Enough?"; Makary, "The High Cost of Disparaging Natural Immunity to Covid."

53. Regalado, "One Doctor's Campaign to Stop a Covid-19 Vaccine Being Rushed Through before Election Day."

54. Prasad and Flier, "Scientists Who Express Different Views on Covid-19 Should Be Heard, Not Demonized."

55. Lenzer, "John Ioannidis and Medical Tribalism in the Era of Covid-19"; Brownlee and Lenzer, "The COVID Science Wars."

56. Blastland et al., "Five Rules for Evidence Communication," 363.

57. Spiegelhalter, "Those Who Tell Us What to Do during the Pandemic Must Earn Our Trust."

58. "Why *Nature* Supports Joe Biden for US President."

59. "Why *Nature* Needs to Cover Politics Now More Than Ever."

60. Zhang, "Political Endorsement by *Nature* and Trust in Scientific Expertise during COVID-19."

61. "Why *Nature* Needs to Stand up for Science and Evidence."

62. McNeil, "How Much Herd Immunity Is Enough?"

63. Altman, "The Exit Polls Show the Need to Confront COVID-19 Denial in Red America."

64. Quoted in Kirkpatrick, "Where Has Seal Been?"

65. Schaeffer, "A Look at the Americans Who Believe There Is Some Truth to the Conspiracy Theory That COVID-19 Was Planned."

66. Chait, "Democrats Learned from Their COVID Errors. Republicans Didn't."

67. *Real Time with Bill Maher*, "Overtime: Andrew Cuomo, Scott Galloway, Melissa DeRosa."

Chapter 4

1. Cuddy, "Your Body Language May Shape Who You Are."

2. Hochman, "Amy Cuddy Takes a Stand."

3. For example, thelostobama, "Did Anyone Try Amelia's 'Superhero Pose' Confidence-Boost Method?," Reddit post, *R/Greysanatomy*, February 10, 2023, https://

www.reddit.com/r/greysanatomy/comments/10z4vbp/did_anyone_try_amelias
_superhero_pose/.

4. Carney, "My Position on 'Power Poses.'" (Unusually and admirably, Carney annotates her online CV with others' critiques of her work as well as replication challenges to studies she has authored.)

5. Ericsson, "The Danger of Delegating Education to Journalists."

6. Engber, "A Whole Field of Psychology Research May Be Bunk."

7. Holson, "Malcolm Gladwell Hands Out Book Blurbs Like Santa Does Presents."

8. Baker, "Internal Review Found 'Falsified Data' in Stanford President's Alzheimer's Research"; Baker, "Stanford President's Research under Investigation."

9. Dyer, "Harvard's Dana-Farber Cancer Institute to Retract Multiple Papers."

10. US Department of Health and Human Services, "Findings of Research Misconduct."

11. Fang, Steen, and Casadevall, "Misconduct Accounts for the Majority of Retracted Scientific Publications."

12. Fanelli, "How Many Scientists Fabricate and Falsify Research?"

13. C. Ferguson, Marcus, and Oransky, "Publishing"; Locke, "Scientists Scammed at Least 110 Academic Papers into Publication Using Fake Peer Reviews."

14. As some commentators see this connection between bad/good research design and strong findings, "What made matters worse is that both scientific journals and the general public are more interested in spectacular claims than in mundane ones." Frijters, Foster, and Baker, *The Great Covid Panic*, 152.

15. Smaldino and McElreath, "The Natural Selection of Bad Science."

16. Ioannidis, "Why Most Published Research Findings Are False."

17. National Institutes of Health, "NIH to End Funding for Moderate Alcohol and Cardiovascular Health Trial."

18. Prasad and Cifu, "Medical Reversal"; Prasad and Cifu, *Ending Medical Reversal*.

19. Bhattacharya, "Up to 140,000 Heart Attacks Linked to Vioxx."

20. Prasad and Cifu, "Medical Reversal," 474.

21. Armstrong, "The Seer-Sucker Theory," 16.

22. Piper, "Science Has Been in a 'Replication Crisis' for a Decade."

23. Gelman and Fung, "Freakonomics"; Scheiber, "Freaks and Geeks."

24. Illing, "Michael Lewis on Why Americans Don't Trust Experts."

25. Lewis recounts the story in Illing, "Michael Lewis on Why Americans Don't Trust Experts" (edited excerpt from a podcast interview by Sean Illing for Vox). Lewis also tells Allen's story throughout his book *The Fifth Risk* (2018) and in the third season of his podcast series *Against the Rules* (https://www.pushkin.fm/podcasts /against-the-rules/against-the-rules-season-3-the-ballad-of-expertise).

26. Fernandes, Lynch, and Netemeyer, "Financial Literacy, Financial Education, and Downstream Financial Behaviors."

27. Illing, "Michael Lewis on Why Americans Don't Trust Experts." (Lewis tells his interviewer: "I agree that you never want to lose your ability to question the things you're being told, but it's also not true that everybody has a right to an opinion about everything. . . . I don't have a right to an opinion about climate change. Neither does Donald Trump. There are people who study this stuff, their whole lives are devoted to trying to understand it. They are state of the art. It is a scientific consensus. My opinion shouldn't exist, but people think they have a right to an opinion about it.")

28. Dahly, Elia, and Johansen, "A Letter of Concern Regarding Increased Risk of COVID-19 among Users of Proton Pump Inhibitors by Almario, Chey, and Spiegel."

29. "The Case against Globaloney."

30. Bendavid, "The Faustian Bargain between Pandemic Scientists and the Media."

31. Ahuja, "We Need to Examine the Beliefs of Today's Tech Luminaries."

32. Osnos, "Survival of the Richest."

33. Acemoglu, "Harms of AI," abstract.

34. Metz, "The ChatGPT King Isn't Worried, but He Knows You Might Be."

35. Begley, "Influential Covid-19 Model Uses Flawed Methods and Shouldn't Guide U.S. Policies, Critics Say."

36. Sumner et al., "The Association between Exaggeration in Health Related Science News and Academic Press Releases."

37. Vinkers, Tijdink, and Otte, "Use of Positive and Negative Words in Scientific PubMed Abstracts between 1974 and 2014."

38. Hyland and Jiang, "'Our Striking Results Demonstrate . . . .'"

39. Two days after resigning the Harvard presidency, Claudine Gay reframed her resignation as a "single skirmish in a broader war to unravel public faith in pillars of American society" that started "with attacks on education and expertise." Rather than take stock of the missteps that had led to her resignation—some of which

involved critiques shared by left-leaning and right-leaning faculty alike—she and others rushed to rewrite legitimate questions about plagiarism as an "attack on . . . expertise." Gay, "What Just Happened at Harvard Is Bigger Than Me."

40. Greenhalgh, Howick, and Maskrey, "Evidence Based Medicine."

41. Fischhoff, Jetelina, and Cetron, "Do Masks Work?"

Chapter 5

1. For instance, although some of the *gilets jaunes* were opposed to a diesel-fuel tax, their movement was not an antienvironmental movement, and some have argued that its politics are aligned with other movements protesting governmental inaction on global warming. Patterson, "Gilet Jaunes."

2. Calling a phenomenon "rational" means seeking to understand it as an intelligible strategic response. It does not mean it is "correct." For an extreme example, political scientists have argued that terrorism is best understood as a "rational" phenomenon, which obviously does not represent a morally favorable judgment. See, e.g., Chenoweth et al., "What Makes Terrorists Tick." The idea is that it is useful to understand terrorists as operating under a strategic calculus toward a particular political end.

3. An almost comical failure to understand this can be seen in Kuper, "The Revenge of the Middle-Class Anti-elitist." For a critique of Kuper's thesis, see Goodwin, "Populism Isn't about Class."

4. Shrum, "Donald Trump Is Not a Populist." See also Goodwin, "Populism Isn't about Class."

5. This problem may be particularly acute with populism because an elected populist candidate becomes, almost by definition, part of the same "elite" that his or her supporters mistrusted.

6. Representative examples of scholars who attempt to strike a level-headed balance but succumb to the temptation to magnify populism's downsides include Jan-Werner Müller in *What Is Populism?*, Barry Eichengreen in *The Populist Temptation*, and Cas Mudde in "The Populist Zeitgeist." Scholars rarely offer praise for populism. Significant exceptions include those who have criticized the antidemocratic tenor of much antipopulist scholarship, such as Thomas Frank in *The People, No*, Roger Eatwell and Matthew Goodwin in *National Populism*, Bernard Harcourt in "Disambiguating Populism," and Robert Howse in "Epilogue: In Defense of Disruptive Democracy." In another significant exception, a few historians and left-leaning political thinkers characterize populism as a revitalization of democracy—for example, Lawrence Goodwyn in *Democratic Promise*, Charles Postel in *The Populist Vision*, and Chantal Mouffe in *For a Left Populism*.

7. Gallie, "Essentially Contested Concepts."

8. Jan-Werner Müller suggests as much in *What Is Populism?* ("Populism is obviously a politically contested concept," 9).

9. A *Guardian* commentator bemoaned the term *populist* because "too often, it merely denotes what the author and their friends dislike, throwing together clowns such as Beppe Grillo with social democrats such as Jeremy Corbyn." Chakrabortty, "Here's the Essential Skill for Assessing Our Politics."

10. Another account along the same lines is Sadurski, *A Pandemic of Populists.*

11. Frank, *The People, No,* 52.

12. Hirschman, *Exit, Voice, and Loyalty.*

13. A short but thorough review of neoliberalism can be found in Menand, "The Rise and Fall of Neoliberalism."

14. Müller, *What Is Populism?,* 2.

15. Müller, 20.

16. Müller, 44, 58.

17. Müller, 84, 99.

18. Müller, "Populism and the People."

19. Eatwell and Goodwin note: "Trump still won around 28 percent of the Latino vote, while Clinton underperformed among this group relative to Obama. Trump also won more than half of the Cuban-American vote in the key state of Florida (although in the longer term this group appears to be drifting towards the Democrats)." Eatwell and Goodwin, *National Populism,* 11.

20. Eatwell and Goodwin, 78.

21. Eatwell and Goodwin, 114–116, quoting Conway, Repke, and Houck, "Donald Trump as a Cultural Revolt against Perceived Communication Restriction."

22. Eatwell and Goodwin, 146.

23. Mitchell, "European Public Opinion Three Decades after the Fall of Communism."

24. Eatwell and Goodwin, *National Populism,* 111, 154, 151, 157.

25. Eatwell and Goodwin, 156, 146.

26. Eatwell and Goodwin, 179, 180, citing Piketty, *Capital in the Twenty-First Century.*

27. Eatwell and Goodwin, 181, 182.

28. Eatwell and Goodwin, 212, 213.

29. Eatwell and Goodwin, 235.

30. Eatwell and Goodwin, 238, 239–240.

31. Eatwell and Goodwin, 249.

32. J. Williams, "How Biden Won Back (Enough of) the White Working Class."

33. J. Williams; J. Williams, *White Working Class*, 29, citing Lareau, *Unequal Childhoods*, 146–151.

34. J. Williams, *White Working Class*, 44.

35. J. Williams, 43, citing and quoting ("class escalator") "Some Colleges Have More Students from the Top 1 Percent Than the Bottom 60."

36. Sandel, *The Tyranny of Merit*, 104.

37. Mendez, Tilman, and Frey, "Biden Slams Trump, Warns 'Equality and Democracy Are under Assault.'"

38. Pew Charitable Trusts, "How the American Middle Class Has Changed in the Past Five Decades."

39. For sustained discussion of this theme, see Bobbitt, *The Shield of Achilles*.

40. Of course, Clinton was hardly alone in seeing neoliberal ideas in this way.

41. Eatwell and Goodwin, *National Populism*, 196.

42. See, for example, O'Neil, *The Globalization Myth*.

43. Roubini, *MegaThreats*, 165.

44. Kotkin, *The Coming of Neo-feudalism*.

45. Gilberstadt, "More Americans Oppose Than Favor the Government Providing a Universal Basic Income for All Adult Citizens."

46. Sandel, *The Tyranny of Merit*. For a similar sentiment, see J. Williams, "How You Treat the 'Non-elite' Is Key to Beating Populism."

47. Hirschman was originally focused on consumers responding to declining product quality. Others have, like us, employed his insights more widely. Joseph Weiler used them to explain the normative underpinnings of the EU legal order. He wrote: "Exit is the mechanism of organizational abandonment in the face of unsatisfactory performance. Voice is the mechanism of intraorganizational correction and recuperation. Apart from identifying these two basic types of reaction to malperformance, Hirschman's basic insight is to identify a kind of zero-sum game between the two. Crudely put, a stronger 'outlet' for Voice reduces pressure on the Exit option and

can lead to more sophisticated processes of self-correction. By contrast, the closure of Exit leads to demands for enhanced Voice. And although Hirschman developed his concepts to deal with the behavior of the marketplace, he explicitly suggested that the notions of Exit and Voice may be applicable to membership behavior in any organizational setting." Weiler, "The Transformation of Europe," 2411.

48. Matthew Goodwin echoes Hirschman in his own account of Brexit and the refusal of "the new elite" to come to terms with the motivating forces behind Brexit. He writes: "Rather than see Brexit as a historic turning point in which millions of people sought to reassert their values and voice against a system which had excluded them for decades, some writers prefer to portray their fellow citizens as mindless, irrational, ignorant lemmings who are being pushed around from one election to the next by lies, misinformation and post-truth politics." Goodwin, *Values, Voice and Virtue*, 2.

Chapter 6

1. "Gov. Pritzker Releases Guidelines to Safely Reopen Additional Businesses and Industries."

2. "Pritzker Closes Indoor Dining throughout Illinois Starting Nov. 4."

3. Masterson, "Restaurant Owners Push Back on Pritzker's Indoor Dining Restrictions."

4. NBC Chicago, "Pritzker Defends Stance on New Indoor Dining Policy."

5. Quoted in Haddon, Wernau, and Hewett, "Restaurant Holdouts Defy Covid-19 Shutdown Orders."

6. "Illinois Restaurant Owner on Why He Is Pushing Back against New Coronavirus Restrictions."

7. This finding has been made many times over the years; a recent example is in Sparkman, Geiger, and Weber, "Americans Experience a False Social Reality by Underestimating Popular Climate Policy Support by Nearly Half" ("We find a form of pluralistic ignorance that we describe as a *false social reality*: a near universal perception of public opinion that is the opposite of true public sentiment. Specifically, 80–90% of Americans underestimate the prevalence of support for major climate change mitigation policies and climate concern. While 66–80% Americans support these policies, Americans estimate the prevalence to only be between 37–43% on average").

8. As one commentator noted about skepticism during the pandemic, "Scepticism is suddenly perilously out of fashion. More than that, it is now deemed dangerous. The reason? The rise of the 'lockdown sceptics,' who in recent weeks have taken a

battering for having made claims about the virus that turned out not to be true. . . . [T]he ferocity of the attacks has left us at a place where all questioning groups are subjected to the same moral condemnation. Whether they are pundits peddling conspiracies, credentialed scientists recommending alternative approaches, or intellectuals worried about the political implications—'lockdown sceptics' is used interchangeably for them all. Any dissent will mark you out as part of the global 'anti-science' movement. So sceptic has become a dirty word." Sayers, "We Need Scepticism More Than Ever."

9. As the political scientist Nicholas Tamio explains, skepticism is an eminently defensible approach to rationality and knowledge: "Sceptics still want to learn about things. The word 'sceptic' comes from the Greek word *skepsis*, meaning 'enquiry.' Sceptics run experiments, test hypotheses, submit and do peer review, and the like. Sceptics follow the rules and methods of science and scholarship, and they laugh with their scholarly friends at the unfounded pronouncements of populists. But sceptics think that part of being intellectually honest is admitting the limits and flaws of one's knowledge." Tampio, "Scepticism Is a Way of Life That Allows Democracy to Flourish."

10. As Rogers Brubaker concludes, "Populism tends to valorize common sense and concrete personal experience, and it tends to be suspicious of abstract and experience-distant forms of knowledge." Brubaker, "Paradoxes of Populism during the Pandemic," 75.

11. Nagel, "What Is It Like to Be a Bat?"

12. For discussion of Descartes, see Dancy and Sosa, eds., *A Companion to Epistemology*, entry on "Rene Descartes" by John Cottingham, 93–97.

13. M. Williams, "Hume's Skepticism."

14. Wittgenstein, *On Certainty*, sec. 115 ("If you tried to doubt everything you would not get as far as doubting anything").

15. Pritchard, *Scepticism*, 4.

16. See, for example, Rutjens, van der Linden, and van der Lee, "Science Skepticism in Times of COVID-19."

17. Sodha, "We Need Scientists to Quiz Covid Consensus, Not Act as Agents of Disinformation."

18. Frankovic, "A Growing Number of Americans Want Stronger Action against Coronavirus."

19. Staerklé et al., "Common Sense as a Political Weapon" ("More research is needed to reach a better understanding of the psychological factors underlying science skepticism," 916).

20. Staerklé et al., 917; Saurette and Gunster, "Ears Wide Shut."

21. Kahan, "The Cognitively Illiberal State."

22. Nyhan, "Facts and Myths about Misperceptions"; Kahan, "Misconceptions, Misinformation, and the Logic of Identity-Protective Cognition."

23. Hawkins et al., *The Ideational Approach to Populism.*

24. The figure is misleading in that the United Kingdom received a rebate from Brussels as well as direct funding. See Henley, "Why Vote Leave's £350m Weekly EU Cost Claim Is Wrong."

25. U. Friedman, "Should the Brexit Vote Have Happened at All?"

26. Marshall and Drieschova, "Post-truth Politics in the UK's Brexit Referendum," 90.

27. Marshall and Drieschova, 91. See also, in general, d'Ancona, *Post-truth.*

28. Eatwell and Goodwin, *National Populism*, 239–240.

29. Antonucci, Horvath, and Krouwel, "Brexit Was Not the Voice of the Working Class nor of the Uneducated." Regarding the middle-class squeeze, see Plunkett, "The Squeezed Middle."

30. Tombs, *This Sovereign Isle*, 49.

31. Richards, Fernández-Reino, and Blinder, "UK Public Opinion toward Immigration."

32. Richards, Fernández-Reino, and Blinder.

33. See, for example, Eatwell and Goodwin, *National Populism.*

34. Tombs, *This Sovereign Isle*, 77. Another way of putting this point is that Brexit was about perceived British exceptionalism. See Crozier, "British Exceptionalism."

35. Staerklé et al., "Common Sense as a Political Weapon," 916. The authors continue: "Indeed, in populist discourse, concrete, immediate and familiar everyday thinking—'common sense'—is portrayed as a form of knowledge that is equal to, if not superior, to expert and scientific knowledge" (916).

36. An overview is given in "Commonsense Knowledge."

37. Misgeld, "Common Sense and Common Convictions," 117; Misgeld discusses Durkheim on 110–112.

38. Kant, *Critique of Judgment*, sec. 40.

39. Kant, sec. 60.

40. *The Late Show with Stephen Colbert*, "Jon Stewart on Vaccine Science and the Wuhan Lab Theory."

41. Shaffer, "Jon Stewart Floats the Covid-19 Wuhan Lab Theory with Stephen Colbert."

42. Zweig, "Anthony Fauci's Deceptions."

43. Almost two years later, Stewart, recalling the backlash he faced over his comments, noted that the biggest problem was our collective "inability to discuss things that are within the realm of possibility without falling into absolutes and litmus-testing each other for our political allegiances as it arose from that." Quoted in Barrabi, "Jon Stewart Recalls Outrage After He Backed COVID-19 Lab Leak Theory."

44. Dotson, *The Divide*, 54.

45. Dotson, 57.

46. Dotson, 10–11.

47. Müller, *What Is Populism?*, 20, emphasis in original.

48. Lemieux, "The Impossibility of Populism," 20.

49. Canovan, *The People*, 140.

50. Canovan, 121.

51. Ackerman, *We the People*.

52. Canovan, *The People*, 121–137, quote on 121, emphasis in original.

53. Canovan, 138.

Chapter 7

1. Eyal, *The Crisis of Expertise*, 25.

2. Eyal, 25.

3. Experts have been a focus of academic commentary for decades. Among other examples, in the early 1990s James Shanteau developed a theory of expertise based on five characteristics, while in 2007 David Snowden and Mary Boone developed a new framework (dubbed the "Cynefin Framework") to improve the quality of expert judgment. In 2011, like others in behavioral economics, Daniel Kahneman assessed the biases of experts and others. See Shanteau, "Competence in Experts"; Snowden and Boone, "A Leader's Framework for Decision Making"; Kahneman, *Thinking, Fast and Slow*.

4. Nichols, *The Death of Expertise*, x–xi.

5. Siegel, "You Must Not 'Do Your Own Research' When It Comes to Science." (Ironically enough, as their central example of the perils of doing your own research, many of these warnings use people who questioned mask wearing.)

6. Joint Commission, "Use an Advocate or Be an Advocate for Others."

7. PatientsLikeMe, https://www.patientslikeme.com/, accessed October 4, 2023.

8. Lyme disease and long COVID are examples: both are real but have also given rise to misinformation and patients overdiagnosing themselves with it. Berg, "Lyme Disease Misinformation"; Gaffney, "We Need to Start Thinking More Critically—and Speaking More Cautiously—about Long Covid."

9. Kelman, "Hard Choices and Deficient Choosers."

10. For discussion, see Marent, Forster, and Nowak, "Conceptualizing Lay Participation in Professional Health Care Organizations."

11. Eyal, *The Crisis of Expertise*, 112.

12. Eyal, 112.

13. Collins and Evans, "The Third Wave of Science Studies."

14. Collins and Evans, 270.

15. Jasanoff, "Breaking the Waves in Science Studies," 391. In a similar vein is Brian Wynne's classic observation about a categorial divide between objective knowledge and cognitively empty emotion or values. See Wynne, "Creating Public Alienation."

16. As Herbert Simon observes, facts do not "come to the administrators carefully wrapped in bundles with the value elements and the factual elements neatly sorted." Simon, *Administrative Behavior*, 4.

17. For several case studies, see Fung and Wright, *Deepening Democracy*.

18. Pew Research Center, "Rebuilding U.S. Fisheries."

19. Ellickson, *Order without Law*, 4.

20. Ostrom, *Governing the Commons*.

21. Burling, "Should Coronavirus Lock Down Protesters Waive Their Medical Care?"

22. Diamond, "Suddenly, Public Health Officials Say Social Justice Matters More Than Social Distance."

23. Greiner et al., "Open Letter."

24. Jennifer Nuzzo (@JenniferNuzzo), Twitter, June 2, 2020, 2:25 p.m., https://twitter.com/JenniferNuzzo/status/1267885076697812993.

25. Marcus and Gonsalves, "Public-Health Experts Are Not Hypocrites."

26. Kramer, *The People Themselves*.

27. In a scathing critique, Aaron Timms notes that Sunstein's books share a certain relentless "sameness." "You immediately begin work on your next book, which will be indistinguishable from this book. Congratulations: You are Cass Sunstein." Timms, "The Sameness of Cass Sunstein."

28. Sunstein, *Risk and Reason*, 30–31, 22. Interestingly, some scientists now think the public was right and that the EPA's estimate of radon's contribution to lung cancer is far off. Considerable controversy remains. See Brody, "Some Scientists Say Concern over Radon Is Overblown by E.P.A."; Stockton, "Trump Wants EPA Radon Program Cut"; Cao et al., "Radon-Induced Lung Cancer Deaths May Be Overestimated."

29. See, e.g., Kelman, "Saving Lives, Saving from Death, Saving from Dying."

30. Shrader-Frechette, "Review of *Risk and Reason* by Cass Sustein."

31. Sunstein, *The Cost–Benefit Revolution*, x.

32. Sunstein, *Averting Catastrophe*, 1.

33. Sunstein, 2, 3, 5.

34. Sunstein, 8, 2.

35. Sunstein, 9, 13–15.

36. Sunstein, 7.

37. Sunstein, 107–108.

38. Sunstein, 15.

39. See, e.g., Timms, "The Sameness of Cass Sunstein."

40. Pamuk, *Politics and Expertise*, 5.

41. See, in general, the essays in Weber, *From Max Weber*.

42. Pamuk, *Politics and Expertise*, 9.

43. Berlin, "Two Concepts of Liberty," 166.

44. Pamuk, *Politics and Expertise*, 196, 199 (citing Grey and MacAskill, "Special Report," on the initial advice against a strict lockdown in the United Kingdom), 197, 199.

45. US House of Representatives, Committee on Oversight and Accountability, "Investigation Reveals Biden's CDC Bypassed Scientific Norms."

46. Eyal, *The Crisis of Expertise*, 111.

47. Quoted in Leonhardt, "The Long Shadow of Covid School Closures."

48. Federalist Society, "Constitutional Protections of Economic Activity."

49. Federalist Society.

50. Federalist Society.

51. McCaffree and Saide, "How Informed Are Americans about Race and Policing?"

52. Pazzanese, "Study Finds Political Bias Skews Perceptions of Verifiable Fact."

53. UVA Center for Politics, "New Initiative Explores Deep, Persistent Divides between Biden and Trump Voters."

54. The bacon example is explored in depth by David Spiegelhalter in his masterful explanation of statistical interpretation for a popular audience. See Spiegelhalter, *The Art of Statistics*, 28–37.

55. Silver, *The Signal and the Noise*, 9.

56. National Academies of Sciences, *Science and Creationism*, 2.

57. Gould, *Hen's Teeth and Horse's Toes*, 255

58. Mulligan and Correia, "Facts."

59. Rorty, "Texts and Lumps," 3, 4.

60. Boyle, "How Are COVID-19 Deaths Counted?"

61. Fiorina, "The Voting Decision." There is a long literature in political science and public choice on whether expressive voting helps explain irrational paradoxes in voting, but it is largely irrelevant for our purposes.

62. Plenty of Sanders supporters would say their votes *were* instrumental, not expressive.

63. Sunstein, *The Cost–Benefit Revolution*, x.

64. Marshall and Drieschova, "Post-truth Politics in the UK's Brexit Referendum," 90.

Chapter 8

1. Cheathem, "Conspiracy Theories Abounded in 19th-Century American Politics."

2. A World Economic Forum report issued in January 2024 ranked "misinformation and disinformation" as the top threat over the next two years—much more of a global threat than war (which, despite all the events of 2023, ranked only fifth). See World Economic Forum, *The Global Risks Report 2024*, 8. In response, Nate Silver quipped, "If the experts think that misinformation is a bigger problem than war, then a way bigger problem than misinformation is that the experts are

fucking idiots." Nate Silver (@NateSilver538), "If the Experts Think That Misinformation . . . ," Twitter, January 11, 2024, 10:01 a.m., https://twitter.com/NateSilver538 /status/1745460915032785112.

3. In a rare pushback against the conventional wisdom, many contributors to a recent special issue of *Critical Review* (including your authors) questioned the "post-truth" narrative. See *Critical Review* 35, nos. 1–2 (2023).

4. Kakutani, "The Death of Truth."

5. Pew Research Center, "Trust and Distrust in America."

6. CBS News, "CBS News Poll, 2018."

7. Packer, "How America Fractured into Four Parts." To his credit, Packer, as a consummate storyteller, also notes that narrative plays a role in that shared reality and that facts intersect with political culture.

8. Nichols, *The Death of Expertise*, xiii.

9. See, e.g., Nyhan, "Facts and Myths about Misperceptions"; Uscinski et al., "Have Beliefs in Conspiracy Theories Increased over Time?"

10. Packer, "How America Fractured into Four Parts."

11. Boot, "The GOP Has Become the Stupid Party."

12. Berinsky, "Telling the Truth about Believing the Lies?," 211.

13. Sasse quoted in Rauch, *The Constitution of Knowledge*, 9; Obama quoted in Beck, "President Obama Tells David Letterman False 'Facts' and Media Bubbles Are a Big Problem, Obviously"; Brooks, "Rotting of the Republican Mind."

14. Schaffner and Luks, "Misinformation or Expressive Responding?"

15. As Nyhan puts it, "A particular analytical challenge is distinguishing between directionally motivated reasoning and differences in information evaluation resulting from differing priors, which are often observationally equivalent despite occurring via different processes." Nyhan, "Facts and Myths about Misperceptions," 226.

16. Quoted in Mansky, "The Age-Old Problem of 'Fake News.'"

17. Hofstadter, "The Paranoid Style in American Politics."

18. See Arnold, "QAnon, the Conspiracy Theory Creeping into U.S. Politics"; Rauhala and Morris, "In the United States, QAnon Is Struggling. The Conspiracy Theory Is Thriving Abroad"; Russonello, "QAnon Now as Popular in U.S. as Some Major Religions."

19. Enders et al., "Who Supports QAnon?" Support for QAnon is meager and stable, revealing a chasm between heavy news coverage of it and polling data. This

comports with studies finding that online fake news and conspiracy theories are less influential than popularly assumed. See Guess, Nagler, and Tucker, "Less Than You Think"; and Guess, Nyhan, and Reifler, "Exposure to Untrustworthy Websites in the 2016 US Election."

20. See Oliver and Wood, "Conspiracy Theories and the Paranoid Style(s) of Mass Opinion."

21. Nyhan, "Facts and Myths about Misperceptions," 232.

22. Guess, Nyhan, and Reifler, "Selective Exposure to Misinformation"; Guess, Nyhan, and Reifler, "Exposure to Untrustworthy Websites in the 2016 US Election."

23. Sean Carroll, "Mindscape 250: Brendan Nyhan on Navigating the Information Ecosystem."

24. Uscinski et al., "Have Beliefs in Conspiracy Theories Increased over Time?"

25. Uscinski et al.

26. Something close to half of respondents (between 43 percent and 54 percent) harbor each of these views. Enders, Uscinski, Seelig, et al., "The Relationship between Social Media Use and Beliefs in Conspiracy Theories and Misinformation," 787. The researchers distinguish a conspiracy theory from misinformation; although misinformation often buttresses conspiracy theories, they are distinct. A conspiracy theory is "a proposed explanation of events that cites as a main causal factor a small group of persons (the conspirators) acting in secret for their own benefit, against the common good" (782).

27. Enders, Uscinski, Klofstad, Wuchty, et al., "Who Supports QAnon?," 845–846.

28. Nyhan, "Facts and Myths about Misperceptions," 228; Guess, Nyhan, and Reifler, "Selective Exposure to Misinformation."

29. Jonathan Haidt thoroughly documents the evidence for this proposition in his Substack newsletter *After Babel* (https://jonathanhaidt.substack.com), while working on a book identifying social media's key role in our growing epidemic of mental health issues. He summarized some of the evidence in testimony before a Senate subcommittee in 2022. Haidt, "Teen Mental Health Is Plummeting, and Social Media Is a Major Contributing Cause."

30. Nyhan, "Facts and Myths about Misperceptions," 222.

31. Kahan, "Fixing the Communications Failure," 296. Kahan calls his work "cultural cognition theory," or the idea that a group's values affect its processing of information and decision-making.

32. Kahan et al., "Motivated Numeracy and Enlightened Self-Government."

33. Nyhan, "Facts and Myths about Misperceptions," 227.

34. Tesler, "Elite Domination of Public Doubts about Climate Change (Not Evolution)," 306, emphasis added.

35. Krupenkin, "Does Partisanship Affect Compliance with Government Recommendations?," 452.

36. Two-thirds of "anti-elites" (populists) share this view in Ekins, "Five Types of Trump Voters."

37. B. Hart, "Poorly Conceived Biden Disinformation Board Put on Pause." Some elites predictably seized on the failure of the ill-conceived initiative as proof that the initiative was needed, claiming it was scuttled by the very forces that required a disinformation department. Lorenz, "How the Biden Administration Let Right-Wing Attacks Derail Its Disinformation Efforts."

38. The researchers also misrepresent the federal government report issued in 2023 (Office of the Director of National Intelligence, "Potential Links between the Wuhan Institute of Virology and the Origin of the COVID-19 Pandemic"), falsely claiming that it concludes that an animal origin of the virus is more likely. Sule et al., "Communication of COVID-19 Misinformation on Social Media by Physicians in the US," 2, 9. (The Office of the Director of National Intelligence report states that the intelligence community unanimously believed both natural and laboratory origins were plausible, and that agencies remain divided in their view about the most likely origin. Sule et al. inaccurately assert that the report "favor[s] a zoonotic origin of the virus" [9].)

39. Chan, "Twitter CEO Says It Was Wrong to Block Links to Biden Story."

40. Haslam and Prasad, "Characteristics of Facebook's Third-Party Medical Fact Checkers."

41. David Zweig (@davidzweig), "The Twitter Files: How Twitter Rigged the Covid Debate," Twitter, December 26, 2022, 9:10 a.m., https://twitter.com/davidzweig/status/1607378386338340867.

42. Arora, "Speech Reduction Act."

43. J. Hart, "Twitter Blacklisting of Bhattacharya."

44. Fang, "Covid-19 Drugmakers Pressured Twitter to Censor Activists Pushing for Generic Vaccine."

45. Both happened during the pandemic. John Ioannidis, one of the most respected contemporary medical scientists, had hour-long interviews removed from YouTube for claims that were hardly misinformation (many of them were hardly controversial). Not surprisingly, given his stature, many other scientists made the decision to stay silent for fear of being attacked or worse.

46. Uscinski and Butler, "The Epistemology of Fact Checking."

47. Holan, Kertscher, and Sherman, "Donald Trump's 'I Was Right about Everything,' Fact-Checked."

48. Stimson and Wager, *Converging on Truth*.

49. Swift, "In U.S., Belief in Creationist View of Humans at New Low."

50. Porter and Wood, *False Alarm*.

51. Nyhan, "Facts and Myths about Misperceptions."

52. See, e.g., Nyhan et al., "Taking Fact-Checks Literally but Not Seriously?" Other studies of the effect of factual corrections on voter preferences are reviewed in Nyhan, "Facts and Myths about Misperceptions."

53. The overuse of this quote actually contains its own irony—a small bit of misinformation. The saying is almost always attributed to Daniel Patrick Moynihan. That's wrong; although Moynihan said it, he didn't originate it. In 2017, some in liberal circles gleefully mocked a Republican senator who attributed the saying to Ronald Reagan. The *Washington Post* found this mockery a delicious "irony" given the reversal in parties: not only did Moynihan not come up with the quote, but Moynihan himself also said he picked it up from a Republican, Alan Greenspan. The phrase, in slightly different form, can be traced back to at least the 1940s. Facts, as John Adams famously said (but also not first!), are indeed stubborn things! See "People Are Entitled to Their Own Opinions but Not to Their Own Facts."

54. As we mention elsewhere in this book, Cass Sunstein is a leading purveyor of this view.

55. Sandel, *The Tyranny of Merit*, 110.

56. Mak, "The Librarian Who Created the Inescapable 'Love Is Love' Yard Sign."

57. Taylor, "How One Woman's Yard Sign Became a Rallying Cry for Allies."

58. Rauch, *The Constitution of Knowledge*, 40.

59. Applebaum, *Twilight of Democracy*, 185.

Chapter 9

1. See Buchanan, "Politics without Romance."

2. See, e.g., MacLean, *Democracy in Chains*; Mayer, *Dark Money*; Oreskes and Conway, *The Big Myth*.

3. Valentine, "'Democracy in Chains' Traces the Rise of American Libertarianism." The NPR ombudsman received so many complaints about the review that NPR published a column acknowledging the many questions that had been raised

about MacLean's sourcing and analysis, ultimately resulting in an editor's note added to the original piece. Jensen, "Readers Rankled by 'Democracy in Chains' Review."

4. Farrell and Teles, "Even the Intellectual Left Is Drawn to Conspiracy Theories about the Right." Henry Farrell and Stephen Teles, left-leaning politics scientists who have written about the intellectual origins of ideas such as public choice and law and economics, were quite harsh in their criticism of MacLean, suggesting she was providing a "conspiracy theory" that has drawn in the "intellectual left." They note that Buchanan's ideas of public choice are indeed widespread and indeed lean right but that MacLean fails to engage with those ideas or take them in good faith, instead labeling conservative economics as providing "a handbook for how to conduct a fifth column assault on democracy." One might add an additional explanation to Farrell and Teles's account. MacLean's claim, even if wrong, leads to a more readable book. A more even-handed discussion of public-choice economics—even one that ultimately comes to quite harsh assessments about the validity of most public-choice theorists' conclusions—would be more accurate, but perhaps less likely to yield a widely reviewed, popular book.

5. We certainly don't mean that only liberals do this; witness suggestions that George Soros is mysteriously behind all liberal ideas. Interestingly, few researchers and commentators seem to be attentive to the most mundane centrist groups that fund far more academic work: How many books have been written about the Aspen Institute or the Ford Foundation? The reason for the silence is presumably not that these organizations are any less interesting but that they fund ideas that are within the academic mainstream that authors such as MacLean personally support.

Funding no doubt matters, but there is a weird double standard in how it is considered. First, how funding affects research is probably quite complicated. Most academics aren't getting funding in the form of an outright bribe; some may only be vaguely if at all aware of where their funding comes from if it's through a center or the university. Even if they are aware, they may be "bribed" by those who know they already agree rather than be paid to change their opinion. Again, this isn't to say that we shouldn't try to purify incentives in academia; it's just to say that finding a trail that points to a particular funder does not mean the research is either wrong or in bad faith.

Moreover, the claim that someone is just doing the bidding of their funders seems to be levied quite selectively. MacLean's acknowledgments mention funding she received from the American Council of Learned Societies, the National Endowment for the Humanities, the National Humanities Center, and the Northwestern University Institute for Policy Research. The latter has gotten millions from the MacArthur Foundation. To understand MacLean's work, do readers need to research MacArthur's policy priorities? Do they need to delve into the personal biography of Carl Pforzheimer III, a financier who donates to the American Council? No: we can't see anything useful that could come from doing so other than to make some unfounded and conspiratorial inferences. Rather, we think the best way to read MacLean's work is on its own terms. But we think it is peculiar that MacLean and others never think to scrutinize their own funding: perhaps because they are confident that funding does not really affect their views, a benefit of the doubt they never grant their opponents.

6. In *Age of Fracture*, Daniel Rodgers traces the ways in which neoliberalism and general ideas of fracturing and disambiguation were taken up on both the political right and the left.

7. Lest it sound as if we are not taking MacLean in good faith and are assuming she played up the title to sell books: MacLean's response to Teles suggests that her work is a genuine statement of how she sees the world. In a Facebook post later shared by Teles, she resorted to the same form of critique to dismiss Teles's critiques. She wrote that Teles "just co-authored a book by a vp at Cato," a libertarian think tank, and that another critique "is on the payroll at the Niskanan [sic] Center," which is "named after the former Cato president" (an image of the post is found in Teles, "A Response to Nancy MacLean"). As Teles points out in his reply, those claims are factually inaccurate in a variety of shoddy ways, but he also sees them as further confirmation that MacLean "cannot, despite all the evidence to the contrary, imagine this as anything but a political dispute, when it is at its core a scholarly disagreement." Teles, "A Response to Nancy MacLean." Nancy MacLean went on to do the same to other critiques of her work, not engaging their substance but instead referring to their authors as "Koch operatives and the riders of their academic 'gravy train.'" Quoted in Bernstein, "Nancy MacLean's Conspiratorial Response to Criticism of 'Democracy in Chains.'" In levying that accusation, she showed no apparent interest in whether these authors had actually received money from Koch or coordinated with each other, much less if this had any impact on what they thought—she simply asserted it.

8. Parmet and Paul, "COVID-19."

9. Compare, for example, Rauch, *The Constitution of Knowledge*.

10. See, for example, Buranyi, "Talk of a Scientific Rift Is a Dangerous Distraction in the Fight against Covid-19."

11. Yamey and Gorski, "Covid-19 and the New Merchants of Doubt."

12. Ioannidis, "A Fiasco in the Making?" For an overview of responses to his op-ed, see Jamison, "A Top Scientist Questioned Virus Lockdowns on Fox News. The Backlash Was Fierce."

13. Oreskes, "The Scientific Consensus on Climate Change."

14. Harrison and Sachs, "A Call for an Independent Inquiry into the Origin of the SARS-CoV-2 Virus"; Office of the Director of National Intelligence, "Potential

Links between the Wuhan Institute of Virology and the Origin of the COVID-19 Pandemic."

15. For the Cochrane analysis, see Jefferson et al., "Physical Interventions to Interrupt or Reduce the Spread of Respiratory Viruses"; for a representative dubious response to the analysis, Tufekci, "Here's Why the Science Is Clear That Masks Work."

16. Oreskes, *Why Trust Science?*, 19, 20.

17. Comte, *Introduction to Positive Philosophy*, 4.

18. See Thornton, "Karl Popper," sec. 3 (For Popper, "all observation is selective and theory-laden and there are no pure or theory-free observations").

19. See Oberheim and Hoyningen-Huene, "The Incommensurability of Scientific Theories," sec. 2.2–2.3.

20. Oreskes, *Why Trust Science?*, 55.

21. Oreskes, 57–58.

22. For the worrisome view that the failures of science are broadly systematic, see Ioannidis, "Why Most Published Research Findings Are False."

23. Oreskes, *Why Trust Science?*, ix, xi.

24. Jamison, "A Top Scientist Questioned Virus Lockdowns on Fox News. The Backlash Was Fierce."

25. These views are described in Hu, "Covid's Cassandra."

26. John Burn-Murdoch (@jburnmurdoch), Twitter, August 26, 2020, 4:03 p.m., https://twitter.com/jburnmurdoch/status/1298712805416169472.

27. Apoorva Mandavilli (@apoorva_nyc), Twitter, September 3, 2020, on file with authors.

28. See, for example, a Twitter thread by the Yale public-health professor Gregg Gonsalves, leveling "shame" on *Jacobin* magazine for publishing an interview containing Kulldorf's "drivel," a "very bad take" that he terms "practically Trumpian." Gregg Gonsalves (@gregggonsalves), Twitter, September 21, 2020, 3:30 p.m., on file with authors.

29. Oreskes briefly acknowledges that pandemics "do, of course, involve economic matters" but then asserts that debates over herd immunity and lockdowns were pure "public health" issues. Oreskes, *Why Trust Science?*, xvii.

30. Oreskes, xvi.

31. Hardwicke and Ioannidis, "Petitions in Scientific Argumentation."

32. Two science journalists have written a useful account of the "science wars" between these two views and of the attempts to suppress debate: see Brownlee and Lenzer, "The COVID Science Wars."

33. Kulldorf, Gupta, and Bhattacharya, "Great Barrington Declaration."

34. Alwan et al., "Scientific Consensus on the COVID-19 Pandemic."

35. Wise, "Covid-19."

36. Oreskes, *Why Trust Science?*, xvi.

37. Oreskes, xvii. On the AIER's defense, see Harrigan and Magness, "Fauci, Emails, and Some Alleged Science." Oreskes argues elsewhere that free markets are not good things. Toward the conclusion to *Merchants of Doubt*, Oreskes and Conway state that "the most serious critique of the central tenet of free market fundamentalism is simply that it is wrong, factually" because "markets do fail" (251). They riff at greater length on this theme in their book *The Big Myth: How American Business Taught Us to Loathe Government and Love the Free Market* (2023), which has been criticized for its "cursory rewrites of well-known history" and "awfully broad and cliched assertions." See, e.g., McLean, "Big Business's Relentless Push to Equate the Free Market with Freedom."

38. For their earlier work, see Aschoff, "We Need a Radically Different Approach to the Pandemic and Our Economy as a Whole"; Lourenço et al., "The Impact of Host Resistance on Cumulative Mortality and the Threshold of Herd Immunity for SARS-CoV-2"; and Sood et al., "Seroprevalence of SARS-CoV-2–Specific Antibodies among Adults in Los Angeles County, California, on April 10–11, 2020."

39. For the views of one such critic, see Pelling and Phelps, "François Balloux."

40. Block, "Vaccinating People Who Have Had Covid-19"; Pugh et al., "The Unnaturalistic Fallacy."

41. Oreskes, *Why Trust Science?*, xvii.

42. N. Ferguson et al., "Report 9."

43. See Wes Pegden (@WesPegden), Twitter, October 15, 2020, 4:31 p.m., https://twitter.com/WesPegden/status/1316839159844274179. Although the economist Paul Romer was also critical of the Great Barrington Declaration, he correctly called out the counterattack letter for its failure to articulate a better plan; in his view, the authors' "preachy tone" masked a "catastrophic intellectual failure by the public health and epi-modeling communities" to articulate an alternative or to engage with the reality of our democracy. The emergence of dueling schools of sciences in the pandemic went hand in hand with increasingly humiliating behavior by scientists on Twitter as their feeds devolved into siren emojis, fights over who has more followers, and name-calling. A few weeks of tweets in 2020 sent from one distinguished

chemist who was widely quoted during the pandemic included descriptions of other scientists as "imbecile[s]," "morons," and "shill[s]" and their ideas as "nonsense" and "idiocy." He rarely elaborated on substance. It was clear from his press appearances that he could make terrific, thoughtful arguments, but Twitter didn't bring out that quality in him.

44. Ioannidis, "Citation Impact and Social Media Visibility of Great Barrington and John Snow Signatories for COVID-19 Strategy."

45. Oreskes, *Why Trust Science?*, 59, 67.

46. Consider Fauci's now-famous statement that to disagree with him was to attack science. See Sullivan, "Fauci: Attacks on Me."

47. Arora, "Did the Government Pressure Twitter to Curtail Speech?"; Brownlee and Lenzer, "The COVID Science Wars"; Harrigan and Magness, "Fauci, Emails, and Some Alleged Science"; Harrison and Sachs, "A Call for an Independent Inquiry into the Origin of the SARS-CoV-2 Virus."

48. Prasad and Flier, "Scientists Who Express Different Views on Covid-19 Should Be Heard, Not Demonized."

49. Yamey and Gorski, "Covid-19 and the New Merchants of Doubt." Although it is tempting to say Yamey and Gorski's work is a misapplication of *Merchants*, the final chapter of *Merchants* employs similar guilt by (unproven) association—for instance, suggesting that a scientist has low credibility because they have been "defended in the *Financial Times*, the *Wall Street Journal*, and the *Economist*." Later in that chapter, Oreskes and Conway draw on the authority of George Soros, without explaining why he and his associated think tanks should not be subject to the very same scrutiny as the free-market think tanks that they dismiss out of hand (Oreskes and Conway, *Merchants of Doubt*, 251–259). This is a common problem in the growing scholarly literature on intellectual influences: it focuses its scrutiny solely on conservative think tanks without ever considering whether comparable effects are possible from liberal funders of academic research or whether funding is the best explanation for the influence of the ideas under study.

50. Thorp, "Remember, Do No Harm?"

51. A similar line-drawing problem is pervasive yet underexamined in related areas, such as the contemporary practice of "fact-checking" and in discussions of what constitutes a conspiracy theory. For examinations of this problem in both areas, see Uscinski and Butler, "The Epistemology of Fact Checking," and Uscinski et al., "Have Beliefs in Conspiracy Theories Increased over Time?"

52. H. Holden Thorp, quoted in Florko, "'Science Was on the Ballot.'"

53. Prasad, Cifu, and Ioannidis, "Reversals of Established Medical Practices"; Prasad and Cifu, *Ending Medical Reversal*.

54. For disagreement with Ioannidis's conclusions, see Greenhalgh and Howard, "Masks for All? The Science Says Yes."

55. S. Lee, "JetBlue's Founder Helped Fund a Stanford Study That Said the Coronavirus Wasn't That Deadly"; Brownlee and Lenzer, "The COVID Science Wars."

56. Fuller, "Models v. Evidence."

57. In particular and contrary to the conventional wisdom in the media, people were less likely to believe medical misinformation than other types of conspiratorial views about COVID-19; that is, "dangerous health misinformation is more difficult to believe than abstract ideas about the nefarious intentions of governmental and political actors." Enders, Uscinski, Klofstad, and Stoler, "The Different Forms of COVID-19 Misinformation and Their Consequences."

58. C. Lee et al., "Viral Visualizations," 2.

59. C. Lee et al., 7.

60. C. Lee et al., 2.

61. C. Lee et al., 10.

62. C. Lee et al., 13, 14. We note that the researchers do not use the word *manipulate* in a pejorative sense. Data are "manipulated" when they are used to make visualizations and other representations. C. Lee et al., 15.

63. C. Lee et al., 14.

64. C. Lee et al., 15.

65. Thorp, "The Charade of Political Neutrality."

Chapter 10

1. Quoted in Wright, "In Defense of Whataboutism."

2. This view has been expressed for many years by political scientists associated with realist theories of foreign policy. For a representative recent example, see Walt, "Liberal Illusions Caused the Ukraine Crisis."

3. McFaul and Applebaum quoted in Lears, "Orthodoxy of the Elites."

4. Lears, "Orthodoxy of the Elites." He continues: "For American democracy to survive, its clercs are going to have to disengage from orthodoxy, stop talking only to one another, and start listening to heretics."

5. Forman-Katz and Jurkowitz, "U.S. Journalists Differ from the Public in Their Views of 'Bothsidesism' in Journalism."

6. Fallon, "2021 Proved That 'Cancel Culture' Is Bullsh*t."

7. "America Has a Free Speech Problem."

8. "A Letter on Justice and Open Debate."

9. "The response was swift, bitter—and, for many of them, unexpected." Ellison and Izadi, "The Harper's Letter."

10. Quoted in Varadarajan, "Make Freedom of Speech Liberal Again."

11. As Jonathan Zimmerman, a Penn professor of history of education, told the *Philadelphia Inquirer* in response to a student protest in 2019, most professors these days are quiet about impediments to open debate because free speech increasingly is "unfortunately and incorrectly" seen as a conservative value. "All of this is an enormous error," he said. "It's a historical error." Quoted in Snyder and Orso, "A 'New Wave' of Activism on Campus."

12. Quoted in Varadarajan, "Make Freedom of Speech Liberal Again." Amia Srinivasan points out that of the incidents in FIRE's database, only 30 percent of the left-initiated incidents resulted in revocation of a speaking invitation. The success rate for "right-wing" disinvitation attempts was higher, at 44 percent. Srinivasan quips: "The left is good at making noise but the right is better at shutting them up." Srinivasan, "Cancelled."

13. FIRE, "Faculty Members More Likely to Self-Censor Today Than during McCarthy Era."

14. The most prominent case involves the University of Pennsylvania, which, starting in 2022, began considering revoking the tenure of the law professor Amy Wax. The case remained unresolved in 2024. See V. Patel, "UPenn Accuses a Law Professor of Racist Statements. Should She Be Fired?"

15. Lukianoff, "The Academic Mind in 2022."

16. FIRE, "Faculty Members More Likely to Self-Censor Today Than during McCarthy Era."

17. Stevens and Schwichtenberg, *2021 College Free Speech Rankings*, 3.

18. Haidt, "The Yale Problem Begins in High School."

19. Powell, "M.I.T.'s Choice of Lecturer Ignited Criticism."

20. Abbot and Marinovic, "The Diversity Problem on Campus." For the Twitter mob's reasoning, see Flaherty, "A Canceled Talk, and Questions about Just Who Is Politicizing Science."

21. Marijolovic, "Professors Are Sharply Divided on DEI Statements in Hiring, Survey Finds"; Freeman, "DEI Dies in the Desert."

22. Flaherty, "A Canceled Talk, and Questions about Just Who Is Politicizing Science." The Princeton invitation came from the conservative Madison Program led by Professor Robert George.

23. Reich, "Judge Duncan's Stanford Visit and the Aftermath, Explained"; Steinbach, "Diversity and Free Speech Can Coexist at Stanford." For a video of the event, see CBN News, "Stanford Dean Joins Students in Heckling of Conservative."

24. Sibarium, "Student Activists Target Stanford Law School Dean in Revolt over Her Apology."

25. Martinez, "Stanford Law School Letter from Dean."

26. Adams, "Sussex Professor Resigns after Transgender Rights Row"; Leiter, "Philosopher Kathleen Stock Resigns Her Position at the University of Sussex."

27. For the list of signatories to the dons' letter of support, see https://www.the pinknews.com/2023/05/17/oxford-university-kathleen-stock-richard-dawkins-letter -support/. Many students also signed a petition rejecting calls for cancellation of the invitation to Stock. See "Student Petition." Just before Stock's scheduled speech to the Oxford Union on May 30, 2023, a group of 100 Oxford academics and staff signed a letter in opposition to Stock's visit; that letter can be accessed at https://docs.google .com/document/d/1myWcqaU0E4Yokw6NavfNwgxuXwJ_Fad5zsiwZt8fl4Y/edit.

28. Adams, "Academics Condemn 'Threats' against Oxford Union in Kathleen Stock Row."

29. Stock, "The Oxford Kids Are Alright."

30. Gavin Williamson, Nadhim Zahawi, and Earl Howe, Higher Education (Freedom of Speech) Act of 2023, passed in the House of Commons on June 13, 2022, and in the House of Lords on December 13, 2022, and it received royal assent on May 1, 2023, https://policymogul.com/legislation/primary/614/higher-education-freedom-of -speech-act-2023.

31. Srinivasan, "Cancelled."

32. FIRE, "FIRE Statement on Florida's Expansion of the Stop WOKE Act."

33. Srinivasan, "Cancelled."

34. Quoted in Clarence-Smith, "Free Speech in Peril as Trans Row Engulfs Oxford University."

35. Of course, Gay's departure was ultimately the result of charges of academic plagiarism.

36. Collins, "Special Post."

37. In a commentary shortly after the hearings, Fareed Zakaria argued that US higher education has lost its standing in the world as the direct result of its embrace

of a progressive ideology that infects every facet of academic life. Zakaria, "Why University Presidents Are under Fire" ("Good intentions have morphed into a dogmatic ideology and turned these universities into places where the pervasive goals are political and social engineering, not academic merit").

38. Sandel, *The Tyranny of Merit*; Markovits, *The Meritocracy Trap*.

39. Quoted in Schuessler, "Harvard Finds More Instances of 'Duplicative Language' in President's Work."

40. Conti, "The Rise of the Sectarian University."

41. Bennet, "When the *New York Times* Lost Its Way."

42. Parker, "The Growing Partisan Divide in Views of Higher Education."

43. Oreskes and Tyson, "Is Academe Awash in Liberal Bias?"

44. Pruneyard Shopping Center v. Robins, 447 U.S. 74 (1980).

45. Zimmer and Isaacs, "Report of the Committee on Freedom of Expression." See also Zimmer, "Statement on Faculty, Free Expression, and Diversity."

46. Stephens, "Go Forth and Argue."

47. Thorp, "The Charade of Political Neutrality" ("This tension has led many universities to adopt the so-called Chicago Principles, which is a mostly innocuous statement by the University of Chicago about welcoming different points of view. But to conservative university stakeholders, it sounds like something that will tamp down the purported liberal bias of the campus and lead to speakers and courses about conservative ideals").

48. All quotes from Thorp, "The Charade of Political Neutrality."

49. Sunstein, *The Cost–Benefit Revolution*, x.

50. Kirshenbaum, "No, Climate Change Will Not End the World in 12 Years"; Bowden, "Ocasio-Cortez."

51. Yglesias, "Misinformation Isn't Just on the Right."

52. Yglesias, "People Need to Hear the Good News about Climate Change"; "Misinformation Isn't Just on the Right."

53. As the economics journalist Greg Ip put it, "The economics of getting to net zero remain, fundamentally, dismal: Someone has to pay for it, and shareholders and consumers decided this year it wouldn't be them." Ip, "Why No One Wants to Pay for the Green Transition."

54. Aristotle, *Politics*, book 1, part 6, quoted in Callard, "Should We Cancel Aristotle?"

55. Callard, "Should We Cancel Aristotle?"; all quotes from Callard come from this article.

56. Saller and Martinez, "An Update for the Stanford Community."

Conclusion

1. Denchak, "Flint Water Crisis."

2. Denchak; Egan, "These Are the 15 People Criminally Charged in the Flint Water Crisis." Some residents no longer trust their own expert, Marc Edwards, who has disputed claims made by a new expert whom Edwards considers an opportunistic fraud. Hohn, "Flint's Water Crisis and the 'Troublemaker' Scientist."

3. Vadala, "The Pennsylvania 'Kids-for-Cash' Judicial Scandal, Explained."

4. Echols, "State Failed to Investigate Complaints in Juvenile Court Kickback Scandal."

5. Pennsylvania's flip to Trump is described in Bradlee, *The Forgotten*.

6. Roe v. Wade, 410 U.S. 113 (1973); Bush v. Gore, 531 U.S. 98 (2000); Dobbs v. Jackson Women's Health Organization, 597 U.S. 215 (2022).

7. Tyson and Kennedy, "Two-Thirds of Americans Think Government Should Do More on Climate"; Burnett, "AP-NORC Poll"; Hartig, "About Six-in-Ten Americans Say Abortion Should Be Legal in All or Most Cases."

8. Bennet, "When the *New York Times* Lost Its Way." Along these lines is Uri Berliner's critique of the decline of NPR. See Berliner, "I've been at NPR for 25 Years. Here's How We Lost America's Trust." Shortly after the publication of his article, Berliner was suspended without pay for five days by NPR. He subsequently resigned from his position.

9. Rodgers, *Contested Truths*, 3. In *Contested Truths*, the historian Daniel Rodgers describes shifting rhetoric in America over the nature of government, the state, and the people.

10. Beiner, *Political Judgement*, 152.

Bibliography

Abbasi, Kamran. "The Curious Case of the Danish Mask Study." *British Medical Journal* 371 (November 26, 2020): art. m4586. https://doi.org/10.1136/bmj.m4586.

Abbot, Dorian S., and Ivan Marinovic. "The Diversity Problem on Campus." *Newsweek*, August 12, 2021. https://www.newsweek.com/diversity-problem-campus-opinion-16 18419.

Acemoglu, Daron. "Harms of AI." National Bureau of Economic Research, Working Paper 29247, September 2021. https://doi.org/10.3386/w29247.

Ackerman, Bruce. *We the People*. Vol. 1 of *Foundations*. Cambridge, MA: Belknap Press, 1993.

Adams, Richard. "Academics Condemn 'Threats' against Oxford Union in Kathleen Stock Row." *The Guardian*, May 17, 2023. https://www.theguardian.com/uk-news /2023/may/17/academics-condemn-threats-against-oxford-union-in-kathleen -stock-row.

Adams, Richard. "Sussex Professor Resigns after Transgender Rights Row." *The Guardian*, October 28, 2021. https://www.theguardian.com/world/2021/oct/28/sussex -professor-kathleen-stock-resigns-after-transgender-rights-row.

Adamy, Janet. "Most Americans Doubt Their Children Will Be Better Off, WSJ-NORC Poll Finds." *Wall Street Journal*, March 24, 2023. https://www.wsj.com/articles /most-americans-doubt-their-children-will-be-better-off-wsj-norc-poll-finds-35500 ba8?mod=article_inline.

Ahuja, Anjana. "We Need to Examine the Beliefs of Today's Tech Luminaries." *Financial Times*, May 10, 2023. https://www.ft.com/content/edc30352-05fb-4fd8-a503 -20b50ce014ab.

Altman, Drew. "The Exit Polls Show the Need to Confront COVID-19 Denial in Red America." *KFF* (blog), November 17, 2020. https://www.kff.org/coronavirus-covid-19 /perspective/the-exit-polls-show-the-need-to-confront-covid-19-denial-in-red-america/.

Alwan, Nisreen A., Rochelle Ann Burgess, Simon Ashworth, Rupert Beale, Nahid Bhadelia, Debby Bogaert, Jennifer Dowd, et al. "Scientific Consensus on the COVID-19 Pandemic: We Need to Act Now." *The Lancet* 396, no. 10260 (2020): e71–e72. https://doi.org/10.1016/S0140-6736(20)32153-X.

"America Has a Free Speech Problem" (editorial). *New York Times*, March 18, 2022. https://www.nytimes.com/2022/03/18/opinion/cancel-culture-free-speech-poll.html.

Anderson, Jeffrey H. "The Harm Caused by Masks." *City Journal*, May 9, 2023. https://www.city-journal.org/article/the-harm-caused-by-masks/.

Andrew, Scottie. "A Lawyer Dressed as the Grim Reaper Is Haunting Florida Beaches to Protest Their Reopening." CNN, May 1, 2020. https://www.cnn.com/2020/05/01/us/grim-reaper-florida-beaches-trnd/index.html.

Antonucci, Lorenza, Laszlo Horvath, and André Krouwel. "Brexit Was Not the Voice of the Working Class nor of the Uneducated—It Was of the Squeezed Middle." *British Politics and Policy at LSE* (blog), October 12, 2017. https://blogs.lse.ac.uk/politicsandpolicy/brexit-and-the-squeezed-middle/.

Appiah, Kwame Anthony. *Cosmopolitanism: Ethics in a World of Strangers*. New York: Norton, 2007.

Applebaum, Anne. *Twilight of Democracy: The Seductive Lure of Authoritarianism*. New York: Random House, 2021.

Armstrong, J. Scott. "The Seer-Sucker Theory: The Value of Experts in Forecasting." *Technology Review* 82, no. 7 (June–July 1980): 16–24. https://repository.upenn.edu/handle/20.500.14332/39470.

Arnold, Laurence. "QAnon, the Conspiracy Theory Creeping into U.S. Politics." *Washington Post*, August 25, 2020. https://www.washingtonpost.com/business/energy/qanon-the-conspiracy-theorycreeping-into-us-politics/2020/08/24/0638de5c-e62c-11ea-bf44-0d31c85838a5_story.html.

Arora, Rav. "Did the Government Pressure Twitter to Curtail Speech?" *City Journal*, September 1, 2022.

Arora, Rav. "Speech Reduction Act." *City Journal*, September 1, 2022. https://www.city-journal.org/article/speech-reduction-act/.

Aschoff, Nicole. "We Need a Radically Different Approach to the Pandemic and Our Economy as a Whole." *Jacobin*, September 19, 2020. https://jacobin.com/2020/09/covid-19-pandemic-economy-us-response-inequality.

Aubrey, Allison. "CDC Urges Vaccinated People to Mask Up Indoors in Places with High Virus Transmission." *All Things Considered*, NPR, July 27, 2021. https://www.npr.org/sections/health-shots/2021/07/27/1021206558/cdc-expected-to-change-mask-guidance-for-vaccinated-people-including-in-schools.

Baker, Theo. "Internal Review Found 'Falsified Data' in Stanford President's Alzheimer's Research, Colleagues Allege." *Stanford Daily*, February 17, 2023. https://stanford daily.com/2023/02/17/internal-review-found-falsified-data-in-stanford-presidents -alzheimers-research-colleagues-allege/.

Baker, Theo. "Stanford President's Research under Investigation." *Stanford Daily*, November 29, 2022. https://stanforddaily.com/2022/11/29/stanford-presidents-research -under-investigation-for-scientific-misconduct-university-admits-mistakes/.

Baldwin, Richard. *The Great Convergence: Information Technology and the New Globalization*. Cambridge, MA: Belknap Press, 2016.

Barnum, Matt. "Did School Closures Help Youngkin Win in Virginia?" Chalkbeat, December 8, 2021. https://www.chalkbeat.org/2021/12/8/22814789/youngkin-vir ginia-election-school-closures.

Barrabi, Thomas. "Jon Stewart Recalls Outrage After He Backed COVID-19 Lab Leak Theory: 'F—k You, I'm Done.'" *New York Post*, February 28, 2023. https://nypost.com /2023/02/28/jon-stewart-recalls-outrage-after-he-backed-covid-19-lab-leak-theory-f -k-you-im-done/.

Baum, Lawrence, and Neal Devins. "Why the Supreme Court Cares about Elites, Not the American People." *Georgetown Law Journal* 98, no. 6 (2010). https://api.semantic scholar.org/CorpusID:152704350.

Baumeister, Roy, and John Tierney. *Willpower: Rediscovering the Greatest Human Strength*. London: Penguin, 2011.

Beck, Kellen. "President Obama Tells David Letterman False 'Facts' and Media Bubbles Are a Big Problem, Obviously." *Mashable*, January 12, 2018. https://mashable .com/article/david-letterman-obama-netflix-false-facts.

Begley, Sharon. "Influential Covid-19 Model Uses Flawed Methods and Shouldn't Guide U.S. Policies, Critics Say." *STAT* (blog), April 17, 2020. https://www.statnews .com/2020/04/17/influential-covid-19-model-uses-flawed-methods-shouldnt-guide -policies-critics-say/.

Beiner, Ronald Steven. *Political Judgement*. 1983. Reprint, London: Routledge, 2010.

Bendavid, Eran. "The Faustian Bargain between Pandemic Scientists and the Media." *Tablet Magazine*, October 17, 2021. https://www.tabletmag.com/sections/science /articles/faustian-bargain-scientists-media.

Bennet, James. "When the *New York Times* Lost Its Way." *The Economist*, December 14, 2023. https://www.economist.com/1843/2023/12/14/when-the-new-york-times -lost-its-way.

Berg, Sara. "Lyme Disease Misinformation Has Physicians Searching for Guidance." American Medical Association, January 12, 2023. https://www.ama-assn.org/deliver

ing-care/public-health/lyme-disease-misinformation-has-physicians-searching
-guidance.

Berger, Peter L., and Thomas Luckmann. *The Social Construction of Reality: A Treatise in the Sociology of Knowledge*. New York: Anchor, 1967.

Berinsky, Adam J. "Telling the Truth about Believing the Lies? Evidence for the Limited Prevalence of Expressive Survey Responding." *Journal of Politics* 80, no. 1 (January 2018): 211–224. https://doi.org/10.1086/694258.

Berlin, Isaiah. "Two Concepts of Liberty" (1958). In *Liberty*, 2nd ed., edited by Henry Hardy, 166–217. Oxford: Oxford University Press, 2002.

Berliner, Uri. "I've been at NPR for 25 Years. Here's How We Lost America's Trust." *The Free Press*, April 9, 2024. https://www.thefp.com/p/npr-editor-how-npr-lost -americas-trust.

Bernstein, David. "Nancy MacLean's Conspiratorial Response to Criticism of 'Democracy in Chains.'" *Washington Post*, July 11, 2017. https://www.washington post.com/news/volokh-conspiracy/wp/2017/07/11/nancy-macleans-conspiratorial -response-to-criticism-of-democracy-in-chains/.

Bhattacharya, Shaoni. "Up to 140,000 Heart Attacks Linked to Vioxx." *New Scientist*, January 25, 2005. https://www.newscientist.com/article/dn6918-up-to-140000 -heart-attacks-linked-to-vioxx/.

Blastland, Michael, Alexandra L. J. Freeman, Sander van der Linden, Theresa M. Marteau, and David Spiegelhalter. "Five Rules for Evidence Communication." *Nature* 587, no. 7834 (November 2020): 362–364. https://doi.org/10.1038/d41586-020-03189-1.

Block, Jennifer. "Vaccinating People Who Have Had Covid-19: Why Doesn't Natural Immunity Count in the US?" *British Medical Journal* 374 (September 13, 2021): art. n2101. https://doi.org/10.1136/bmj.n2101.

Bobbitt, Philip. *The Shield of Achilles: War, Peace, and the Course of History*. Paperback ed. New York: Anchor, 2003.

Bokat-Lindell, Spencer. "Is It Time to End Outdoor Masking?" *New York Times*, April 20, 2021. https://www.nytimes.com/2021/04/20/opinion/mask-outdoor-mandate .html.

Bologna, Caroline. "The Rudest Things You Can Do at a Hotel." *Huffington Post*, October 7, 2021. https://www.huffpost.com/entry/rudest-things-you-can-do-hotel_l _615b23dfe4b050254235fa82.

Boot, Max. "The GOP Has Become the Stupid Party—and Proud of It." *Washington Post*, October 4, 2021. https://www.washingtonpost.com/opinions/2021/10/04/gop -proud-of-its-own-stupidity/.

Bowden, John. "Ocasio-Cortez: 'World Will End in 12 Years' If Climate Change Not Addressed." *The Hill* (blog), January 22, 2019. https://thehill.com/policy/energy -environment/426353-ocasio-cortez-the-world-will-end-in-12-years-if-we-dont-address/.

Bowen, Alison. "That Cat Lawyer Video Was Funny. Here's Why Mental Health Experts Say You Should Watch More Like It." *Chicago Tribune*, February 16, 2021. https://www.chicagotribune.com/coronavirus/ct-life-laughter-importance-videos -distractions-tt-20210216-2jljkdddfzgzrahymjegde44tm-story.html.

Boyle, Patrick. "How Are COVID-19 Deaths Counted? It's Complicated." Association of American Medical Colleges, accessed October 20, 2023. https://www.aamc.org /news/how-are-covid-19-deaths-counted-it-s-complicated.

Bradlee, Ben, Jr. *The Forgotten: How the People of One Pennsylvania County Elected Donald Trump and Changed America.* New York: Little, Brown, 2018.

Braumoeller, Bear F. *Only the Dead: The Persistence of War in the Modern Age.* New York: Oxford University Press, 2019.

Brenan, Megan. "Americans' Confidence in Higher Education Down Sharply." Gallup, July 11, 2023. https://news.gallup.com/poll/508352/americans-confidence -higher-education-down-sharply.aspx.

Brennan, Jason. *Against Democracy.* Princeton, NJ: Princeton University Press, 2016.

Brennan, Jason. "The Right to Vote Should Be Restricted to Those with Knowledge." *Aeon*, September 29, 2016. https://aeon.co/ideas/the-right-to-vote-should-be-restricted -to-those-with-knowledge.

Brody, Jane E. "Some Scientists Say Concern over Radon Is Overblown by E.P.A." *New York Times*, January 8, 1991. https://www.nytimes.com/1991/01/08/science /some-scientists-say-concern-over-radon-is-overblown-by-epa.html.

Broockman, David E., Gregory Ferenstein, and Neil Malhotra. "Predispositions and the Political Behavior of American Economic Elites: Evidence from Technology Entrepreneurs." *American Journal of Political Science* 63, no. 1 (2019): 212–233.

Brooks, David. "The Rotting of the Republican Mind." *New York Times*, November 26, 2020. https://www.nytimes.com/2020/11/26/opinion/republican-disinformation .html.

Brooks, David. "What If We're the Bad Guys Here?" *New York Times*, August 4, 2023.

Brooks, John T., Jay C. Butler, and Robert R. Redfield. "Universal Masking to Prevent SARS-CoV-2 Transmission—the Time Is Now." *JAMA* 324, no. 7 (2020): 635–637. https://doi.org/10.1001/jama.2020.13107.

Brownlee, Shannon, and Jeanne Lenzer. "The COVID Science Wars." *Scientific American*, November 30, 2020.

Brubaker, Rogers. "Paradoxes of Populism during the Pandemic." *Thesis Eleven* 164, no. 1 (June 2021): 73–87. https://doi.org/10.1177/0725513620970804.

Buchanan, James M. "Politics without Romance: A Sketch of Positive Public Choice Theory and Its Normative Implications." In *The Theory of Public Choice—II*, edited by James M. Buchanan and Robert D. Tollison, 11–22. Ann Arbor: University of Michigan Press, 1984.

Bundgaard, Henning, Johan Skov Bundgaard, Daniel Emil Tadeusz Raaschou-Pedersen, Christian Von Buchwald, Tobias Todsen, Jakob Boesgaard Norsk, Mia M. Pries-Heje, et al. "Effectiveness of Adding a Mask Recommendation to Other Public Health Measures to Prevent SARS-CoV-2 Infection in Danish Mask Wearers: A Randomized Controlled Trial." *Annals of Internal Medicine* 174, no. 3 (March 2021): 335–343. https://doi.org/10.7326/M20-6817.

Buranyi, Stephen. "Talk of a Scientific Rift Is a Dangerous Distraction in the Fight against Covid-19." *The Guardian*, September 29, 2020. https://www.theguardian.com/commentisfree/2020/sep/29/rival-scientists-lockdowns-scientific-covid-19.

Burling, Stacey. "Should Coronavirus Lock Down Protesters Waive Their Medical Care? Some Medical Ethicists Think So." *Philadelphia Inquirer*, May 22, 2020. https://www.inquirer.com/health/coronavirus/should-coronavirus-lockdown-protesters-forgo-medical-care-medical-ethicists-think-so-ventilators-penn-colorado-state-nyu-20200522.html.

Burnett, Sara. "AP-NORC Poll: Most in US Say They Want Stricter Gun Laws." *AP News*, August 23, 2022. https://apnews.com/article/gun-violence-covid-health-chicago-c912ecc5619e925c5ea7447d36808715.

Cadelago, Christopher. "'We Would've Done Everything Differently': Newsom Reflects on Covid Approach." *Politico*, September 10, 2023. https://www.politico.com/news/2023/09/10/newsom-covid-california-00114888.

Call, Andrew C., Scott A. Emett, Eldar Maksymov, and Nathan Y. Sharp. "Meet the Press: Survey Evidence on Financial Journalists as Information Intermediaries." November 1, 2021. https://doi.org/10.2139/ssrn.3279453.

Callard, Agnes. "Should We Cancel Aristotle?" *New York Times*, July 21, 2020. https://www.nytimes.com/2020/07/21/opinion/should-we-cancel-aristotle.html.

Canovan, Margaret. *The People*. Cambridge: Polity, 2005.

Cao, Xiaodong, Piers MacNaughton, Jose Cedeno Laurent, and Joseph G. Allen. "Radon-Induced Lung Cancer Deaths May Be Overestimated due to Failure to Account for Confounding by Exposure to Diesel Engine Exhaust in BEIR VI Miner Studies." *PLOS ONE* 12, no. 9 (2017): art. e0184298. https://doi.org/10.1371/journal.pone.0184298.

Carney, Dana. "My Position on 'Power Poses.'" Accessed April 25, 2024. http://faculty.haas.berkeley.edu/dana_carney/pdf_My%20position%20on%20power%20poses.pdf.

"The Case against Globaloney." *The Economist*, April 20, 2011. https://www.economist.com/business/2011/04/20/the-case-against-globaloney.

CBN News. "Stanford Dean Joins Students in Heckling of Conservative, Used Free Speech to Reject Free Speech." YouTube, March 17, 2023. https://www.youtube.com/watch?v=orzuClSpGCc.

CBS News. "CBS News Poll, 2018." Roper Center for Public Opinion Research, 2019. https://doi.org/10.25940/ROPER-31116742.

Centers for Disease Control and Prevention (CDC). "Provisional COVID-19 Death Counts by Age in Years, 2020–2023." July 12, 2023. https://data.cdc.gov/NCHS/Provisional-COVID-19-Death-Counts-by-Age-in-Years-/3apk-4u4f.

Chait, Jonathan. "Democrats Learned from Their COVID Errors. Republicans Didn't." *New York Magazine Intelligencer* (blog), July 24, 2023. https://nymag.com/intelligencer/2023/07/democrats-corrected-their-covid-errors-republicans-didnt.html.

Chakrabortty, Aditya. "Here's the Essential Skill for Assessing Our Politics: Knowing the Difference between Lies and Bullshit." *The Guardian*, December 22, 2022. https://www.theguardian.com/commentisfree/2022/dec/22/politics-difference-between-lies-bullshit.

Chan, Kelvin. "Twitter CEO Says It Was Wrong to Block Links to Biden Story." *AP News*, October 17, 2020. https://apnews.com/article/business-media-social-media-censorship-ec529ef85c1e72cefe0ae9450e118b9c.

Cheathem, Mark R. "Conspiracy Theories Abounded in 19th-Century American Politics." *Smithsonian Magazine*, April 11, 2019. https://www.smithsonianmag.com/history/conspiracy-theories-abounded-19th-century-american-politics-180971940/.

Chenoweth, Erica, Nicholas Miller, Elizabeth McClellan, Hillel Frisch, Paul Staniland, and Max Abrahms. "What Makes Terrorists Tick." *International Security* 33 (April 1, 2009): 180–202. https://doi.org/10.1162/isec.2009.33.4.180.

Cirillo, Pasquale, and Nassim Nicholas Taleb. "The Decline of Violent Conflicts: What Do the Data Really Say?" November 27, 2016. https://doi.org/10.2139/ssrn.2876315.

Clarence-Smith, Louisa. "Free Speech in Peril as Trans Row Engulfs Oxford University." *Telegraph*, May 16, 2023. https://www.telegraph.co.uk/news/2023/05/16/free-speech-oxford-university-trans-row-kathleen-stock/.

Clark, Jocalyn. "How Covid-19 Bolstered an Already Perverse Publishing System." *British Medical Journal* 380 (March 28, 2023): art. p689. https://doi.org/10.1136/bmj.p689.

"Class of 2025 by the Numbers." *Harvard Crimson*, accessed August 1, 2023. https://features.thecrimson.com/2021/freshman-survey/lifestyle/.

Cohen, Rachel M. "Why Reopening Schools Has Become the Most Fraught Debate of the Pandemic." *American Prospect*, October 28, 2020. https://prospect.org/api/content/89b4aab8-18a4-11eb-b096-1244d5f7c7c6/.

Collins, H. M., and Robert Evans. "The Third Wave of Science Studies: Studies of Expertise and Experience." *Social Studies of Science* 32, no. 2 (2002): 235–296.

Collins, Ronald K. L. "Special Post: Stephen Rohde, 'University Presidents Were Right to Condemn Hate Speech and Defend Free Speech.'" Foundation for Individual Rights and Expression, December 8, 2023. https://www.thefire.org/news/blogs/ronald-kl-collins-first-amendment-news/special-post-stephen-rohde-university-presidents.

"Commonsense Knowledge." Oxford Reference, accessed September 5, 2023. https://www.oxfordreference.com/display/10.1093/acref/9780195123715.001.0001/acref-9780195123715-e-306.

Comte, Auguste. *Introduction to Positive Philosophy*. Translated by Frederick Ferré. Indianapolis, IN: Hackett, 1988.

Conti, Greg. "The Rise of the Sectarian University." *Compact Magazine*, December 28, 2023. https://compactmag.com/article/the-rise-of-the-sectarian-university.

Conway, Lucian Gideon, III, Meredith A. Repke, and Shannon C. Houck. "Donald Trump as a Cultural Revolt against Perceived Communication Restriction: Priming Political Correctness Norms Causes More Trump Support." *Journal of Social and Political Psychology* 5, no. 1 (2017): 244–259. https://doi.org/10.5964/jspp.v5i1.732.

Crozier, Andrew J. "British Exceptionalism: Pride and Prejudice and Brexit." *International Economics and Economic Policy* 17, no. 3 (2020): 635–658. https://doi.org/10.1007/s10368-020-00469-z.

Cuddy, Amy. "Your Body Language May Shape Who You Are." TED Talk, June 2012. https://www.ted.com/talks/amy_cuddy_your_body_language_may_shape_who_you_are.

Cullum, James. "Alexandria School Board Member Lorber Apologizes for Comments on Cautious ACPS Reopening." *ALXnow* (blog), January 13, 2021. https://www.alxnow.com/2021/01/13/alexandria-school-board-member-lorber-apologizes-for-comments-on-cautious-acps-reopening/.

Dahly, Darren, Mario Elia, and Michael Johansen. "A Letter of Concern Regarding Increased Risk of COVID-19 among Users of Proton Pump Inhibitors by Almario, Chey, and Spiegel." July 11, 2020. https://doi.org/10.5281/zenodo.3940578.

d'Ancona, Matthew. *Post-truth: The New War on Truth and How to Fight Back*. London: Ebury Press, 2017.

Dancy, Jonathan, and Ernest Sosa, eds. *A Companion to Epistemology*. Oxford: Blackwell Reference, 1992.

deBoer, Fredrik. *How Elites Ate the Social Justice Movement*. New York: Simon & Schuster, 2023.

Denchak, Melissa. "Flint Water Crisis: Everything You Need to Know." NRDC, November 8, 2018. https://www.nrdc.org/stories/flint-water-crisis-everything-you-need-know.

Diamond, Dan. "Suddenly, Public Health Officials Say Social Justice Matters More Than Social Distance." *Politico*, June 4, 2020. https://www.politico.com/news/magazine/2020/06/04/public-health-protests-301534.

Diaz, Johnny. "Trying to Stay Warm? Here Are Some Tips from Experts." *New York Times*, February 16, 2021. https://www.nytimes.com/2021/02/16/us/stay-warm-power-outage.html.

Domhoff, G. William. *Who Rules America? The Triumph of the Corporate Rich*. 8th ed. New York: McGraw Hill, 2022.

Dotson, Taylor. *The Divide: How Fanatical Certitude Is Destroying Democracy*. Cambridge, MA: MIT Press, 2021.

Dyer, Owen. "Harvard's Dana-Farber Cancer Institute to Retract Multiple Papers after Blogger Alleges Data Fabrication." *British Medical Journal* 384 (2024): q249. https://doi.org/10.1136/bmj.q249.

Eatwell, Roger, and Matthew J. Goodwin. *National Populism: The Revolt against Liberal Democracy*. London: Pelican, 2018.

Echols, Noah. "State Failed to Investigate Complaints in Juvenile Court Kickback Scandal." Juvenile Justice Information Exchange, March 22, 2010. https://jjie.org/2010/03/22/getting-the-juvenile-justice-system-to-grow-up/.

Edsall, Thomas B. "Elites Are Making Choices That Are Not Good News." *New York Times*, November 2, 2022. https://www.nytimes.com/2022/11/02/opinion/artificial-intelligence-automation-jobs-populism.html.

Egan, Paul. "These Are the 15 People Criminally Charged in the Flint Water Crisis." *Detroit Free Press*, June 14, 2017. https://www.freep.com/story/news/local/michigan/flint-water-crisis/2017/06/14/flint-water-crisis-charges/397425001/.

Eichengreen, Barry. *The Populist Temptation: Economic Grievance and Political Reaction in the Modern Era*. New York: Oxford University Press, 2018.

Ekins, Emily. "The Five Types of Trump Voters: Who They Are and What They Believe." Democracy Fund Voter Study Group, June 2017. https://www.voterstudygroup.org/publication/the-five-types-trump-voters.

Ellickson, Robert C. *Order without Law: How Neighbors Settle Disputes*. Cambridge, MA: Harvard University Press, 1994.

Ellison, Sarah, and Elahe Izadi. "The *Harper's* 'Letter,' Cancel Culture and the Summer That Drove a Lot of Smart People Mad." *Washington Post*, July 24, 2020. https://www.washingtonpost.com/lifestyle/style/the-harpers-letter-cancel-culture-and-the-summer-that-drove-a-lot-of-smart-people-mad/2020/07/23/9df5d6e4-c84c-11ea-b037-f9711f89ee46_story.html.

Enders, Adam M., Joseph E. Uscinski, Casey A. Klofstad, and Justin Stoler. "The Different Forms of COVID-19 Misinformation and Their Consequences." *Harvard Kennedy School Misinformation Review* 1, no. 8 (2020). https://misinforeview.hks.harvard.edu/article/the-different-forms-of-covid-19-misinformation-and-their-consequences/.

Enders, Adam M., Joseph E. Uscinski, Casey A. Klofstad, Stefan Wuchty, Michelle I. Seelig, John R. Funchion, Manohar N. Murthi, et al. "Who Supports QAnon? A Case Study in Political Extremism." *Journal of Politics* 84, no. 3 (July 2022): 1844–1849. https://doi.org/10.1086/717850.

Enders, Adam M., Joseph E. Uscinski, Michelle I. Seelig, Casey A. Klofstad, Stefan Wuchty, John R. Funchion, Manohar N. Murthi, et al. "The Relationship between Social Media Use and Beliefs in Conspiracy Theories and Misinformation." *Political Behavior* 45, no. 2 (2023): 781–804. https://doi.org/10.1007/s11109-021-09734-6.

Engber, Daniel. "A Whole Field of Psychology Research May Be Bunk. Scientists Should Be Terrified." *Slate*, March 6, 2016. http://www.slate.com/articles/health_and_science/cover_story/2016/03/ego_depletion_an_influential_theory_in_psychology_may_have_just_been_debunked.html.

Ericsson, K. Anders. "The Danger of Delegating Education to Journalists." *Dr. p.l. (Paul) Thomas* (blog), November 3, 2014. https://radicalscholarship.com/2014/11/03/guest-post-the-danger-of-delegating-education-to-journalists-k-anders-ericsson/.

Eyal, Gil. *The Crisis of Expertise*. Cambridge: Polity, 2019.

Fallon, Kevin. "2021 Proved That 'Cancel Culture' Is Bullsh*t." *Daily Beast*, December 29, 2021. https://www.thedailybeast.com/2021-proved-once-and-for-all-that-cancel-culture-is-total-bullshit.

Fanelli, Daniele. "How Many Scientists Fabricate and Falsify Research? A Systematic Review and Meta-analysis of Survey Data." *PLOS ONE* 4, no. 5 (2009): art. e5738. https://doi.org/10.1371/journal.pone.0005738.

Fang, Ferric C., R. Grant Steen, and Arturo Casadevall. "Misconduct Accounts for the Majority of Retracted Scientific Publications." *Proceedings of the National Academy of Sciences* 109, no. 42 (2012): 17028–17033. https://doi.org/10.1073/pnas.1212247109.

Fang, Lee. "Covid-19 Drugmakers Pressured Twitter to Censor Activists Pushing for Generic Vaccine." *The Intercept*, January 16, 2023. https://theintercept.com/2023/01/16/twitter-covid-vaccine-pharma/.

Farrell, Henry, and Steven Teles. "Even the Intellectual Left Is Drawn to Conspiracy Theories about the Right. Resist Them." Vox, July 14, 2017. https://www.vox.com/the-big-idea/2017/7/14/15967788/democracy-shackles-james-buchanan-intellectual-history-maclean.

Federalist Society. "Constitutional Protections of Economic Activity: How They Promote Individual Freedom." Panel discussion, October 16, 1987. https://www.c-span.org/video/?1422-1/constitutional-economic-rights.

Ferguson, Cat, Adam Marcus, and Ivan Oransky. "Publishing: The Peer-Review Scam." *Nature* 515, no. 7528 (2014): 480–482. https://doi.org/10.1038/515480a.

Ferguson, N., D. Laydon, G. Nedjati Gilani, N. Imai, K. Ainslie, M. Baguelin, S. Bhatia, et al. "Report 9: Impact of Non-pharmaceutical Interventions (NPIs) to Reduce COVID19 Mortality and Healthcare Demand." Imperial College London, March 16, 2020. https://doi.org/10.25561/77482.

Fernandes, Daniel, John Lynch, and Richard Netemeyer. "Financial Literacy, Financial Education, and Downstream Financial Behaviors." *Management Science*, August 1, 2014. https://doi.org/10.1287/mnsc.2013.1849.

Ferré-Sadurní, Luis. "Health Agency under Cuomo 'Misled the Public' on Nursing Home Deaths." *New York Times*, March 15, 2022. https://www.nytimes.com/2022/03/15/nyregion/nursing-home-deaths-cuomo-covid.html.

Feynman, Richard P. *The Pleasure of Finding Things Out: The Best Short Works of Richard P. Feynman.* Edited by Jeffrey Robbins. New York: Basic, 2005.

Fiorina, Morris P. "The Voting Decision: Instrumental and Expressive Aspects." *Journal of Politics* 38, no. 2 (1976): 390–413. https://doi.org/10.2307/2129541.

FIRE. "Faculty Members More Likely to Self-Censor Today Than during McCarthy Era." Foundation for Individual Rights and Expression, February 28, 2023. https://www.thefire.org/news/report-faculty-members-more-likely-self-censor-today-during-mccarthy-era.

FIRE. "FIRE Statement on Florida's Expansion of the Stop WOKE Act." Foundation for Individual Rights and Expression, May 15, 2023. https://www.thefire.org/news/fire-statement-floridas-expansion-stop-woke-act.

Fischhoff, Baruch, Katelyn Jetelina, and Martin Cetron. "Do Masks Work? Randomized Controlled Trials Are the Worst Way to Answer the Question." *STAT* (blog), May 2, 2023. https://www.statnews.com/2023/05/02/do-masks-work-rcts-randomized-controlled-trials/.

Flaherty, Colleen. "A Canceled Talk, and Questions about Just Who Is Politicizing Science." *Inside Higher Ed*, October 6, 2021. https://www.insidehighered.com/news /2021/10/06/mit-controversy-over-canceled-lecture.

Florko, Nicholas. "'Science Was on the Ballot': How Can Public Health Recover from a Rebuke at the Polls?" *STAT* (blog), November 4, 2020. https://www.statnews .com/2020/11/04/public-health-recover-rebuke-at-polls/.

Forman-Katz, Naomi, and Mark Jurkowitz. "U.S. Journalists Differ from the Public in Their Views of 'Bothsidesism' in Journalism." Pew Research Center, July 13, 2022. https://www.pewresearch.org/short-reads/2022/07/13/u-s-journalists-differ-from -the-public-in-their-views-of-bothsidesism-in-journalism/.

Fortinsky, Sarah. "Stacey Abrams Comes under Fire for Not Wearing a Mask in Now-Deleted Photos with Masked Schoolchildren." CNN, February 7, 2022. https://www .cnn.com/2022/02/06/politics/stacey-abrams-school-photos/index.html.

Frank, Thomas. *The People, No: A Brief History of Anti-populism*. New York: Metropolitan Books/Holt, 2020.

Frankovic, Kathy. "A Growing Number of Americans Want Stronger Action against Coronavirus." *The Economist*/YouGov Poll, March 11, 2020. https://today.yougov .com/health/articles/28375-growing-number-americans-want-stronger-action-agai.

Fraser, Giles. "Michael Ignatieff's Confessions—Liberalism, Populism and Multiculturalism." *UnHerd* (podcast), May 11, 2020. https://unherd.com/podcasts/michael -ignatieffs-confessions-liberalism-populism-and-multiculturalism/.

Freeman, James. "DEI Dies in the Desert." *Wall Street Journal*, August 17, 2023. https://www.wsj.com/articles/dei-dies-in-the-desert-84168eeb.

Friedman, Lisa. "Trump Tries to Improve His Environmental Record with a New Water Rule, but Experts Reject Its Efficacy." *New York Times*, September 28, 2020. https://www.nytimes.com/2020/09/28/us/politics/trump-tries-to-improve-his-envi ronmental-record-with-a-new-water-rule-but-experts-reject-its-efficacy.html.

Friedman, Thomas L. *The World Is Flat: A Brief History of the Twenty-First Century*. New York: Farrar, Straus and Giroux, 2005.

Friedman, Uri. "Should the Brexit Vote Have Happened at All?" *The Atlantic*, June 27, 2016. https://www.theatlantic.com/international/archive/2016/06/brexit-vote -referendum-democracy/488654/.

Frijters, Paul, Gigi Foster, and Michael Baker. *The Great Covid Panic: What Happened, Why, and What to Do Next*. Austin, TX: Brownstone Institute, 2021.

Fuller, Jonathan. "Models v. Evidence." *Boston Review*, May 5, 2020.

Fung, Archon, and Erik Olin Wright, eds. *Deepening Democracy: Institutional Innovations in Empowered Participatory Governance*. London: Verso, 2011.

Gaffney, Adam W. "We Need to Start Thinking More Critically—and Speaking More Cautiously—about Long Covid." *STAT* (blog), March 22, 2021. https://www.statnews.com/2021/03/22/we-need-to-start-thinking-more-critically-speaking-cautiously-long-covid/.

Gallie, W. B. "Essentially Contested Concepts." *Proceedings of the Aristotelian Society* 56 (1955): 167–198.

Gay, Claudine. "What Just Happened at Harvard Is Bigger Than Me." *New York Times*, January 3, 2024. https://www.nytimes.com/2024/01/03/opinion/claudine-gay-harvard-president.html.

Gelman, Andrew, and Kaiser Fung. "Freakonomics: What Went Wrong?" *American Scientist*, February 6, 2017. https://www.americanscientist.org/article/freakonomics-what-went-wrong.

Gilberstadt, Hannah. "More Americans Oppose Than Favor the Government Providing a Universal Basic Income for All Adult Citizens." Pew Research Center, August 19, 2020. https://www.pewresearch.org/short-reads/2020/08/19/more-americans-oppose-than-favor-the-government-providing-a-universal-basic-income-for-all-adult-citizens/.

Gilens, Martin, and Benjamin I. Page. "Testing Theories of American Politics: Elites, Interest Groups, and Average Citizens." *Perspectives on Politics* 12, no. 3 (September 2014): 564–581. https://doi.org/10.1017/S1537592714001595.

Giridharadas, Anand. *Winners Take All: The Elite Charade of Changing the World.* New York: Knopf, 2018.

Gladwell, Malcolm. *Outliers: The Story of Success.* New York: Little, Brown, 2008.

Goldhaber, Dan, Thomas J. Kane, Andrew McEachin, Emily Morton, Tyler Patterson, and Douglas O. Staiger. *The Consequences of Remote and Hybrid Instruction during the Pandemic.* Cambridge, MA: Center for Education Policy Research, Harvard University, May 2022. https://cepr.harvard.edu/files/cepr/files/5-4.pdf?m=1651690491.

Goodwin, Matt. "Europe's Turning Right—Here's Why." *Matt Goodwin* (blog), December 12, 2023. https://www.mattgoodwin.org/p/europes-turning-right-heres-why.

Goodwin, Matthew. "Populism Isn't about Class." *UnHerd* (podcast), February 21, 2020. https://unherd.com/2020/02/populism-isnt-about-class/.

Goodwin, Matthew. *Values, Voice and Virtue: The New British Politics.* New York: Penguin, 2023.

Goodwyn, Lawrence. *Democratic Promise: The Populist Moment in America.* New York: Oxford University Press, 1976.

Gould, Stephen Jay. *Hen's Teeth and Horse's Toes: Further Reflections in Natural History.* New York: Norton, 1983.

"Governor Cuomo Announces Updated COVID-19 Micro-cluster Focus Zones." Governor's Press Office, New York, November 18, 2020. https://www.governor.ny.gov/news/video-audio-photos-rush-transcript-governor-cuomo-announces-updated-covid-19-micro-cluster.

"Gov. Pritzker Releases Guidelines to Safely Reopen Additional Businesses and Industries as State Advances to Next Phase of Restore Illinois." June 22, 2020. https://www.illinois.gov/news/press-release.21714.html.

"Greek Prime Minister Announced Minimum Wage Increase." Independent Balkan News Agency, January 28, 2019. https://nezavisen.mk/greek-prime-minister-announced-minimum-wage-hike/.

Greenhalgh, Trisha, and Jeremy Howard. "Masks for All? The Science Says Yes." fast.ai, April 13, 2020. https://www.fast.ai/posts/2020-04-13-masks-summary.html.

Greenhalgh, Trisha, Jeremy Howick, and Neal Maskrey. "Evidence Based Medicine: A Movement in Crisis?" *British Medical Journal* 348 (June 13, 2014): art. g3725. https://doi.org/10.1136/bmj.g3725.

Greiner, Aaron, Alison Roxby, Alison Simmons, and Aaron W. Stewart. "Open Letter." Accessed October 10, 2023. https://drive.google.com/file/u/0/d/1Jyfn4Wd2i6bRi12ePghMHtX3ys1b7K1A/view?pli=1&usp=embed_facebook.

Grey, Stephen, and Andrew MacAskill. "Special Report: Johnson Listened to His Scientists about Coronavirus—but They Were Slow to Sound the Alarm." Reuters, April 7, 2020. https://www.reuters.com/article/us-health-coronavirus-britain-path-speci-idUSKBN21P1VF.

Groseclose, Tim. *Left Turn: How Liberal Media Bias Distorts the American Mind*. New York: St. Martin's Griffin, 2012.

Gross, Neil, and Solon Simmons. "The Social and Political Views of American Professors." September 27, 2007. https://www.researchgate.net/publication/228380360_The_Social_and_Political_Views_of_American_Professors.

Guess, Andrew, Jonathan Nagler, and Joshua Tucker. "Less Than You Think: Prevalence and Predictors of Fake News Dissemination on Facebook." *Science Advances* 5, no. 1 (2019): art. eaau4586. https://doi.org/10.1126/sciadv.aau4586.

Guess, Andrew M., Brendan Nyhan, and Jason Reifler. "Exposure to Untrustworthy Websites in the 2016 US Election." *Nature Human Behaviour* 4, no. 5 (May 2020): 472–480. https://doi.org/10.1038/s41562-020-0833-x.

Guess, Andrew M., Brendan Nyhan, and Jason Reifler. "Selective Exposure to Misinformation: Evidence from the Consumption of Fake News during the 2016 U.S. Presidential Campaign." Report, Dartmouth College, January 8, 2018. https://apo.org.au/node/126961.

Gurri, Martin. *The Revolt of the Public and the Crisis of Authority in the New Millenium.* 2nd ed. San Francisco: Stripe Press, 2018.

Guzman, Joseph. "Fauci Says He Doesn't Regret Advising against Masks Early on in the Coronavirus Pandemic." *The Hill* (blog), July 16, 2020. https://thehill.com /changing-america/well-being/prevention-cures/507728-fauci-has-no-regrets-about -advising-against/.

Haddon, Heather, Julie Wernau, and Lucy Hewett. "Restaurant Holdouts Defy Covid-19 Shutdown Orders." *Wall Street Journal*, November 29, 2020. https://www .wsj.com/articles/restaurant-holdouts-defy-covid-19-shutdown-orders-11606658401.

Haidt, Jonathan. "Teen Mental Health Is Plummeting, and Social Media Is a Major Contributing Cause." Testimony before the Judiciary Committee, Subcommittee on Technology, Privacy, and the Law, U.S. Senate, 117th Cong., 2nd sess., May 4, 2022.

Haidt, Jonathan. "The Yale Problem Begins in High School." *Heterodox Academy*, November 24, 2015. https://heterodoxacademy.org/blog/the-yale-problem-begins-in -high-school.

Haidt, Jonathan, and Greg Lukianoff. *The Coddling of the American Mind: How Good Intentions and Bad Ideas Are Setting Up a Generation for Failure.* New York: Penguin, 2018.

Harcourt, Bernard. "Disambiguating Populism." *Critique & Praxis* (blog), Columbia Center for Contemporary Critical Thought, May 22, 2019. https://blogs.law.colum bia.edu/praxis1313/bernard-e-harcourt-disambiguating-populism/.

Hardwicke, Tom E., and John P. A. Ioannidis. "Petitions in Scientific Argumentation: Dissecting the Request to Retire Statistical Significance." *European Journal of Clinical Investigation* 49, no. 10 (October 2019): art. e13162. https://doi.org/10.1111 /eci.13162.

Harrigan, James, and Phillip W. Magness. "Fauci, Emails, and Some Alleged Science." *American Institute for Economic Research* (blog), December 19, 2021.

Harrison, Neil L., and Jeffrey D. Sachs. "A Call for an Independent Inquiry into the Origin of the SARS-CoV-2 Virus." *Proceedings of the National Academy of Sciences* 119, no. 21 (2022): art. e2202769119. https://doi.org/10.1073/pnas.2202769119.

Harsanyi, David. "We Must Weed Out Ignorant Americans from the Electorate." *Washington Post*, May 20, 2016. https://www.washingtonpost.com/opinions/we -must-weed-out-ignorant-americans-from-the-electorate/2016/05/20/f66b3e18-1c7a -11e6-8c7b-6931e66333e7_story.html.

Hart, Benjamin. "Poorly Conceived Biden Disinformation Board Put on Pause." *Intelligencer*, May 18, 2022. https://nymag.com/intelligencer/2022/05/poorly-conceived -biden-disinformation-board-put-on-pause.html.

Hart, Justin. "The Twitter Blacklisting of Jay Bhattacharya." *Wall Street Journal*, December 9, 2022. https://www.wsj.com/articles/the-twitter-blacklisting-of-jay-bhattacharya-medical-expert-covid-lockdown-stanford-doctor-shadow-banned-censorship-11670621083.

Hartig, Hannah. "About Six-in-Ten Americans Say Abortion Should Be Legal in All or Most Cases." Pew Research Center, June 23, 2020. https://www.pewresearch.org/short-reads/2022/06/13/about-six-in-ten-americans-say-abortion-should-be-legal-in-all-or-most-cases-2/.

Haslam, Alyson, and Vinay Prasad. "Characteristics of Facebook's Third-Party Medical Fact Checkers." *Digital Health* 8 (August 17, 2022): art. 20552076221120318. https://doi.org/10.1177/20552076221120318.

Hassell, Hans J. G., John B. Hobbein, and Matthew R. Miles. "There Is No Liberal Media Bias in Which News Stories Political Journalists Choose to Cover." April 2020. https://doi.org/10.1126/sciadv.aay9344.

Hawkins, Kirk A., Ryan E. Carlin, Levente Littvay, and Cristóbal Rovira Kaltwasser, eds. *The Ideational Approach to Populism: Concept, Theory, and Analysis*. London: Routledge, 2018.

Hayes, Chris. *Twilight of the Elites: America after Meritocracy*. New York: Crown, 2013.

Henley, Jon. "Why Vote Leave's £350m Weekly EU Cost Claim Is Wrong." *The Guardian*, June 10, 2016. https://www.theguardian.com/politics/reality-check/2016/may/23/does-the-eu-really-cost-the-uk-350m-a-week.

Hersh, Eitan D. *Politics Is for Power: How to Move beyond Political Hobbyism, Take Action, and Make Real Change*. New York: Scribner, 2020.

Hilgartner, Stephen, J. Benjamin Hurlbut, and Sheila Jasanoff. "Was 'Science' on the Ballot?" *Science* 371, no. 6532 (2021): 893–894. https://doi.org/10.1126/science.abf8762.

Hinkel, Dan. "What Can Be Deduced from the Length of Jury Deliberations in the Rittenhouse Case? Not Much, Experts Say." *New York Times*, November 18, 2021. https://www.nytimes.com/2021/11/18/us/jury-deliberations-kyle-rittenhouse.html.

Hirschman, Albert O. *Exit, Voice, and Loyalty: Responses to Decline in Firms, Organizations, and States*. Cambridge, MA: Harvard University Press, 1972.

Hochman, David. "Amy Cuddy Takes a Stand." *New York Times*, September 19, 2014. https://www.nytimes.com/2014/09/21/fashion/amy-cuddy-takes-a-stand-TED-talk.html.

Hofstadter, Richard. "The Paranoid Style in American Politics." *Harper's Magazine*, November 1964. https://harpers.org/archive/1964/11/the-paranoid-style-in-american-politics/.

Hohn, Donovan. "Flint's Water Crisis and the 'Troublemaker' Scientist." *New York Times*, August 16, 2016. https://www.nytimes.com/2016/08/21/magazine/flints-water-crisis-and-the-troublemaker-scientist.html.

Holan, Angie, Tom Kertscher, and Amy Sherman. "Donald Trump's 'I Was Right about Everything,' Fact-Checked." Politifact, June 14, 2021. https://www.politifact.com/article/2021/jun/14/donald-trumps-i-was-right-about-everything-fact-ch/.

Holson, Laura M. "Malcolm Gladwell Hands Out Book Blurbs Like Santa Does Presents." *New York Times*, December 16, 2015. https://www.nytimes.com/2015/12/17/fashion/malcolm-gladwell-hands-out-book-blurbs-like-santa-does-presents.html.

Howard, Jeremy. "Masks Help Stop the Spread of Coronavirus—the Science Is Simple and I'm One of 100 Experts Urging Governors to Require Public Mask-Wearing." *The Conversation*, May 14, 2020. http://theconversation.com/masks-help-stop-the-spread-of-coronavirus-the-science-is-simple-and-im-one-of-100-experts-urging-governors-to-require-public-mask-wearing-138507.

Howard, Jonathan. *We Want Them Infected: How the Failed Quest for Herd Immunity Led Doctors to Embrace the Anti-vaccine Movement and Blinded Americans to the Threat of COVID.* Hickory, NC: Redhawk, 2023.

Howse, Robert. "Epilogue: In Defense of Disruptive Democracy—a Critique of Anti-populism." *International Journal of Constitutional Law* 17, no. 2 (2019): 641–660. https://doi.org/10.1093/icon/moz051.

Hu, Jane. "Covid's Cassandra: The Swift, Complicated Rise of Eric Feigl-Ding." *Undark Magazine*, November 25, 2020.

Hyland, Ken, and Feng (Kevin) Jiang. "'Our Striking Results Demonstrate . . .': Persuasion and the Growth of Academic Hype." *Journal of Pragmatics* 182 (September 1, 2021): 189–202. https://doi.org/10.1016/j.pragma.2021.06.018.

Igielnik, Ruth. "70% of Americans Say U.S. Economic System Unfairly Favors the Powerful." Pew Research Center, January 9, 2020. https://www.pewresearch.org/short-reads/2020/01/09/70-of-americans-say-u-s-economic-system-unfairly-favors-the-powerful/.

Illing, Sean. "The Elites Have Failed." Interview of Martin Gurri. *Future Perfect* (podcast), Vox, March 26, 2021. https://www.vox.com/future-perfect/22301496/martin-gurri-the-revolt-of-the-public-global-democracy.

Illing, Sean. "Michael Lewis on Why Americans Don't Trust Experts." *The Gray Area* (podcast), Vox, April 24, 2022. https://www.vox.com/vox-conversations-podcast/23030205/vox-conversations-michael-lewis-against-the-rules-experts.

"Illinois Restaurant Owner on Why He Is Pushing Back against New Coronavirus Restrictions." Fox News, December 1, 2020. https://www.foxnews.com/video/6213276149001.

Ioannidis, John P. A. "Citation Impact and Social Media Visibility of Great Barrington and John Snow Signatories for COVID-19 Strategy." *British Medical Journal Open* 12, no. 2 (2022): art. e052891. https://doi.org/10.1136/bmjopen-2021-052891.

Ioannidis, John P. A. "A Fiasco in the Making? As the Coronavirus Pandemic Takes Hold, We Are Making Decisions without Reliable Data." *STAT*, March 17, 2020. https://www.statnews.com/2020/03/17/a-fiasco-in-the-making-as-the-coronavirus -pandemic-takes-hold-we-are-making-decisions-without-reliable-data/.

Ioannidis, John P. A. "Why Most Published Research Findings Are False." *PLOS Medicine* 2, no. 8 (2005): art. e124. https://doi.org/10.1371/journal.pmed.0020124.

Ioannidis, John P. A., Eran Bendavid, Maia Salholz-Hillel, Kevin W. Boyack, and Jeroen Baas. "Massive Covidization of Research Citations and the Citation Elite." *Proceedings of the National Academy of Sciences* 119, no. 28 (2022): art. e2204074119. https://doi.org/10.1073/pnas.2204074119.

Ip, Greg. "Why No One Wants to Pay for the Green Transition." *Wall Street Journal*, November 30, 2023. https://www.wsj.com/business/autos/why-no-one-wants-to-pay -for-the-green-transition-aed6ba74.

Jamison, Peter. "A Top Scientist Questioned Virus Lockdowns on Fox News. The Backlash Was Fierce." *Washington Post*, December 16, 2020.

Jasanoff, Sheila. "Breaking the Waves in Science Studies: Comment on H. M. Collins and Robert Evans, 'The Third Wave of Science Studies.'" *Social Studies of Science* 33, no. 3 (2003): 389–400.

Jefferson, Tom, Liz Dooley, Eliana Ferroni, Lubna A. Al-Ansary, Mieke L. van Driel, Ghada A. Bawazeer, Mark A. Jones, et al. "Physical Interventions to Interrupt or Reduce the Spread of Respiratory Viruses." *Cochrane Database of Systematic Reviews*, no. 1 (2023). https://doi.org/10.1002/14651858.CD006207.pub6.

Jensen, Elizabeth. "Readers Rankled by 'Democracy in Chains' Review." NPR, August 14, 2017. https://www.npr.org/sections/publiceditor/2017/08/14/542634650/readers -rankled-by-democracy-in-chains-review.

Joint Commission. "Use an Advocate or Be an Advocate for Others." Accessed January 9, 2024. https://www.jointcommission.org/resources/for-consumers/take-charge /use-an-advocate-or-be-an-advocate-for-others/.

Kahan, Dan. "Fixing the Communications Failure." *Nature* 463, no. 7279 (January 2010): 296–297. https://doi.org/10.1038/463296a.

Kahan, Dan M. "The Cognitively Illiberal State." *Stanford Law Review* 60, no. 1 (2007): 115–154.

Kahan, Dan M. "Misconceptions, Misinformation, and the Logic of Identity-Protective Cognition." May 24, 2017. Cultural Cognition Project Working Paper

Series no. 164, Yale Law School, Public Law Research Paper no. 605, Yale Law & Economics Research Paper no. 575. https://doi.org/10.2139/ssrn.2973067.

Kahan, Dan M., Ellen Peters, Erica Cantrell Dawson, and Paul Slovic. "Motivated Numeracy and Enlightened Self-Government." *Behavioural Public Policy* 1, no. 1 (May 2017): 54–86. https://doi.org/10.1017/bpp.2016.2.

Kahneman, Daniel. *Thinking, Fast and Slow.* New York: Farrar, Straus and Giroux, 2011.

Kakutani, Michiko. "The Death of Truth: How We Gave Up on Facts and Ended Up with Trump." *The Guardian*, July 14, 2018. https://www.theguardian.com/books/2018/jul/14/the-death-of-truth-how-we-gave-up-on-facts-and-ended-up-with-trump.

Kamenetz, Anya. "Nation's Pediatricians Walk Back Support for In-Person School." Coronavirus Updates, NPR, July 10, 2020. https://www.npr.org/sections/coronavirus-live-updates/2020/07/10/889848834/nations-pediatricians-walk-back-support-for-in-person-school.

Kant, Immanuel. *Critique of Judgment.* Translated by Werner S. Pluhar. Indianapolis, IN: Hackett, 1987.

Kaplan, Karen. "Face Mask Trial Didn't Stop Coronavirus Spread, but It Shows Why More Mask-Wearing Is Needed." *Los Angeles Times*, November 20, 2020. https://www.latimes.com/science/story/2020-11-20/face-masks-didnt-stop-coronavirus-spread-in-danish-clinical-trial.

Karem, Brian. "Dumbass Nation." *Salon*, October 28, 2021. https://www.salon.com/2021/10/28/dumbass-nation-our-biggest-national-security-problem-is-americas-vast-and-militant-ignorance/.

Kekatos, Mary. "Masks Are Effective but Here's How a Study from a Respected Group Was Misinterpreted to Say They Weren't." ABC News, March 14, 2023. https://abcnews.go.com/Health/masks-effective-study-respected-group-misinterpreted/story?id=97846561.

Kelman, Mark. "Hard Choices and Deficient Choosers." *Northwestern Journal of Law & Social Policy* 14, no. 2 (2019): 190–264. https://scholarlycommons.law.northwestern.edu/cgi/viewcontent.cgi?article=1183&context=njlsp.

Kelman, Mark. "Saving Lives, Saving from Death, Saving from Dying." Sibley Lecture Series, March 25, 2009. https://digitalcommons.law.uga.edu/lectures_pre_arch_lectures_sibley/34.

Kertzer, Joshua D. "Re-assessing Elite–Public Gaps in Political Behavior." *American Journal of Political Science* 66, no. 3 (2022): 539–553. https://doi.org/10.1111/ajps.12583.

Kertzer, Joshua D., and Jonathan Renshon. "Experiments and Surveys on Political Elites." *Annual Review of Political Science* 25, no. 1 (2022): 529–550. https://doi.org /10.1146/annurev-polisci-051120-013649.

Kestenbaum, David, and Baldur Hedinsson. "A New Mom, Bjork's Dad and the President of Iceland." *Planet Money*, NPR, April 15, 2011. https://www.npr.org/sections /money/2011/05/23/135449405/the-friday-podcast-a-new-mom-bjorks-dad-and-the -president-of-iceland.

Kirkpatrick, Emily. "Where Has Seal Been? Watching Your Instagram Stories (and 'Plandemic')." *New York Times*, June 8, 2020. https://www.nytimes.com/2020/06/08 /style/seal-instagram-stories-plandemic-coronavirus.html.

Kirshenbaum, Sheril. "No, Climate Change Will Not End the World in 12 Years." *Scientific American* Blog Network, August 13, 2019. https://blogs.scientificamerican .com/observations/no-climate-change-will-not-end-the-world-in-12-years/.

Kisielinski, Kai, Susanne Wagner, Oliver Hirsch, Bernd Klosterhalfen, and Andreas Prescher. "Possible Toxicity of Chronic Carbon Dioxide Exposure Associated with Face Mask Use, Particularly in Pregnant Women, Children and Adolescents—a Scoping Review." *Heliyon* 9, no. 4 (April 2023): art. e14117. https://doi.org/10.1016/j .heliyon.2023.e14117.

Kotkin, Joel. *The Coming of Neo-feudalism: A Warning to the Global Middle Class.* New York: Encounter, 2020.

Krakauer, Steve. "Rabbit Hole: Coastal Elites Despise 'Yellowstone' Because the Good Guys Are Bad and Bad Guys Are Good." *Fourth Watch* (blog), March 15, 2023. https://fourthwatch.substack.com/p/coastal-elites-despise-yellowstone.

Kramer, Larry D. *The People Themselves: Popular Constitutionalism and Judicial Review.* Oxford: Oxford University Press, 2005.

Kristof, Nicholas. "When Trump Was Right and Many Democrats Wrong." *New York Times*, November 18, 2020.

Krupenkin, Masha. "Does Partisanship Affect Compliance with Government Recommendations?" *Political Behavior* 43, no. 1 (2021): 451–472. https://doi.org/10.1007 /s11109-020-09613-6.

Kulldorf, Martin, Sunetra Gupta, and Jay Bhattacharya. "Great Barrington Declaration." October 4, 2020. https://gbdeclaration.org/.

Kundnani, Hans. "Europe May Be Headed for Something Unthinkable." *New York Times*, December 13, 2023. https://www.nytimes.com/2023/12/13/opinion/european -union-far-right.html.

Kuper, Simon. "The Revenge of the Middle-Class Anti-elitist." *Financial Times*, February 13, 2020. https://www.ft.com/content/b57e6126-4d2e-11ea-95a0-43d18ec715f5.

Lantry, Lauren. "As Dr. Fauci Prepares to Exit, He Reflects on His Legacy and Covid Decisions He Would Change." ABC News, October 16, 2022. https://abcnews.go.com /Politics/dr-fauci-prepares-exit-reflects-legacy-covid-decisions/story?id=91553536.

Lareau, Annette. *Unequal Childhoods: Class, Race, and Family Life, with an Update a Decade Later.* 2nd ed. Berkeley: University of California Press, 2011.

Lasch, Christopher. *The True and Only Heaven: Progress and Its Critics.* New York: Norton, 1991.

The Late Show with Stephen Colbert. "Jon Stewart on Vaccine Science and the Wuhan Lab Theory." YouTube, June 15, 2021. https://www.youtube.com/watch?v =sSfejgwbDQ8.

Lazarus, Jeffrey V., Diana Romero, Christopher J. Kopka, Salim Abdool Karim, Laith J. Abu-Raddad, Gisele Almeida, Ricardo Baptista-Leite, et al. "A Multinational Delphi Consensus to End the COVID-19 Public Health Threat." *Nature* 611, no. 7935 (November 2022): 332–345. https://doi.org/10.1038/s41586-022-05398-2.

Lears, Jackson. "Orthodoxy of the Elites." *New York Review of Books*, January 14, 2021.

Lee, Crystal, Tanya Yang, Gabrielle Inchoco, Graham M. Jones, and Arvind Satyanarayan. "Viral Visualizations: How Coronavirus Skeptics Use Orthodox Data Practices to Promote Unorthodox Science Online." Paper presented at CHI '21, May 8–13, 2021, Yokohama, Japan, 1–18. https://doi.org/10.1145/3411764.3445211.

Lee, Stephanie M. "JetBlue's Founder Helped Fund a Stanford Study That Said the Coronavirus Wasn't That Deadly." *BuzzFeed News*, May 15, 2020. https://www .buzzfeednews.com/article/stephaniemlee/stanford-coronavirus-neeleman-ioannidis -whistleblower.

Leiter, Brian. "Philosopher Kathleen Stock Resigns Her Position at the University of Sussex." *Leiter Reports: A Philosophy Blog*, September 28, 2021. https://leiterreports .typepad.com/blog/2021/10/philosopher-kathlelen-stock-resigns-her-position-at-the -university-of-sussex.html.

Lemieux, Pierre. "The Impossibility of Populism." *Independent Review* 26, no. 1 (2021): 15–25.

Lenzer, Jeanne. "John Ioannidis and Medical Tribalism in the Era of Covid-19." *Undark Magazine*, June 11, 2020. https://undark.org/2020/06/11/john-ioannidis -politicization/.

Leonhardt, David. "The Long Shadow of Covid School Closures." *New York Times*, April 28, 2023. https://www.nytimes.com/2023/04/28/briefing/pandemic-school -closures-randi-weingarten.html.

Leonhardt, David. "Two Covid Americas." *New York Times*, January 25, 2022. https://www.nytimes.com/2022/01/25/briefing/covid-behavior-vaccinated-unvaccinated.html.

"A Letter on Justice and Open Debate." *Harper's Magazine*, July 7, 2020. https://harpers.org/a-letter-on-justice-and-open-debate/.

Levitz, Eric. "How the Diploma Divide Is Remaking American Politics." *New York Magazine*, October 19, 2022. https://nymag.com/intelligencer/2022/10/education-polarization-diploma-divide-democratic-party-working-class.html.

Lewis, Michael. *The Big Short: Inside the Doomsday Machine*. London: Norton, 2010.

Lewis, Michael. *The Fifth Risk*. New York: Norton, 2018.

Li, David K., and Bianca Britton. "L.A. Mayor Eric Garcetti Defends Maskless Pictures: 'I Hold My Breath.'" NBC News, February 3, 2022. https://www.nbcnews.com/news/us-news/l-mayor-eric-garcetti-defends-maskless-pictures-hold-breath-rcna14729.

Lind, Michael. *The New Class War: Saving Democracy from the Managerial Elite*. New York: Portfolio, 2020.

Locke, Susannah. "Scientists Scammed at Least 110 Academic Papers into Publication Using Fake Peer Reviews." Vox, December 7, 2014. https://www.vox.com/2014/12/7/7344963/scientists-scammed-at-least-110-academic-papers-into-publication.

Lorenz, Taylor. "How the Biden Administration Let Right-Wing Attacks Derail Its Disinformation Efforts." *Washington Post*, May 18, 2022. https://www.washingtonpost.com/technology/2022/05/18/disinformation-board-dhs-nina-jankowicz/.

Lourenço, José, Francesco Pinotti, Craig Thompson, and Sunetra Gupta. "The Impact of Host Resistance on Cumulative Mortality and the Threshold of Herd Immunity for SARS-CoV-2." *medRxiv*, July 16, 2020. https://doi.org/10.1101/2020.07.15.20154294.

Lukianoff, Greg. "The Academic Mind in 2022: What Faculty Think about Free Expression and Academic Freedom on Campus." Foundation for Individual Rights and Expression, 2022, accessed November 16, 2023. https://www.thefire.org/research-learn/academic-mind-2022-what-faculty-think-about-free-expression-and-academic-freedom.

Lupton, Danielle L., and Clayton Webb. "Wither Elites? The Role of Elite Credibility and Knowledge in Public Perceptions of Foreign Policy." *International Studies Quarterly* 66, no. 3 (2022): art. sqac057. https://doi.org/10.1093/isq/sqac057.

Lynch, Lily. "How the AfD Won Over Germany." *UnHerd* (podcast), July 26, 2023. https://unherd.com/2023/07/how-the-afd-won-over-germany/.

MacLean, Nancy. *Democracy in Chains: The Deep History of the Radical Right's Stealth Plan for America*. New York: Penguin, 2018.

Mak, Aaron. "The Librarian Who Created the Inescapable 'Love Is Love' Yard Sign Is Hoping for a Post-Trump Comeback." *Slate*, May 12, 2021. https://slate.com/news -and-politics/2021/05/yard-sign-love-is-love-post-trump-sales.html.

Makary, Marty. "The High Cost of Disparaging Natural Immunity to Covid." *Wall Street Journal*, January 26, 2022. https://www.wsj.com/articles/the-high-cost-of-dis paraging-natural-immunity-to-covid-vaccine-mandates-protests-fire-rehire-employ ment-11643214336.

Mandavilli, Apoorva. "C.D.C. Says Cloth Masks Are Not as Effective as Others." *New York Times*, January 14, 2022. https://www.nytimes.com/live/2022/01/14/world /omicron-covid-vaccine-tests.

Mandavilli, Apoorva. "The Price for Not Wearing Masks: Perhaps 130,000 Lives." *New York Times*, October 23, 2020. https://www.nytimes.com/2020/10/23/health /covid-deaths.html.

Mansky, Jackie. "The Age-Old Problem of 'Fake News.'" *Smithsonian Magazine*, May 7, 2018. https://www.smithsonianmag.com/history/age-old-problem-fake-news-180 968945/.

Marcus, Julia. "The Dudes Who Won't Wear Masks." *The Atlantic*, June 23, 2020. https://www.theatlantic.com/ideas/archive/2020/06/dudes-who-wont-wear-masks /613375/.

Marcus, Julia, and Gregg Gonsalves. "Public-Health Experts Are Not Hypocrites." *The Atlantic*, June 11, 2020. https://www.theatlantic.com/ideas/archive/2020/06 /public-health-experts-are-not-hypocrites/612853/.

Marent, Benjamin, Rudolf Forster, and Peter Nowak. "Conceptualizing Lay Participation in Professional Health Care Organizations." *Administration & Society* 47, no. 7 (2015): 827–850. https://doi.org/10.1177/0095399713489829.

Marijolovic, Kate. "Professors Are Sharply Divided on DEI Statements in Hiring, Survey Finds." *Chronicle of Higher Education*, February 28, 2023. https://www.chroni cle.com/article/professors-are-sharply-divided-on-dei-statements-in-hiring-survey -finds.

Markovits, Daniel. *The Meritocracy Trap: How America's Foundational Myth Feeds Inequality, Dismantles the Middle Class, and Devours the Elite*. New York: Penguin, 2019.

Marshall, Hannah, and Alena Drieschova. "Post-truth Politics in the UK's Brexit Referendum." *New Perspectives* 26, no. 3 (2018): 89–106.

Martinez, Jenny S. "Stanford Law School Letter from Dean." March 23, 2023. https://law.stanford.edu/wp-content/uploads/2023/03/Next-Steps-on-Protests-and-Free-Speech.pdf.

Masciotra, David. "'Real Americans' vs. 'Coastal Elites': What Right-Wing Sneers at City Dwellers Really Mean." *Salon*, November 20, 2016. https://www.salon.com/2016/11/20/real-americans-vs-coastal-elites-what-right-wing-sneers-at-city-dwellers-really-mean/.

Masterson, Matt. "Restaurant Owners Push Back on Pritzker's Indoor Dining Restrictions." WTTW News, October 30, 2020. https://news.wttw.com/2020/10/30/restaurant-owners-push-back-pritzker-s-indoor-dining-restrictions.

Mayer, Jane. *Dark Money: The Hidden History of the Billionaires behind the Rise of the Radical Right.* New York: Doubleday, 2016.

McCaffree, Kevin, and Anondah Saide. "How Informed Are Americans about Race and Policing?" Skeptic Research Center, February 20, 2021. https://www.skeptic.com/research-center/reports/Research-Report-CUPES-007.pdf.

McCullough, Marie. "Drexel Researchers Estimate Philadelphia's Coronavirus Lockdown Saved 6,200 Lives." *Philadelphia Inquirer*, May 12, 2020. https://www.inquirer.com/news/drexel-model-estimates-philadelphias-coronavirus-lockdown-saved-6200-lives-20200512.html.

McGahan, Jason. "Exclusive: Cecily Myart-Cruz's Hostile Takeover of L.A.'s Public Schools."*Los Angeles Magazine*, August 26, 2021. https://lamag.com/featured/cecily-myart-cruz-teachers-union.

McLean, Bethany. "Big Business's Relentless Push to Equate the Free Market with Freedom (Review of 'The Big Myth' by Oreskes and Conway)." *Washington Post*, March 10, 2023. https://www.washingtonpost.com/books/2023/03/10/big-myth-business-oreskes-conway/.

McNeil, Donald G. "How Much Herd Immunity Is Enough?" *New York Times*, December 24, 2020. https://www.nytimes.com/2020/12/24/health/herd-immunity-covid-coronavirus.html.

Menand, Louis. "The Rise and Fall of Neoliberalism." *New Yorker*, July 17, 2023. https://www.newyorker.com/magazine/2023/07/24/the-rise-and-fall-of-neoliberalism.

Mendez, David, Rachel Tilman, and Kevin Frey. "Biden Slams Trump, Warns 'Equality and Democracy Are under Assault.'" NY 1, August 31, 2022. https://ny1.com/nyc/all-boroughs/news/2022/08/31/joe-biden-philadelphia-speech-democracy-soul-of-the-nation.

Metz, Cade. "The ChatGPT King Isn't Worried, but He Knows You Might Be." *New York Times*, March 31, 2023. https://www.nytimes.com/2023/03/31/technology/sam-altman-open-ai-chatgpt.html.

Micale, Mark S., and Philip Dwyer. "History, Violence, and Stephen Pinker." *Historical Reflections/Réflexions Historiques* 44, no. 1 (2018): 1–5. https://doi.org/10.3167/hrrh.2018.440102.

Mikhailova, Anna, Christopher Hope, Michael Gillard, and Louisa Wells. "Exclusive: Government Scientist Neil Ferguson Resigns after Breaking Lockdown Rules to Meet His Married Lover." *Telegraph*, May 5, 2020. https://www.telegraph.co.uk/news/2020/05/05/exclusive-government-scientist-neil-ferguson-resigns-breaking/.

Milanovic, Branko. *Visions of Inequality: From the French Revolution to the End of the Cold War*. Cambridge, MA: Belknap Press, 2023.

Mills, C. Wright. *The Power Elite*. 1956. Reprint, New York: Oxford University Press, 2000.

Misgeld, Dieter. "Common Sense and Common Convictions: Sociology as a Science, Phenomenological Sociology and the Hermeneutical Point of View." *Human Studies* 6, no. 1 (1983): 109–139. https://doi.org/10.1007/BF02127757.

Misra, Rishabh. "News Category Dataset." arXiv, last updated October 6, 2022. https://arxiv.org/abs/2209.11429.

Mitchell, Travis. "European Public Opinion Three Decades after the Fall of Communism." Pew Research Center's Global Attitudes Project, October 14, 2019. https://www.pewresearch.org/global/2019/10/14/the-european-union/.

Morozov, Evgeny. *To Save Everything, Click Here: The Folly of Technological Solutionism*. New York: PublicAffairs, 2014.

Mouffe, Chantal. *For a Left Populism*. Paperback ed. London: Verso, 2019.

Mounk, Yascha. "The Undemocratic Dilemma." *Journal of Democracy* 29, no. 2 (April 2018): 98–112.

Mudde, Cas. "The Populist Zeitgeist." *Government and Opposition* 39, no. 4 (2004): 541–563. https://doi.org/10.1111/j.1477-7053.2004.00135.x.

Müller, Jan-Werner. "Populism and the People." *London Review of Books,* May 23, 2019. https://www.lrb.co.uk/the-paper/v41/n10/jan-werner-mueller/populism-and-the-people.

Müller, Jan-Werner. *What Is Populism?* Philadelphia: University of Pennsylvania Press, 2016.

Mulligan, Kevin, and Fabrice Correia. "Facts." In *Stanford Encyclopedia of Philosophy Archive*, edited by Edward N. Zalta, Winter 2021 ed. https://plato.stanford.edu/archives/win2021/entries/facts/.

Murray, Noel. "Is *Yellowstone* a Red-State Show? It's Complicated." *Time*, November 10, 2022. https://time.com/6229017/yellowstone-red-state-fandom/.

Nagel, Thomas. "What Is It Like to Be a Bat?" *Philosophical Review* 83, no. 4 (1974): 435–450. https://doi.org/10.2307/2183914.

National Academies of Sciences. *Science and Creationism: A View from the National Academy of Sciences.* 2nd ed. Washington, DC: National Academies Press, 1999.

National Deaf Children's Society. "Face Masks and Communication—Coronavirus Info for Families of Deaf Children." March 24, 2022. https://www.ndcs.org.uk/blog /face-masks-and-communication-coronavirus-info-for-families-of-deaf-children/.

National Institutes of Health. "NIH to End Funding for Moderate Alcohol and Cardiovascular Health Trial." June 15, 2018. https://www.nih.gov/news-events/news -releases/nih-end-funding-moderate-alcohol-cardiovascular-health-trial.

Nayak, Anika. "The Essential Items Doctors Never Travel Without." *HuffPost*, January 27, 2022. https://www.huffpost.com/entry/items-doctors-never-travel-without_l _61f1817ce4b067cbfa176a0b.

NBC Chicago. "Pritzker Defends Stance on New Indoor Dining Policy in Many Illinois Regions." October 29, 2020. https://www.nbcchicago.com/news/local/pritzker -defends-stance-on-new-indoor-dining-policy-in-many-illinois-regions/2361271/.

Nichols, Tom. *The Death of Expertise: The Campaign against Established Knowledge and Why It Matters.* New York: Oxford University Press, 2017.

Nichols, Tom. "How to Confront the Growing Threat to American Democracy." Interview of Geoff Kabaservice. *The Vital Center* (podcast), with Tom Nichols, Niskanen Center, September 29, 2021. https://www.niskanencenter.org/how-to-confront -the-growing-threat-to-american-democracy-with-tom-nichols/.

Nichols, Tom. *Our Own Worst Enemy: The Assault from within on Modern Democracy.* Oxford: Oxford University Press, 2021.

Nocera, Joe, and Bethany McLean. *The Big Fail: How Our Supply Chains Collapsed When We Needed Them Most.* New York: Penguin Business, 2023.

Noor, Poppy. "The Beach-Going Grim Reaper on His Florida Protest: 'Someone Has to Stand Up.'" *The Guardian*, May 7, 2020. https://www.theguardian.com/us-news /2020/may/07/florida-grim-reaper-beach-interview.

Nyhan, Brendan. "Facts and Myths about Misperceptions." *Journal of Economic Perspectives* 34, no. 3 (August 2020): 220–236. https://doi.org/10.1257/jep.34.3 .220.

Nyhan, Brendan, Ethan Porter, Jason Reifler, and Thomas J. Wood. "Taking Fact-Checks Literally but Not Seriously? The Effects of Journalistic Fact-Checking on Factual Beliefs and Candidate Favorability." *Political Behavior* 42 (September 2020): 939–960. https://doi.org/10.1007/s11109-019-09528-x.

Obama, Barack. "Remarks by the President." White House Press Office, May 15, 2016. https://obamawhitehouse.archives.gov/the-press-office/2016/05/15/remarks-president -commencement-address-rutgers-state-university-new.

Oberheim, Eric, and Paul Hoyningen-Huene. "The Incommensurability of Scientific Theories." In *Stanford Encyclopedia of Philosophy Archive*, edited by Edward N. Zalta, Fall 2018 ed. https://plato.stanford.edu/archives/fall2018/entries/incommensurability/.

Office of the Director of National Intelligence. "Potential Links between the Wuhan Institute of Virology and the Origin of the COVID-19 Pandemic." June 2023. https://www.dni.gov/files/ODNI/documents/assessments/Report-on-Potential-Links -Between-the-Wuhan-Institute-of-Virology-and-the-Origins-of-COVID-19-20230 623.pdf.

Oliver, J. Eric, and Thomas J. Wood. "Conspiracy Theories and the Paranoid Style(s) of Mass Opinion." *American Journal of Political Science* 58, no. 4 (2014): 952–966.

Oliver, J. Eric, and Thomas J. Wood. *Enchanted America: How Intuition and Reason Divide Our Politics*. Chicago: University of Chicago Press, 2018.

O'Neil, Shannon K. *The Globalization Myth: Why Regions Matter*. New Haven, CT: Yale University Press, 2022.

Oreskes, Naomi. "The Scientific Consensus on Climate Change." *Science* 306, no. 5702 (2004): 1686.

Oreskes, Naomi. *Why Trust Science?* Paperback ed. Princeton, NJ: Princeton University Press, 2021.

Oreskes, Naomi, and Erik M. Conway. *The Big Myth: How American Business Taught Us to Loathe Government and Love the Free Market*. New York: Bloomsbury, 2023.

Oreskes, Naomi, and Erik M. Conway. *Merchants of Doubt: How a Handful of Scientists Obscured the Truth on Issues from Tobacco Smoke to Global Warming*. New York: Bloomsbury, 2010.

Oreskes, Naomi, and Charlie Tyson. "Is Academe Awash in Liberal Bias?" *Chronicle of Higher Education*, September 14, 2020. https://www.chronicle.com/article/is-academe -awash-in-liberal-bias.

Osnos, Evan. "Survival of the Richest." *New Yorker*, January 22, 2017. https://www .newyorker.com/magazine/2017/01/30/doomsday-prep-for-the-super-rich.

Oster, Emily. "Your Unvaccinated Kid Is Like a Vaccinated Grandma." *The Atlantic*, March 18, 2021. https://www.theatlantic.com/ideas/archive/2021/03/go-ahead -plan-family-vacation-your-unvaccinated-kids/618313/.

Osterholm, Michael T. "My Views on Cloth Face Coverings for the Public for Preventing COVID-19." Center for Infectious Disease Research and Policy, July 22,

2020. https://www.cidrap.umn.edu/covid-19/commentary-my-views-cloth-face-cover ings-public-preventing-covid-19.

Ostrom, Elinor. *Governing the Commons: The Evolution of Institutions for Collective Action.* Cambridge: Cambridge University Press, 1990.

"Outdoor Mask Mandate Issued for Most Public Outdoor Settings." *Oregon Health News Blog,* August 24, 2021. https://covidblog.oregon.gov/outdoor-mask-mandate -issued-for-most-public-outdoor-settings/.

Packer, George. "How America Fractured into Four Parts." *The Atlantic,* August 2021.

Palus, Shannon. "Do We Really Still Need to Wear Masks Outside?" *Slate,* April 17, 2021. https://slate.com/technology/2021/04/masks-outside-covid-risk-low.html.

Pamuk, Zeynep. *Politics and Expertise: How to Use Science in a Democratic Society.* Princeton, NJ: Princeton University Press, 2021.

Pandey, Erica. "Private Schools Pull Students Away from Public Schools." *Axios,* January 2, 2021. https://www.axios.com/2021/01/02/private-schools-coronavirus-public -schools.

Parker, Kim. "The Growing Partisan Divide in Views of Higher Education." Pew Research Center's Social & Demographic Trends Project, August 19, 2019. https:// www.pewresearch.org/social-trends/2019/08/19/the-growing-partisan-divide-in -views-of-higher-education-2/.

Parmet, Wendy E., and Jeremy Paul. "COVID-19: The First Posttruth Pandemic." *American Journal of Public Health* 110, no. 7 (July 2020): 945–946. https://doi.org /10.2105/AJPH.2020.305721.

Patel, Chirag J., Belinda Burford, and John P. A. Ioannidis. "Assessment of Vibration of Effects due to Model Specification Can Demonstrate the Instability of Observational Associations." *Journal of Clinical Epidemiology* 68, no. 9 (September 2015): 1046–1058. https://doi.org/10.1016/j.jclinepi.2015.05.029.

Patel, Vimal. "UPenn Accuses a Law Professor of Racist Statements. Should She Be Fired?" *New York Times,* March 13, 2023. https://www.nytimes.com/2023/03/13/us /upenn-law-professor-racism-freedom-speech.html.

Patrinos, Harry Anthony. "The Longer Students Were Out of School, the Less They Learned." World Bank Group, Europe and Central Asia Region, Office of the Chief Economist, Policy Research Working Paper 10420, April 2023. https://documents1 .worldbank.org/curated/en/099534004242341552/pdf/IDU0807776730889d04a240 ad3305c282c112fe8.pdf.

Patterson, Matthew. "Gilets Jaunes, Extinction Rebellion and Neoliberal Climate Policy." Policy @ Manchester Articles: Digital Futures, December 20, 2018. https://

blog.policy.manchester.ac.uk/europe-stream/2018/12/gilets-jaunes-extinction-rebellion
-and-neoliberal-climate-policy/.

Pazzanese, Christina. "Study Finds Political Bias Skews Perceptions of Verifiable
Fact." *Harvard Gazette*, June 3, 2020. https://news.harvard.edu/gazette/story/2020/06
/study-finds-political-bias-skews-perceptions-of-verifiable-fact/.

Pelling, Rowan, and Peter Phelps. "François Balloux." *Perspective Magazine*, February
4, 2022. https://perspectivemag.co.uk/the-interview-francois-balloux/.

"People Are Entitled to Their Own Opinions but Not to Their Own Facts."
Quote Investigator, March 17, 2020. https://quoteinvestigator.com/2020/03/17/own
-facts/.

Pew Charitable Trusts. "How the American Middle Class Has Changed in the Past
Five Decades." September 20, 2022. https://pew.org/3q3k1Z2.

Pew Research Center. "Rebuilding U.S. Fisheries: Success Stories." March 16, 2012.
http://pew.org/2yHxhqz.

Pew Research Center. "Trust and Distrust in America." July 2019. https://www
.pewresearch.org/politics/2019/07/22/americans-struggles-with-truth-accuracy-and
-accountability/.

Piketty, Thomas. *Capital in the Twenty-First Century*. Cambridge, MA: Belknap Press,
2014.

Pinker, Steven. *The Better Angels of Our Nature: Why Violence Has Declined*. New York:
Viking Penguin, 2011.

Piper, Kelsey. "Science Has Been in a 'Replication Crisis' for a Decade. Have We
Learned Anything?" Vox, October 14, 2020. https://www.vox.com/future-perfect
/21504366/science-replication-crisis-peer-review-statistics.

Plunkett, James. "The Squeezed Middle: The Pressure on Ordinary Workers in America and Britain." *Journal of Social Policy* 43, no. 1 (January 2014): 218–220. https://
doi.org/10.1017/S004727941300072X.

Porter, Ethan, and Thomas J. Wood. *False Alarm: The Truth about Political Mistruths in
the Trump Era*. Cambridge: Cambridge University Press, 2019.

Postel, Charles. *The Populist Vision*. Oxford: Oxford University Press, 2007.

Powell, Michael. "M.I.T.'s Choice of Lecturer Ignited Criticism. So Did Its Decision to
Cancel." *New York Times*, October 20, 2021. https://www.nytimes.com/2021/10/20
/us/dorian-abbot-mit.html.

Prasad, Vinay, and Adam Cifu. *Ending Medical Reversal: Improving Outcomes, Saving
Lives*. Baltimore: Johns Hopkins University Press, 2015.

Prasad, Vinay, and Adam Cifu. "Medical Reversal: Why We Must Raise the Bar Before Adopting New Technologies." *Yale Journal of Biology and Medicine* 84, no. 4 (December 2011): 471–478.

Prasad, Vinay, Adam Cifu, and John P. A. Ioannidis. "Reversals of Established Medical Practices: Evidence to Abandon Ship." *JAMA* 307, no. 1 (2012): 37–38. https://doi.org/10.1001/jama.2011.1960.

Prasad, Vinay, and Jeffrey Flier. "Scientists Who Express Different Views on Covid-19 Should Be Heard, Not Demonized." *STAT* (blog), April 27, 2020. Reprinted in *3 Quarks Daily*, April 29, 2020. https://3quarksdaily.com/3quarksdaily/2020/04/scientists-who-express-different-views-on-covid-19-should-be-heard-not-demonized.html.

Pritchard, Duncan. *Scepticism: A Very Short Introduction.* Oxford: Oxford University Press, 2019.

"Pritzker Closes Indoor Dining throughout Illinois Starting Nov. 4." Illinois Policy, November 2, 2020. https://www.illinoispolicy.org/pritzker-closes-indoor-dining-throughout-illinois-starting-nov-4/.

Pugh, Jonathan, Julian Savulescu, Rebecca C. H. Brown, and Dominic Wilkinson. "The Unnaturalistic Fallacy: COVID-19 Vaccine Mandates Should Not Discriminate against Natural Immunity." *Journal of Medical Ethics* 48, no. 6 (2022): 371–377. https://doi.org/10.1136/medethics-2021-107956.

Quammen, David. "The Ongoing Mystery of Covid's Origin." *New York Times*, July 25, 2023. https://www.nytimes.com/2023/07/25/magazine/covid-start.html.

"Randi Weingarten's Incredible Covid Memory Loss." *Wall Street Journal*, April 30, 2023. https://www.wsj.com/articles/randi-weingartens-incredible-covid-memory-loss-teachers-union-pandemic-education-reopen-1015ce21.

Rauch, Jonathan. *The Constitution of Knowledge: A Defense of Truth.* Washington, DC: Brookings Institution Press, 2021.

Rauhala, Emily, and Loveday Morris. "In the United States, QAnon Is Struggling. The Conspiracy Theory Is Thriving Abroad." *Washington Post*, November 13, 2020. https://www.washingtonpost.com/world/qanon-conspiracy-global-reach/2020/11/12/ca312138-13a5-11eb-a258-614acf2b906d_story.html.

Real Time with Bill Maher. "Overtime: Andrew Cuomo, Scott Galloway, Melissa DeRosa." YouTube, October 27, 2023. https://www.youtube.com/watch?v=QQApZhXLcic.

Regalado, Antonio. "One Doctor's Campaign to Stop a Covid-19 Vaccine Being Rushed Through before Election Day." *MIT Technology Review*, October 19, 2020. https://www.technologyreview.com/2020/10/19/1010646/campaign-stop-covid-19-vaccine-trump-election-day/.

Reich, Greta. "Judge Duncan's Stanford Visit and the Aftermath, Explained." *Stanford Daily*, April 5, 2023. https://stanforddaily.com/2023/04/05/judge-duncan-stanford-law-school-explained/.

Reiner, Robert C., Ryan M. Barber, James K. Collins, Peng Zheng, Christopher Adolph, James Albright, Catherine M. Antony, et al. "Modeling COVID-19 Scenarios for the United States." *Nature Medicine* 27, no. 1 (January 2021): 94–105. https://doi.org/10.1038/s41591-020-1132-9.

Richards, Lindsay, Mariña Fernández-Reino, and Scott Blinder. "UK Public Opinion toward Immigration: Overall Attitudes and Level of Concern." Migration Observatory, January 20, 2020. https://migrationobservatory.ox.ac.uk/resources/briefings/uk-public-opinion-toward-immigration-overall-attitudes-and-level-of-concern/.

Robinson, Eugene. "'Real' Americans Are a Myth. Don't You Dare Buy It." *Washington Post*, May 15, 2018. https://www.washingtonpost.com/opinions/real-americans-are-a-myth-dont-you-dare-buy-it/2018/05/14/b4c3099e-57a3-11e8-8836-a4a123c359ab_story.html.

Rodgers, Daniel T. *Age of Fracture*. Cambridge, MA: Belknap Press, 2012.

Rodgers, Daniel T. *Contested Truths: Keywords in American Politics since Independence*. Cambridge, MA: Harvard University Press, 1998.

Rorty, Richard. "Texts and Lumps." *New Literary History* 17, no. 1 (1985): 1–16. https://doi.org/10.2307/468973.

Rosenblatt, Adam, and Robert Green. *Supreme Court Survey*. New York: C-Span PSB, 2018.

Rothwell, Jonathan, and Sonal Desai. "How Misinformation Is Distorting COVID Policies and Behaviors." Brookings Institution, December 22, 2020. https://www.brookings.edu/articles/how-misinformation-is-distorting-covid-policies-and-behaviors/.

Roubini, Nouriel. *MegaThreats: Ten Dangerous Trends That Imperil Our Future, and How to Survive Them*. New York: Little, Brown, 2022.

Rouhanifard, Paymon. "Blue States Are Failing Their Students by Not Reopening Schools." *Time*, April 12, 2021. https://time.com/5954077/reopen-schools-blue-states/.

Rubin, Jennifer. "Andrew Cuomo Gets It Right: Govern by Science, Not Your Gut." *Washington Post*, May 5, 2020. https://www.washingtonpost.com/opinions/2020/05/05/reject-governing-by-gut-instinct/.

Rummler, Orion. "CDC Director Suggests Face Masks Offer More COVID-19 Protection Than Vaccine Would." Axios, September 16, 2020. https://www.axios.com/2020/09/16/coronavirus-vaccine-redfield-cdc-masks.

Russonello, Giovanni. "QAnon Now as Popular in U.S. as Some Major Religions." *New York Times*, May 27, 2021, https://www.nytimes.com/2021/05/27/us/politics /qanon-republicans-trump.html.

Rutjens, Bastiaan T., Sander van der Linden, and Romy van der Lee. "Science Skepticism in Times of COVID-19." *Group Processes & Intergroup Relations* 24, no. 2 (2021): 276–283. https://doi.org/10.1177/1368430220981415.

Sacerdote, Bruce, Ranjan Sehgal, and Molly Cook. "Why Is All COVID-19 News Bad News?" National Bureau of Economic Research, Working Paper 28110, November 2020. https://doi.org/10.3386/w28110.

Sadurski, Wojciech. *A Pandemic of Populists*. Cambridge: Cambridge University Press, 2022.

Saller, Richard, and Jenny Martinez. "An Update for the Stanford Community." *Stanford Report*, October 11, 2023. https://news.stanford.edu/report/2023/10/11 /update-stanford-community/.

Sandel, Michael J. *The Tyranny of Merit: What's Become of the Common Good?* New York: Farrar, Straus and Giroux, 2020.

Saturday Night Live. "Dr. Anthony Fauci Cold Open." YouTube, April 25, 2020. https://www.youtube.com/watch?v=uW56CL0pk0g.

Saurette, Paul, and Shane Gunster. "Ears Wide Shut: Epistemological Populism, Argutainment and Canadian Conservative Talk Radio." *Canadian Journal of Political Science / Revue canadienne de science politique* 44, no. 1 (March 2011): 195–218.

Sayers, Freddie. "We Need Scepticism More Than Ever." *UnHerd* (podcast), January 19, 2021. https://unherd.com/2021/01/we-need-scepticism-more-than-ever/.

Schaeffer, Katherine. "A Look at the Americans Who Believe There Is Some Truth to the Conspiracy Theory That COVID-19 Was Planned." Pew Research Center, July 24, 2020. https://www.pewresearch.org/short-reads/2020/07/24/a-look-at-the-americans -who-believe-there-is-some-truth-to-the-conspiracy-theory-that-covid-19-was-planned/.

Schaeffer, Katherine. "Nearly All Members of the 118th Congress Have a Bachelor's Degree—and Most Have a Graduate Degree, Too." Pew Research Center, February 2, 2023. https://www.pewresearch.org/short-reads/2023/02/02/nearly-all-members-of-the -118th-congress-have-a-bachelors-degree-and-most-have-a-graduate-degree-too/.

Schaffner, Brian F., and Samantha Luks. "Misinformation or Expressive Responding? What an Inauguration Crowd Can Tell Us about the Source of Political Misinformation in Surveys." *Public Opinion Quarterly* 82, no. 1 (2018): 135–147. https://doi .org/10.1093/poq/nfx042.

Scheiber, Noam. "Freaks and Geeks." *New Republic*, April 2, 2007. https://newrepublic .com/article/62561/freaks-geeks.

Schleifer, Theodore. "Andrew Cuomo Is Leaning on Tech Billionaires to Help New York Rebuild." Vox, May 6, 2020. https://www.vox.com/recode/2020/5/6/21249410 /coronavirus-andrew-cuomo-bill-gates-eric-schmidt-tech-billionaires.

Schonhaut, Luisa, Italo Costa-Roldan, Ilan Oppenheimer, Vicente Pizarro, Dareen Han, and Franco Díaz. "Scientific Publication Speed and Retractions of COVID-19 Pandemic Original Articles." *Pan American Journal of Public Health* 46 (2022). https:// doi.org/10.26633/RPSP.2022.25.

Schuessler, Jennifer. "Harvard Finds More Instances of 'Duplicative Language' in President's Work." *New York Times*, December 21, 2023. https://www.nytimes.com /2023/12/20/us/harvard-claudine-gay-plagiarism.html.

Science Media Centre. "Expert Reaction to a Study Looking at Mandatory Face Masks and Number of COVID-19 Infections in New York, Wuhan and Italy." *Science Media Center Roundups for Journalists* (podcast), June 12, 2020. https://www.science mediacentre.org/expert-reaction-to-a-study-looking-at-mandatory-face-masks-and -number-of-covid-19-infections-in-new-york-wuhan-and-italy/.

Scott, Dylan. "Why Are so Few People Getting the Latest Covid-19 Vaccine?" Vox, November 17, 2023. https://www.vox.com/policy/2023/11/17/23964294/covid-19 -vaccine-2023-us-vaccination-rates.

Sean Carroll, "Mindscape 250: Brendan Nyhan on Navigating the Information Ecosystem." YouTube, September 18, 2023. https://www.youtube.com/watch?v=s7 T4qqhp_48.

Shaffer, Claire. "Jon Stewart Floats the Covid-19 Wuhan Lab Theory with Stephen Colbert." *Rolling Stone*, June 15, 2021. https://www.rollingstone.com/tv-movies/tv -movie-news/jon-stewart-stephen-colbert-wuhan-lab-1184553/.

Shanteau, James. "Competence in Experts: The Role of Task Characteristics." *Organizational Behavior and Human Decision Processes* 53, no. 2 (1992): 252–266. https://doi .org/10.1016/0749-5978(92)90064-E.

Shapiro, Eliza. "N.Y.C. Schools, Nation's Largest District, Will Not Fully Reopen in Fall." *New York Times*, July 8, 2020. https://www.nytimes.com/2020/07/08/nyregion /nyc-schools-reopening-plan.html.

Shrader-Frechette, Kristin. "Review of *Risk and Reason*, by Cass Sunstein." *Notre Dame Philosophical Reviews*, April 9, 2003. https://ndpr.nd.edu/reviews/risk-and-reason/.

Shrum, Robert. "Donald Trump Is Not a Populist." *Politico*, August 29, 2017. https:// www.politico.com/magazine/story/2017/08/29/donald-trump-not-a-populist-215552.

Sibarium, Aaron. "Student Activists Target Stanford Law School Dean in Revolt over Her Apology." *Washington Free Beacon*, March 14, 2023. https://freebeacon.com /campus/student-activists-target-stanford-law-school-dean-in-revolt-over-her-apology/.

Siegel, Ethan. "You Must Not 'Do Your Own Research' When It Comes to Science." *Forbes*, April 30, 2020. https://www.forbes.com/sites/startswithabang/2020/07/30 /you-must-not-do-your-own-research-when-it-comes-to-science/.

Silver, Nate. *The Signal and the Noise: Why so Many Predictions Fail—but Some Don't.* New York: Penguin Random House, 2012.

Silver, Nate. "Twitter, Elon and the Indigo Blob." *Silver Bulletin* (blog), October 1, 2023. https://www.natesilver.net/p/twitter-elon-and-the-indigo-blob.

Simon, Herbert A. *Administrative Behavior.* 4th rev. ed. New York: Free Press, 1997.

Smaldino, Paul E., and Richard McElreath. "The Natural Selection of Bad Science." *Royal Society Open Science* 3, no. 9 (2016): art. 160384. https://doi.org/10.1098/rsos .160384.

Snowden, David J., and Mary E. Boone. "A Leader's Framework for Decision Making." *Harvard Business Review*, November 1, 2007. https://hbr.org/2007/11/a-leaders-frame work-for-decision-making.

Snyder, Susan, and Anna Orso. "A 'New Wave' of Activism on Campus: Students Are Aggressively Seeking Their Demands." *Philadelphia Inquirer*, December 23, 2019. https://www.inquirer.com/education/protest-students-college-campus-fossil-fuels -speakers-fraternities-20191223.html.

Sodha, Sonia. "We Need Scientists to Quiz Covid Consensus, Not Act as Agents of Disinformation." *The Guardian*, November 22, 2020. https://www.theguardian.com /commentisfree/2020/nov/22/we-need-scientists-to-quiz-covid-consensus-not-act -as-agents-of-disinformation.

"Some Colleges Have More Students from the Top 1 Percent Than the Bottom 60. Find Yours." *New York Times*, January 18, 2017. https://www.nytimes.com/interactive /2017/01/18/upshot/some-colleges-have-more-students-from-the-top-1-percent-than -the-bottom-60.html.

Somin, Ilya. "Why Political Ignorance Is a Serious Problem." *Balkinization* (blog), October 4, 2013. https://balkin.blogspot.com/2013/10/why-political-ignorance-is -serious.html.

Sood, Neeraj, Paul Simon, Peggy Ebner, Daniel Eichner, Jeffrey Reynolds, Eran Bendavid, and Jay Bhattacharya. "Seroprevalence of SARS-CoV-2–Specific Antibodies among Adults in Los Angeles County, California, on April 10–11, 2020." *JAMA* 323, no. 23 (2020): 2425–2427. https://doi.org/10.1001/jama.2020.8279.

Sparkman, Gregg, Nathan Geiger, and Elke U. Weber. "Americans Experience a False Social Reality by Underestimating Popular Climate Policy Support by Nearly Half." *Nature Communications* 13, no. 1 (2022): art. 4779. https://doi.org/10.1038 /s41467-022-32412-y.

Spiegelhalter, David. *The Art of Statistics: How to Learn from Data*. New York: Basic, 2019.

Spiegelhalter, David. "Those Who Tell Us What to Do during the Pandemic Must Earn Our Trust." *The Guardian*, November 26, 2020. https://www.theguardian.com /commentisfree/2020/nov/26/pandemic-earn-trust-facts-vital-covid.

Srinivasan, Amia. "Cancelled." *London Review of Books*, June 29, 2023. https://www .lrb.co.uk/the-paper/v45/n13/amia-srinivasan/cancelled.

Staerklé, Christian, Matteo Cavallaro, Anna Cortijos-Bernabeu, and Stéphane Bonny. "Common Sense as a Political Weapon: Populism, Science Skepticism, and Global Crisis-Solving Motivations." *Political Psychology* 43, no. 5 (2022): 913–929. https:// doi.org/10.1111/pops.12823.

Steerpike. "Fact Check: What Did Michael Gove Actually Say about 'Experts'?" *The Spectator*, September 2, 2021. https://www.spectator.co.uk/article/fact-check-what-did -michael-gove-actually-say-about-experts/.

Steinbach, Tirien. "Diversity and Free Speech Can Coexist at Stanford." *Wall Street Journal*, March 23, 2023. https://www.wsj.com/articles/diversity-and-free-speech-can -coexist-at-stanford-steinbach-duncan-law-school-protest-dei-27103829.

Stephens, Bret. "Go Forth and Argue." *New York Times*, June 2, 2023. https://www .nytimes.com/2023/06/02/opinion/free-speech-campus.html.

Stevens, Sean, and Anne Schwichtenberg. *2021 College Free Speech Rankings*. Philadelphia: Foundation for Individual Rights in Education, College Pulse, and Real-ClearEducation, September 21, 2021. https://www.thefire.org/research-learn/2021 -college-free-speech-rankings.

Stimson, James A., and Emily M. Wager. *Converging on Truth: A Dynamic Perspective on Factual Debates in American Public Opinion*. Cambridge: Cambridge University Press, 2020.

Stock, Kathleen. "The Oxford Kids Are Alright." *UnHerd* (podcast), May 31, 2023. https://unherd.com/2023/06/the-oxford-kids-are-alright/.

Stockton, Nick. "Trump Wants the EPA Radon Program Cut. So Do Some Scientists." *Wired*, July 31, 2017. https://www.wired.com/story/to-radon-or-radont-that-is-the -question/.

"Student Petition." May 29, 2023. https://docs.google.com/forms/d/e/1FAIpQLSeKa XG5WWznqnyDsuh_wg0s0eNxNIn2ZR_GEp9I2uwiy8zpnQ/viewform?pli=1&pli =1&usp=embed_facebook.

Sule, Sahana, Marisa C. DaCosta, Erin DeCou, Charlotte Gilson, Kate Wallace, and Sarah L. Goff. "Communication of COVID-19 Misinformation on Social Media by

Physicians in the US." *JAMA Network Open* 6, no. 8 (2023): e2328928. https://doi.org
/10.1001/jamanetworkopen.2023.28928.

Sullivan, Peter. "Fauci: Attacks on Me Are Really Also 'Attacks on Science.'" *The Hill*
(blog), June 9, 2021. https://thehill.com/policy/healthcare/557602-fauci-attacks-on
-me-are-really-also-attacks-on-science/.

Sumner, Petroc, Solveiga Vivian-Griffiths, Jacky Boivin, Andy Williams, Christos A.
Venetis, Aimée Davies, Jack Ogden, et al. "The Association between Exaggeration in
Health Related Science News and Academic Press Releases: Retrospective Observational Study." *British Medical Journal* 349 (December 10, 2014): art. g7015. https://
doi.org/10.1136/bmj.g7015.

Sunstein, Cass R. *Averting Catastrophe: Decision Theory for COVID-19, Climate Change,
and Potential Disasters of All Kinds*. New York: New York University Press, 2021.

Sunstein, Cass R. *The Cost–Benefit Revolution*. Cambridge, MA: MIT Press, 2018.

Sunstein, Cass R. *Risk and Reason: Safety, Law, and the Environment*. Cambridge: Cambridge University Press, 2004.

Swift, Art. "In U.S., Belief in Creationist View of Humans at New Low." Gallup, May
22, 2017. https://news.gallup.com/poll/210956/belief-creationist-view-humans-new
-low.aspx.

"Take the Quiz: What We Don't Know." *Newsweek*, March 20, 2011. https://www
.newsweek.com/take-quiz-what-we-dont-know-66047.

Tampio, Nicholas. "Scepticism Is a Way of Life That Allows Democracy to Flourish."
Aeon, March 25, 2022. https://aeon.co/essays/scepticism-is-a-way-of-life-that-allows
-democracy-to-flourish.

Taylor, Chris. "How One Woman's Yard Sign Became a Rallying Cry for Allies." Mashable, June 16, 2020. https://mashable.com/article/in-this-house-we-believe-black-lives
-matter-kindness-is-everything-sign.

Teles, Steven. "A Response to Nancy MacLean." Niskanen Center, September 17,
2018. https://www.niskanencenter.org/a-response-to-nancy-maclean/.

Tesler, Michael. "Elite Domination of Public Doubts about Climate Change (Not
Evolution)." *Political Communication* 35, no. 2 (2018): 306–326. https://doi.org/10
.1080/10584609.2017.1380092.

Tetlock, Philip E. *Expert Political Judgment: How Good Is It? How Can We Know?* New
ed. Princeton, NJ: Princeton University Press, 2006.

"These Expert-Approved Gadgets Can Help Upgrade Your Kitchen for Less." *New
York Times*, September 11, 2023. https://www.nytimes.com/wirecutter/money/expert
-approved-gadgets-to-upgrade-kitchen/.

Thornton, Stephen. "Karl Popper." In *Stanford Encyclopedia of Philosophy Archive*, edited by Edward N. Zalta and Uri Nodelman, Fall 2022 ed. https://plato.stanford.edu/archives/fall2022/entries/popper/.

Thorp, H. Holden. "The Charade of Political Neutrality." *Chronicle of Higher Education*, September 16, 2022. https://www.chronicle.com/article/the-charade-of-political-neutrality.

Thorp, H. Holden. "Remember, Do No Harm?" *Science* 38, no. 6617 (2022): 231. https://www.science.org/doi/10.1126/science.adf3072.

Thrasher, Stephen W. "Andrew Cuomo Should Resign." *Scientific American*, March 4, 2021. https://www.scientificamerican.com/article/andrew-cuomo-should-resign/.

Timms, Aaron. "The Sameness of Cass Sunstein." *New Republic*, June 20, 2019. https://newrepublic.com/article/154236/sameness-cass-sunstein.

Timms, Aaron. "Us vs. Him." *The Baffler*, April 23, 2018. https://thebaffler.com/latest/us-vs-him-timms.

Tombs, Robert. *This Sovereign Isle: Britain in and out of Europe.* London: Allen Lane, 2021.

Tuccille, J. D. "'The Science' Suffers from Self-Inflicted Political Wounds." *Reason*, November 20, 2023. https://reason.com/2023/11/20/the-science-suffers-from-self-inflicted-political-wounds/.

Tufekci, Zeynep. "The C.D.C. Needs to Stop Confusing the Public." *New York Times*, August 4, 2021. https://www.nytimes.com/2021/08/04/opinion/cdc-covid-guidelines.html.

Tufekci, Zeynep. "Here's Why the Science Is Clear That Masks Work." *New York Times*, March 10, 2023. https://www.nytimes.com/2023/03/10/opinion/masks-work-cochrane-study.html.

Turner, Camilla. "Rishi Sunak: Mistake to 'Empower Scientists' in Covid Pandemic." *Telegraph*, August 25, 2022. https://www.telegraph.co.uk/politics/2022/08/25/rishi-sunak-mistake-empower-scientists-covid-pandemic/.

Tyson, Alec, and Brian Kennedy. "Two-Thirds of Americans Think Government Should Do More on Climate." Pew Research Center, June 23, 2020. https://www.pewresearch.org/science/2020/06/23/two-thirds-of-americans-think-government-should-do-more-on-climate/.

US Census Bureau. "Census Bureau Releases New Educational Attainment Data." February 24, 2022. https://www.census.gov/newsroom/press-releases/2022/educational-attainment.html.

Uscinski, Joseph E., and Ryden W. Butler. "The Epistemology of Fact Checking." *Critical Review* 25, no. 2 (June 2013): 162–180. https://doi.org/10.1080/08913811.2013 .843872.

Uscinski, Joseph, Adam Enders, Casey Klofstad, Michelle Seelig, Hugo Drochon, Kamal Premaratne, and Manohar Murthi. "Have Beliefs in Conspiracy Theories Increased over Time?" *PLOS ONE* 17, no. 7 (2022): art. e0270429. https://doi.org/10 .1371/journal.pone.0270429.

US Department of Health and Human Services. "Findings of Research Misconduct." *Federal Register*, September 6, 2012. https://www.federalregister.gov/documents/2012 /09/06/2012-21992/findings-of-research-misconduct.

US House of Representatives, Committee on Oversight and Accountability. "Investigation Reveals Biden's CDC Bypassed Scientific Norms to Allow Teachers Union to Re-write Official Guidance." September 5, 2023. https://oversight.house.gov/release /investigation-reveals-bidens-cdc-bypassed-scientific-norms-to-allow-teachers-union -to-re-write-official-guidance/.

UVA Center for Politics. "New Initiative Explores Deep, Persistent Divides between Biden and Trump Voters." September 30, 2021. https://centerforpolitics.org/crystal ball/new-initiative-explores-deep-persistent-divides-between-biden-and-trump -voters/.

Vadala, Nick. "The Pennsylvania 'Kids-for-Cash' Judicial Scandal, Explained." *Philadelphia Inquirer*, August 18, 2022. https://www.inquirer.com/news/pennsylvania/pa -kids-for-cash-scandal-judges-mark-ciavarella-michael-conahan-20220818.html.

Valentine, Genevieve. "'Democracy in Chains' Traces the Rise of American Libertarianism." NPR, June 18, 2017, online only. https://www.npr.org/2017/06/18/5319 29217/democracy-in-chains-traces-the-rise-of-american-libertarianism.

Varadarajan, Tunku. "Make Freedom of Speech Liberal Again." *Wall Street Journal*, August 5, 2022. https://www.wsj.com/articles/make-free-speech-liberal-again-john -stuart-mill-aclu-nadine-strossen-classical-liberalism-universities-censorship-social -media-11659710472.

Varoufakis, Yanis. *Talking to My Daughter about the Economy: or, How Capitalism Works—and How It Fails*. Translated by Jacob Moe and Yanis Varoufakis. London: Farrar, Straus and Giroux, 2017.

Viner, Russell, Simon Russell, Rosella Saulle, Helen Croker, Claire Stansfield, Jessica Packer, Dasha Nicholls, et al. "School Closures during Social Lockdown and Mental Health, Health Behaviors, and Well-Being among Children and Adolescents during the First COVID-19 Wave: A Systematic Review." *JAMA Pediatrics* 176, no. 4 (2022): 400–409. https://doi.org/10.1001/jamapediatrics.2021.5840.

Vinkers, Christiaan, Joeri Tijdink, and Willem Otte. "Use of Positive and Negative Words in Scientific PubMed Abstracts between 1974 and 2014: Retrospective Analysis." *British Medical Journal (Clinical Research Ed.)* 2015 (December 14, 2015): art. h6467. https://doi.org/10.1136/bmj.h6467.

Wallace-Wells, David. "Dr. Fauci Looks Back: 'Something Clearly Went Wrong.'" *New York Times*, April 25, 2023. https://www.nytimes.com/interactive/2023/04/24/magazine/dr-fauci-pandemic.html.

Walt, Stephen M. *The Hell of Good Intentions: America's Foreign Policy Elite and the Decline of U.S. Primacy.* Illus. ed. New York: Farrar, Straus and Giroux, 2018.

Walt, Stephen M. "Liberal Illusions Caused the Ukraine Crisis." *Foreign Policy*, January 19, 2022. https://foreignpolicy.com/2022/01/19/ukraine-russia-nato-crisis-liberal-illusions/.

Ward, Ian. "How Elites Misread Public Opinion." *Politico*, June 17, 2022. https://www.politico.com/news/magazine/2022/06/17/elites-kertzer-renshon-political-science-00039943.

Weber, Max. *From Max Weber: Essays in Sociology.* Edited by H. H. Gerth and C. Wright Mills. New York: Oxford University Press, 1946.

Weiler, J. H. H. "The Transformation of Europe." *Yale Law Journal* 100 (June 1991): 2403–2483.

"Why *Nature* Needs to Cover Politics Now More Than Ever." *Nature* 586, no. 7828 (2020): 169–170. https://doi.org/10.1038/d41586-020-02797-1.

"Why *Nature* Needs to Stand up for Science and Evidence." *Nature* 615, no. 7953 (2023): 561. https://www.nature.com/articles/d41586-023-00789-5.

"Why *Nature* Supports Joe Biden for US President." *Nature* 586, no. 7829 (2020): 335. https://doi.org/10.1038/d41586-020-02852-x.

Williams, Joan. "How You Treat the 'Non-elite' Is Key to Beating Populism." *Financial Times*, November 21, 2022. https://www.ft.com/content/35a5fc19-06b6-4d9e-b55f-ce03b871dba0.

Williams, Joan C. "How Biden Won Back (Enough of) the White Working Class." *Harvard Business Review*, November 10, 2020. https://hbr.org/2020/11/how-biden-won-back-enough-of-the-white-working-class.

Williams, Joan C. "What so Many People Don't Get about the U.S. Working Class." *Harvard Business Review*, November 10, 2016. https://hbr.org/2016/11/what-so-many-people-dont-get-about-the-u-s-working-class.

Williams, Joan C. *White Working Class: Overcoming Class Cluelessness in America.* Cambridge, MA: Harvard Business Review Press, 2019.

Williams, Michael. "Hume's Skepticism." In *The Oxford Handbook of Skepticism*, edited by John Greco, 80–107. Oxford: Oxford University Press, 2008.

Williams, Sierra. "Are 90% of Academic Papers Really Never Cited? Reviewing the Literature on Academic Citations." *Impact of Social Sciences* (blog), April 23, 2014. https://blogs.lse.ac.uk/impactofsocialsciences/2014/04/23/academic-papers-citation-rates-remler/.

Wise, Jacqui. "Covid-19: Experts Divide into Two Camps of Action—Shielding versus Blanket Policies." *British Medical Journal* 370 (September 21, 2020): art. m3702. https://doi.org/10.1136/bmj.m3702.

Wittgenstein, Ludwig. *On Certainty*. Edited by G. E. M. Anscombe and G. H. von Wright. Translated by Denis Paul. New York: Harper & Row, 1969.

World Economic Forum. *The Global Risks Report 2024*. 19th ed. Geneva: World Economic Forum, January 2024. https://www3.weforum.org/docs/WEF_The_Global_Risks_Report_2024.pdf.

Wright, Robert. "In Defense of Whataboutism." *Nonzero Newsletter*, February 28, 2022. https://nonzero.substack.com/p/in-defense-of-whataboutism.

Wynne, Brian. "Creating Public Alienation: Expert Cultures of Risk and Ethics on GMOs." *Science as Culture* 10, no. 4 (2001): 445–481. https://doi.org/10.1080/09505430120093586.

Xu, Meimei. "More Than 80 Percent of Surveyed Harvard Faculty Identify as Liberal." *Harvard Crimson*, July 13, 2022. https://www.thecrimson.com/article/2022/7/13/faculty-survey-political-leaning/.

Yamey, Gavin, and David Gorski. "Covid-19 and the New Merchants of Doubt." *British Medical Journal Opinion* (blog), September 13, 2021. https://blogs.bmj.com/bmj/2021/09/13/covid-19-and-the-new-merchants-of-doubt/.

Yglesias, Matthew. "Misinformation Isn't Just on the Right." *Slow Boring* (blog), February 27, 2023. https://www.slowboring.com/p/misinformation-isnt-just-on-the-right.

Yglesias, Matthew. "People Need to Hear the Good News about Climate Change." *Slow Boring* (blog), March 1, 2023. https://www.slowboring.com/p/people-need-to-hear-the-good-news?utm_medium=email.

Zakaria, Fareed. "Why University Presidents Are under Fire." CNN, December 8, 2023. https://www.cnn.com/2023/12/08/opinions/israel-palestine-antisemitism-american-universities-zakaria/index.html.

Zhang, Floyd Jiuyun. "Political Endorsement by *Nature* and Trust in Scientific Expertise during COVID-19." *Nature Human Behaviour* 7, no. 5 (May 2023): 696–706. https://doi.org/10.1038/s41562-023-01537-5.

Zimmer, Robert J. "Statement on Faculty, Free Expression, and Diversity." November 29, 2020. https://president.uchicago.edu/en/from-the-president/announcements/2006 -2021/112920-free-expression.

Zimmer, Robert J., and Eric D. Isaacs. "Report of the Committee on Freedom of Expression." University of Chicago, accessed January 10, 2024. https://provost.uchicago .edu/sites/default/files/documents/reports/FOECommitteeReport.pdf.

Zweig, David. "Anthony Fauci's Deceptions." The Free Press, August 7, 2023. https:// www.thefp.com/p/anthony-faucis-deceptions.

Index

Abbot, Dorian, 202, 209
ABC News, 53
Academia. *See also specific institutions*
  Academic Freedom Alliance, 208
  censorship in, 212–214, 259n12,
    259n14
  conservative faculty in, 17–18
  credentialism in, 16, 83–84
  culture of, 2–3
  deBoer on, 229n22
  economics of, 80
  elitism in, 4, 11–12, 19, 63–67
  epistemic humility in, 83–85
  epistemology in, 8
  expertise in, 245n3
  faculty experts in, xvi
  first principles for, 214–216
  freedom of speech in, 259n11
  groupthink in, 200–206
  Higher Education Freedom of Speech
    Act, 203–204
  ideological diversity in, 18, 199–207
  journalism and, xii, 28–29, 81–82
  knowledge of, 67–72
  opinions from, 51
  politics in, 22
  populism in, 239n6
  replication crisis in, 63
  reputation of, 78–81, 181–182
  research from, 28
  science in, 181–183

  skepticism of, 192–193
  in United States, 260n37
Acemoglu, Daron, 14, 80
Ackerman, Bruce, 122–123
Adams, John, 159, 252n53
Ad hominem attacks, 3–4, 57, 174
Age of Fracture (Rodgers), 254n6
AIER, 187
Alien and Sedition Acts, 159
Allen, Arthur A., 75
Alternative facts, 155–156
Altman, Sam, 80–81
American Civil Liberties Union, 199
American dream, 99–102
American Federation of Teachers, 42,
  141–142
American Institute for Economic
  Research (AIER), 187
American Political Science Review
  (journal), 13–14
Anarchy, State, and Utopia (Nozick), 208
Anecdotal research, 76–77
Anti-elitism, 96, 99, 102
Antiestablishment voters, 2
Anti-experts, 185–187, 226n3
Antimaskers, 53, 193–195
Antipluralists, 92
Anti-Trump resistance, 170–171
Antivaxxers, 5
Applebaum, Anne, 197–198
Argumentative space, 227n8